OXFORD MONOGRAPHS ON MUSIC

Time in Indian Music

Time in Indian Music

Rhythm, Metre, and Form in North Indian Rāg Performance

MARTIN CLAYTON

OXFORD
UNIVERSITY PRESS

OXFORD
UNIVERSITY PRESS

Great Clarendon Street, Oxford OX2 6DP
Oxford University Press is a department of the University of Oxford.
It furthers the University's objective of excellence in research, scholarship,
and education by publishing woldwide in

Oxford New York

Athens Auckland Bangkok Bogotá Buenos Aires Calcutta
Cape Town Chennai Dar es Salaam Delhi Florence Hong Kong Istanbul
Karachi Kuala Lumpur Madrid Melbourne Mexico City Mumbai
Nairobi Paris São Paulo Shanghai Singapore Taipei Tokyo Toronto Warsaw

and associated companies in Berlin Ibadan

Oxford is a registered trade mark of Oxford University Press
in the UK and certain other countries

Published in the United States
by Oxford University Press Inc., New York

First published 2000

British Library Cataloguing in Publication Data
Data available

Library of Congress Cataloging in Publication Data
ISBN 0–19–816686–9

1 3 5 7 9 10 8 6 4 2
Typeset by Kolam Information Services Pvt Ltd
Printed in Great Britain by
TJ International Ltd, Padstow, Cornwall

Acknowledgements

To Dr Richard Widdess I owe much of my knowledge of the history and theory of Indian music; his support, guidance, and criticism have contributed incalculably to this work. To Shri Deepak Choudhury I owe most of my practical training in the *sitār* and in the arts of *rāg* and *tāl*—and much more besides. Thank you both.

I am indebted to others who assisted with or commented on my doctoral research, conducted between 1988 and 1992, on which much of this book is based; in particular Dr David Hughes, Dr Owen Wright, and Dr Neil Sorrell for their comments and advice; Dr Shubha Choudhury and her staff at the Archives and Research Centre for Ethnomusicology (ARCE) in New Delhi, Anant Vaidyanathan at the Sangeet Research Academy (SRA) in Calcutta, and the staff of the National Centre for Performing Arts (NCPA) in Mumbai for their assistance, and the British Academy and the School of Oriental and African Studies (SOAS) for financial support.

As for subsequent research work, I thank the Open University's Arts Faculty Research Committee for generously supporting my efforts to complete this book. Dr Janet Topp Fargion, Dr Ian Cross, Dr Kevin Dawe, Dr Rupert Snell, and numerous others have also given me valuable assistance, in different ways, without which I could not have completed the work. I would particularly like to thank the anonymous readers who commented on earlier versions of this text. Thanks also to the editors of the *British Journal of Ethnomusicology*, the *Bulletin of the School of Oriental and African Studies*, and *Cahiers de Musiques Traditionelles* for permission to use parts of my earlier publications from those journals in revised form, and to all the artists and record companies who generously allowed me to use extracts from their recordings. Thanks also to Mr K. R. Norman for his diacritics font.

Musicians who have contributed directly to this study include Deepak Choudhury, Pandit Ravi Shankar, Pandit Ram Narayan; *tablā* players Pandit Swapan Choudhury, Pandit Anindo Chatterjee, Arup Chattopadhyay, and Bikram Ghosh; and singers Dr Ritwik Sanyal (of Banaras Hindu University) and Veena Sahasrabuddhe. Along with these artists, I must thank my previous teachers Uma Shankar Mishra and the late Pandit Manikrao Popatkar for their encouragement, and many musical friends and colleagues, both here, in Calcutta and elsewhere.

It's been a lot of work, and a lot of fun. Thanks to everyone who helped.

Martin Clayton

The Open University
August 1999

Contents

List of tables

List of examples

Note on orthography

Indian technical terms are italicized throughout, and spelt as transliterated from their most common Hindi spellings (alternative spellings have not in general been noted).

Transliteration is according to the standard system set out in R. S. McGregor's *An Outline of Hindi Grammar* (Oxford 1972/1986, p. 8), in the same author's *The Oxford Hindi–English Dictionary* (Oxford 1993, pp. xvi–xvii) and in R. Snell and S. Weightman's *Hindi* (London 1989, p. 5 ff).

English-style plurals have been employed throughout. The inherent vowel '*a*', generally omitted from final syllables in transliterations from Hindi (thus *tāl*, not *tāla*), is included where the transliteration is from a Sanskrit title or author, or from a song text (since these vowels are generally pronounced in singing).

In quotations from works in English, the original spelling and type style have been retained.

Note on music notations

Music examples are given in a number of different forms, according to the information to be presented. Elements of Western staff notation, and of the Hindustānī notation system devised in the early twentieth century by Pandit V. N. Bhatkande, are combined in various ways.

In all cases *tāl* (metric structure) is indicated according to the Hindustānī system. In all but the simplest examples, rhythmic notation is given using Western symbols. Where necessary either text, instrumental, or percussion stroke names (*bols*), or *sargam* (solfège) syllables are included; in a few examples melody has been indicated in Western staff notation.

The symbols used are as follows:

Tāl structure: Hindustānī signs for *sam* (X), *khālī* (0), and *tālī* (numerals 1, 2, etc.) are given in the top line of all music examples, and these signs apply to everything vertically below them unless otherwise indicated. *Mātrā* ('beat') numbers are given in the second line of most transcriptions, and are referred to in the text as 'm.1, m.2', etc. Vertical lines separate *vibhāgs* (sections).

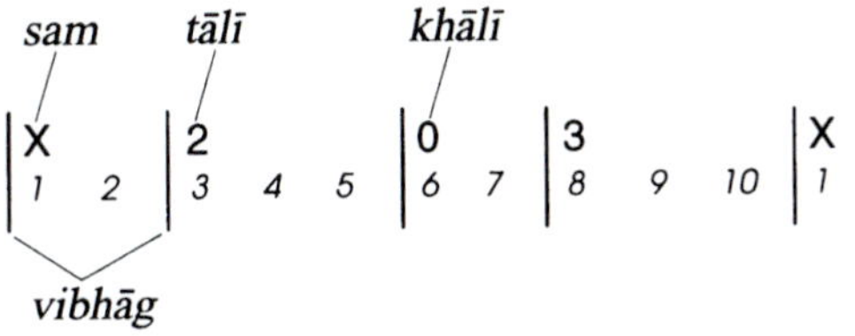

Rhythmic notation is not generally given for *ṭhekās* (basic drum patterns), in which case the system is as follows. The *bols* (strokes) of each *mātrā* are grouped together and the *mātrās* separated by spaces. Rests or prolonged strokes are indicated by a dash (–), and the *mātrā* is divided equally by the sum total of all strokes and dashes. Thus:

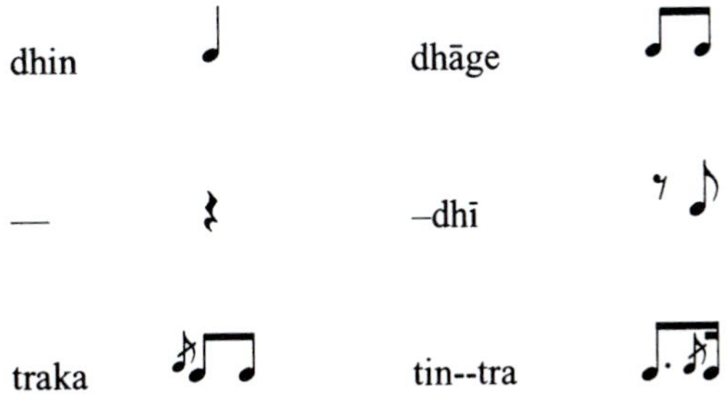

Transcriptions observe the following conventions:

sign	**meaning**
	tie
	slur or phrase mark
 yā—	melisma
>	accent
⁒	repeat (previous *mātrā* or *vibhāg*)
c24	cycle (*āvart*) number
♩ = 49+ MM	*mātrā* notated as crotchet (quarter-note); 49 or more beats per minute
	*mīṇḍ* (melismatic ornament)
	*kṛntan* (pull-off or hammer-on)
	*zamzamā* (combination of *kṛntans*)
Sa Re Ga Ma Pa Dha Ni s r g m p d n	*sargam* (solfège syllables, in ascending order; superscript dot indicates high octave, subscript dot low octave)
da, ra, diri, dra etc.	*bols* (instrumental strokes); da=inward or downward, ra=outward or upward
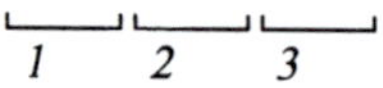 *1 2 3*	*tihāī* elements

1

Introduction

1.1 A *rāg* performance

Before any performance of *rāg* music in North India can begin,[1] a number of rituals are enacted, marking the time from the entrance of the performers to the sounding of the first pitch of the recital. Performers must be introduced—often with a lengthy speech, in which the speaker (on behalf of the programme's patron) charts the lineage and lists the achievements and honours of the soloist (and, to a lesser extent, accompanists) whose services have been secured for the event. Musicians may be presented with garlands, which they will accept gratefully before removing as a gesture of humility. Accompanists take the stage, standing respectfully until the soloist makes his entrance, acknowledges the audience's welcome, sits and gestures to his colleagues that they should do likewise.[2]

We are still far from ready for the recital to begin. Our soloist must first settle into his space—removing his watch and placing it in front of him, placing a notebook with song texts or a case with spare strings and plectra nearby, adjusting microphone positions—all the while trying to focus his concentration on the *rāg* to be performed and achieve the state of mind necessary for a good performance. And then the final tuning process begins. Instruments will already have been tuned in the course of a sound check, and perhaps retuned back stage. But their tuning will inevitably have slipped under the heat of the stage lights, and in any case, a few minutes spent concentrating on the sound of the *tānpūrā* drone enables the musicians to relax and focus their concentration. Once again the musicians will take turns, soloist first, and then (with his approval) accompanists.

The soloist welcomes his listeners and tells them what he is going to present. He may simply announce the *rāg* (mode), or *rāg* and *tāl* (metric cycle); or he may describe the composition, perhaps suggesting its origins in a particular tradition ('My Guruji taught me . . .') or simply in the past ('This is a very old composition . . .'). Special gestures of respect may be offered at this point, to honoured guests or senior musicians present, or to the artist's forebears.

We are now ready for the performance. *Rāg* performances often begin slowly, with the first few phrases doing little more than establishing and emphasizing the principal drone note Sa. But the drone itself has, by this point, already become

[1] The terms '*rāg* music', 'Hindustānī music', and 'North Indian music' are used interchangeably in this book.

[2] For simplicity's sake I have used masculine pronouns here and elsewhere to stand for musicians and listeners of either gender.

thoroughly fixed in the listener's mind, since it has sounded throughout the tuning process—not just the Sa, and one or two other important pitches such as (the fifth) Pa and (the leading note) Ni, but a dense cloud of harmonics produced by the *tānpūrās* which seems to envelop performers and audience alike. At this moment I sense that the melody is already present in the drone, asking to be sung; I hum along with the drone, and feel that I know which *rāg* is to be performed before it has been announced. And even when I'm wrong, it seems as though the *rāg* actually presented was merely another of several possibilities, all latent, all potential.

For us (the audience), and for the performers, this is how it should be: the musicians should not appear to be at work, recalling formal structures or grammatical rules for the *rāg*, or counting beats... it should seem as though the *rāg* simply emerges, naturally and effortlessly, from the primordial cloud of harmonics that is the drone; that the *rāg* is one, a single entity with its own character; that the performer merely allows this character to be expressed through his actions. Of course it's not always like that: every musician gives workaday performances, has to fulfil commitments when he's not in the mood, when the instruments won't stay in tune or the room just doesn't feel right; and if he's professional enough, many in the audience won't know the difference. But when it happens right, it just seems to happen, and performers and listeners feel as if they are utterly engaged in the same entrancing, transforming sounds.

If I put aside any notion of analytical listening, my overriding impression, particularly of vocal performance, is of an intricate gestural dance. Melody doesn't simply go, or move, from third to fourth to fifth and back again to third. It glides, it swoops and dives, it climbs up and falls back down. The development of a *rāg* is a sequence of *gestures*, figures mimed by the singer as he traces a graceful arc, stretches out an arm to let the melody out before pulling it back. Melodic figures seem to have a spatial presence, a presence which is not static but dynamic, a tracing of patterns in the air; if a melody has an image (and *rāgs* have often been painted as human or divine figures), it is an image *being viewed*, explored, and experienced in time by the observer's eye. It's not coincidental that images of movement abound in Indian descriptions of music; the flight of a bird, the rush of a waterfall, the gait of God, human or animal, even the rattle of a moving train.

A musician, for sure, knows he is singing (for instance) the notes Ga Ma Pa, Ga; as a listener you may be able to extract this *sargam*, the solfège code. But you don't, because the melody grabs your attention, not as a succession of pitches but as a succession of gestures. Gestural patterns seem to relate to one another in almost an organic way, growing out of one another. From time to time new ideas or images appear, then for a while each successive gesture emerges as if inevitably from the last, until that sequence has run its course and it's time to return to the refrain and to a state of repose, to take stock and to allow a new idea to take shape. As a listener, this is where a moment of magic is experienced, because just as that train of thought reaches its final destination, just as the soloist returns to the refrain of his composition, you become aware that the drummer is also reaching the cadential point of his sequence, and that soloist and drummer are going to reach a point of climax and repose *at exactly the same moment.*

For many people, to listen to this music, eyes closed, is the epitome of relaxed, contemplative engagement with (and through) music. But I can't keep my eyes off the action, the strands of gestural communication which proceed, simultaneously or intermittently. Singers trace figures in the air, raise arms in supplication, shake violently as they strain to produce *gamak tāns* in their lowest register. Listeners raise their arms, palms upward, in admiration, crying 'wah, wah' (bravo!), congratulating the musicians, or just muttering or sighing their approval. Performers acknowledge the appreciation, smile to the audience and to their colleagues in acknowledgement; accompanists shake their heads and smile. The soloist gestures to his drummer to adjust the tempo, to a *tānpūrā* player to play louder, to one of his accompanists that they may take the lead for a moment while he takes a rest. Two *tānpūrā* players smile at each other and shake their heads in admiration and acknowledgement. Anyone with a free hand may clap or slap a thigh from time to time to mark the progress of the *tāl.*

As I watch a performance in progress I'm constantly aware of this many-layered dance of gestures. Physical movements control performance, mediate or regulate the social interaction and hierarchy of musicians and listeners, generate and respond to musical figures which themselves seem almost to trace a path through space. Musical performance in India, perhaps everywhere, is physical, embodied, and transactional, it depends on the act of performing and the active engagement of listeners.

Back with our performance, our soloist seems now to have moved on to something a little brisker, and more exciting. And as we listen, it seems to get faster and faster; the soloist nods to the drummer, who changes his stroke pattern and increases the tempo further. We become increasingly aware of this process of *intensification.*

Those magical coming-together moments are still there, sometimes dramatized by the triple repetitions they call *tihāīs*—darada ONE, darada TWO, darada THREE, at which point we hit that point of climax and repose they call *sam.* Some people seem to have been counting the *tāl* out with successions of gently sounding claps and silent waves; they don't seem so amazed, but still smile and shake their heads in admiration of the performers' skill and audacity. The music becomes more and more intense until, finally, it can go no further and soloist and drummer, together, play an incredible, dramatic pattern that seems to be made of *tihāīs* within *tihāīs* within *tihāīs*, and which ends with a crash, a cheer, a smile, and a thunder of applause.

1.2 Some prefatory remarks

I hope you will forgive the none-too-subtle sleight of hand by which in the previous passage I glossed over the many differences, some slight and others rather significant, between the different genres and styles of Hindustānī *rāg* performance. Different performances may follow rather different courses, some concentrating on the initial unaccompanied *ālāp* for up to an hour or even more, others moving on to accompanied, metrical forms within a few minutes, some using dozens of *tihāīs* of astonishingly varied form and others barely one in an entire recital, and so on. There are some pretty important differences between vocal and instrumental performance; sometimes there are two soloists; there may be various configurations of accompanists; there may be no stage lights or (more rarely) no amplification. But having offered that disclaimer, I have to say most of what I wrote above holds for most North Indian *rāg* music, most of the time; and I think that for all its generalizations my introduction has the merit of concentrating attention (mine as well as yours) on the kind of event, and the kind of experience, to which the various theories and analyses which follow refer.

What I hope these comments achieve is a focus on the performative and transactional aspects of music. Even in studies of musical time, the analytical trap of addressing the product of a musical performance, its form and structure as if 'out of time', is a difficult one to avoid. At any moment in any performance, musicians are engaged in an *act* of music-making, in which they produce sonic gestures or utterances. These gestures are generally the result of bodily movement, and they are both expressive (on the part of the performer) and conditioned by the performer's interaction with his or her physical and social environment (including other performers and audience members). (I should explain that I use the term 'gesture' to refer here to both a physical action and its sonic results.)

Listeners may respond to these gestures in many ways: to qualities of timbre, intonation, dynamics, and so on; to the relationship of a particular gesture to what has gone before; and to its relationship to what was expected. Self-evident as these observations may seem, the apparent implication that music needs to be understood as an ongoing process of performance, interpretation, and interaction, in which listeners play an active role in interpreting structure and meaning, is still too often ignored. It seems to me an equally great temptation in ethnomusicological analysis, to allow ideological assumptions prevailing in particular music cultures to lead us to forget that these conditions must apply to any performance.

This book is concerned with the time dimension of *rāg* music. Since this repertoire features rather a complex system of metrical organization (*tāl*) a lot of the text deals with that dimension of the music—but my study is, or at least is intended to be, rather more than that. I've tried to write about musical time organization on at least three different levels: the organization of performances as a whole, the nature and function of metre, and the generation and manipulation of rhythmic patterns. I have also considered the interrelationships between these levels: the way rhythmic patterns are generated from or assimilated to metrical structure; the contributions of metre and tempo to large-scale organization, and so on. And I have been concerned with rhythm and metre in the context of the overall aesthetic aims and ideology of performance—of the ideas which shape, directly or indirectly, any performance.

If I begin the study with one assumption above all others, it is of sameness—that human beings in different environments, in making music, have a great deal in common with each other. Therefore I have neither set out to make value judgements ('Indian rhythm is complex, therefore it is good'), nor have I emphasized alterity or assumed that a supposed fundamental difference between Oriental and Occidental cultures must be reflected in the respective art music repertoires. On the contrary: although I find that Indian and Western art music repertoires are sufficiently distinct to be to some extent mutually unintelligible—it is extremely difficult, for instance, to follow the more complicated *tāl* structures without having been trained to do so—I am convinced that such differences are the result of the working out within particular cultural contexts of subtly different responses to certain universal constraints on music-making—such as those on perception, cognition, and memory—slight differences whose results are nonetheless compounded over historical time to produce significantly different sonic results.

In rhythm and metre as in other domains, it seems clear that certain misapprehensions have been allowed to spread (amongst Westerners) about Indian music. Partly this is a result of simple misunderstanding: because understanding depends to some extent on both experience and training, Westerners without extensive experience have tended to misunderstand, or completely fail to understand, Indian rhythm. In an earlier era this misunderstanding was manifested in a belief that, since the music was unintelligible it must be devoid of form and organization. Thus William Hamilton Bird, a collector and arranger of Indian songs for the harpsichord, felt moved to complain in 1789 that it 'cost him great pains to bring them into any form as to TIME, which the music of Hindostan is extremely deficient in . . .' (from *The Oriental Miscellany,* quoted by Bor 1988 : 56).

While this impression has long since been dispelled, it has been replaced by a view that Indian rhythm is indeed organized, but in such a complex manner that a mere Westerner could not hope to comprehend it. In the words of one recent author, 'It is necessary . . . to say a few words about the mysteries of Indian music. Its *talas*, its rhythmic sequences—incomprehensible for Western listeners—can be as long as 108 beats; yet the Indian ear is constantly aware of where the *sam* falls . . . as easily as if it were simple 4/4 or 6/8 time' (Berendt 1987 : 202).

It is hardly necessary for me to add that both of these positions are profoundly influenced by Western attitudes towards Indian culture current in the late eighteenth and late twentieth centuries respectively; the image of the Indian as backward, unsophisticated, and inferior to the European largely gave way over this period to that of the Indian as spiritual, mystical, and capable of highly sophisticated thought inaccessible to materialistic Western minds. Since I share neither of these unfortunate misapprehensions, I would hope that this book would work against them, although I fear that so much of my argument seems to suggest complexity that it will inevitably, and inadvertently, reinforce a view I would much prefer to challenge. So, let me at least try to make this clear at the outset: the rhythmic organization of North Indian *rāg* music is undoubtedly a difficult and complicated subject, but I do not see this as in any way a unique or distinguishing feature.

In fact I can think of no objective criteria for judging the relative complexity or sophistication of rhythm in, for example, Indian *rāg* music, Western tonal art music, and that of African drum ensembles, each of which is organized according to a subtle and complex system (only parts of which, in each case, are verbalized or notated). The distinctive feature of the first, at the risk of simplification, is that it uses metric structures both more various, and at times more complex than either of the others, and that those metric structures are explicitly specified to a greater degree. But to say that rhythmic organization *as a whole* is more complex in *rāg* music than in any other repertoire would be a misconception, and show a lack of understanding of the variety of levels of organization found elsewhere, and of the very different ways in which broadly comparable levels of complexity can be realized in different repertoires. As an instance, I might say that the fact that Indian metric structures appear, on the whole, more elaborate than those of Western music, has its obverse side, namely that the subtlety and ambiguity of metre encountered in some Western music far exceeds that of Indian music. To an educated listener, there can be *no* metrical ambiguity in Indian music, which together with the apparent rigidity of the *tāl* structures closes off various possibilities exploited in the European tradition.[3]

Returning to my earlier point, nor do I take as a given the structuralist position that certain underlying cultural patterns are reflected in music sounds. As an instance of this, the argument has been put forward that (if I may paraphrase a little crudely) Indian people subscribe to Hindu thought, which has certain specific things to say about (for instance) the nature of time; that in any culture music reflects such ideas; and that therefore a Hindu world-view is encoded in Indian music.

I have always found the coherent simplicity of such an argument deeply attractive, and yet must admit to being troubled by a number of significant difficulties. Can we speak of Indians as a mass, Indian culture as a homogeneous whole, the 'Indian mind' as one, when the evidence of variety and difference and of the indeterminate boundaries of the 'Indian' is quite unavoidable? Can we assimilate 'Indian' thought to a particular set of ancient Hindu doctrines, when not only are many Indians Muslim, Sikh, Christian, or atheist, but the very nature of Hindu belief and practice has changed markedly since those doctrines were first expressed? If music reflects deep cultural patterns (whatever those patterns may be), how does that happen? (While it's conceivable that one can

[3] If this sounds like an extreme relativist position—all music is equally complex—that is not my intention. Rather, I am suggesting that we have no objective measure for complexity and that an apparent 'deficiency' in this respect may be illusory.

consciously create a piece of music to 'reflect' an abstract idea, and this has happened in many different places at different times, surely in most cases the mechanism would have to be quite unconscious.)

Along rather similar lines, David Epstein takes as one of the principal assumptions of his recent study of time in Western tonal music the proposition that 'musical time is a special case of time in general' (1995 : 21), and can therefore be expected to reflect contemporary philosophical speculations and scientific theories on the subject. While this position helps to generate many fascinating insights, it does perhaps put the cart before the horse. For me, music cannot simply reflect time in general: rather, musical time is the result of a negotiation between physical and psychological constraints on the one hand, and human individuals' attempts to describe and order their experience on the other. Cultural norms and ideologies undoubtedly have an important part to play in this process, but they cannot be a simple determinant of musical structure; nor can the nature of time actively determine (rather than constrain) musical structure.

Abstract ideas can certainly come to be represented in (or perceived in) musical structures, and patterns experienced in other realms of life may also be felt in music. However, this kind of cultural symbolism can never be absolute. The structure of a piece of music, let alone its meaning, can never be fixed since it inevitably depends on the interpretation (conscious or unconscious) of the listener. If music reflects deep cultural patterns in any meaningful way then those patterns must be perceived by the listener; and yet a listener may perceive such patterns partly because of a predisposition to interpret any event in terms of a limited number of archetypal patterns (in other words, the 'deep' pattern resides in the hearer rather than in the musical sounds); moreover he may be inclined to hear certain things in music because he has learned from the prevailing ideology that they are expected to be there (the hearer perceives the pattern he believes *must* be there). To separate patterns in music from patterns in the listener, and to separate features necessarily in the music from patterns expected to be in the music, are not easy tasks. For this reason, I suggest that the idea of music as symbolically representing cultural ideologies is both necessary and deeply problematic. This theme, and the others outlined above, is one to which I will return.

1.3 The aims and scope of the present study

Research on North Indian rhythm in modern times has been limited, and for the most part superficial.[4] The basic information on *tāl* found in many published

4 This is true both of Indian musicology and Western ethnomusicology (if indeed there can be a clear division between the two). The most extensive recent Indian study is that of Subhadra Chaudhary (1997), who describes the modern North Indian *tāl* system (and those of several other Indian traditions) in the context of ancient and medieval theory. The overwhelming majority of Indian writers who address the topic of *tāl* do so by reproducing and/or compiling in written form

works does not in itself add up to a theory of rhythm and metre, any more than description of the European system of bars and time signatures constitutes a theory of rhythmic organization in Western art music. I have tried to go far beyond such discussions in this book, and I hope in doing so to complement the impressive body of recent work on time in Western music theory[5] and in music psychology, as well as in ethnomusicology.[6]

I have set out to present a theoretical model of the rhythmic organization of North Indian art music, from the perspective of one who has spent many years studying, playing, listening, and responding to this music, not to mention discussing music with rather more capable performers than myself. It therefore synthesizes the perspectives of Indian theory, as expressed in written works and in oral tradition, with analytical perspectives from Western music theory, ethnomusicology, and cognitive psychology. Indian theoretical concepts lie at the core of my description, yet I hope to have made the result intelligible to both an Indian and a non-Indian readership.

The music with which this study is concerned is that of the so-called 'classical' genres of Hindustānī music. These include vocal genres such as *dhrupad*, *dhamār*, *sādrā*, *khyāl*, *tarānā*, and *ṭhumrī*, as well as instrumental music including both *gats* and adaptations of vocal forms. Solo percussion performance is excluded from detailed discussion, as is *kathak* dance, and vocal genres such as *gīt*, *ghazal*, *qavvālī*, and *bhajan*, which are generally considered to lie beyond the boundaries of the 'classical'—there are nonetheless a number of occasions where I have referred to one or other of these genres. The distinction between the 'classical' music discussed here and non-classical forms is of course a construction, and in practice the boundaries are blurred and negotiable: while adherence to canonical *rāg* and *tāl* systems is a standard benchmark for 'classical' status, much music which would be classed as non-classical nevertheless uses *rāg*- and/or *tāl*-like structures (see e.g. Thompson 1995, Groesbeck 1999). Nonetheless, the use of Hindustānī *tāls* in popular, devotional, and other realms falls outside the scope of this study.

This study is not primarily concerned with drums, drumming, or drum repertoires, on which a considerable amount of research has been published in

information which may be verbalized by musicians in pedagogical contexts, and therefore rarely go beyond simple prescriptions of *tāls*. There are too many such works to be listed here, although perhaps the best summaries can be found in the works of Nikhil Ghosh (e.g. 1968, 1975*a*, 1975*b*).

[5] Interest in the subject seems to have been building gradually in recent decades: works to which I will refer include those of Cooper and Meyer (1960), Yeston (1976), Lerdahl and Jackendoff (1983), Lester (1986), Kramer (1988), Epstein (1995), and Hasty (1997), and indeed the earlier but much admired thoughts on rhythm and metre of Victor Zuckerkandl (1956).

[6] Comparative studies in rhythm and metre have declined in prominence somewhat since the days of Sachs (1953), Kolinski (1959, 1973), and Lomax (1982); nevertheless important ethnomusicological studies have been made, such as those of Catherine Ellis on Australian aboriginal music (1984) and those of Stone (1985), Arom (1991), Agawu (1995*a*, 1995*b*), and others on various African repertoires. Studies of Indian rhythm include a number of excellent works on drumming and drum repertoires (e.g. Stewart 1974; Gottlieb 1977, 1985, 1993; Kippen 1988), and several books and articles by Lewis Rowell and by Richard Widdess to which I will make reference.

recent decades. Where the drums *tablā* and *pakhāvaj* are discussed here, it is their contribution to the rhythmic organization of the music as a whole—vocal or instrumental—which will be under consideration. Readers will also note that I have given relatively little space to the discussion of unmetred music, in other words *ālāp* (but see my discussion at §7.2 and in Chapter 12). This is not due to a lack of interest in the subject, and nor can I claim that such a study would be irrelevant here—rather I believe that the analysis of unmetred music (so-called 'free rhythm'), which has proved and remains an immensely difficult problem,[7] requires further development of both theoretical perspectives and analytical techniques before I or anyone else can do it full justice.

In the next two chapters I introduce some important perspectives on which the later discussion draws, considering both Indian cultural norms and ideologies which may be of relevance to rhythmic organization (Chapter 2) and a number of general theories and controversies on rhythm and metre (Chapter 3). In Chapter 4 I introduce the basic theory of the North Indian *tāl* system, outlining the model of rhythmic organization implicit therein, and its limitations, and building on this work to propose an outline of a theoretical model of North Indian rhythmic organization.

Subsequent chapters refer back to the perspectives introduced in Chapters 2 to 4, in discussing the most important aspects of rhythmic organization in this music. They cover in turn, *tāl* (metric structure, Chapter 5), *lay* (tempo and rhythmic density, Chapter 6), performance practice in general (Chapter 7), composition structure (Chapter 8), development techniques (Chapter 9), and *laykārī* (rhythmic variation, Chapter 10).

Thus Chapters 2 to 4 set the foundations for the study, and 5 to 10 describe North Indian rhythmic organization in terms of a theoretical model, illustrating this with reference to specific rhythmic parameters in actual musical performance. Chapter 11 applies this theoretical model in a case study of an individual musician's repertoire (that of sitārist Deepak Choudhury), in order to illustrate the usefulness of rhythmic analysis in addressing issues of historical continuity and innovation, and the relationships between various genres and styles—both issues which are extremely important in this musical tradition, and difficult to discuss without either the distortions generated by musicians' need to validate their own practices, or a resort to vague and impressionistic writing. Finally, in Chapter 12 I return to general issues, drawing on observations from the study of *rāg* music which may shed light on general problems of musical time.

[7] See Clayton 1996.

2

Theoretical perspectives I: musical time in Indian cultural perspective

2.1 Introduction

I turn now to the wider cultural context within which Indian rhythmic organization operates—and to a critical discussion of how, if at all, cultural ideology, patterns, and norms may be reflected in music. As I noted in Chapter 1, a relationship is often postulated between ideology and cultural norms on the one hand and musical theory and practice on the other. This relationship is characterized in different ways: for Stanley Hoffman, for instance, music is tied into a web of culture, and musical knowledge is inseparable from any other kind of knowledge;

> it is not possible to isolate something called music from something else called culture. Musical knowledge *is* cultural knowledge. Furthermore, the way in which a person knows music is not different from the way he knows in general. That is, musical knowledge is based on the same epistemology which underlies and pervades the entire culture. (1978 : 69)[1]

While for Catherine Ellis, patterns of thought are encoded in music so that they may subtly influence participants' ways of thinking;

> it seems that in common with many other musics in the world—and perhaps even *all* other musics in the world—Aboriginal music uses elements of time structure to manipulate the performers' and/or listeners' sense of time and thereby to enable specific desired patterns of thought to be implanted in the minds of the participants. (1984 : 150)

Thus music has been described both as reflecting a more general cultural ideology, and as being the channel through which ideology is disseminated. It still remains, however, to show how such ideologies influence music structure, if indeed such influence can be demonstrated at all.

In the Indian context both of these positions are expressed, the former 'reflectionist' position most of all. To give but one example, an emphatic articulation of the view that Indian *rāg* music embodies in some sense a world-view, representing in audible form metaphysical ideas about the world, is contained in the comment of one of India's greatest musicians, Pandit Ravi Shankar, that 'The highest aim of our music is to reveal the essence of the universe it reflects' (1969 : 17).

[1] See also Merriam (1964 : 13), and Such and Jairazbhoy (1982 : 104).

I have already expressed my scepticism about invocations of 'Indian culture' or appeals to the preferences of 'the Indian' —simplistic notions which can all too easily divert attention from the (well-known) diversity of the subcontinent's religious, social, linguistic, and indeed musical systems. I neither believe nor propose, as some have done, that a performance of Indian music represents, in the form of a large-scale aural analogy, cosmological process as conceived in Hindu philosophy. This is not to say that no musicians believe it to be so, but I believe such a view to be a possible rather than a necessary or universally shared interpretation.

Nevertheless, given that we are considering an art music tradition patronized by social élites and codified within an ancient literary-theoretical tradition, we must allow for the possibility that this music system has—at various times over the course of its history—been influenced by the religious tenets, philosophical notions, and ideologies to which those élites subscribed. Indeed, since the problem of time is fundamental to all philosophical systems, and temporal organization an equally important aspect of all music systems, connections between music and metaphysics are at least as likely to be manifested here as in any other domain. Thus the Indian concept of 'cyclical' time is of importance in a musical context. Other metaphysical concepts—such as the interdependence of the phenomena of form and process—may also perhaps find expression in music systems and theories, and ultimately influence the temporal organization of music.

There are in fact several important ways in which the rhythmic organization of North Indian music may be thought to reflect wider ideological considerations, of which I will consider below three particularly important instances;

- the perceived necessity for accurate and unambiguous time measurement in music (as in ritual);
- the conception of musical performance and of the world in general as a process of manifestation and dissolution, rather than as a discrete and enduring product;
- the conception of *tāl* structures, and of time in general, as cyclically repeating.

I should note first of all a logical distinction between the first of these points and the other two. The importance of accurate time-keeping seems to be a result of *rāg* music's historically quasi-ritual function, and is therefore a practical and functionally determined preference; the concepts of musical performance as process, and of musical time as cyclical, are derived from a tendency to conceive music as reflecting—by means of its own structure and organization—man's conception of the universe. In other words they are, in so far as they may be identified in music, symbolic, whereas the first point is pragmatic.

This important distinction may reflect the historical evolution of Indian art music, from its earlier status as an aspect of religious ritual into a music tradition patronized by royal courts and, more recently, the urban middle classes. Where music forms a part of or an accompaniment to religious ritual, rules for its performance may be determined by religious considerations, but its actual structure need not necessarily represent these concepts. Only in the case of an art-music tradition, albeit one aware of its religious roots, will the music *itself* be taken to embody and symbolize metaphysical concepts. It seems possible that as Indian music has evolved, one of the forces influencing that evolution has been the desire to 'reveal the essence of the universe'—the universe as conceptualized and constructed within a particular cultural context—through musical structures.

2.2 Time measurement

Indian music theory historically shows a strong preference for the accurate and unambiguous measurement of time. This principle seems to stem from the role of music as a religious act, analogous to and to some extent derived from Vedic ritual. As Lewis Rowell writes in his study of ancient Indian music (*gāndharva*),[2]

> Like earlier Vedic rituals, from which it may have sprung, the performance of gāndharva was considered a sacrifice. The ritual actions, text, poses, dancing, miming and music were specified in unusual detail, and precise performance was required in order for the production to achieve its objective—adṛṣṭa-phala (unseen benefit) (1988*a* : 141)

The ancient connection between musical performance and religious observance has left its legacy in the patterns of hand gestures used in Indian music for counting time—the cheironomy. Just as every action and every word of a religious ritual must be perfectly performed in order to ensure a beneficial effect, so no effort may be spared in ensuring the correct progression of a musical performance.[3] Although the *tāl* structures are nowadays generally much less complex than those employed in *gāndharva*, clap (or gesture) patterns are still a feature of most *rāg* music today.

The belief that ill effects could arise from inaccurate time-keeping was surely instrumental in the development, from ancient times, of a rigid and unambiguous rhythmic structure backed up by the complex system of cheironomy of which a vestige survives to this day. (This may also be a factor in the traditional assumption that a moderate underlying tempo should be maintained in music performance. Complex metrical structures are more easily maintained at moderate tempi, and acceleration might be construed as a distortion of that structure.)

Subhadra Chaudhary explains another aspect of the philosophical importance accorded to time measure. For her, as for Bharata, the putative author of

[2] This question is also discussed in detail by Mukund Lath (1978 : 82 ff., 101 ff.).

[3] Chaudhary (1997 : 6) touches on this point citing Śaṅgadeva's 'Saṅgītaratnākara' (13th cent.) and Kallinātha's commentary thereon, 'Kalānidhi' (c. 1450). Commenting on a passage from the Saṅgītaratnākara (5/38–9), Kallinātha explains that a second singer must assist the main singer in keeping *tāl*, because if a mistake were to occur, not only would the '*adtṛṣṭa phala*' be lost, but a '*pratyavāya*' (ill effect) could occur (these terms are common to religious ritual).

the ancient dramaturgical treatise Nātyaśāstra, 'There is no sound which is outside time measure and no time measure without sound.'

Here Bharata has indicated an extremely subtle truth. A little thought is enough to understand that sound is not possible without time, but why cannot time be measured without sound? Time is boundless and it is impossible to have knowledge of it. It has to be divided into segments in order to be perceived. Division requires actions. Sound is indispensable for action however subtle it may be . . . Thus these two elements—Vāk [speech, utterance] and Kāla [time] combine to produce Nāda [sound] which is the basis of the functioning of the whole universe. (1997 : 350–1)

Thus, according to traditional Hindu philosophy, the production of sound and the measurement of time are inextricably linked to each other and to the functioning of the universe. Little wonder then that the measurement of time has played an important part in Hindu ritual, nor that music theorists through the ages should have given such a prominent place to questions of time measurement. This remains a factor in modern musical practice, and is perhaps the clearest link between ideology and the practice of music.

2.3 Musical performance as process

Rāg performance—with its gradual exposition, development, acceleration, and ultimate subsidence into the drone—has sometimes been considered to represent the Indian metaphysical concept of the creation and ultimate dissolution of matter in the universe. Lewis Rowell best puts the case for viewing the opening improvisation (*ālāp*) of a performance as representing matter undergoing differentiation and emerging as structure in 'a process of pure *becoming*' (1981 : 207).[4] I would like to discuss the possibility that this analogy may actually have helped to shape Indian music practice over the course of history.

Indian music is considered to be pre-existent in a rather different sense to that of a European composition which is stored in written form. Form, indeed, is the keyword here—a classical symphony has a form which is conceived as essentially permanent and unchanging, and a considerable part of its value is understood in terms of that form or structure—the ways in which different parts are perceived to relate to one another and to the whole; the progression from beginning to a logically determined end point; the sheer beauty of the piece of music as a sound object. To be sure there are considerable differences in this respect between such 'closed' forms and 'open' forms such as the rondo and passacaglia, or strophic song, but even in the latter cases many Europeans seem predisposed to regard pieces of music as indivisible, bounded wholes distinguished by the structural relationships between their parts. Performance, then, is widely conceived in the West as the gradual revelation of a pre-existent structure

[4] In another passage the same author writes 'To [the Indian] music is pure natural *process* and process is what he values' (1989 : 28).

in audible form, whose essential parameters (duration included) are known in advance.

A *rāg* performance works rather differently. A *rāg* is pre-existent, to be sure (whether regarded as recently, and humanly composed, or essentially a gift from God), but it is neither an object, nor a fixed structure built of notes in the sense of a symphony or string quartet. The *rāg* is a dynamic, temporal, generative principle which can have no satisfactory representation in static or synchronic form. The *rāg* can only be apprehended in performance, *in time*. Performance is therefore conceived as a process of making audible, of evoking, of manifesting: and the primary criterion by which a performance is judged is the extent to which it permits the *rāg* itself to do what it is uniquely able to do, which is to create affect (*bhāv*), to move the hearts of those who hear it.

This conception of music as process rather than product has profound implications for rhythmic organization, as we shall see. For analytical purposes, one of the implications of a view of music as process, is that a fragment of music should not in principle be analysed without reference to its context—which should be understood here not as position within a form or structure, but as stage in musical *process*. Within the context of the *tāl*, an episode of rhythmic play (*laykārī*) is not only an artefact created and performed by the musician, but also a solution to a problem of process—how to develop a rhythmic idea and achieve a satisfactory cadence, coinciding with the start of the new *tāl* cycle—a solution which often itself evolves as the cadential point comes ever closer (as I will show below).

Having said this much (and Rowell has gone further in writing that Indian music is 'pure process', 1989 : 28), I think it is important to qualify this observation. For, just as Indian musical terminology suggests a conception of performance as process (Rowell cites examples such as *vistār*, 'expansion', and *prastār*, 'permutation'), it points at the same time to an understanding of various musical elements as enduring 'objects'. Thus a vocal composition is a *bandiś* ('restriction, structure') or a *cīz* ('article, thing'); the names for development techniques such as *bol banāo* ('building the text'), *bol bāṇṭ* ('distributing the text'), *baṛhat* ('growth') and indeed *vistār* and *prastār* all appear to indicate that some *thing* is being manipulated (restricted, distributed) or exhibiting behaviour (growing); in other words, while musical performance is a process or set of processes, these processes involve the presentation and manipulation of some musical object or other.

Form and process are necessarily entwined in music—any musical gesture may be initially perceived as process and subsequently rationalized as form,[5] and this is true of Indian music as it is of Western. Some Indian theorists have in fact described music performance in these terms. Vamanrao Deshpande, for instance, interprets performance as a process in which 'Each *avartana* [cycle] must . . . excel the one that has gone before. This process goes on until the last

[5] See e.g. David Clarke 1989.

avartana in which the very acme of tension is reached, to be followed by a grand resolution which completes the entire recital' (1987 : 33). Yet this process is for him aimed at the description of form: 'When [musicians] speak of *gayaki* [vocal style] or *bandish* there is little doubt that what they have in mind is the formal organization of a musical piece. Musicians and connoisseurs have always accorded the highest value to *gayaki*-s which showed perfectness of form . . .' (1987 : 40).

Thus the performance is not a product, but parts of it, such as the *bandiś* (fixed composition), are, while the *rāg* itself is in a sense objectified. Performance in Indian music is not therefore 'pure process', if such a phenomenon can be said to exist; it is a process whereby latent musical entities (such as a *rāg*) are made manifest—revealed, described, and invoked. In the course of this process composed musical 'products' (such as a *bandiś*) are presented, repeated, varied, and extended. And the aim—in aesthetic, rather than spiritual terms—is that through these processes the potential affective power of music should be evoked. Indian music is, then, fundamentally an art of process, but we should not forget that process involves the manipulation of objectified musical materials, nor that such process is valued for its affective power.

2.4 Cyclicity in musical and cosmic time

A number of musicologists have pointed to an apparent connection between cyclic *tāl* structures and cyclic time in Hindu thought. Rowell, for instance, writes that 'the cyclic organization of the underlying *tāl* is a microcosmic parallel to the macrocosmic cycles within which Indian time unfolds' (1981 : 207), citing linguistic observation to support his argument (the common term for a metric unit, *āvart* or *āvard*, translates as 'cycle' or 'period'). David Such and Nazir Jairazbhoy, appealing to the view that 'since music forms a part of the social and cultural environment, it reflects the conceptual structures of a community' (1982 : 104), state equally plainly that: 'Since music is symbolic and reflects the conceptual structures and organization of a community, one would expect to find similar cyclic structures in certain aspects of Indian music. The most obvious instance of a cycle appears in the concept underlying *tāla* . . .' (1982 : 105). B. C. Deva explains the logic of the basic description of *tāl* as cyclic as follows: 'when a rhythmic experience is arranged so that there is a feeling of "coming back" to the origin, the arrangement becomes repetitive or cyclic; for it is only in a circle that one returns to the beginning . . .' (1974 : 38); while Such and Jairazbhoy suggest that in a *tāl*,

> beat 1 . . . represents both the end of the cycle and the beginning of the next; indeed, the principles of the tāla cycle contrast sharply with the rhythmic principles of most Western music which generally end on the last beat. The tāla tends to provide a degree of perpetual motion characteristic of cycles. In terms of analogy, a single tāla cycle can thus be compared to a single human life with the high and low points within the time cycle being

similar to life cycle events . . . Furthermore, successive cycles of the tāla can be seen as the successive lives experienced by the individual soul—a comparison made even more meaningful when applied to North Indian classical music where the tempo of succeeding cycles gradually rises to a climax, like the individual soul rising up the ladder of *vārnas* [sc. varṇas; social classes] until final liberation. (1982 : 106–7)

This argument—in its various forms—raises rather fundamental questions; in order to consider it, it will be necessary to reflect a little on both time in Indian philosophy, and the significance of the description of musical time as cyclical.

2.4.1 Time in Indian thought

According to Indian cosmology, time is indeed cyclical not only on the levels of days, months, and years, but also on the higher level of the enormously long aeons or world cycles (*kalpa*). Fred Clothey suggests[6] that 'Time and its measure are important dimensions of ritual observance throughout Hinduism' (1983 : 47), while the ideas of cyclicity—extending from lunar, stellar, and solar cycles up to the world cycles—and of ritual time as microcosm of cosmic time, are recurrent features of Hindu ritual.

As Anindita Balslev points out, Western writers have often misunderstood and misrepresented Indian cyclic time, taking it to indicate a 'philosophy of sheer recurrence',[7] and assuming that world cycles repeat themselves exactly. In the Indian philosophical tradition however, world cycles repeat, but 'the wheel of becoming, in the Indian context, does not involve a mechanical repetition of the particular/the individual, neither does it preclude salvation' (Balslev 1983 : 147). Cycles are the same in type, but not in detail, and processes such as salvation unfold continuously within the framework of cyclical time. Moreover, while the cyclicity of time suggests that things are essentially unchanging (see Nakamura 1981 : 77), 'the very repetitiveness of the cycles suggests the world's eternal renewability' (Clothey 1983 : 77).

Indian musical organization can certainly be construed as paralleling this concept. Music unfolds in a process of continuous development and does not repeat exactly, but this development takes place largely within the context of a cyclically repeating temporal structure—the *tāl*. (Thus the implication of the analogy should be not only of the cyclicity of *tāl*, but equally of a conceptual separation between the continuous process of *rāg* development, and the recurrent temporal substructure of *tāl*.) Moreover, the ultimate nature of the *rāg* is thought of as unchanging, while it is constantly renewed in performance as cycle inevitably follows cycle.

On the other hand, the idea of music structure reflecting cyclical time does not seem to have been prevalent in India in the first millennium CE (the period from

[6] In the course of an anthropological study of a South Indian Śaiva cult.
[7] Toynbee (1972 : 157–8), quoted in Balslev (1983 : 149).

which the earliest surviving sources on Indian music date). In so far as ancient Indian music reflected cosmological ideas, it is primarily in the emphasis placed on the measurement of time noted above. As Rowell points out, the Indian *tāl* system 'shifted from a set of complex modular formal structures [the ancient *mārga tāla* system] to an integrated system designed to facilitate improvisation over a repeated rhythmic cycle' (1992 : 192): while this important change seems to have taken place by the thirteenth century, there is no evidence for it in the Nāṭyaśāstra or in other first-millennium sources.

As Rowell concedes, the onus is on proponents of the 'cultural symbolism' argument (such as himself) to explain why ancient Indian *tāl* was not conceived as cyclic (although cosmic time was), and why the concept of musical cyclicity developed rather slowly—apparently during the very period, historically, when the hold of classical Brahmanical Hinduism began to weaken in Northern India, challenged both by a series of Muslim conquests and by the emergence of popular devotional strains of Hindu worship. The answer Rowell presents, in the most convincing of his formulations, lies in 'a mutual feedback and a development of what we might call "resonances" between a musical tradition and its controlling ideology' (1988*b* : 330). In other words, such symbolic representations are subject to a considerable time lag, so that music may come to 'reflect' ideas which have been superseded in other realms of thought.

While this theory is not implausible in itself, there are at least two other possible explanations, namely:

1. that musical structures changed for reasons largely unconnected with the symbolic representation of cosmic time, and the fact that the new structures lent themselves more easily to metaphors of cyclicity was no more than a happy coincidence;
2. the idea that performance should actually *represent* cyclic time, rather than (as in the ancient Indian system) *regulate* cosmic time, is at least partly due to the influence of Sufi thought. This possibility in particular deserves a little consideration.

Sufism flourished in India shortly after the first Muslim invasions, and was well established by the thirteenth century CE, since which time certain strains of Sufism (that of the Chishti sect in particular) have had a close and continuing relationship with Indian musical culture. Images of cyclicity and circularity play an important part in Sufi thought, as explained by the Indian Sufi thinker and musician Hazrat Inayat Khan, writing in the early years of the twentieth century:

> In the traditions of the Sufis *Raqs*, the sacred dance of spiritual ecstasy . . . is traced to the time when contemplation of the Creator impressed the wonderful reality of His vision so deeply on the heart of [thirteenth-century mystic] Jelal-ud-Din Rumi that he became entirely absorbed in the whole and single immanence of nature, and took a rhythmic turn which caused the skirt of his garment to form a circle, and the movements of his hands and neck made a circle. It is the memory of this moment of vision which is celebrated in the dance of dervishes. (1991 : 153)

As in some strands of Hindu thought, for Inayat Khan binary alternation and cyclicity are aspects of the same phenomenon.[8]

> the whole universe is a single mechanism working by the law of rhythm; the rise and fall of the waves, the ebb and flow of the tide, the waxing and waning of the moon, the sunrise and the sunset, the change of the seasons, the moving of the earth and of the planets—the whole cosmic system and the constitution of the entire universe are working under the law of rhythm. Cycles of rhythm, with major and minor cycles interpenetrating, uphold the whole creation in their swing. (1991 : 155)

In Regula Qureshi's study of Sufi *qavvālī* music (which is closely related to the classical *rāg* tradition, although strictly speaking outside the scope of this book), she discusses the importance of *zikr*, or verbal invocation, thus:

> The dynamic principle of *zikr* is repetition, a motion in time of an essentially circular nature. Sufis themselves explain this as *lai kā halqa* (encirclement of pace or rhythm) a cyclical temporal pattern that carries the verbal repetition even when the words are not actually spoken. What marks each temporal pattern is *zarb* (stroke, blow, also heart beat), meant to stir the heart at the culmination of each verbal invocation. In the classical *zikr* recitation it is marked by a vocal accent and reinforced by a strong downward nod. (1994 : 505)

According to Qureshi's interpretation at least, the principles of *zikr* also extend into musical performance 'The drum pattern (*theka*) provides an independent acoustic frame for the meter and in fact functions much like an ostinato underlying the melodic setting of the song, at the same time it also incorporates the duple accentuation that invokes *zikr*' (1994 : 514).

I cannot claim that this suggestion is any more than speculative, but it seems to me that the notion of cyclic repetition in music being based entirely on ancient Hindu concepts of time is difficult to support, and that the ideological resonance of the concept of cyclicity is rather more complex than such a proposition would suggest. Whereas for the Hindu musicians of 2,000 years ago cosmic time was essentially cyclical, while music embodied ideas of ritual as cosmic regulation, for Sufi thinkers, flourishing rather later, the mystic's duty was to represent cyclicity through repeated verbal invocation and repetitive musical patterns, and spatially in the circular patterns of a dancer's dress and hand positions. Just as Hindu and Sufi ideas experienced degrees of mutual influence over history, Sufi music both drew on earlier Indian repertoires and influenced the development of new styles: thus, even in so far as cultural ideology may be said to be represented in music (and I will discuss the limits of that contention itself below), Indian music's 'cyclicity' surely cannot be so simple as a reflection of ancient Hindu thought.

2.4.2 Images of cyclicity in music

Let me now risk stating the obvious by saying that no music is cyclical in any empirically verifiable sense. The cycle is a spatial-temporal metaphor used in

[8] For another perspective on the relationship between alternation and cyclicity see Gell (1992 : 34–5).

order to clarify, mediate, and communicate subjective musical experience. Musical metre is no more a circle, or a wheel (see Deva 1981 : 270), than it is a ruler or tape-measure (see *Grove 6*), or indeed a helix or a wave (see below); rulers, wheels, helixes, and waves are metaphors used to explain musical metre, and it does not follow that because theorists in different cultures use different metaphors, metre actually functions differently from place to place.

I would suggest, on the contrary, that these (and other) metaphors represent attempts to explain two complementary aspects of musical metre. Metre, on the one hand, appears to *measure* time—that is, an event can be located in time relative to another event (two beats later, one bar before) thanks to metre; on the other hand, metre involves the *recurrence* of temporal patterns (the first beat of any measure is equivalent to the first beats of all other measures). Music therefore appears both to go from A to B in a measured manner, and to keep coming back to the same 'place' in time. Most metaphors for metre emphasize one or other of these two aspects, and I would suggest that (very roughly speaking) Western music theory has emphasized metre's aspect as time measurement and played down the aspect of recurrence, while Indian music theory has given expression to both aspects more equally.

In other words, if there is a difference between metre in Indian and Western music it may lie not so much in one being cyclical and the other not, but in the fact that Indian theorists have not been troubled by the apparent paradox of musical time as both linear and recurrent, whereas Western theorists have been inclined to play down the sense of recurrence, let alone cyclicity, in favour of a more singular conception of linear development. There is nothing in Deva's position (see above) that could not be equally well said of Western music, while Such and Jairazbhoy's contention that the emphasis on beat 1 as both beginning and ending contrasts sharply with Western music is highly contentious. For sure, elementary theory appears to describe a 4/4 metre as a sequence of 4 crotchet beats (beginning on the first, presumably, and ending on the last!); but regularly metrical music is organized according to a *recurring* pattern of beats, and our experience of a 4/4 metre inevitably involves a sense that following the fourth beat we will experience the first of a new measure.

'Cyclical' metre is not, then, unique to India. For examples of cyclical descriptions of musical time in other parts of the world I might cite Catherine Ellis's view of Aboriginal music (1984), and Laz Ekwueme's description of African rhythm (1975–6). Similarly, several musicologists have in fact described metre in Western music as cyclical, and increasingly so in recent years (see e.g. Hasty 1997; Yako 1997). The themes Christopher Hasty discusses, in a lengthy examination of the issue, could all equally well apply to Indian music: cycles as the return of 'the same' time-span; as regulation; as homogeneous despite the heterogeneity of their contents; and so on (1997 : 8–9). So too, indeed, could his suggestion that 'A cycle must be differentiated internally in order to mark a duration that can be equal to the duration of another instance of the cycle' (1997: 9).

Similarly, just as we find the *sam* (beat 1) described in Indian music as having a dual function as beginning and ending, Wallace Berry can ask of Western music, 'In the metric unit, what does "one"—the "one" of counting—signify? (Riemann's term *Hervortreten*, a "stepping forth", is suggestive. Moreover, merged arrival and departure, in fulfillment of anacrusis and the thrust of downbeat impetus, is an apt conceit by which to characterize many notated measure beginnings)' (1985 : 7).

In fact, it seems as if the idea of cyclicity has always been available for the description of Western music, while until recently theorists have been strikingly resistant to take it on board. This is most clearly illustrated by the work of Victor Zuckerkandl, whose 'wave theory' of metre is often admiringly cited (if not widely applied) by Western music theorists. In the exposition of his theory, the place given to cyclicity is extremely revealing. Here he ponders the nature of simple duple metre:

> To be able to come back, one must first have gone away; now we also understand why we count one-*two*, and not one-*one*. Here 'two' does not mean simply 'beat number 2', but also 'away from'. The entire process is therefore an 'away from-back to', not a flux but a cycle [*Diagram*] a constantly repeated cycle, for the 'one' that closes one cycle simultaneously begins another. (1956 : 168)

Having got this far, however, Zuckerkandl is clearly unhappy with his own image of cyclically repeating time: 'But since in time there can be no real going back, and hence, strictly speaking, no real cyclical motion either, since, therefore, every new beat does bring us to a new point in time, the process can be better understood and visualized as a wave [*Diagram*] which also best corresponds to our sensation of meter' (1956 : 168).

It is surely not surprising, given such a reluctance on the part of earlier Western theorists to accept cyclical time, that Western students of Indian music were struck forcefully by Indian theorists' acceptance of the same concept. It will be useful, in fact, to contrast Zuckerkandl's reasoning with that of Subhadra Chaudhary, in her discussion of the same topic.

> The circle and cycle are two important visual concepts which aid one in comprehending the concept of tāla. Although both have round shapes the circle is formed by returning to starting point whereas the cycle is formed by moving forward gradually in a spiral [illustrated as a helix].
>
> The āvartana [cycle] of tāla bears similarity to the circle since we return to the . . . starting point. The measuring of time is the main purpose of tāla and, since the time which has been elapsed in one āvarta[na] of tāla cannot be recaptured, there is a forward movement in time, as a result of which there is a 'cycle' of tāla, not a 'circle'. (1997 : 35)

Comparing the reasoning of Zuckerkandl and Chaudhary, it would seem that conceptions of musical metre are actually (or at least can be) rather similar in the West and in India. Both these writers use visual images to illustrate the dual nature of musical time as embodying both recurrence and change. The Indian concept of the metric cycle, which seems to relate to cosmological ideas of time as described above, seems to me to attempt to balance or reconcile the two aspects, whereas many Western music theorists in the past chose rather to ignore, denigrate, or otherwise evade the issue of recurrence.

The predominance of a linear conception of time in Western culture is also historically specific. Stephen Jay Gould discusses the tensions between conceptions of linearity (illustrated metaphorically by the arrow) and recurrence (by the cycle) in his account of the development of modern geology, *Time's Arrow, Time's Cycle* (1987). Gould makes the point that the former has dominated Western (Judeao-Christian) thought, tracing the idea back to the Bible ('Many scholars have identified time's arrow as the most important and distinctive contribution of Jewish thought...', 1987: 11), while also stressing that the image of time's cycle has always remained a part of Western ideas. Another useful distinction made by Gould is that between time's arrow as simply a 'chain of unique events', and the implication of 'progress' which dates from much later. There is clearly a connection between linear conceptions of musical time and wider concerns in European thought—it may not be too great a simplification, in fact, to associate the linear conception of time with tonal music of the common-practice period, and with wider tendencies in modern (in the sense of post-Enlightenment) thought.

Cyclicity as a reconciliation between linear progression and recurrence is intimately linked to other aspects of metrical perception, including the conceptual separation between metre and rhythm which has exercised many Western theorists (see Chapter 3). If we regard metre as the regular, repetitive, and predictable framework against which rhythm is measured, Jeffrey Pressing suggests the possibilities thus afforded are widely exploited.

> The recurrence of the same or related sonic events in music is often considered to create a kind of cyclic time that stands in contrast to linear time. This idea is widespread in non-Western music (e.g. the West African time line, the Indian *tala*) and in the music of our own [i.e. Western] culture (e.g. passacaglia, ostinato, strophic form, theme and variations, rondo form)... Since it is repetition that allows cyclicity to be perceived, it can be useful heuristically to classify the nature of repetition used in music, as an index of the degree of cyclicity of time. Thus we may view a certain passage as being periodic, quasi-periodic, aperiodic. (1993: 111)

This leads him to propose metrical music as exhibiting two-dimensional time, in which 'there are two primary time positions that affect the function of notes: absolute time position, and placement within the bar' (1993: 111),[9] a situation which inspires him to produce a graphical illustration in the form of a helix—exactly the same image used by Chaudhary.

The supposed contrast between time in Indian and Western music is then to a great extent illusory. Metre, in Western music, is an integral component of our sense of 'motion', of music moving from beginning to end in a controlled and

[9] Pressing does concede that this situation is complicated rather by the fact that a note or motive's position within the phrase or section need also be considered.

controllable manner. Metre involves recurrence, for sure, as 4/4 bar follows 4/4 bar, but this aspect of metre remains almost hidden because of a reluctance of theorists (until very recently) to deal with the duality of time in metre. In Indian music, similarly, *tāl* measures time as it moves to its conclusion; similarly, *tāl* 'cycle' follows cycle. The difference is that Indian musicians and theorists have never had a problem with such recurrence, because their 'common-sense' notions of time do not preclude cyclical recurrence on every imaginable level. The primary contrast, therefore, is not in musical structure but in the metaphorical explanation of that structure.

What appears to have happened in India, to extend Rowell's hypothesis, is that Indian theorists moved from a recognition that *tāl* could be conceived in this way to a belief that this was, after all, a natural state of affairs—since time in all other dimensions of experience was cyclical. Having reached this position—influenced by whatever combination of Hindu and Sufi ideologies—it is possible that the conception of *tāl* as cyclical fed back from music theory into practice as performers began to be persuaded that time in music *ought* to be so. As this happened, features which appeared to indicate cyclicity were enhanced and those which weakened it disparaged (or ignored), so that musical repertoires slowly evolved to reinforce this concept. To cite but one effect of this shift, metrical patterns which had reached a climax at their end point were reorganized so that the emphasized point was regarded as the beginning.[10] *Tāl*—which had been practised as a predetermined succession of different metrical patterns—came to be a single, endlessly replicable pattern used to organize improvised performance.

The relationship between music structure and ideology is surely dynamic and interactional. Music structure is not a given which influences its listeners' world-view (as Ellis would have it); nor is ideology a given which is reflected in music structure. The musical sounds people actually produce are determined by so many different variables, interacting in so many ways, that simple reflectionism is untenable. What is more credible is the proposition that these sound patterns are received and interpreted by the same perceptual and cognitive systems which deal with other stimuli; that people tend to perceive or to impose patterns on sound which they perceive in other domains of experience; that consequently they come to expect certain types of patterning to be present in music; and that performers will attempt to fulfil such expectation by implanting such patterning in music.

And yet, there are no simply agreed norms for culturally preferred patterns. Ideologies change, and are constantly subject to redefinition and renegotiation. Moreover, whatever the intention there are limits on the kinds of patterns which

[10] As Emmie te Nijenhuis points out, 'In modern Indian music [the *sam*] mostly occurs at the beginning of the rhythmic cycle, whereas in the ancient *mārgatālas* the *saṃnipāta* (abbr. *saṃ*) generally falls on the last [time unit]' (1974 : 67). In North Indian music *sam*, which is often described as a 'point of equilibrium' (see Deshpande 1987 : 32; Rowell 1992 : 188) marks the *beginning* of the cycle, but it also marks the *end* of a rhythmic phrase or cadence.

can be reliably encoded in and decoded from music sounds. As Qureshi suggests, 'ideology clearly emerges as the most immediate cultural key to notions of time and their musical realizations. But . . . ideology and normative concepts need to be tested against the sound experience itself, if the time content of music is to be decoded' (1994 : 526). Music, like ideology, is constantly being re-created and redefined, and I see these two processes as parallel yet interacting, and music theory as a conduit for this interaction.

2.4.3 Linearity, narrativity, and cyclicity

I will return now to a suggestion floated above, and propose that musical time exhibits two complementary aspects. One is periodicity, regularity, and recurrence, corresponds to the domain of metre, and gives rise to the concept of cyclicity. The other is gestural, figural, and (in principle) unpredictable and relates to the domain of rhythm. Rhythmic gestures tend to relate to one another in a more linear fashion: rather than (as in metre) the same pattern being due for return, in rhythm one gesture can be followed by either a repetition of the same, a variation thereon, or a distinct but complementary pattern.

Rather than singling out Indian music as uniquely cyclical, it may be more instructive to test the idea that Western music is unusually linear. European theorists have from the early modern era until recently tended to avoid the notion of cyclicity and stress linearity: natural, logical, progressive development leading to final resolution. For Barney Childs, this preference has led musicians to assimilate musical structures to the kind of narrative curve found in other temporal arts.

> The Western European intellectual and cultural tradition has seemingly found most fundamental a basic structural organization of a work of time art, what might be called a *narrative curve*. Greek tragedy, the 'classic' short story, the television crime drama, the Romantic tone poem, furnish examples of this organization, which presumably is held to exist as a stylized reflection of how the tradition views life itself . . . (1977 : 195)

Similarly for Michel Imberty,

> It is easy to assume that for the average [Western] listener every musical work has something like an *exposition*, a *development*, a *recapitulation*, or a succession from idea A to idea B with an obligatory return to idea A. This structure, which has been sustained for over three centuries of tonal music and has been imposed by the very nature of tonal syntax, is perhaps not very far removed from the structures of narratives which are arranged according to a similar system (exposition, tension-crisis, denouement or catastrophe). Even though there is necessarily something approximate about this comparison, nevertheless it is possible to show that the *memorisation*, as well as the *segmentation* of the musical piece, is achieved in accord or in conflict with those models acquired by the subjects in their general culture. (1993 : 35)

Although comparisons between music and narrative structure can seem a little forced (a 'return to idea A' seems to me to be somewhat different in kind to a 'denouement or catastrophe'; moreover the much higher levels of redundancy and repetition in almost any music than in literature seems to me a major difficulty), it seems clear that the idea that a piece of music should move through a logical order of events towards closure has been an important one in European music practice and theory.

These ideas of linearity, the concomitant stress on teleological listening, and their denial in much twentieth-century Western music, are discussed at some length by Jonathan Kramer (1988). Of Kramer's many fascinating ideas, one which most clearly relates to this study is his distinction between linear and non-linear time in music. Linearity, for Kramer, is related to the functions of the brain's left hemisphere;[11] it is deductive and sequential, and understands time as 'containing a sequence of events'. Non-linearity is located in the right hemisphere, is holistic and continuous, and understands time as 'containing a complex of events' (1988 : 9–10). Kramer lists characteristics of these two concepts as follows;

Linearity	Nonlinearity
teleological listening	cumulative listening
horizontal	vertical
motion	stasis
change	persistence
progressive	consistency
becoming	being
left brain	right brain
temporal	atemporal

Kramer (1988 : 63)

His implication seems to be that music can exploit either or both of these complexes, and that any piece of music exhibits both linear and non-linear features. Linear features, for Kramer, are those aspects of music which seem to be determined by what has gone before, while nonlinear features are determined by characteristics of the piece as a whole. Thus harmonic motion, cadence, and closure are linear features, while (for instance) the metre of a consistently metrical piece, or the composition of an ensemble, are non-linear features. Tonal music (so far as it may be generalized) exploits linearity almost to the greatest possible degree, since it is built on logical development, teleological listening and development towards final cadence and closure. Closure, for Kramer, 'is most comfortably associated with tonality'.

A composition in which the cadence of one phrase is appreciably stronger than the cadence of a previous phrase is a piece that exhibits a greater degree of closure than one in which each successive cadence is of equivalent finality. A strong cadence tends to close off not only its phrase but also several preceding phrases, thus creating a phrase group. The . . . final cadence of a piece is generally the strongest, since it must end the

[11] Kramer's use of the left brain/right brain dichotomy may be, in fact, one of the weaker components of this theory (Ian Cross, personal communication).

entire work . . . Thus closure, like tonality itself, is hierarchical . . . no music is as richly or unequivocally hierarchical as tonal music. (1988 : 137–8)

These ideas are instructive when applied to Indian music. I should say first of all that I agree with Kramer that any piece of music exhibits both linear and non-linear features; I am certainly not about to propose any simple dichotomy (tonal music as linear, Indian as non-linear, for example). Yet it does appear that, *relative to Western tonal music*, Indian music seems to display non-linear features more prominently and linear features less so. This seems to me inherent in assumptions about the nature of *rāg*, *tāl*, and composition (*bandiś*). Thus, a single *rāg* determines the melody of an entire performance, without modulation; a single *tāl* remains in force, its cycles repeating indefinitely; a 'composition' is not a whole performance, but a relatively brief fragment which remains operative as a source of variations and elaborations. Conversely, Indian music has no equivalent to the Western concept of large-scale harmonic motion away from and back to a tonic chord; a piece which begins in *rāg* A continues in *rāg* A, and ends in *rāg* A, thus there can be no resolution equivalent to a final cadence. Closure is hierarchical only up to the level of a brief episode of elaboration; the closure of each successive episode carries roughly equal weight and no hierarchy of closure is established; consequently the ending cadence, although often longer, more elaborate, and dramatic than what has gone before, does not logically include all previous cadences.

This is not to say that Indian *rāg* music shows no linear features. *Rāg* development is in a sense a linear procedure, in many styles proceeding by a process of expansion from a small kernel around the Sa (system tonic) until the *rāg* occupies the whole gamut. Thus, an episode whose range extends up to the fourth degree Ma may be expected to be followed by one extending up to the fifth, Pa. Within each episode of development, whether focused on melody, rhythm, or text, performers tend to follow a procedure of presenting an idea, and developing it (through variation, elaboration, and so on) as far as possible before bringing the episode to an end with a cadential gesture.

The large-scale processes of *rāg* music which I will describe under the general heading of *intensification* are difficult to classify in Kramer's terms, since they are in a sense linear without being teleological. *Rāg* music tends to become faster, for instance, but there is no target speed for which the performer aims, and there is no point at which the 'final' speed can be said to have been attained. On the contrary, the music seems to accelerate until either the limit of the performers' technical ability has been reached, the soloist becomes bored with the process, or the time limit set for the concert or recording has been reached.

The differences between Western tonal and Indian *rāg* music seem therefore to concern the levels at which linearity and non-linearity operate, and the relative value ascribed to these two aspects of musical time. Indian music is linear and progressive at a local level, while non-linear features predominate at higher levels; tonal music extends the principle of linearity to control the hierarchical organization of pieces as a whole. This does seem to be related to differences in cultural ideology: where Western thought since the Enlightenment has valued progress and development, and music theorists have sought to demonstrate the logical organization and coherence of great works, Indian theorists have sought to emphasize music's value as a *state*. Thus, a *rāg* simply *is*: the performer's task is to bring the *rāg* to the listeners' consciousness and allow us to focus our attention on the *rāg*'s qualities. If some performances are better than others, it is because some establish the mood or affect of the *rāg* more powerfully. For the listener, since there is no large-scale sense of teleology, no expectation of recapitulation and final cadence, the ideal condition is not so much being entrained to teleological process as being absorbed in an ongoing state of *rāg*-ness—one which tends towards *timelessness*.

3

Theoretical perspectives II: general theories of rhythm and metre

3.1 Introduction

I believe that it should be the aim of any specific study in rhythm to shed light on general issues, and this is certainly my intention here. This is not an aim which has been pursued with much vigour in recent years: such cross-cultural comparison has yet to regain the impetus it received from ethnomusicologists such as Curt Sachs, Mieczyslaw Kolinski, and Alan Lomax; studies in Western music often put forward ideas of general applicability which are however seldom tested in the context of non-Western repertoires; while studies in psychology have tended to be studies in the psychology of Western music.

While this study is founded on Indian concepts, then, I will also discuss how those concepts can be translated into general concepts of cross-cultural applicability. In explaining *tāl* as a model of metric structure—in 'translating' the concept—I believe that understanding of the Indian concept is broadened. The benefit is felt both ways moreover: the findings of Indian music studies enhance those of other ethnomusicological studies, and help us move to more sophisticated ideas of rhythmic organization in general. Study of Indian rhythm must contribute to the development of general theoretical models of rhythmic organization, while conversely, Western and other ideas about metre help us to understand *tāl* better.

A variety of perspectives to emerge from work in other fields—including Western music theory, cognitive psychology, and non-Indic ethnomusicology—will therefore be of interest to the present study. Three areas in particular are significant here:

- Theories of metre (in all three of these fields).
- The distinction between so-called additive and divisive rhythm, formulated most famously by Curt Sachs.
- Psychological perspectives on the relationship between metre, perception, and memory.

3.2 Metre: an ethnomusicological perspective

3.2.1 Problems of metre in ethnomusicology

Metre, along with tempo and rhythm itself, is one of the core concepts we use to describe rhythmic phenomena. But what is metre? To many, particularly those familiar with staff notation, it is simply the dimension of music which is represented by a time signature. This is rather misleading—the time signature is, historically, a notational convention which aids the co-ordination of ensembles but need not indicate metre (although it often does, particularly in much eighteenth- and nineteenth-century music). However, since time signatures and related symbols are so widely taken to be indications of metre, they do provide useful clues regarding common-sense Western notions of this concept.

A time signature has two components, specifying between them the number of beats forming each bar and the note value used to notate this 'beat'.[1] The time signature thus specifies both that a particular time unit is regarded as a 'beat' (which may be calculated, where a metronome figure is given), and that a defined number of these beats is grouped together to form a 'bar'. Thus far we are dealing with a notational convention, according to which notational symbols are grouped to aid reading.

In much Western art music of course, the bar is also taken to be a *metric* unit, and the time signature to specify the metre. It is assumed that the first beat of the bar is the primary 'strong' beat, and that this 'strong' beat is complemented by one or more subsidiary strong beats and 'weak' beats. Metre has often been described by musicologists either as a *pattern of strong and weak beats*, or as a *grouping of beats* for the purpose of measuring time.[2]

Metre for many Western musicians and musicologists seems therefore to be a simple concept, a supposition which is confirmed by the brevity of entries on metre in many music dictionaries.[3] My purpose here is not to examine the

[1] The way this is achieved does of course vary between simple and compound metres; a point discussed at some length by Arom (1991). I have tried to use the term 'measure' for a metrical unit in general (i.e. an intended or perceived metrical unit) and 'bar' to describe an aspect of notation. Bars exist in notation but not in musical sound, although in some repertoires bar(-lines) are used to represent graphically the perceived metrical structure. I have used the terms 'pulse' and 'beat' interchangeably. Epstein suggests a distinction between the two—that a pulse is a characteristic of the performed rhythm, while a beat is a time point, the 'primary level of meter' (1995 : 29)—a position which has gained a degree of acceptance. While agreeing that some such distinction may be useful, I find Epstein's use of the terms counter-intuitive: beat suggests to me an intentional action (occurring at a time point), and pulse a perceived or unintentional action. Thus I prefer to distinguish, where necessary, between a time point and a sonic event (which necessarily has duration), with both beat and pulse referring to events perceived or understood as occurring at defined time points.

[2] See e.g. Cooper and Meyer (1960 : 4), who stress the former; *Grove 6* (1980, vol. xii : 222) which stresses the latter; and the more sophisticated definitions given by Yeston (1976 : 32–3) and Lerdahl and Jackendoff (1983 : 12).

[3] See *Grove 6* (1980) in particular; the definition in the *New Harvard Dictionary* (1986) is more sophisticated, but still perfunctory.

concept of metre in Western music in detail,[4] although it is worth noting that most music theorists and psychologists specializing in rhythmic analysis have long since abandoned the assumption that time signatures fully or reliably indicate metre.[5] What concerns me more here is the acceptance by many ethnomusicologists that metre is indeed a simple concept which may be applied to a wide range of musics, which may as a consequence be notated with Western-style time signatures and bar-lines. Metre and its representation is in fact a complex area in Western music theory, so that to apply Western concepts and notational conventions in a simplistic way in ethnomusicological studies must be methodologically unsound.

Time signatures may undoubtedly sometimes be appropriate to the description of non-Western musics. What is clear, however, is that this may not be *assumed* to be the case, without an examination of the issues involved. The problems encountered by ethnomusicologists in notating the rhythm of musics from around the world have been severe, even if many have remained unaware of them.[6] If in many cases the results have been unsatisfactory, one reason for this must be a failure to address the issues which are inevitably involved in adapting non-Western music to Western notational conventions.

These notational conventions have been employed in the graphical representation of non-Western music for centuries.[7] The practice increased during the era of the greatest growth of ethnomusicological transcription—that immediately following the invention of the phonograph in the late nineteenth century—and has continued in popularity ever since, despite numerous innovations in transcription methodology. Few authors, however, have discussed the function of time signatures and bar-lines in their transcriptions. While in many cases they may be taken to indicate the transcriber's perception of metre, given the ambiguity of their application in Western music this cannot be assumed to be the case.

Otto Abraham and Erich von Hornbostel's suggestions on transcription for comparative musicologists (1909–10) for instance, would appear to indicate that these pioneers did not use notational conventions in so strictly defined a way. When they write that 'Each grouping is delineated by a bar line. Whatever appears between two given bar lines represents a melodic-rhythmic unit' (1994 : 436), this could be taken to suggest that grouping or phrase structure, rather than metric structure is being represented. Yet these authors indicate elsewhere that the time signature *is* in fact clearly intended to represent metre ('The indication of

[4] As a number of musicologists have begun to do—see Lerdahl and Jackendoff, Yeston, Epstein, Kramer, and Hasty to name but a few. For a useful survey of Western rhythmics see Arom (1991 : 179–212).

[5] For instance, Wallace Berry suggests that 'It is fundamental that the meter is often independent of the notated bar-line', and that an important aspect of metrical analysis is the determination of the 'real' metre, whether or not it accords with the notated metre (1976 : 324).

[6] Ethnomusicologists who have written on these difficulties include Kolinski (1973), Pantaleoni (1987), and Arom (1991, esp. 206–11).

[7] A famous example is to be found in Rousseau's *Dictionnaire de Musique* (1768). It is worth remembering that the association of bar-lines with metric structure became widespread in Europe only in the 17th cent.

regularly recurring meter may be placed at the beginning of the piece', 1994: 436). Abraham and Hornbostel did not, evidently, distinguish between these different aspects of structure (metre and grouping). Yet unfortunately this confusion has continued, with the result that in a large number of ethnomusicological transcriptions the reader is not clear what the notation is meant to signify regarding rhythmic structure, let alone whether it does so reliably.

In instances where music to be transcribed appears to be clearly metrical, where the number of pulses per unit can be identified, and where (for whatever reasons) the transcriber wishes to use some form of staff notation, it would appear to be an obvious decision to indicate metre by means of time signature and bar-lines. Kofi Agawu, for instance, argues forcefully and cogently for the use of standard notation in the representation of African music (1995*a*, 1995*b*). Yet care must still be taken. Notating musical metre according to such conventions involves the taking of a number of crucial decisions. How do we decide which time unit is to be taken as the 'beat', and how to notate it? How do we decide whether a grouping of 2, 3, or 4 beats is enough to specify a metre, or whether a higher level grouping (of 6, 8, 12, or 16 perhaps) is also metrically significant? Where does the measure begin and end, and which pulse is a 'beat' and which an 'off-beat'? Surely our Western notation system is profoundly influenced by the assumptions of our own concept of metre (and vice versa), and this can cause problems, particularly in ethnomusicological studies. (An instance is the assumption that the first beat of a measure is a primary 'strong' beat. In gamelan music, the *last* beat/note of a time unit tends to be the most important structurally. Does the transcriber make this stressed pulse the first of his measure, confusing the rhythmic structure of the piece, or the last, risking the misreading of the notation?)

3.2.2 Three theories on metre

There is obviously a need to clarify our concept of metre in such a way that we have definable and meaningful terms with which to describe a variety of musics, and notational tools applicable to as many as possible. Three important strands of research have taken us part of the way to achieving this. Firstly we are indebted to Mieczyslaw Kolinski, for making an important connection between metre and Gestalt psychology (1973). Kolinski described metre as a background against which the rhythmic surface is perceived. According to this view metre is a kind of reference grid which profoundly influences the perception and cognition of rhythm, the 'ground' to rhythm's 'figure'. In most cases of course, metre must itself be inferred by the listener from the rhythmic surface. This suggests a complex mechanism in musical cognition, whereby metre is inferred subjectively from the rhythmic surface, which is itself then interpreted with reference to this very metrical framework.

Psychological research tends to confirm that all metrical music has a dual structure in cognition, in which rhythm is superimposed on an underlying beat.

As Jay Dowling and Dane Harwood point out, 'The dual structure of underlying beat and superimposed rhythm is fundamental to the cognitive organization of music...' (1986 : 186). Similarly, Eric Clarke describes metre as 'a framework around which individual notes are organized, and through which they gain an appropriate durational quantification' (1987 : 228).

This idea is of great importance in understanding Hindustānī music's rhythmic organization. This idea of such a dual structure is an integral, if implicit, part of conventional *tāl* theory, and will be built into the theoretical model developed below.[8] It seems reasonable to describe *tāl* as the conceptual substructure upon which rhythm is overlaid, and to discuss the relationship between the *tāl* and the 'surface' rhythm, and how (if at all) the *tāl* organizes or generates that rhythm.

Fred Lerdahl and Ray Jackendoff (1983) have, by disentangling metric and grouping structure in Western tonal music, been able to develop arguably the most convincing metric theory to date, one which is now widely accepted in Western music theory (although it is not yet clear to what extent their theory may be applicable to other musics). According to this theory metre is described in terms of the interaction of two or more concurrent levels of pulsation, in such a way as to generate 'beats' which are relatively strong or weak (the 'stronger' beats being so in an abstract structural sense, not necessarily louder or otherwise more stressed than the 'weaker' beats). A time point which is perceived as a beat on two different levels of pulsation is 'structurally stronger' than a point which is felt as a beat on only one level. For music to have metre therefore, it must be perceived to have at least two such pulse levels: often there will be three or more. This analysis and the dot notation used to illustrate it prove powerful tools in the metric analysis of Western tonal music, and have been adapted below.

Thus with Kolinski's image of metre as a background or framework for rhythm, and Lerdahl and Jackendoff's theory of metre as interacting pulse streams and their system for its notation and analysis, we have the beginnings of a concept of metre of wide applicability. These ideas may also be seen in the light of a third, perhaps more radical approach still, that of Simha Arom (1991). Arom suggests that although Central African polyrhythm is clearly organized in a periodic manner, the concept and term 'metre' are inappropriate in this context (he prefers 'isoperiodicity'). Metre, as we have seen, implies a hierarchy of strong and weak beats (an 'accentual matrix' in Arom's terms). Central African polyrhythm on the other hand consists of a web of interlocking, periodic rhythmic patterns, organized around a single primary pulse level. Since there is only one pulse level, and no regular 'accentual matrix', this organization cannot (according to Arom) be described as a type of metre.[9]

Arom's careful review of the history of Western rhythmics, and equally clear redefinition of certain basic rhythmic terminology, points the way forward for

[8] Rowell, writing on early Indian music, describes it as a 'counterpoint—audible events superimposed over a conceptual substructure' (1988*a* : 143).

[9] See Arom's discussion of metre, p. 204, and of African rhythmics, pp. 206 ff.

studies of this kind. Yet, precisely because the kind of music to which he directs his attention is in his view not *metrical*, his coverage of metre (and of dependent concepts such as syncopation) is rather brief.

Metre as discussed by Arom is, effectively, a regular pattern of accentuation. Defined in this way, one would assume that metre is dependent on a continuing, regular, and audible accentuation pattern, and consequently that once such a pattern ceases to be heard, metre ceases to exist. This would clearly be too simple a view of metre however, as Arom himself concedes when he writes that 'the measure *may be inaudible* but is nonetheless still taken as the temporal reference of the musical durations' (1991 : 204, italics added). Arom claims in the same section that '*What is called metre in music is . . . the simplest form of rhythmic expression*. In other words, musical metre has no independent status' (1991 : 204). While the latter point is strictly true, it is worth reiterating that metre *can* in fact have a status independent of audible accentuation patterns: although it may be inferred on the basis of a recurrent accentual pattern, it is not to be confused with that pattern. Thus, even in a situation where such an accentual pattern, once established, ceases to be heard, the metrical structure derived from that accentuation may continue to be supplied by the listener, who has come to expect its continuation.

This caveat does not necessarily affect Arom's subsequent argument, however. If, as I have suggested, we accept Lerdahl and Jackendoff's proposition that metre depends on the perception of at least two pulse levels, and if Arom is correct in stating that only one such level is present in traditional Central African music, then according to our definition such music is indeed not metrical.[10] This does, however, show up once again the need for caution in the definition and use of such concepts. Arom talks of music based on 'A strictly periodic structure (isoperiodicity) . . . set up by the repetition of identical or similar musical material' (1991 : 211): it would be quite possible to draft a definition of metre loose enough to include such organization. I am however inclined to accept Arom's 'isoperiodicity' as a term describing such periodic, pulsation-based organization. This has the advantage of freeing the term 'metre' for organization fulfilling further conditions—roughly speaking, that pulses should be organized according to a regular hierarchical scheme (i.e. some pulses are more structurally important than others; these more important pulses themselves generate a second level of pulsation).

3.2.3 The subjectivity of metre

Another important point to come out of this discussion is the importance of the listener. Metre is more than a simple accentual pattern, and moreover it is not

[10] Arom's supposition that the principles of rhythmic organization described by him are the same in 'most traditional African music' (1991 : 211) would however be disputed by some. Agawu, for instance, insists on a simple metrical background for most Northern Ewe music (against which interest is created by a more complex rhythmic foreground).

necessarily measurable or objectively demonstrable. On the contrary, metre depends for its existence on the agency of a human interpreter. Psychological studies on metric interpretation suggest that the process is far more complex than might otherwise have been assumed (as indeed, the relationship between music sound and its cognitive representation is in general rather complex). The construction of a cognitive representation of metre is far from being a simple process based on the recognition of louder (or otherwise accented) sounds.

It is clear that it is possible for a single piece of music to be interpreted metrically in more than one way.[11] Indeed, the greater part of Lerdahl and Jackendoff's work on tonal music is devoted to the exposition of 'well-formedness rules' and 'preference rules', describing the ways in which listeners tend to choose one possible metric interpretation rather than another. Even if Lerdahl and Jackendoff's basic approach is sound, it is not clear how listeners of differing cultural backgrounds apply such rules: which (if any) are universally valid, and how those which are not universal vary between cultures. If metrical interpretation depends on the identification of key musical parameters (such as patterns of intensity or duration, the repetition of melodic or harmonic features, or something else), then it seems more than possible that people of different cultural backgrounds assign importance to these parameters in different ways.[12]

3.3 Metre vs. rhythm in Western and Indian music

The distinction between metre and rhythm has been a matter of debate in Western music theory for several centuries, as Christopher Hasty demonstrates in his extensive discussion of the topic (1997). My own discussion above accepted the clear and unequivocal nature of the distinction rather easily perhaps, partly because I feel that such a distinction is useful in clarifying what we mean by the term 'metre', and partly because such a firm separation accords with Indian intuitions on the subject and lends itself well to the analysis of Indian music. It is nevertheless a subject that deserves further consideration.

One Indian writer who makes the metre-rhythm distinction (albeit in different terms) is Vamanrao Deshpande:

> Nature exhibits one kind of rhythm in events repeating themselves at regular intervals of time and the other in movements of an irregular kind ... In music we find both kinds of movements reflected in the forms of tala and laya respectively. The regular rhythm is the tala or theka, which may be called the 'standard rhythm'. The irregular rhythm is laya and may be called the 'functional rhythm' ... The movement of music takes place within the cycles of tala but with irregular movements. (1987 : 70)

The distinction he draws is of course that between metre (*tāl*) and rhythm (for which he uses the term *lay*, in a sense which he himself admits to be rather

[11] See e.g. Handel 1989 : 411 ff. [12] See Hopkins 1982.

idiosyncratic; see Chapter 6). For Deshpande, the musician's job is to control or regulate these irregular rhythms in order to create perfect forms:

> the musical sounds . . . possess a sort of a form and shape of their own. These can be described as 'audible' shapes and forms. A successful *bandish* [composition or, in Deshpande's terms, performance as a whole] is that in which an 'audible organization' is organically and coherently formed out of these audible shapes and forms . . . (1987 : 100)

Deshpande's position—that the actual musical sounds form 'audible shapes' which have irregular rhythm and which must be entrained to the regular rhythm of *tāl*—is one often expressed by Indian music theorists. The traditional Sanskrit saying '*śrutir mātā layaḥ pitā*'—'*śruti* (i.e. pitch) is the mother and *lay* the father (of music)'—expresses this same idea (*lay* here is meant in the rather more usual sense of rhythm as regularity and tempo). Similarly for Arun Kumar Sen, 'Tāla binds music by definite rules and restrictions of Time. Just as lack of definite time sequence in life leads to a lack of happiness and prosperity, so too music without tāla makes it meaningless and ineffective . . . Tāla disciplines music and entices the audience by its organized form, stability and outstanding qualities' (1994 : 13–14).

Tāl then is almost universally regarded as a positive attribute, a force for stability and regulation, allowing otherwise untamed and irregular rhythmic impulses to be constrained in a well-organized form. This would seem to be closely related to the earlier Hindu view of musical time measurement as ritually necessary—the result is expressed in musical rather than metaphysical terms, and yet the value accorded to time measurement and regulation is similarly high.

Western views have been rather more equivocal; the natural, organic rhythmic impulse has tended to be accorded the higher value, while metrical rigidity has been seen as inimical to good musical performance. Metre, for many Western theorists, has been seen as a regrettable necessity rather than as the valuable source of order it has been to most Indian writers. Perhaps the most neutral view is that of David Epstein, who sees these two dimensions of rhythmic organization in a productive state of tension.

> [Music] imparts upon a potentially undifferentiated continuum two species of demarcation; the mensural demarcation of beat and, subsequently, meter; and the demarcation of time related to experience, perceived qualitatively through the events of a given musical work. It poses both metrical and experiential frames simultaneously, placing them variously in states of co-ordination or of opposition and tension. (1987 : 56)

This notion may be supported by another strand of research in music psychology. Jeanne Bamberger suggests, on the basis of experiments with children, the existence of two modes of rhythmic understanding, termed figural and metrical.[13] According to this theory, metric understanding depends on the relationship of rhythm to an underlying beat, while figural understanding does

[13] These modes are described as particular instances of a general dichotomy between 'figural and formal modes of organizing present phenomena' (Bamberger 1991 : 15).

not, relying more on general Gestalt principles such as the grouping of like elements. Drawing a correlation between these two modes of rhythmic interpretation, and the domains of 'rhythm' and 'metre' reinforces the view that phrases or patterns may be understood both in terms of their own internal structures and their relationship to metrical frameworks.

Even in cultures with highly developed theories of metre, such as in India, people may understand and organize rhythm in non-metrical ways. In the Indian context this may for instance help us to explain the similarities between the 16-beat *tīntāl* (and its several variants), the 14-beat *dīpcandī*, and even the 10-beat *jhaptāl*: although clearly representing different *metres*, each has the same gestural pattern (clap-clap-wave-clap), and similar sequences of *tablā* strokes in its basic drum pattern. That they are considered to be closely related is apparent from the fact that *tāl* names such as *dīpcandī*, *cāñcar*, and *addhā* may refer to structures of either 14 or 16 *mātrās*.[14]

Metre, as Eric Clarke suggested, may be regarded as 'a cognitive framework around which events are organized', yet as Stephen Handel and Gregory Lawson point out, it is not really possible to separate rhythmic figure and ground. 'Each rhythmic level . . . functions as both a figure and a ground; it becomes part of the perceived rhythm, yet simultaneously is part of the supporting framework for other rhythmic levels. This makes theorizing about rhythm extremely difficult' (1983 : 118).

For these psychologists, then, rhythm arises as a result of the interaction of different levels in context, and any attempt to separate rhythm and metre is over-simplistic. As Western musicologists have been rather more ready than their Indian counterparts to point out, it is difficult to construct and maintain a boundary between metre and rhythm. Metre is not itself audible, and therefore cannot be construed other than on the evidence of rhythmic sounds and actions; conversely metre tends to direct rhythm, and even to suggest or to generate rhythm. Thus a constant interaction between metre and rhythm must continue in the cognitive processing of any metrical music, and I believe that this is as true of Indian music as European. The nature of the relationship between metre and rhythm will be a recurring theme in later chapters.

3.4 Metre, cognition, and the present

A relationship is sometimes postulated between the perception of metre and the psychological (alternatively perceptual, subjective, conscious, or specious) present, a phenomenon 'commonly understood as a time interval in which sensory information, internal processing, and concurrent behavior appear to be integrated within the same span of attention' (Michon 1978 : 89). Since the psychological present is somewhat flexible, being dependent on the rate and kind of

[14] See Manuel 1983*a* : 10.

information being processed, it is not possible to set precise parameters; but it is usually taken to span a period of a few seconds.[15] John Michon believes the present plays a crucial role to the extent that 'the process of discovering or constructing the temporal pattern of a sequence of events is consciously experienced as the *specious present*' (1978 : 90), citing metre as a temporal pattern in this sense. His suggestion seems to be that since a pulse can only be perceived as such within a certain durational limit corresponding to the 'present', this must also limit the duration of any metrically significant time-span.[16]

If metre depends on the perception of two or more nested pulse levels, the longest of which is the measure (period or cycle), then if Michon is correct the measure should theoretically not exceed the limits of the present, commonly estimated at around 2–3 seconds in duration. In Alf Gabrielsson's words, features of rhythm such as grouping and accent

> take place within a relatively short period of time, what... William James once called 'the specious present'... This duration is short, in most cases only a few seconds... The meaning of this condition for rhythm is easily demonstrated. Clap any rhythm you like. Then make it successively slower and slower, and it won't take long until you discover that it gets very difficult to clap it any longer; the pattern dissolves, leaving only a number of isolated events. You may make a conscious mental effort to still keep them together, but in that case there is a *conceived* (cognitively constructed) rhythm rather than a spontaneously perceived one. (1993 : 97)

Candace Brower attempts to go even further than this, correlating different levels of musical structure to different cognitive mechanisms. Thus foreground structure depends on sensory or echoic memory (which to some psychologists is related to or synonymous with the present); middleground structure with short-term memory; and background structure with long-term memory (1993). While such suggestions are rather speculative, it seems likely that musical cognition should ultimately be explainable in terms of the interaction of various mechanisms of perception and memory.

The problem for a study of *tāl* is that *tāl* cycles are rarely as short in duration as 3 seconds, and are frequently much longer. Taking commonly accepted definitions of metre and applying them to *tāl* one is tempted to conclude that in many cases a *tāl* cannot be described as a metre, since the recurrence of the cycle cannot be directly perceived through the functioning of the present, of sensory memory or even perhaps of short-term memory. Work in this area is still in progress, and it would be premature to build too much speculation on what

[15] Pöppel suggests a figure of around 3 seconds, citing the timing of 'Ceremonial greetings, playful gestures directed towards others, and many other types of behavior characterized by intentionality...' as corroborative evidence (1989 : 87). Dürr and Gerstenberg suggest a rather higher figure: 'Modern psychologists have suggested 12 seconds as the longest span of time which can be distinctly perceived as a single unit' (1980 : 805). Dowling and Harwood write of 'a psychological present normally lying in the 2–5 sec range but occasionally stretching out to 10 or 12 sec'. They do allow, however, that 'The length of the psychological present varies with context and can be manipulated by composers and performers in particular contexts within stylistic limits' (1986 : 181).

[16] The most precise set of figures I have seen are 0.2–1.8 seconds (in Parncutt 1987 : 133–4).

are themselves rather speculative theories. What does seem clear however, is that a cycle lasting 2 seconds and a cycle lasting 60 seconds are likely to be perceived and understood very differently—the latter will be cognitively constructed rather than directly perceived, perhaps.[17]

3.5 Additive or complex metre

3.5.1 From additive and divisive rhythm . . .

The distinction sometimes made between 'additive' and 'divisive' rhythm is important here, not least since Indian rhythm is often described as 'additive' (in implicit or explicit contrast with 'divisive' rhythm in Western music). Curt Sachs distinguished divisive rhythm, in which time is divided into equal parts (also called 'qualitative'), from additive rhythm, made by adding unequal time-spans (also called 'quantitative') (1953 : 24–6, 93). He saw Indian rhythm as additive, because of the addition of groups of different lengths in many *tāl* structures. Hence his rather extreme (and misleading) comment that 'A musical system so thoroughly metrical as India's cannot create "divisive" rhythms . . . No Indian pattern can be divided into halves, thirds, or quarters; they all are 'irregular' from our Western viewpoint' (1953 : 102).

For A. H. Fox Strangways, writing in 1914, this supposed Indian predilection for additive rhythm (although the term had not yet been coined) was a consequence of a duration-based prosodic system (in contrast to Western stress-based organization).

> It is sometimes thought that these uneven times—5, 7, 10, 14, and so on—are full of suggestion for European composers. This on the whole may be doubted, because duration is not the same thing as stress. All these Indian rhythms have their *raison d'être* in the contrast of long and short duration, and to identify these with much and little stress is to vulgarize the rhythms. (1914 : 222)

> Stress pulses, and demands regularity; duration is complementary, and revels in irregularity. In order to get the true sense of duration we have to get rid of stress, and this would mean that we must find some other means (as the Hindus do) of marking the beginning of the bar than by accenting it. (1914 : 223)

Fox Strangways and Sachs seem to be thinking on the same lines, drawing a distinction between stress-based 'divisive' rhythm and duration-based 'additive' structures. Harold Powers follows Sachs to the extent of asserting that 'an *āvarta* is not in principle divisible into subsections of equal length but has rather to be

[17] It may be that a fuller understanding of the processes involved will be possible if we supplement the idea of the perceptual present with more complex concepts such as Alan Baddeley's 'multi-component working memory model' (1990 : 67), and integrate this with Mari Riess Jones's theory of attentional periodicity (see e.g. Jones and Yee 1993). This is somewhat beyond the scope of the present work, unfortunately, but it does seem clear that the psychological significance of absolute duration and tempo needs to be taken into account in any study of rhythm and metre.

assembled by adding up its *vibhāg* or *aṅga* [parts or sections; see Chapter 5]' (1980 : 119). Lewis Rowell, also taking on board Sachs's terminology, suggests that part of Indian music's uniqueness lies 'not so much in her exploitation of additive rhythms as in the development of an appropriate theoretical framework for their codification' (1992 : 209). This view is however questioned by Richard Widdess, who suggests that apart from a limited number of irregular metres, 'the musical rhythm of Indian *art*-music is predominantly "divisive" rather than "additive"' (1981*b* : 133).[18]

It is clear that most of the comments cited here refer to metrical organization rather than rhythm in general. If we extend the discussion to cover the organization of rhythmic patterns, the proposed distinction between stress-based 'divisive' patterns and duration-based 'additive' patterns may have different implications. I am not sure, in fact, that such a distinction can be made, at least in terms of addition and division—if it can, then perhaps it applies best to the transformation or variation of patterns (is a crotchet potentially divisible into two quavers, or must it endure as a crotchet in any transformation?) rather than their basic form. It is easier to see how rhythmic patterns can be interpreted as stress- or duration-based, along Fox Strangways's lines, although I very much doubt that patterns can be classified as one or the other so much as interpreted in two different ways.

Rhythm, then, may be interpreted either as an alternation of stresses or as a succession of durations—but either of these positions assumes a degree of analytical listening, and perhaps underestimates our capacity to apprehend patterns as wholes. This facility is hinted at by Bamberger's concept of figural understanding, which we might extend to suggest that rhythmic patterns may be apprehended as figures or gestures, from which elements of both stress and duration may potentially be extracted. This may be extended perhaps to the cognition of recurrent patterns such as contribute to the cognition of metre. Manfred Clynes and Janice Walker put forward the idea of a rhythmic pulse which is pre-programmed as a unitary event; 'the iteration of a rhythmic pulse in general represents a unitary event preprogrammed *not* as an *alternation* of activity and rest, as musical notation implies, but as a replication of a *single* dynamic form accurately stored in memory' (1982 : 176). They continue; 'analysis in terms of "strong" and "weak" alone cannot do justice to the great subtleties of relative timing, accent, and the details of form of the pulse, which determine its actual character' (1982 : 192).

These theoretical speculations, as to whether the organization of musical time is best regarded as a division of time measures or the addition of shorter

[18] Another distinction made earlier by Sachs (1943 : 41–3), was between the categories 'logogenic' and 'melogenic'; he found speech-derived rhythm (logogenic) more uneven, more constant in tempo and flatter in hierarchy than that derived from music (melogenic). He also introduced a concept of numerical rhythm, which is distinguished by a counted number of syllables, the 'absence of meter' and the 'absence, scarcity or vagueness of accents' (1953 : 26, 57). In his later work Sachs talks of three types of rhythmic organization—purely numerical; relying on actual or suggested stresses; and metre (i.e. additive rhythm) (1962 : 113 ff.).

time units; as the succession of durable events or the alternation of relatively more and less intense events; as the interaction of different pulse levels or as the replication of a unitary rhythmic pulse, can be widely applied in music theory and analysis. To the extent that these options can often be regarded as equally valid ways of describing the same phenomena, it is however problematic to use such notions as a basis for comparison of musical cognition (as opposed to theory and ideology). It may be that questions of additive metre have tended to come up in discussions of Indian music simply because traditional Western models of metre have been unable to accommodate Indian *tāl* structures, and if this is so the additive/divisive dichotomy may be illusory.

This inability to accommodate *tāl* patterns is apparent even in Lerdahl and Jackendoff's metrical speculations. These authors, as I noted above, consider metre to be the product of the interaction of two or more pulse levels. Since their conception of a pulse is as a series of time points separated by notionally equal time units, they can account for simple and compound metres as used in Western music, but not (for instance) the North Indian *jhaptāl*, with its 10 beats divided $2+3+2+3$. For this Indian pattern to be analysed in Lerdahl and Jackendoff's terms, we have to alter one of their 'well-formedness' rules for metre in order to allow an irregular pulse level as metrical; this means breaking with the assumption of pulses being separated by equal durations.

In view of such difficulties, it might appear tempting to appeal to Sachs's additive-divisive dichotomy to explain *jhaptāl*, but this presents new problems. Since North Indian music also uses a pattern of 16 beats divided $4+4+4+4$ (*tīntāl*), an application of the additive-divisive dichotomy would suggest either that *jhaptāl* is fundamentally of a different metrical species to *tīntāl*, for which we have no evidence and which would appear to run contrary to the intuitions of Indian performers; or else that apparently binary metres somehow work quite differently in Indian music to Western, which seems to me equally unsatisfactory. Even if we could establish that *jhaptāl* and *tīntāl* originate in different metrical systems, it would remain for us to explain how both can be accommodated under the heading '*tāl*' without apparent difficulty.

3.5.2 ... to irregular or complex metre

Listening to a piece of music in 4/4 we may certainly experience, as Lerdahl and Jackendoff suggest, at least two interacting pulse levels, contributing to a sense of metre; the metrical pattern may itself be experienced as a kind of figure or Gestalt; we may moreover experience at the same moment the recurrence of this metrical pattern and the independent flow of melodic and rhythmic groups and phrases. I believe, however, that the idea that the measure is divided (into two, and into two again) is misleading, partly because it assumes the measure's duration as a given *prior to* its division; surely the measure exists either as an internally differentiated whole or not at all.

The Indian listener, assuming a known *tāl*, performed at medium tempo, with divisions marked by hand gestures, has an experience of a similar kind despite the greater complexity of the metrical pattern. The difference is that in Indian music (as, incidentally, in much West and Central Asian, and Balkan music), one of the principal pulse levels which contributes to a sense of metre may be, in Western terms, irregular. Listening to *jhaptāl* for instance, besides pulsations at the level of the beat and the cycle, the listener is aware of the 2 + 3 + 2 + 3 division, a level at which some pulses appear to be longer than others.

This kind of metrical construction may be related to one or more of a number of other phenomena—in particular, the use of apparently related metres (so-called 'aksak') in the Balkans and the Middle East as dance rhythms, where 'long' beats correlate to 'heavy' dance steps; and the distinction between long and short syllables in the prosody of some languages (including Sanskrit and Hindi). It may also be related to the metric structure of African percussion ensemble music, which has been the subject of considerable academic debate. According to Simha Arom such music is organized (in Central Africa at least) with reference to a single pulse level; patterns repeat, usually every 8 or 12 pulses or a fraction thereof. There is no underlying 'accentual matrix' such as one would expect in a metre (1989 : 91). Yet Ruth Stone, working in West Africa, refers to the 'double-bell pattern' or so-called 'time-line' around which ensemble music in this region seems to be organized:

Stone regards this pattern as representing a pulse

and comments that 'it does not follow that [the] background grid of an equally spaced pulse must then determine that the beat constituted of several pulses at the next level in the hierarchy must also be equally spaced' (1985 : 140). Arom in fact notes the same phenomenon, describing it as 'rhythmic oddity' (because the group of 12 pulses is effectively split into a 7 and a 5; 8 can be split into 5 + 3, and so on), but does not interpret the time-line as a non-isochronous pulse. Jonathan Magill and Jeffrey Pressing have on the other hand gone so far as to test the hypothesis that the underlying mental model for West African drumming is based on the 'irregular' time-line rather than on a regular pulse (1997), finding some evidence to support this contention.

Irregularity in this case may perform the function of differentiation: since stress or dynamic accent seems to play little or no role in determining metre in African percussion ensembles, a cycle can only be internally differentiated by varying the *length* of the beats. It may be, therefore, that the use of 'unequal beats' as an integral part of metric structure is actually rather widespread, being found in India and several other regions of Asia, much of Africa, and Eastern Europe (and, perhaps, rather unusually absent from most tonal music in the European tradition). Indian music has used for centuries the device of long vs. short 'beats' alongside other means of differentiation (e.g. sounded vs. silent gestures in cheironomy, resonant vs. damped drum strokes).

Justin London offers some insights into what he calls 'complex' metre—that 'in which one level is nonisochronous' (1995 : 66). London's formulation avoids one of the problems of Lerdahl and Jackendoff's when he says that 'meter minimally consists of two levels: B [beat] and M [measure] (where M = some modular ordering of Bs)' (1995 : 68). I believe that this concept of metre, which accommodates such 'complex' or 'irregular' patterns may ultimately be more satisfactory than the additive-divisive dichotomy. Also useful is London's comment that: 'There appears to be a general correlation between metric complexity and fragility: complex meters require "explicit specification" of their invariant features ... and once established, these patterns can be varied only within extremely narrow limits' (1995 : 69).

As I will show, this statement is an apt description of Indian *tāl*, and neatly establishes the correlation between two of the most important differences between Indian and Western metre—that the former is both more complex and more explicitly established.

3.6 Summary: six statements on metre

Metre as commonly understood in the West is clearly not a universal concept, nor is it a phenomenon observable in all world musics. It should, however, be possible to develop a concept of metre which *is* applicable beyond our own culture, since the organization of rhythm with respect to a periodic pattern of differentiated (e.g. 'strong' and 'weak', or perhaps 'long' and 'short') beats is certainly not limited to Western music. At this stage it will be most useful to assess the state of our knowledge and to propose general hypotheses to test against our findings on North Indian music (and to refine in the future). In the light of this discussion, the following statements regarding musical metre—consistent with our current understanding of the concept—will serve as useful points of comparison with North Indian music.

1. Much music (but not all) is organized with respect to a periodic and hierarchical temporal framework, in such a way that a cognitive representation of this framework may be generated in the mind of the listener. This organization and its representation are termed 'metre'.

2. Metre can be said to exist when two or more continuous streams of pulsation are perceived to interact; these streams are composed of time points (beats) separated by durations definable as multiples of a basic time unit. Time points which are perceived as beats on more than one level are 'stronger' than

those which are beats on only one level; metre can thus be regarded as necessarily hierarchical.

3. Beats may be differentiated by stress and/or duration (i.e. they can be perceived as strong and weak, and/or long and short).

4. The relationship between metre and rhythm has two complementary aspects: metre is inferred (largely subjectively) on the basis of evidence presented by rhythm, while rhythm is interpreted in terms of its relationship to that metre.

5. The inference of metre is a complex phenomenon which is influenced by the musical experience and training of the listener, and more indirectly perhaps by his or her general experience and cultural background. Consequently both metric theory and practice are culturally determined to a great extent, although they are ultimately founded on the same psycho-physiological universals.

6. The cognition of metre appears to be dependent on one or more of the following factors: the extent of the perceptual present (determining that pulses are unlikely to be separated by more than 2–3 secs.); the function of short-term memory; and the ability to comprehend recurring patterns as single Gestalts which combine notions of stress and duration.

4

Tāl theory as a model of rhythmic organization

4.1 An outline of *tāl* theory

All North Indian *rāg* music may be classified as either *nibaddh* (bound by *tāl*) or *anibaddh* (unbound); in principle, all metrically organized music falls into the first category, and is set to one of a number of authorized metric frameworks called *tāls*. *Tāls* are conceived as cyclically recurring patterns of fixed length. The overall time-span of each cycle (*āvart*) is made up of a certain number of smaller time units (*mātrās*), and these *mātrās* are organized into sections (*vibhāgs* or *aṅgs*). *Mātrā* may be translated as 'beat' in most contexts, but I have tried to avoid this here since there are circumstances in which it may cause confusion. *Vibhāg* may be translated as 'section'; the *vibhāg* is a subdivision of the *āvart*. Thus in principle the *tāl* is a hierarchical structure organized on three temporal levels, from the smallest time unit (*mātrā*), to the section (*vibhāg*), to the complete cycle (*āvart*). The *tāl* cycle may be conceived as either a sum of its *vibhāgs* (or *mātrās*), or as a single unit divided into smaller (but not necessarily equal) time units.

Each *vibhāg* is marked at its start by a hand gesture, either a clap (*tālī*) or a wave (*khālī*), the sequence of which makes up a 'clap pattern'[1] which may be employed by performers and/or listeners to count out the *tāl*. The first *mātrā* of the cycle is designated *sam*.[2] Each *tāl* also has a *ṭhekā*—a basic recognizable pattern of strokes (*bols*) for the *tablā* or *pakhāvaj*.[3] These features are illustrated in Example 4.1, using the example of the 10-*mātrā jhaptāl*.

Jhaptāl is a *tāl* comprising cycles of 10 *mātrās*, which are divided into four *vibhāgs*, two of 2 *mātrās* and two of 3 *mātrās*, in the sequence 2 + 3 + 2 + 3. The clap pattern consists of hand gestures on each *vibhāg*, as follows; *tālī* + *tālī* + *khālī* + *tālī* (clap + clap + wave + clap). The *vibhāgs* are assigned notational symbols as follows; 1st *tālī* (*sam*) = X, 2nd *tālī* = 2, *khālī* = 0, and 3rd *tālī* = 3 (giving in all: X 2 0 3—see the preliminary 'Note on music notations'). The *ṭhekā* is made up of *bols*, that is strokes of the *tablā* or *pakhāvaj*, which are

[1] This term is borrowed from Widdess (1981*b*).

[2] *Sam* is marked by a *tālī* in all except *rūpak tāl*, where it is signified by a *khālī*.

[3] A number of musicologists use the term *thapiyā* (or *thāpiyā*) as the *pakhāvaj* equivalent of the *tablā ṭhekā* (the *pakhāvaj* is the barrel drum used to accompany *dhrupad* and *dhamār* performance); see e.g. Srivastav 1980 : 55. However, there is some dispute as to whether the two share the same function; see Stewart (1974 : 86) and Bhowmick (1981 : 56).

TABLE 4.1   Some common *bols* (strokes) for the *tablā* and *pakhāraj*

performance technique		instrument	
hands	damping	*tablā*	*pakhāvaj*
(right hand)	undamped	tā/nā, tin, tū, etc.	din, tā
	damped	teṭe	tiṭa
(left hand)	undamped	**ge/ghe**	**ge**
	damped	ke/ka	ka
combination		**dhā** (tā + ghe),	**dhā**,
(r.h. + l.h.)		**dhin** (tin + ghe),	tiṭakitagadigana
		tirakita	

represented by onomatopoeic syllables ('dhin, nā' etc.).[4] The main drum *bols* may be illustrated as in Table 4.1; those shown in bold are *bharī* ('full') *bols*, the remainder are *khālī* ('empty'). The basic *ṭhekā* of *jhaptāl* is given in Example 4.1.

jhaptāl: 10 *mātrās*, 2+3+2+3

X	2	0	3	X
dhin nā	dhin dhin nā	tin nā	dhin dhin nā	dhin

⌐____⌐ *mātrā* (beat)
⌐_____⌐ *vibhāg* (section)
⌐_____⌐ *āvart* (cycle)

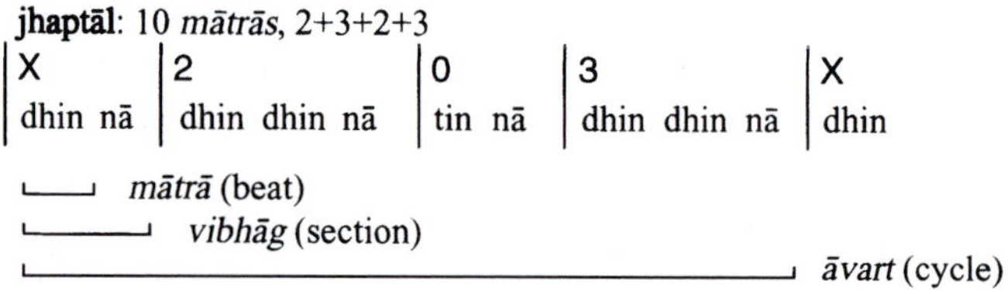

EXAMPLE 4.1   *Jhaptāl* in *sargam* notation, showing structure and *ṭhekā*

This introduces the principal concepts and terms of modern North Indian *tāl* theory. In practice, *tāls* are usually cited in written form as in the upper part of Example 4.1; they are taught orally by reciting the *ṭhekā* to the accompaniment of the clap pattern. (A list of the most common North Indian *tāls* is given in Chapter 5, with more detailed discussion of these features.)

The next most important concept in Hindustānī rhythmic theory is that of *lay*, which governs the speed of the music. Historically, *lay* refers to the rate of succession of the *tāl* structure (i.e. tempo), but often in practice it is used to describe what we would call rhythmic density, or as a general term for 'rhythm' (see Chapter 6). Both *lay* and the related concept of *laykārī* have important implications for the ways in which rhythmic organization is understood in North Indian music. *Laykārī* is usually translated as rhythmic play or rhythmic variation—it is dependent on the idea of surface rhythm being generated directly from the *tāl* structure by means including subdivision of the *mātrā* (see Chapter 10).

[4] The variety of *bols*, method of production and naming vary between the different *tablā* and *pakhāvaj* traditions (see e.g. Gottlieb 1977; Stewart 1974; Kippen 1988).

4.1.1 Implications of *tāl* theory

Even this brief introduction to *tāl* theory—and most general works on Indian music barely go further than this—tells us a great deal about assumptions on rhythmic organization within North Indian music culture. The main points are as follows;

- The principles of metric organization are the same for all metred music (with only the choice of particular *tāl* and *lay* varying);
- metred music has a dual structure, whose explicit metric element is manifested as the *tāl* and regulates rhythm;
- this metric structure (*tāl*) repeats cyclically;
- time is kept by means of clap patterns, which represent the internal structure of the *tāl* cycle;
- each *tāl* has an associated *ṭhekā,* or identifying drum pattern;
- the concept of *lay* governs the tempo (i.e. the rate of succession of the *tāl*), while that of *laykārī* governs the generation of surface rhythm by means of subdivision of the *tāl*'s time-spans.

These then are some of the assumptions of conventional *tāl* theory. They cover not only the way *tāl* works (e.g. it can be manifested by clap patterns and/or *ṭhekā*), but also more fundamental assumptions—that music should be organized by an explicit metric structure (conceptually distinct from rhythm), that this should be done accurately and unambiguously, and that all *nibaddh* (metrically bound) music is organized by the same system. Example 4.2 illustrates the dual structure implied by these assumptions, *tāl* underlying surface rhythm.

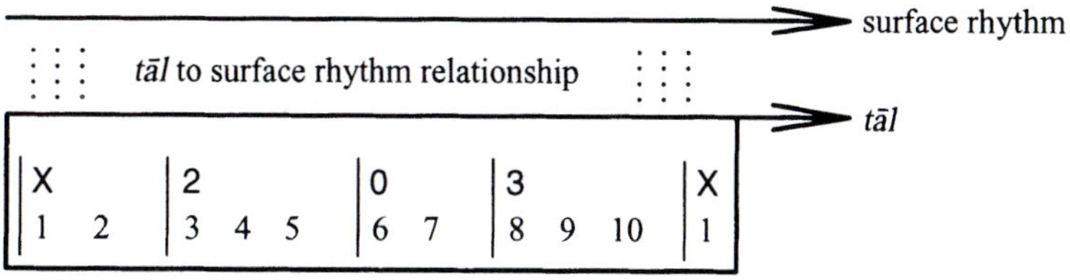

Example 4.2 A theoretical model for rhythmic organization, incorporating *tāl* and its relationship with surface rhythm

4.1.2 Limitations of *tāl* theory

One might be forgiven for assuming that such a multi-faceted, yet apparently coherent, model would adequately describe North Indian music's rhythmic organization. There are, however, a number of areas in which it fails to do so; its very coherence is in some ways illusory.

First we may question the assumption that all metred music is organized in the same way. If this were so, one would expect clap patterns and *ṭhekās* to perform more or less the same functions in all cases. This is manifestly not the case in practice: clap patterns are not used at all at very slow tempi (e.g. in *ati-vilambit khyāl*), and are rarely employed in lighter styles of music such as *ṭhumrī* and *dādrā*; *ṭhekās* on the other hand may be used either to the exclusion of any other form of accompaniment (e.g. in *vilambit khyāl*), or barely at all (e.g. in some *dhrupad*).

Clearly, one must look at the functions of the clap pattern and *ṭhekā* in practice, and at how the variation of rhythmic parameters (such as tempo), alters those functions. The relationship between these two phenomena is also unclear; it seems in some *tāls*, such as *jhaptāl*, that the so-called *khālī bols* (those without bass resonance; 'tā, nā, tin' and so on) occupy *vibhāgs* marked by the *khālī* gesture (sections marked with a wave). If a correlation between *tāl* structure and drum timbre is assumed on this basis however, it is not borne out in other *tāls*.

There appear moreover to be different types of *tāl*—some are symmetrical, with the second half of the cycle marked by the *khālī* gesture (as in the case of *jhaptāl*), and some are not; some are played on the *tablā* and some on the *pakhāvaj*; some are characterized by pitch modulation of the *bāyā̃* (left-hand drum head on the *tablā*) and some not (see Stewart 1974 : 93 ff.). *Tāls* may also be associated with particular genres and forms, and most may only be played within a limited tempo range. There is at least prima facie evidence for saying that the apparent uniformity of the *tāl* system conceals significant differences between the types of rhythmic organization employed in the different genres of North Indian music.

Other issues need clarifying too, in two important and related areas. First, there appears to be no articulated theoretical concept governing the relationship between *tāl* and surface rhythm except that of *laykārī*; yet this concept only applies in particular circumstances—when the *mātrā* is subdivided at a definite rate, and the surface rhythm is derived from that rate of subdivision, usually as an aspect of rhythmic play (see Chapter 10). There are many types of music which may be described as organized or generated by '*laykārī*', since the term is used somewhat flexibly in practice, but they do not add up to the whole of Hindustānī music. Therefore a significant amount of *tāl*-bound music lacks a theoretical basis for the relationship between *tāl* and surface rhythm, which is an important omission from the theoretical model.

Secondly, no theoretical concept sanctions acceleration of the *tāl*, despite the fact that such acceleration is a very widespread phenomenon in North Indian music (see Chapter 6). Historically it has been assumed by Indian musicologists that if and when music speeded up, it did so through an increase in rhythmic density alone, and the tempo of the *tāl* was by implication constant. This is no longer a reasonable assumption to make, yet the theory of North Indian *tāl*, while not explicitly denying the possibility of acceleration, has certainly not integrated the phenomenon into the received theoretical model.

These last two points suggest that certain features of *tāl* theory may relate to archaic musical concepts, or at least that old concepts may have developed somewhat different significance by the late twentieth century to that which they had when initially proposed. A model of *tāl* as set out above—with tempo assumed to be constant, all acceleration achieved through rhythmic density alone, and a clearly defined relationship between surface rhythm and *tāl*—is internally coherent. It is also the model which is most clearly suggested by the concepts of *tāl*, *lay*, and *laykārī*. However, while *tāl* theory is sufficient for didactic and most descriptive purposes within Indian music culture, it fails to explain a number of important rhythmic phenomena; *tāl* theory is in fact more coherent than the practice it describes. In order to establish an analytical model of rhythmic organization for Hindustānī music, it is necessary to modify and to extend conventional *tāl* theory, both to accommodate the enormous diversity in the tradition, and to bring that theory up to date.

4.2 *Tāl* as metric structure

Tāl is a system for organizing musical time, and this organization involves two major aspects. First, a succession of time-spans is measured out; and secondly, these time-spans are ordered in a hierarchical relationship. Thus, while it may be other things as well—and we must leave aside for the moment the importance of cyclicity, and the variation of drum timbres in the *ṭhekā*—these two principles suggest that *tāl* is a special form of metric structure.

Returning to Lerdahl and Jackendoff's metric notation system, I noted above that in their theory of metre, two or more pulse levels are recognized in the music, and each pulse level is marked by a row of dots (below the main music notation). Beats which are 'stronger' within the hierarchy thus have a deeper column of dots than those which are 'weaker'. Example 4.3 applies the dot notation system to *jhaptāl* at a medium fast tempo (*c*.100 MM).[5] *Jhaptāl* is shown to consist of a maximum of four levels of pulsation—the *mātrā*, half-*āvart* and full *āvart* (which are all regular), and the *vibhāg* (which in this case is irregular). All *tāls* should similarly have at least three metric levels (*mātrā*, *vibhāg*, and *āvart*), and possibly a fourth (the half-cycle level applies only to symmetrical structures).

X		2			0		3			X		
1	2	3	4	5	6	7	8	9	10	1		
•	•	•	•	•	•	•	•	•	•	•	*mātrā*	100 MM
•		•			•		•			•	*vibhāg*	
•					•					•	half-*āvart*	20 MM
•										•	*āvart*	10 MM

EXAMPLE 4.3 *Jhaptāl* interpreted as metric structure, illustrated using Lerdahl and Jackendoff's dot notation

Lerdahl and Jackendoff's analysis also generated a new perspective on the meaning of 'tempo'—the perceived tempo being the rate of succession of one of

[5] 'MM' is an abbreviation for 'Mälzel's metronome', not '*mātrās* per minute'.

these pulse rates, selected according to psychological and/or physiological criteria.[6] It will be instructive to apply this type of analysis to North Indian *tāl* structures, for several reasons: it will help to clarify the way in which *tāl* functions as metric structure, the perception of tempo (hence the concept of *lay*), and the relationship of *tāl* to surface rhythm (particularly in *laykārī*). In Example 4.3 the *mātrā* rate (in this case 100 MM) defines the tempo (*lay*). Surface rhythm is organized in relation to this hierarchical structure. This is most obvious in *laykārī*, where surface rhythm is generated by subdivision of the *mātrā* pulse (illustrated in Example 4.4).

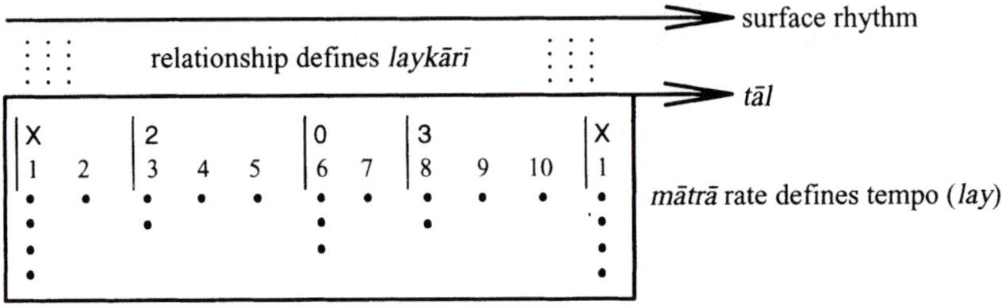

Example 4.4 The relationship between *tāl* (metric structure) and surface rhythm, as governed by *laykārī*

If one could assume a constant tempo and a definable *tāl*-to-surface rhythm relationship, and if the pulse rate of the *mātrā* remained within a range perceptible as a metric pulse rate (i.e. within the 'present' perhaps), then this model would effectively define rhythmic organization for North Indian music. However, in modern practice any or all of these conditions may be broken; as this occurs, the model must be modified accordingly, in order to adequately describe rhythmic organization.

The model illustrated above is significant largely as an ideal—albeit an ideal which may have been an accurate reflection of practice at some point in the past, and one which is still applicable, with slight modifications, to much North Indian music. Terms such as *lay* and *laykārī* are best understood in the context of this idealized model, and therefore it is of considerable importance. This prototypical model of *tāl* as explicit metric structure will however need to be modified and extended.

4.2.1 Syllabic style and a 'syllabic' model of rhythmic organization

Implicit in the model of *tāl* illustrated in Example 4.4 is the idea of a close relationship between *tāl* and the surface rhythm organized thereby. This

[6] Lerdahl and Jackendoff define such a rate as the tactus; 'The listener tends to focus on one (or two) intermediate level(s) in which beats pass by at a moderate rate. This is the level at which the conductor waves his baton, the listener taps his foot, and the dancer completes a shift in weight. . . . Adapting the Renaissance term, we call such a level the *tactus*' (1983 : 21).

relationship is frequently determined by the concept of *laykārī*. In *laykārī*, the surface rhythm patterns are generated by the execution of a number of mathematical operations on the *tāl* structure, such as division of the pulse, arrangement of rhythmic pulses into groups and phrases, and the manipulation and permutation of those phrases (described in detail in Chapter 10).

Just as this theoretical model of *tāl* applies in practice to some but not all North Indian music, so the implicit '*laykārī*' model of rhythmic organization (illustrated in Example 4.5) can be regarded as a special case. It is appropriate to some but by no means all North Indian music; its theoretical pre-eminence suggests that it may have applied more widely in the past. For these reasons I will for the moment look on this model as an 'ideal', and treat other modes of rhythmic organization as deviations from or adjustments to this ideal.

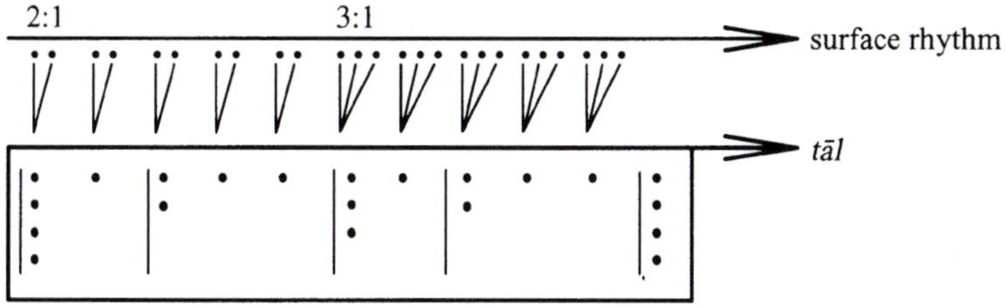

EXAMPLE 4.5 An illustration of subdivision of the pulse in *laykārī*; an increase in the rate of subdivision (in this case 2 : 1 to 3 : 1) is used to accelerate the surface rhythm

In order for this mode of organization to function, it is implicit that the surface rhythm can be regarded as derived from a stream of distinct pulses (e.g. the top row in Example 4.5); if it is not and cannot be, then this model becomes irrelevant. These pulses must be manifested in the form of discrete musical elements, such as notes, text syllables, or drum strokes, and the clear differentiation of such building blocks is facilitated by the employment of *bols*. *Bols* are syllables—sung text or *sargam* (solfège) syllables, drum syllables or the syllables used to represent note names or instrumental strokes in teaching—and the idea that music is built up of distinct units, each of which comprises or may be represented by a spoken syllable (*bol*), is of great importance in Indian music. I will call the rhythmic style influenced by this concept of music 'syllabic'.

Syllabic rhythmic style implies a particular model of rhythmic organization, which may also be termed 'syllabic'. 'Syllabic' music is conceived as comprising distinct units, which have temporally definable attack points as well as other qualities of tone, timbre, dynamics, and so on.[7] These units are called *bols*, because they constitute or can be represented by spoken syllables. The basic characteristic of this type of rhythm is that it is based on the durable qualities of

[7] Note the specific sense in which the term 'syllabic' is employed here. Constantin Brailoiu, writing on Romanian folk rhythm, used the term in a rather different sense: 'As for syllabic . . . we are dealing with rhythmic effects whose sole principle is the variable quantity of the syllable . . . the rhythm takes its source from the metre and is only to be explained by it' (1984 : 168).

syllables; in vocal styles such as *dhrupad* the use of the text syllables is all important, while instrumental styles tend to be dominated by stroke patterns. Rhythmic variety is produced by the manipulation of these *bols*, as I will demonstrate below.

There is a strong tendency in syllabic styles for the structure of the *bandiś* (composition) to be well defined. This is illustrated in the most syllabic of vocal forms, *dhrupad*—although a certain amount of latitude is always allowed for expressive nuance, the position of each syllable of a *dhrupad bandiś* within the *tāl* cycle is fixed. *Sitār gats* show a similar level of definition; the most common *gat* type, the *masītkhānī gat*, is defined by the sequence of *sitār bols* (right-hand strokes) and their relationship with the *tāl* (see Chapter 8).

There is evidence that this syllabic conception of music was predominant in India until relatively recent times (probably the last 150–200 years), and that this correlates with the traditionally syllabic nature of much Indian art and language. As Lewis Rowell suggests, 'There is a profound relationship between the phonetic structure of the Sanskrit language as described by the ancient grammarians, the syllabic Indian scripts, and the diverse ways in which syllables have dominated the music and musical thought of India since early times...' (1988*a*: 149). Although no longer as dominant as it once was, this model retains some relevance in North Indian music. This model has, however, been modified in modern music in at least two ways: first by decreasing the tempo, which breaks down the relationship between *tāl* and surface rhythm, favouring a 'melismatic' style and a distinct 'melismatic' model of rhythmic organization; and secondly by a more subtle modification of the model brought about by the increasing importance of the *ṭhekā* and the use of the *tablā* drum (an 'accentual' model).

4.2.2 Melismatic style and a 'melismatic' model of rhythmic organization

One of the most popular forms of Hindustānī vocal music today, the *vilambit* or *ati-vilambit* ('slow' or 'very slow') *khyāl*, appears in many of its manifestations to be organized in a way quite distinct from the syllabic model outlined above. There is apparently no close relationship between the *tāl* and surface rhythm, nor is that surface rhythm conceived as a string of discrete units or syllables. On the contrary, the melodic style is highly melismatic (many notes are sung to one text syllable, where text is employed, or to an open vowel sound), and their individual articulation points are not always clearly defined temporally.

In general the *tāl* to surface rhythm relationship in music of melismatic style is neither as simple nor as clearly definable as in the syllabic model. That is not to say that no such correlation exists, but the type of mathematical relationship outlined in the previous section clearly does not apply here. The development of such a melismatic style in *nibaddh* (metred) forms marks a departure from previous Indian musical tradition.

This style of music has developed, almost certainly within the last 100 years, for specific aesthetic reasons. The musicians who took the lead in this development, in particular *khyāl* singers Abdul Wahid Khan (d. 1949) and Amir Khan (1912–73), did so because they found that the conventional modes of rhythmic organization limited their scope for expression. They developed a style of singing in which, by slowing down the tempo markedly, they created 'space'—i.e. longer time-spans—in which to develop arguably the most emotionally expressive form of classical singing heard in North India.[8] (A similar deceleration in the performance of *kaharvā* and *cāñcar tāls* occurred in *ṭhumrī*; see Manuel 1989 : 83.)

Deceleration of the *tāl*, coupled with the expressive and melismatic singing style, broke down the conventional model of rhythmic organization. Indeed the changes brought about were so radical that it is remarkable that this type of music is still performed in *tāl*, and that *tāl* has proved sufficiently adaptable in practice to permit such changes in its function.

Melismatic music may be characterized as follows. The *tāl* measures out a long time-span (c. 40–70 secs.) into a number of equal time units (usually 12, 14, or 16 *mātrās* in *vilambit khyāl*). The point reached in the cycle is signalled by the *tablā*'s *ṭhekā*.[9] In this time-span melodic phrases are developed, showing various degrees of co-ordination with the *ṭhekā* and the *tāl* structure. The area where *tāl* and melodic rhythm show the greatest co-ordination is around *sam* (beat one), where a section of the fixed composition (the *mukhṛā*) is repeated. Although each phrase will still begin with a *bol* or text syllable, these syllables never acquire the rhythmic significance they do in syllabic styles. This mode of rhythmic organization is illustrated graphically in Example 4.6.

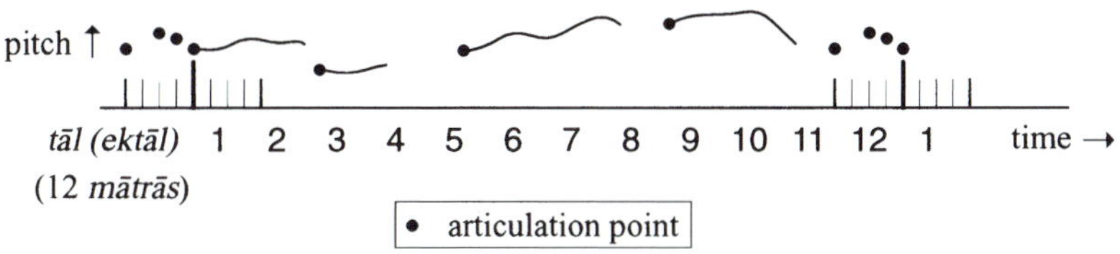

Example 4.6 A graphic illustration of a 'melismatic' model of rhythmic organization

Melismatic rhythm could be described as *rāg*- or melody-oriented—the simplest building blocks of the music are the melodic patterns specific to each *rāg*. Therefore each note need not be articulated with a new *bol*; a singer may stretch one text syllable melismatically to a considerably lengthy and complex melodic pattern, an effect imitated by the *mīṇḍ* (portamento) produced on the *sitār*

[8] Deshpande writes 'Influence of Vahid [= Abdul Wahid] Khan's *alapi* is so profound on Amir Khan that in slow *khyal* he is almost a replica . . . The tempo is unusually slow and therefore the *laya* element is unobtrusive and can be safely ignored except at the *sam* beat or thereabouts' (1987 : 65). Wade measured Abdul Wahid's Darbārī Kānhṛā in *jhūmrā tāl* at $\frac{1}{4}$ *mātrā* = 84, i.e. *mātrā* = 21 MM (1984*a* : 211).

[9] On the role of the *tablā*, Bhowmick has written 'While accompanying with a 'Bāḍā-khayāl' of long durations Ek-tāla (48 beats), Jhumrā-Tāla (56 beats) and Tilvārā-Tāla (64 beats), a Tablā accompanist loses the charm of the music if he is made to perform a dull game of enumeration' (1975 : 40).

and other instruments.[10] A 'melismatic' rhythmic style predominates in much *vilambit khyāl* (depending on the *gharānā* or individual style), *ṭhumrī* (in modern *bol banāo* style), and to some extent in instrumental styles based on *khyāl* or *ṭhumrī*.

4.2.3 The *tablā ṭhekā* and a hybrid model of rhythmic organization

We must now consider more subtle changes to the syllabic model, changes which have established a hybrid mode of rhythmic organization, which is current in most genres of Hindustānī music today. Broadly speaking, these changes are associated with the increased importance of the *ṭhekā* in modern *tāl*, and the associated rise of symmetrical *tāl* structures and of the importance of stress and pitch modulation in the drum patterns. All these changes were brought about by the adoption of the *tablā* as the accompanying drum for most genres of Hindustānī music, and the development of its style and repertoire.

These issues are addressed in Rebecca Stewart's doctoral dissertation (1974): her account of the development of the *tablā* and its repertoire, and its rise to pre-eminence in North Indian music over the last 150–250 years, is also the most important analytical study of *tāl* in modern North Indian practice attempted to date. Stewart not only distinguishes differences in techniques and repertoire between the *tablā* and *pakhāvaj* (the older barrel drum still used to accompany *dhrupad* and *dhamār*, and a close relative of the South Indian *mṛdangam*). She also distinguishes between different *tāl* types, broadly associated with either of these two drums, and argues that the *tablā* has acted as an agent of an alien rhythmic system (basically Middle Eastern in origin), and that its adoption has entailed considerable changes in the North Indian rhythmic system.[11]

Stewart's 'traditional Indian', *pakhāvaj*-based rhythmic system, is characterized as follows: the *tāls* have asymmetrical structures marked by agogic accents (i.e. some *vibhāgs* are longer than others); the drum plays elaborative patterns rather than a *ṭhekā*, and these *tāls* are subject to divisive manipulation (cf. *laykārī*). This model is contrasted with a so-called 'alien', *tablā*-based rhythmic system: *tāls* are characterized by the dynamic, timbre, and pitch variations of the *ṭhekā*, having symmetrical structures and being varied not divisively but by the interpolation of extra strokes (*bols*).[12]

[10] *Mīṇḍ* is a technique in which pitch is varied by means of lateral deflection of the playing string along the fret.

[11] Although Stewart's thesis is for the most part convincing, her characterization of the *tablā*'s rhythmic system as non-Indian is perhaps an exaggeration; moreover she ignores the possibility that her 'traditional Indian' rhythmic system may have absorbed influence from Persia and Central Asia in medieval times (i.e. pre-18th cent.). This is not the place however for a review of Stewart's work as a whole.

[12] See Stewart (1974: pp. xvii, 129 etc.). This idea of a difference in rhythmic styles between *pakhāvaj* and *tablā* is given another dimension by Gottlieb, who suggests a broad distinction between the more *pakhāvaj*-influenced *tablā* styles (especially *Banāras* and *Pañjāb*), and the rest. These two styles are the most rhythmically complex, using more cross-rhythms and *laykārīs* using divisions of 5, 7, and 9, amongst others (1977: 79).

Comparing these characterizations with the 'syllabic' model described above, there seems to be a correlation between that and Stewart's 'traditional Indian' system. It is striking that the syllabic model covers all major aspects of rhythmic organization (metre, tempo, the organization of surface rhythm) in a coherent manner, without integrating the concept of *ṭhekā*. Clearly this prototypical syllabic model and Stewart's 'traditional Indian' system are essentially the same thing, their characterizations arrived at by two different routes. Moreover I see no reason to doubt her argument that *ṭhekās*, pitch modulation, and symmetrical *tāl* structures have been adopted via the *tablā*, effectively within the last 200 years. (Subhadra Chaudhary suggests, in fact, that the first documentary evidence for the use of the *ṭhekā* dates from as late as 1857; 1997 : 148–9.)

Each of these three 'new' phenomena associated with the *tablā* may coexist with the tenets of syllabic organization (dual structure, explicit and hierarchical metric structure marked by clap patterns, generation of surface rhythm from *tāl* structure). This they do in practice, and in fact a hybrid model of rhythmic organization has evolved (and continues to evolve), with these new features superimposed on an older rhythmic system of which they are not a prerequisite, but with which they may coexist.

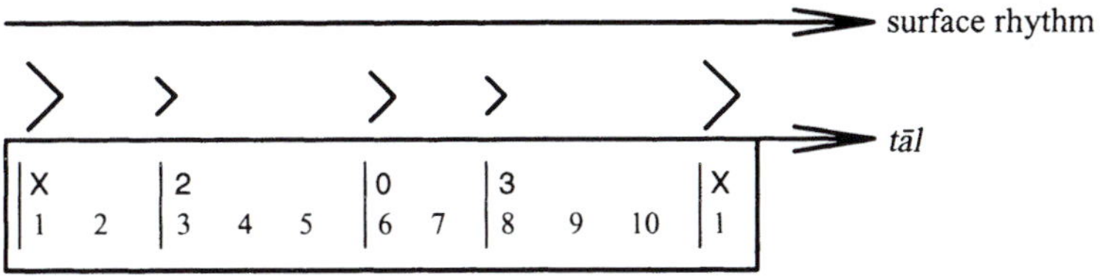

Example 4.7 In this hybrid model *tāl* is not only a quantitative (durational) but also a qualitative (accentual) hierarchy

This hybrid model (illustrated in Example 4.7) is closely related to the syllabic model outlined above, but modified by the prominence of the *tāl*'s accentual pattern, as expressed in the *ṭhekā*. This could be termed 'syllabic-accentual'. The *tāl*'s characteristic accentual pattern is called its *chand*, a term which may also be used to describe any accentual rhythmic pattern (see Chapter 10). Qualitative distinctions between *mātrās* are not expressed simply as differences in drum timbre; they are felt to be weighted, and this weighting (*vazan*) indicates relative structural importance.[13] The concepts of *chand* and *vazan* are important in modern-day *tāl*, and are sometimes used in criticism of slow *khyāl*, which is accused of being sung in *tāl* without these qualities.[14]

[13] One way of achieving this is by dynamic stress, another by lengthening the more important beats slightly. This lengthening is not perceived as such, but rather as an accent which enhances the life of the *tāl*. Gottlieb writes that 'Chhand is an important characteristic of gharānā style as it pertains to the distinctive manner in which the rhythmic patterns are varied slightly in performance from their strictly measured divisions of timing' (1977 : 81). See also Jairazbhoy's timing of *tīntāl* (1983 : 117 ff.).

[14] e.g. by the late K. G. Ginde (lecture demonstration Bombay 31 Dec. 1990).

This model represents a hybrid of pre-*tablā* syllabic rhythmic organization with the concept of *ṭhekā* (and in some cases symmetrical structure and pitch modulation) which was introduced with the *tablā*. In many respects it retains the features of the old *tāl* system, yet it cannot be regarded as a purely quantitative mode of organization; with the addition of the *ṭhekā*, it becomes a qualitative and accentual hierarchy of beats, and this is a significant modification.[15]

4.2.4 Summary: a unified model of rhythmic organization in North Indian music

Three conceptually distinct models of rhythmic organization have been outlined, which are called here syllabic, melismatic, and hybrid (syllabic-accentual). The syllabic model is associated with a syllabic rhythmic style, the melismatic model with a melismatic rhythmic style; the latter 'hybrid' model is formed by the superimposition of the *tablā*'s *ṭhekā* on the earlier syllabic paradigm.

The theoretical model implied by the traditional Indian rhythmic concepts—*tāl*, *lay*, and *laykārī*— is described here as syllabic, since it is logically dependent on a conception of music as a stream of distinct units, capable of representation by spoken syllables (*bols*). *Tāl* is the manifestation of explicit metric structure, controlling the temporal dimension of music. *Tāl* represents a quantitative organization of beats, counted out with the help of hand gestures for the sake of accuracy. Implicit in the syllabic model are notionally constant tempo (*lay*), and a clearly definable relationship between *tāl* and surface rhythm (i.e. *laykārī*). *Ṭhekā* does not have a necessary role in defining or characterising *tāl*.

In many ways the antithesis of the syllabic model is the melismatic model. *Tāl* remains as the primary agent of temporal organization, but its functions are considerably modified. It is a succession of beats, some distinguished in the *ṭhekā* as cues (see Chapter 5), but not perceived as a hierarchical structure. Clap patterns are redundant; tempo remains constant, and slow, but the *tāl* to surface rhythm relationship is less clearly definable.

In much Hindustānī music, the rhythmic organization is a more subtle variant of the traditional syllabic model. All the essential features of syllabic style are retained, and superimposed on this model is the characterization of *tāls* by their *ṭhekās*. It is essentially a hybrid system, combining syllabic and accentual features. Recognition of this fact is essential to the understanding of a number of apparent contradictions and anomalies within the system, as we shall see in Chapter 5.

All three of these models are significant in the rhythmic organization of North Indian music; yet the music cannot be divided simply into three parts, each of the three organized by a different paradigm. For instance, the most syllabic North Indian vocal genre, *dhrupad*, frequently uses stereotypical drum patterns, albeit not as consistently as the *ṭhekā* is used in *khyāl* or instrumental genres. Although

[15] Arrows mark accents of different weights.

basically syllabic, it is possible to describe the rhythmic organization of *dhrupad* in terms of a hybrid model, noting that the durational element of the *tāl* predominates over the accentual.

The most melismatic vocal genre, namely *ati-vilambit khyāl*, has developed further since the time of Amir Khan, in much of whose music *tāl* could be said to be in some respects dysfunctional (see Chapter 6). While many *khyāl* singers of the present day retain a melismatic rhythmic style and a very slow tempo, they also encourage an accompaniment style in which regular subdivision of the *mātrā* is established by an elaborated *ṭhekā*. This is an important change which has stabilized the status of the *tāl*; although the rhythmic organization of this type of music is still distinct from that of the rest of North Indian music, it is also possible to consider it as a particular variant or transformation of the hybrid model described above. Whereas in the latter case *tāl* is a hierarchical structure, largely characterized by the *ṭhekā*, in the melismatic model this hierarchy becomes transformed into a simple time-measuring apparatus, and *ṭhekā* becomes merely a supplier of cues.

Rather than talk of three distinct models of rhythmic organization in North Indian music then, it may be preferable to talk of a single variable model with a number of parameters which can be significantly adjusted. This unified theoretical model describes what is essentially a hybrid system, synthesized over many centuries both through the absorption of new elements into Hindustānī music, and through the latter's autonomous development. It encompasses a metric hierarchy with both quantitative and qualitative (durational and accentual) characteristics, and an explicitly dual structure in which surface rhythm overlays that metric pattern (Example 4.8).

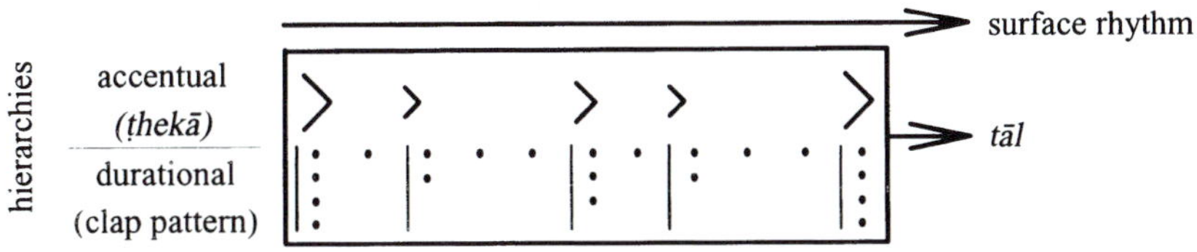

Example 4.8 An illustration of a unified model of rhythmic organization, combining aspects of quantitative (durational) and qualitative (accentual) hierarchy

Two of the most important variables in this model are tempo and the use of the *ṭhekā*. If the tempo is very slow, the structure loses most of its accentual character, and the *ṭhekā* retains only its function as the source of cues for time measurement—as in the melismatic model described above. If the *ṭhekā* is not used extensively, the accentual aspect is again weakened, and the clap pattern regains its historical importance as the main aid to time keeping—as in the syllabic model. At a moderate tempo and with the *ṭhekā* audible, however, a balance may be achieved between the different aspects of *tāl* structure. By adjusting certain rhythmic parameters, this model can therefore describe all metred (*nibaddh*) *rāg* music. The conventional perception of the *tāl* system as homogeneous and applicable equally to all forms of North Indian music, although misleading, is nevertheless important. The very idea of homogeneity, and of a system in consonance with historical principles, is important to Indian music culture. The premium attached to a unitary and coherent theory not only obscures the diversity of musical practice, it has also in fact played a positive role in assisting the development of a modern hybrid system.

5

Tāl in practice: quantitative, qualitative, and cyclic functions

5.1 *Tāl* in practice

5.1.1 Common *tāls* of North Indian music

About 20 *tāls* are commonly used in North Indian music at the present time: although rather larger numbers are often cited, these would include many rare *tāls* used mainly in drum solos and offer a misleading picture (in truth, even several of those listed in Example 5.1 are rarely heard). The common *tāls* comprise binary, ternary, quintal, and septimal[1] structures as well as combinations of the above (i.e. compound metres, such as *ektāl*, which combines binary and ternary features) and a few apparently anomalous structures, including some apparently conceived as arithmetical progressions (e.g. *matta tāl* of 9 *mātrās*, usually split $2 + 3 + 4$). Many *tāls* are associated with particular genres, and most are limited in the range of tempi at which they may be performed.

As I outlined in Chapter 4, *tāl* measures out musical time by means of recurring cycles comprising numbers of equal *mātrās* (time units). These *mātrās* are grouped into a sequence of *vibhāgs*, each of which is marked at its start by a hand gesture when counting out the *tāl*. *Tāls* are often most easily recognized, however, by their characteristic basic drum patterns, called *ṭhekās*. Example 5.1 is an alphabetical list of the most common Hindustānī *tāls*, illustrating structural features (number of *mātrās*, *vibhāg* groupings and hence clap patterns), and *ṭhekās*. The list is necessarily simplified, and does not include all possible variants.[2] Similar compilations can be found in most introductory texts on Hindustānī music.

As I proposed in Chapter 4, *tāl* is essentially a hybrid system, incorporating both quantitative or durational features (illustrated by the clap patterns), and qualitative or accentual features (by *ṭhekās*), and exists as both abstract structure and realized stress-time pattern. The essence of a *tāl* is therefore most often

[1] The terms 'quintal' and 'septimal', meaning based on groups of 5 and 7 respectively, were suggested to me by Richard Widdess and are, I believe, of his invention. I am not aware of any other suitable Western terms, but see the Indian terminology introduced later (Chapter 6).

[2] These *ṭhekās* from Ghosh 1968 : 68–70 (*addhā, dādrā, rūpak, tilvāḍā tāls*); Kaufmann 1967 : 254–8 (*āḍā cautāl, dīpcandī*); Ritwik Sanyal (personal communication, *brahma tāl, matta tāl*); Bhatkande (1953–8 : v. 10–12) (*cautāl, tīvrā tāl*); Powers 1980 : 125 (*dhamār tāl*); Wegner 1982 : 58–61 (*iqvāī*); Gottlieb 1977 : 226 (*jhūmrā tāl*); Alkutkar *c.* 1960 : 40 (*ādi tāl*), and Swapan Choudhury (personal communication, *savārī* and *pañcam savārī tāls*).

āḍā cautāl: 14 *mātrās*, 2+2+2+2+2+2+2

X	2	0	3	0	4	0	X
dhī trkt	dhī nā	tū nā	kat tā	trkt dhī	nā dhin	dhin nā	dhī

addhā tāl: see *tīntāl*

ādi tāl: 16 *mātrās*, 4+4+4+4

X	2	0	3	X
dhā dhi ṭa dhā	ge dhi ṭa dhā	ka ti ṭa tā	tiṭa kata gadi gana	dhā

brahma tāl: 14 *mātrās*, 2+3+4+5

X 0	2 3 0	4 5 6 0	7 8 9 10 0	X
dhā kiṭa	taka dhuma kiṭa	taka dhet tā dhet	tā tiṭa kata gadi gana	dhā

cāñcar tāl: see *dīpcandī tāl*

cārtāl kī savārī: see *savārī tāl*

cautāl: 12 *mātrās*, 2+2+2+2+2+2

X	0	2	0	3	4	X
dhā dhā	din tā	kiṭa dhā	din tā	tiṭa kata	gadi gana	dhā

dādrā tāl: 6 *mātrās*, 3+3

X	0	X
dhā dhin nā	tak dhina dhin	dhā

dhamār tāl: 14 *mātrās*, 5+2+3+4

X	2	0	3	X
ka dhi ta dhi ta	dhā –	ge ti ṭa	ti ṭa tā –	ka

dīpcandī (cāñcar or jat) tāl: 16 *mātrās*, 4+4+4+4; or 14 *mātrās*, 3+4+3+4

X	2	0	3	X
dhā (–) dhin –	dhā dhā dhin –	tā (–) tin̕ –	dhā dhā dhin –	dhā

ektāl: 12 *mātrās*, 2+2+2+2+2+2

X	0	2	0	3	4	X
dhin dhin	dhāge trkt	tū nā	kat tā	dhāge trkt	dhin nā	dhin

iqvāī tāl: see *tīntāl*

jat tāl: see *dīpcandī tāl*

jhaptāl: 10 *mātrās*, 2+3+2+3

X	2	0	3	X
dhin nā	dhin dhin nā	tin nā	dhin dhin nā	dhin

jhūmrā tāl: 14 *mātrās*, 3+4+3+4

X	2	0	3	X
dhā dhā trkt	dhin dhin dhāge trkt	tin tā trkt	dhin dhin dhāge trkt	dhā

EXAMPLE **5.1** Common Hindustānī *tāls*, showing *vibhāg* divisions, clap patterns, and *ṭhekās*

kaharvā tāl: 8 *mātrās*, 4+4

X	0	X
dhā ge na tin	na ke dhin na	dhā

matta tāl: 9 *mātrās*, 2+3+4

X 0	2 3 0	4 5 6 0	X
dhā ghira	naka ghira naka	tiṭa kata gadi gana	dhā

pañcam savārī tāl: 15 *mātrās*, 4+4+4+3

X	2	0	3 (4)	X
dhī nā dhīdhī kat	dhīdhī nā,dhī dhīnā tin--tra	tinnā trkt tinnā kattā	dhīdhī nā,dhī dhīnā	dhā

pañjābī tīntāl: see *tīntāl*

rūpak tāl: 7 *mātrās*, 3+2+2

X/0	1	2	X/0
tin tā trkt	dhin nā	dhin nā	tin

savārī tāl (cārtāl kī savārī): 11 *mātrās*, 4+4+3

X	0	2 (3)	X
dhī trkt dhin nā	tū nā kat tā	dhīdhī nā,dhī dhīnā	dhī

sitārkhānī tāl: see *tīntāl*

sūltāl (sūrphaktā tāl): 10 *mātrās*, 2+2+2+2+2

X	0	2	3	0	X
dhā dhā	din tā	kiṭa dhā	tiṭa kata	gadi gana	dhā

tilvāḍā tāl: see *tīntāl*

tīntāl: 16 *mātrās*, 4+4+4+4

X	2	0	3	X
dhā dhin dhin dhā	dhā dhin dhin dhā	dhā tin tin tā	tā dhin dhin dhā	dhā

variants of tīntāl: (all 16 *mātrās*)

(a) **addhā, pañjābī or sitārkhānī**

X	2	0	3	X
dhā -dhī -ga dhā	dhā -dhī -ga dhā	dhā -tī -ka tā	tā -dhī -ga dhā	dhā

(b) **iqvāī**

X	2	0	3	X
dhā dhin -trekre dhin	dhāge dhin -trekre tin	tā tin -trekre dhin	dhāge dhin -trekre dhin	dhā

(c) **tilvāḍā**

X	2	0	3	X
dhā trkt dhin dhin	dhā dhā tin tin	tā trkt dhin dhin	dhā dhā dhin dhin	dhā

tīvrā tāl: 7 *mātrās*, 3+2+2

X	2	3	X
dhā din tā	tiṭa kata	gadi gana	dhā

thought of as the combination of clap pattern and *ṭhekā—tāls* are 'quoted' and transmitted by recitation of the *ṭhekā* to the accompaniment of the appropriate hand gestures.[3] Since each *tāl* has both of these essential features, *tāl* often appears to be a unified and homogeneous system, whereas in truth it is quite diverse. Thus in some *tāls*, the *ṭhekā* is merely a standardized elaborative pattern, illustrating the essential internal divisions as marked by the clap pattern; in others the position is reversed, with the clap patterns emphasizing the structure primarily represented by the *ṭhekā*.

The application of a single terminology gives rise to some confusing anomalies. Some of these will be discussed below; they are indicative of the synthesis of the earlier syllabic system with the later *ṭhekā*-based system. There are anomalies arising from other causes too, most of which are not altogether mysterious; and these appear logical when seen in the context of the performance practice of the genre to which each *tāl* is applied. No single *tāl* is used in all genres, and the rhythmic and aesthetic requirements of each genre are somewhat different. There may be features of the system which can only be explained as historical accidents (for instance, features that have been retained despite apparently losing their functional significance), yet most will be found to have some function in performance.

5.1.2 Functions of *tāl*

The functions of *tāl* fall into three main categories, as follows, and the discussion below will be divided accordingly.

- Functions of a quantitative (durational) hierarchy; time measurement and time division, expressed through the structures of both clap patterns and *ṭhekās*.
- Functions of a qualitative (accentual) hierarchy; rhythmic character and dynamic form, as determined by the *ṭhekā*'s accentual pattern.
- Cyclicity; factors which reinforce a sense of recurrence can be interpreted as performing a 'cyclical' function.

The relative importance of each of these functions, which may be coexistent and even complementary, varies with the musical context.

5.2 Quantitative functions: time measurement and division

The primary function of *tāl* is to measure out and thereby to regulate time; but how does it achieve this? In principle the *tāl* continues its repetitive progress throughout any metrically bound piece of music: sometimes this is made clear by

[3] In fact, each *ṭhekā* has many variations in practice, and many *tāls* have more than one possible counting pattern. Within each *gharānā* or *bāj*, however, both are more or less standardized at any given tempo.

performers and/or audience visibly keeping time by means of hand gestures, at other times by the repetition of the *ṭhekā* by the accompanist, or by both means or neither (although where the *tāl* is not being made accessible through clap patterns or *ṭhekā*, it has generally already been established by these means). Thus *tāl* is both an abstract and a concrete phenomenon, which may function on several different levels.

The issue of time measurement has two dimensions, namely the measurement of the longest metrically significant time-span (the *āvart*), and the maintenance of structure within that span. Since the unambiguous structuring of this time-span is clearly necessary for its accurate preservation, one must look first at how the *āvart* is structured and at the methods used to establish and reinforce that structure.

5.2.1 Clap patterns (cheironomy)

Counting or clapping patterns have been a feature of the Indian *tāl* system since ancient times: cheironomy seems to have been associated in the first instance with Vedic ritual (Gerson-Kiwi 1980: 192). The Nāṭyaśāstra (written by the fifth century CE) gives patterns for each *tāl* using up to 8 different gestures, 4 sounded and 4 unsounded;[4] these have since been reduced in North Indian practice to two, one sounded and the other silent. These actions are simply a clap and a wave of the hand; they are called *tālī* and *khālī* respectively, and represented in modern North Indian notation by numerals (for *tālīs*) and by 0 for *khālī* (X is used for *sam* whether this falls on a *tālī* or a *khālī*). The primary function of clap patterns and their significance, now as in the past, is that they facilitate the counting out of the *tāl* cycles, helping to ensure that the *tāl* structure remains intact and that beats are not inadvertently lost or added. Interestingly, the function of the silent gesture has changed over the course of history. In modern practice the *khālī* contrasts with the *tālī* and helps therefore to specify the *tāl* structure. In ancient practice the principal contrast was between left and right hand claps, while the silent gestures were reserved for 'expanded' (augmented) states (Rowell 1992: 193–4).

In modern Hindustānī music, clap patterns are particularly useful (even indispensable), in measuring time when audible clues are at a minimum—when *ṭhekās* are not used consistently, for example, or do not in themselves provide sufficient guidance. Indeed since the use of the *ṭhekā* is a much more recent phenomenon than that of clap patterns, it is fair to say that it is clap patterns that have traditionally been the principal means of time-keeping in Indian music:[5] this is indeed still the case in *dhrupad-dhamār*, as it is in South Indian music.

[4] See e.g. Rowell (1988*a*: 147 or 1992: 193–4). According to Nijenhuis's interpretation, there were 3 sounded and 4 unsounded gestures (1974: 62).

[5] 'The function of cheironomy was to measure out, in visible, audible and unambiguous fashion, the musical time . . . '; Widdess (1981*c*: 507) on Nānyadeva's Pāṇikā songs (*c*.1100 AD).

All *tāls* have clap patterns; in most cases they are standardized, although some *tāls* do have a number of variant patterns (see e.g. *dhamār tāl*, below). The primary requirement of a clap pattern is that the identity of *sam* should be clearly and unambiguously established, and therefore the pattern should not repeat within the cycle. To this end, the patterns require divisions of different lengths and/or the use of two or more hand gestures—*vibhāgs* must differ in kind and/or duration. For this reason, simply three claps are sufficient to establish the asymmetrical *tīvrā tāl* (3 + 2 + 2), whereas a second gesture is required for *tīntāl*, since a pattern of simply four equidistant claps would be almost entirely redundant (see Widdess 1981*b* : 133).

Clap patterns often also support the accentual pattern of the *ṭhekā* (or vice versa, the effect is mutual), so that the claps or waves occur on beats felt to be accented, and/or the *khālī* gesture may signify the *ṭhekā*'s '*khālī*' section (that distinguished by strokes without bass resonance). Clap patterns may support the *ṭhekā* in this way, or they may on occasions contradict its implicit structure (see below). They may do no more than keep time, or they may in fact influence the music profoundly, for instance by suggesting rhythmic patterns for compositions. At the other extreme, in melismatic *ati-vilambit khyāls*, although the *vibhāg* division is retained in principle, the clap patterns are redundant; they simply fail to fulfil their function at a tempo slower than about 30 MM.

5.2.2 *Ṭhekā* and time measurement

The *ṭhekā*, or basic drum pattern, may assist time measurement by means of the aural clues it provides. Indeed the *ṭhekā* itself is an audible indication of the *tāl*, but in practice certain features are particularly useful in this regard, especially *khālī* sections and certain other *bol* combinations which may act as signals (e.g. the phrase 'tirakita').

Khālī sections provide the basic aural clues in the *ṭhekās* of a number of *tāls*, for instance *tīntāl:* in this case the *ṭhekā* breaks down into 4 equal sections, and the only distinguishing factor is the absence of undamped *bāyā̃* strokes ('ge/ghe') in the third quarter (in practice, *mātrās* 10–13 rather than 9–12). This sequence, 'tin tin tā, tā' is the most significant audible clue to the point reached in the *tāl*.

In *vilambit khyāl tāls* too, *khālī* sections can be useful cues, for example *mātrās* 5–8 of *ektāl* and 8–10 of *jhūmrā tāl*. However, because the tempo here is generally very slow, additional cues are needed, most significantly the easily distinguishable *bol* phrase 'tirakita' which occurs on *mātrās* 4 and 10 of *ektāl* and on *mātrās* 3, 7, 10, and 14 of *jhūmrā tāl*. The fact that this cue tends to be repeated in the cycle might be a source of confusion,[6] but in combination with the *khālī vibhāg* it supplies sufficient guidance (see Example 5.2).[7]

[6] This observation was suggested to me by the singer Veena Sahasrabuddhe (interview, Mar. 1991).

[7] *Khālī bols* are italicized, and the phrase 'tirakita' (trkt) is bold. Note that the last *mātrā* of *ektāl* is normally changed from 'nā' to 'dhā' in elaborated versions.

ektāl: 12 *mātrās*, 2+2+2+2+2+2

X	0	2	0	3	4	X
dhin dhin	dhāge **trkt**	*tū nā*	*kat tā*	dhāge **trkt**	dhin dhā	dhin

jhūmrā tāl: 14 *mātrās*, 3+4+3+4

X	2	0	3	X
dhā dhā **trkt**	dhin dhin dhāge **trkt**	*tin tā* **trkt**	dhin dhin dhāge **trkt**	dhā

EXAMPLE **5.2** Cueing features of *vilambit ektāl* and *jhūmrā tāl*

A different situation pertains in *dhrupad*, where the *ṭhekā* is not used so extensively as in *khyāl*; clap patterns play a much more important role in time-keeping. However, even there aural clues play their part: the recognizable stroke 'din' on *mātrās* 3 and 7 of *cautāl*, and the typical cadential phrase 'tirakita gadigana' covering the last four *mātrās* of *cautāl* and several other *dhrupad tāls* are cases in point. Both these features may be maintained in some form even in the absence of the *ṭhekā* as such; for instance the phrase 'tirakita gadigana' may be heard in drum improvisation at double speed at the end of a cycle, occupying 2 *mātrās* rather than 4 (see Example 5.3).[8] In this case the cadential function of the phrase is not dependent on its *lay* (i.e. rhythmic density).

cautāl: 12 *mātrās*, 2+2+2+2+2+2

X	0	2	0	3	4	X
dhā dhā	**din** tā	kiṭa dhā	**din** tā	tiṭa kata	*tirakita gadigana*	dhā

EXAMPLE **5.3** *Cautāl ṭhekā*, with final 4-*mātrā* pattern varied

The use of the *ṭhekā* varies greatly, particularly between genres, and in fact the basic *ṭhekā* patterns as quoted above are almost invariably elaborated in practice. As Rebecca Stewart shows, two fundamentally different types of elaboration are employed (1974). Elaboration in *tablā tāls* (e.g. *tīntāl*, *jhaptāl*, *rūpak tāl*) tends to comprise a filling-in between the structurally important *bols* which make up the basic *ṭhekā* (the amount of elaboration being largely dependent on the tempo). Elaboration of *ṭhekās* in asymmetrical *pakhāvaj tāls* (e.g. *cautāl*, *dhamār tāl*) tends to allow more displacement of the *ṭhekā bols*.

This distinction is illustrated in Example 5.4, with examples of elaborated *ṭhekās* of *cautāl* (as played on *pakhāvaj*) and *rūpak tāl* (as played on the *tablā*). In the *cautāl* example the phrase 'tiṭakatagadigana' is doubled in speed, and consequently *bols* are displaced. In the *rūpak tāl* example, the *ṭhekā* is elaborated by substitution and interpolation of *bols*.[9]

[8] The most prominent cueing features are in bold.

[9] The elaborated *rūpak tāl* example is from Stewart (1974: 106). The *bols* 'tiṭa' and 'tira' are equivalent; the latter is more usual at higher speeds and vice versa.

cautāl: 12 *mātrās*, 2+2+2+2+2+2

X	0	2	0	3	4	X
dhā dhā	din tā	kiṭa dhā	din tā	*tiṭa kata*	*gadi gana*	dhā

X	0	2	0	3	4	X
dhā dhā	din tā	kiṭa dhā	din tā	tiṭa kata	*tirakita gadigana*	dhā

rūpak tāl: 7 *mātrās*, 3+2+2

X/0	1	2	X/0
tin tā trkt	dhin nā	dhin nā	tin

X/0	1	2	X/0
tī--kra tintin tā-taka	dhindhin dhāge	dhin dhāge	tin

EXAMPLE **5.4** Illustrations of plain and elaborated *ṭhekās* of *cautāl* and *rūpak tāl*

5.2.3 The relationship between clap pattern and *ṭhekā*

Clap patterns frequently parallel changes in the type of *bols* used in the *ṭhekā*: for instance *khālī bols* can signify the *khālī vibhāg*, as was noted above. The *khālī vibhāg* (that marked by a wave, and the symbol '0') may thus correlate with a section of the *ṭhekā* using *khālī* or *band bols*, those lacking the resonant bass sound of the *bāyā̃* (left-hand drum; e.g. 'nā, tā, tin, ke, tirakiṭa'). The bass tones occur in the *bharī* or *khulī*[10] *bols* ('ge, dhā, dhin' etc.) which (theoretically) fall in the remaining, *tālī vibhāgs*. Yet in practice, the relationship between clap pattern and *ṭhekā* can vary between coincidence (*jhaptāl*), overlapping (*tīntāl*), and contradiction (*ektāl*).

The correlation between *khālī vibhāg* and *bols* is exact in *jhaptāl*, one of several symmetrical *tāls* made unambiguous by the *tālī/khālī* distinction (see Example 5.5). In such *tāls*, the *khālī* section is an exact counterpart of the first *tālī* section: the *bols* of the *khālī vibhāg* are those of the first *vibhāg* without their *bāyā̃* (left hand, i.e. bass) element, so that 'dhin' becomes 'tin', 'dhā' becomes 'tā' and so on. The correlation of *khālī vibhāg* with *khālī bols* is also clear in *rūpak tāl*, which is unique in having a *khālī* section coinciding with *sam* (Example 5.6).

jhaptāl: 10 *mātrās*, 2+3+2+3

X	2	0	3	X
dhin nā	dhin dhin nā	*tin nā*	dhin dhin nā	dhin

EXAMPLE **5.5** *Jhaptāl*, *ṭhekā* with *khālī vibhāg* italicized

[10] In general *khālī/band* (empty/closed) *bols* are represented by unvoiced consonants, and *bharī/khulī* (full/open) *bols* by voiced consonants.

rūpak tāl: 7 *mātrās*, 3+2+2

X/0	1	2	X/0
tin tā trkt	dhin nā	dhin nā	tin

EXAMPLE 5.6 *Rūpak tāl, ṭhekā* with *khālī vibhāg* italicized

Tīntāl and *dhamār tāl* provide examples of looser forms of correlation. In *tīntāl*, the correlation is not so exact as in *jhaptāl* or *rūpak tāl*—the *khālī* bols are shifted back by one *mātrā* (Example 5.7). In *dhamār tāl*, the *khālī bols* cover half the cycle and overlap by one *mātrā*, with the result that *sam*, marked by a *tālī* gesture, is actually played on a *khālī bol* (Example 5.8).

tīntāl: 16 *mātrās*, 4+4+4+4

X	2	0	3	X
dhā dhin dhin dhā	dhā dhin dhin dhā	dhā *tin tin tā*	*tā* dhin dhin dhā	dhā

EXAMPLE 5.7 *Tīntāl, ṭhekā* with *khālī bols* italicized

dhamār tāl: 14 *mātrās*, 5+2+3+4

X	2	0	3	X
ka dhi ta dhi ta	dhā –	ge *ti ṭa*	*ti ṭa tā* –	*ka*
A		B		

EXAMPLE 5.8 *Dhamār tāl, ṭhekā* with *khālī bols* italicized

In Example 5.8 B appears to be a *khālī* counterpart to A:[11] the connection between *ṭhekā* and counting pattern is somewhat tenuous, but at least the *sam*/*khālī* dichotomy of the clap pattern appears to be represented in the *ṭhekā*. *Dhamār tāl* may be counted by means of at least three other clap patterns, however. One, popular in the temple tradition known as *havelī saṅgīt,* is 3 + 2 + 2 + 3 + 2 + 2 , alternating *tālīs* and *khālīs* (i.e. X + 0 + 2 + 0 + 3 + 0).[12] Another variant ignores *khālī* completely to give 5 + 5 + 4,[13] yet another is 2 + 3 + 2 + 3 + 4 (X + 0 + 2 + 0 + 3);[14] none of these shows a more logical correlation with the *ṭhekā*.

Ektāl is an extremely anomalous example, showing no apparent correlation between the structures of its counting pattern and its *ṭhekā*, in which the

ektāl: 12 *mātrās*, 2+2+2+2+2+2

X	0	2	0	3	4	X
dhin dhin	dhāge trkt	*tū nā*	*kat tā*	dhāge trkt	dhin nā	dhin

EXAMPLE 5.9 *Ektāl, ṭhekā* with *khālī bols* italicized

[11] This observation was suggested to me by Richard Widdess.

[12] From Ritwik Sanyal, personal communication. See also Chaudhary, who cites an 'older' version of *dhamār* divided 3 + 2 + 3 + 2 + 2 + 2 (1997 : 305).

[13] From Ravi Shankar, personal communication.

[14] See Bhowmick (1975 : 40).

khālī bols cover the middle third of the cycle (*mātrās* 5–8; see Example 5.9). *Ektāl*'s alternative clap pattern, sometimes used at fast tempo, 3 + 3 + 3 + 3 (X + 2 + 0 + 3),[15] shows no better correlation to the *ṭhekā*'s structure (although the *ṭhekā* may be performed with dynamic accents suggesting a ternary structure). The standard *ektāl* clapping pattern is identical to that of *cautāl*, where the two *khālī vibhāgs* do correlate with *khālī bols* of the *pakhāvaj*. Although the historical development of these and other *tāls* has yet to be properly established, it seems likely that *ektāl* has borrowed the counting pattern of *cautāl*, to which its *ṭhekā* is apparently thoroughly unrelated.[16] Anomalous as this undoubtedly is, it illustrates the fact that both *ṭhekā* and clap pattern may function simultaneously, without necessarily showing any structural correlation.

All these examples illustrate the point that the purpose of the clap pattern is to support one of the *tāl*'s principal functions, namely time measurement. The distinctions in drum timbre in the *ṭhekā* also play a part in time measurement—in fact their function in that respect can be very similar—yet there is no overriding reason why the two patterns should coincide (unless of course one is derived from the other historically), and this is reflected in practice. The correlation of the silent hand gesture *khālī* with the *khālī* drum strokes applies only to certain *tāls*: it is a relatively recent development, and has occurred probably as a result of *ṭhekās* being created to support existing clap patterns, and vice versa.

These two phenomena are in essence features of two distinctly different rhythmic systems, in one of which a hierarchical structure is expressed through the clap pattern, while in the other, an accentual pattern is determined by the *ṭhekā*. Since a process of interpenetration and hybridization between these two systems has been going on for some time (perhaps 150–200 years), it is not always possible to classify *tāls* unequivocally as belonging to one group or the other. In the hybridization process, *tāls* of the first group have acquired *ṭhekās*, and symmetrical, *ṭhekā*-based *tāls* have been given clap patterns; others have been imported into classical music from folk music, there to acquire both of these 'classical' features. The merging of the two systems is not however complete, and the anomalies or mis-matches between *ṭhekā* and clap pattern are the by-products of this historical process.

5.3 Qualitative functions: rhythmic character and accentual patterns

5.3.1 Observations on the character of *tāls*

Tāl, although historically a quantitative metric hierarchy underpinning syllabically conceived rhythm, is often defined by qualitative factors such as accentual

[15] See Stewart (1974: 117), and Renshaw (1966: 82) who quotes the great *sarod* player Ali Akbar Khan giving three versions of *ektāl*, 2 + 2 + 2 + 2 + 2 + 2; 3 + 3 + 3 + 3; and 6 + 6.

[16] Stewart in fact suggests that *ektāl*'s affinity with *dādrā* is closer than that with *cautāl* (1974: 111, 117–18). Powers comments on this same anomaly (1980: 122).

patterns, pitch, and timbre variation. Each *tāl* is more than a collection of *mātrās*, and more than a recurring cycle of fixed length: by a variety of means each *tāl*, at a particular tempo, acquires its own aesthetic character. In many cases, this character is in fact determined largely by the quantitative metric pattern itself and by the tempo. In others, it is created by factors such as accentual patterns inherent in the *ṭhekā*.

It is a truism to say that each *tāl* has its own character, something readily affirmed by musicians—but what is meant by 'character', and which factors contribute to it? If it were possible to leave aside the conventional associations between *tāl*, genre, and style, what would be left of the character of the *tāl per se*? Is there similarity between *tāls* with the same number of *mātrās*, or between all ternary, all quintal structures, and so on? Do similar connections exist between *tāls* with related *ṭhekās*, regardless of the number of *mātrās*? How important is performance tempo?

In the slow *ektāl* and *jhūmrā tāl* used in *baṛā* ('great', i.e. slow tempo) *khyāl*, there is little more to the respective *tāls*' character than the effect of the tempo itself: repose, ease, apparent lack of rhythmic restraint. Folk-derived *tāls* such as *kaharvā* and *dādrā* have a lively, driving quality due to the powerful accents and the *bāyā̃* pitch modulation of their *ṭhekās*.[17] *Dhrupad tāls* such as *cautāl* have qualities which may be dependent to some extent on their *ṭhekā*, such as *cautāl*'s measured alternation of *tālī-khālī-tālī-khālī* groups, followed by the cadential 'tirakita gadigana' driving towards *sam*. However, as the *ṭhekā* is not used as extensively as in *khyāl*, much of the rhythmic character is created by the wide variation allowed from the basic drum pattern, together with the energy and rhythmic invention of the performance. In these respects, *cautāl* does share a lot with related *pakhāvaj tāls*, such as *tīvrā tāl*, or *jhaptāl* in its *pakhāvaj* form. The common use of the cadential formula 'tirakita gadigana' is illustrated in Example 5.10.[18]

Seven-*mātrā tāls* In *tāls* performed at medium tempo, the number of beats becomes more important, and this is illustrated in the case of the seven-*mātrā tāls rūpak* and *tīvrā*, both of which have the same 3+2+2 structure. My, admittedly, subjective impression is that one effect of this structure is that the group of three *mātrās*, being longer than the rest, produces a sensation akin to both deceleration and relaxation at the beginning of the cycle (an effect which is increased in *rūpak tāl* by the use of a *khālī bol* on *sam*). The two groups of 2 *mātrās*, being shorter, conversely suggest tension and acceleration, so that the combined effect is one of a continual alternation of speeding up and slowing

[17] Manuel writes; 'Kaharvā tāl appears in a number of variants. . . . most of these iambically accent sam by preceding it with a stressed upbeat on the penultimate mātrā . . . . This iambic, "heartbeat" rhythm pervades North Indian folk music; drummers often intensify the iambic effect by depressing the left hand drum head on the sam in order to increase skin tension and raise the pitch of that beat' (1983*b* : 304).

[18] This *jhaptāl ṭhekā* comes from Bhagvandas and Pagaldas (1960 : 49).

cautāl: 12 *mātrās*, 2+2+2+2+2+2

X	0	2	0	3	4	X
dhā dhā	din tā	kiṭa dhā	din tā	tiṭa kata	gadi gana	dhā

tīvrā tāl: 7 *mātrās*, 3+2+2

X	2	3	X
dhā din tā	tiṭa kata	gadi gana	dhā

jhaptāl: 10 *mātrās*, 2+3+2+3

X	2	0	3	X
dhā din	tā tiṭa din	tā tiṭa	kata gadi gana	dhā

EXAMPLE **5.10** Three *pakhāvaj ṭhekās*

down, tension and relaxation. (One might expect to find a similar quality of 'seven-ness' in the 14-beat *tāls*: but as we have seen, *jhūmrā*'s tempo is too slow for this to be noticeable, while in *dhamār* the structure is ambiguous, and the greater possibilities of division and recombination of 14 beats are exploited.)

Ten-*mātrā tāls* As for 10-*mātrā tāls, jhaptāl* is usually played at medium tempo,[19] and features a symmetrical *tālī/khālī* division into 2 + 3 + (2) + 3. There is more to it than this: it is sometimes said to have a unique quality, its distinctive *chand*. Ashok Ranade talks of coming to *sam* 'in a pouncing manner' in *jhaptāl*.[20] *Jhaptāl* certainly has a unique character, but the comparison with another 10-*mātrā tāl, sūltāl,* is interesting. *Sūltāl* has two principal differences from *jhaptāl*; a different structural division and a faster tempo.[21] It appears on this basis to be radically different, yet in fact there is an affinity between the two *tāls*, or more precisely between *sūltāl*'s cycle and half of *jhaptāl*'s cycle (Example 5.11). The

sūltāl	X 2 + 2	2 + 2 + 2	X 2 + 2	2 + 2 + 2	X
jhaptāl	X 1 + 1	1 + 1 + 1	0 1 + 1	1 + 1 + 1	X

EXAMPLE **5.11** An illustration of the affinity between the structures of *sūltāl* and *jhaptāl*

[19] Generally—although some *khyāl* singers use *jhaptāl* for *vilambit khyāls*.

[20] Ranade quotes an unnamed 'old-timer', who pronounced that '*jhaptāl* comes pouncing, and *jhūmrā* swaying'—'*jhaptaal jhapse aataa hai, aur jhumra jhoomke*'; '*jhapse*' is either a misspelling or a variant of '*jhapaṭse*' (pouncing or swooping, from the verb '*jhapaṭnā*') for the purpose of alliteration (1984: 145).

[21] My tempo measurements give a range of 224–411 MM for *sūltāl*, contrasting with *jhaptāl*'s 38–104 MM (vocal) or 80–160 MM (instrumental). See Chapter 6.

division of the group of 5 into the iambic 2 + 3 pattern,[22] provides a connecting factor between these two *tāls*.

Twelve-*mātrā tāls* As for the mathematics of the number twelve, it allows binary or ternary subdivisions, or both (either consecutively or simultaneously). *Cautāl* makes use of this by employing a rigidly binary *tāl* structure, in both clap pattern and *ṭhekā*, but allowing frequent use of a ternary division in the melodic rhythm (see §8.2). *Ektāl* uses the same counting pattern as *cautāl*, but has an intriguing *ṭhekā*. Its structure may be regarded as either 4 + (4) + 4, as in the version used in *vilambit khyāl*, with the middle third ('tū nā kat tā') effectively sounding as a *khālī vibhāg*; as 6 + 6 (with the symmetry of the 'dhāge tirakitā' phrases suggesting this interpretation); or as 3 + 3 + 3 + 3, suggested by the clearly audible 'nā' stroke[23] on every third *mātrā* (3, 6, 9 and 12). Alternatively, the 4 + 4 + 2 + 2 counting pattern may be manifested as a series of dynamic accents, effectively imposing this structure on the *ṭhekā* (see Example 5.12).[24] This metrical ambiguity is itself one of the key aspects of the character of *ektāl* at medium or fast tempi.

ektāl: 12 *mātrās*, 2+2+2+2+2+2

X	0	2	0	3	4	X
dhin dhin	dhāge trkt	tū nā	kat tā	dhāge trkt	dhin nā	dhin

444	*bharī*		*khālī*		*bharī*	
4422	**dhin**		**tū**		**dhā**	**dhin**
66	dhāge trkt			dhāge trkt		
3333	*dhā*	*nā*		*dhā*		*nā*

EXAMPLE **5.12** *Ektāl*, illustrating four possible interpretations of its structure

5.3.2 *Ṭhekā* as accentual pattern

Looking specifically at the *ṭhekā*, a number of factors contribute to the *tāl*'s character or qualitative definition. *Ṭhekās* may be conceived analytically in terms of accentual patterns, and a number of different kinds of accents may be recognized. According to Grosvenor Cooper and Leonard Meyer's definition of accent as something which 'marks for consciousness' (1960 : 8), North Indian *ṭhekās* employ three main types of audible accent, as follows;

- dynamic accent; variation in loudness or attack between *bols*,
- timbre accent; variation in *bol* timbre (for example the distinction between *bharī* and *khālī bols*),
- pitch accent; e.g. *bāyā̃* pitch modulation in *tāls* such as *kaharvā*.

[22] Cf. Powers' term 'superparticular proportion' (1980 : 121).
[23] This 'nā' may appear as its synonym 'tā' or as 'dhā' in combination with the *bayā̃* stroke 'ghe'.
[24] Deepak Choudhury sees this as the essence of the *tāl*'s structure (personal communication).

Different drum *bols* vary in dynamic level regardless of any special intent on the part of the musician; this is a phenomenon inseparable in this context from timbre accents. There are also however instances where the drummer deliberately places dynamic accents in order to draw attention to a particular beat. This may be a regular accent (an integral part of the *ṭhekā*), or an accent specific to the musical context.

Special dynamic accents of this kind may do one of several things, such as providing a dramatic conclusion to a piece of improvisation by emphasizing *sam*; helping to keep the soloist in *tāl* by discreetly emphasizing *sam* or a cueing phrase (e.g. 'tirakita'); or attempting to confuse the soloist by accenting a beat which is not normally accented, a legitimate tactic in several performance styles.

The most obvious factor in the *ṭhekā* to distinguish one beat from another is the use of different drum *bols*, which have different timbres. The grossest aspect of timbre changes is that between *bharī* ('full') and *khālī* ('empty') *bols*. In many cases the *khālī* stroke may be heard as a timbre accent; for example the 'din' in *cautāl*'s *ṭhekā* (*mātrās* 3, 7) or the 'tin...' in *tīntāl* (m. 10–11) clearly draw attention to those beats and are both an aid to time-keeping and a contributor to rhythmic character.

There are many more subtle variations in timbre, since there are many possible drum strokes. The type of *bols* and their combination, and their derivation from either *tablā* or *pakhāvaj*, are important contributors to the *tāl*'s character. One reason for this is that the *pakhāvaj* is severely limited in its possible degree of pitch modulation, compared with the *tablā*. Such modulation, achieved by varying the pressure applied to the left drum head (*bāyā̃*) with the heel of the hand, is a prominent feature of most styles of *tablā* playing. This plays an important role in the characterization of several *tāls*, including *kaharvā* and *tīntāl*, where it may be seen as a kind of pitch accent.[25] An illustration of pitch modulation in *kaharvā tāl* is given below in Example 5.13.[26] A similar pattern of pitch modulation may be heard on Audio track 1, in the 6-*mātrā dādrā tāl*.

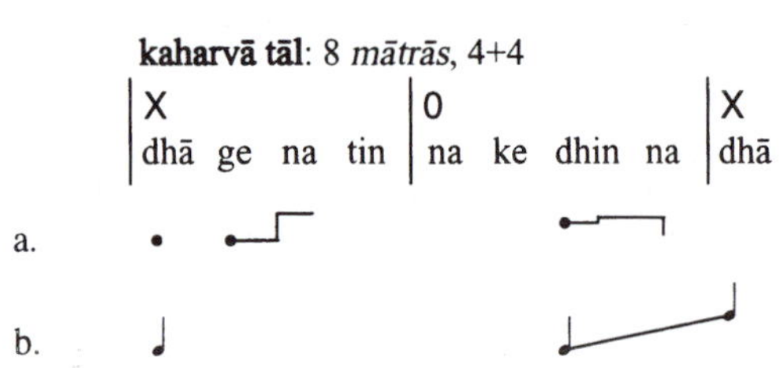

Example 5.13 Two representations of *bāyā̃* pitch modulation in *kaharvā tāl*

25 See Stewart (1974 : 89–91).
26 These illustrations from (*a*) Stewart (1974 : 90) and (*b*) Manuel (1983*b* : 304).

5.4 Cyclicity

I argued in Chapter 2 that all *tāls*, like any metric structures, may be considered as cyclic structures. Cyclicity is a concept rather than a percept: it cannot be directly perceived in music. Even if this is the case, however, it may be that some *tāls* lend themselves more readily to the concept, and if so cyclicity is another variable, linked to other variables. For instance, the length of the 'cycle' varies from less than 2 seconds to over a minute; due to factors such as the limits on the psychological present and short-term memory, the significance of these *tāls*' perceived cyclicity is surely very different (in fact, the latter can perhaps not be directly apprehended at all).

In Indian *tāls* the most important beat, *sam*, is both first and last; it is usually written as first, but more often than not functions as last in that it is the beat upon which rhythmic tensions are resolved. It is this ambiguity of the function of *sam* and the cadence-oriented improvisatory style, which are the practical manifestations of this preference for cyclicity. Factors which influence the importance of cyclicity include tempo, genre, type of composition, improvisation, and accompaniment style: cyclicity is another variable of Indian rhythmic organization.

5.4.1 *Ṭhekā* and cyclicity: the case of *tīntāl*

If an important implication of cyclicity is the dual role of *sam* as start and end point of the pattern, then *tāls* with a high degree of cyclicity might be expected to balance the sense of counting from *sam* ('**dhā** dhin dhin dhā . . . ') with one of approach to *sam* (' . . . dhin dhin dhā **dhā**'). The most important ways of doing this in a *ṭhekā* are to use cadential patterns (especially in *pakhāvaj ṭhekās*, e.g. 'tira kita gadi gana **dhā**') or with a combination of dynamic and timbre accents with pitch modulation (in many *tablā ṭhekās*). The principle of end-accented rhythm, while not so central as in much South-East Asian music, is an important one in North India. For example, in *tīntāl* the *bol* 'dhā' of *mātrās* 1, 5, and 9 may be heard as the last of a 4 *mātrā* group 'dhin dhin dhā **dhā**'. This makes the last 3 *mātrās* of the cycle effectively function as an anacrusis leading to *sam* (Example 5.14).

tīntāl: 16 *mātrās*, 4+4+4+4

X	2	0	3	X
dhā dhin dhin dhā	dhā dhin dhin dhā	dhā *tin tin tā*	*tā* dhin dhin dhā	dhā

EXAMPLE **5.14** *Tīntāl, ṭhekā* with an alternative grouping shown by square brackets

This interpretation appears to be supported by research into rhythm perception by Paul Fraisse, who suggests that rhythmic groups of 2 weak (W) and 2 strong (S) beats tend to be perceived as WWSS or SSWW, but not as SWWS (1978 : 237).[27] While the traditional structure of *tīntāl*, comprising four groups of

[27] This phenomenon was in fact first noted by Bolton as early as 1894.

four beats, remains in force, I suggest that the *ṭhekā* implies an overlapping grouping ('dhin dhin dhā dhā'), given a probable preference in most listeners for grouping like elements together, according to the well-known Gestalt principle.[28] Put another way, the implicit grouping of the *ṭhekā* overlaps the basic metric structure indicated by the clap pattern, which also explains the apparent shift in *khālī vibhāg* by one *mātrā*. The hand gesture comes on the strongest beat of the *ṭhekā* group, the last, with the final *mātrā* of the last group being the most important of all, *sam*. This is one of many instances of the importance of end-accented (anacrustic) patterns in Indian rhythm.

The tension between the conventional interpretation of *tīntāl*'s divisions and counting pattern ('**dhā** dhin dhin dhā') and the grouping implicit in the *ṭhekā* ('dhin dhin dhā **dhā**') need not be resolved, since it is this very tension which is felt to augment the sense of cyclicity in *tīntāl*. In *tīntāl* one is constantly aware of both the journey from and the anticipated arrival at *sam*, and this dual perception is stronger here than in most other *tāls*—which may go some way to explaining the current predominance of this *tāl* in practice.

5.4.2 Cyclicity in practice

Cyclicity, as a variable of rhythmic style in North Indian music, may be manifested either in standard cadential patterns resolving on *sam*, or (as in *tīntāl*) in overlapping grouping patterns. It is also influenced by other variables, especially tempo. This sense of cyclicity is perhaps at its weakest in *baṛā khyāl tāls*, because the slow tempo makes perception of the cycle as an integral unit too difficult. Although the structural principles of these *tāls* are no different, it is difficult to feel any sense of cyclicity here. The function of creating an expectation of *sam* is achieved through other means; a tightening up of the rhythmic structure is indicated by a temporarily more syllabic style, an increase in the rhythmic density, even on occasion a slight acceleration towards the end of the cycle, associated with the reiteration of the composition's *mukhṛā* (anacrusis). If such long, slow cycles can be conceived as cycles at all, it is intellectually, by extrapolation from the *mukhṛā*.

In fast tempo pieces, however, the rapid recurrence of a repeated drum pattern makes recurrence palpable and cyclicity easier to conceive. Indeed in some cases, the lack of a clear dynamic accent on *sam* can be a handicap in counting *tāl*, as one has a sense of looking for the join in a continually revolving circle. The musical significance of a feeling of cyclicity is that it encourages and supports a highly organized form of improvisation, the main structural pivot of which is the

[28] This interpretation is shared by Powers, who writes; 'DHĪN DHĪN DHĀ DHĀ coming up to *sam* is the nuclear formula, not DHĀ DHĪN DHĪN DHĀ beginning from *sam*' (1980 : 123). There is another designation where *sam* is counted as the second clap of the cycle, viz. X 3 0 1 (= 1 X 3 0). The second *tālī* of the cycle is called *pichlī* (lit. last), and the third *tālī* called *pahlī* (lit. 'first'). Confusing as this is, it does have a certain logic to it. It confirms that the *tāl* may be conceived as a cycle, since the implication is that the last *tālī* is reckoned as the first of a sequence of three (see Bhowmick 1981 : 56; Ghosh 1968 : 67; and Sargeant and Lahiri 1931 : 433).

sam at the end of each cycle. A soloist may begin a section of development or improvisation at any point (depending on the genre), but the way it ends—synchronized with the *tāl* cycle—is much more significant. The most common ways are with a climax either on *sam* or before the starting point of the composition, the *mukhṛā*.

5.5 Summary: *tāl* functions and the theoretical model of rhythmic organization

I have illustrated above a clear relationship between the quantitative function of time measurement and clap patterns. The accentual patterns associated with most *tāls* are on the other hand largely dependent on the *ṭhekā*. No such clear correlation can be established with the function of cyclicity: cyclicity is not an objective property of *tāl* but a conceptual or metaphoric phenomenon—the music is cyclic largely because people believe it is (or should be) cyclic. Nevertheless, it seems to be easier to conceive of some *tāls* as cyclic than others.

However, neither the correlation between clap pattern and time measurement, nor that between a *tāl*'s *ṭhekā* and accentual pattern and character, are exclusive—they are intimately related. The *ṭhekā* often plays a part in supporting the time-measuring function, and the clap pattern in turn may support the accentual pattern; since the concept of cheironomy pre-dates that of the *ṭhekā* in classical music, it is indeed likely that in some cases *ṭhekās* have evolved or been devised to complement older *tāls* which previously had none. In the case of *tāls* which have been absorbed from folk music into the classical realm, the complementary process may have occurred—clap patterns being created in order to support the accentual pattern of the *ṭhekā*. However, since there are numerous examples where the structures implied by these features do not concur, producing apparent anomalies, there are surely many more historical factors involved than these.

The usage of clap pattern and *ṭhekā* varies with context, as does the relationship between these phenomena and the main categories of *tāl* functions. This variability is to some extent associated with the different performance practice of different genres, and with the implications of different tempi. North Indian *tāl* is indeed a complex and multi-dimensional system of metric organization.

The *tāl* system is best represented as a hybrid model incorporating quantitative and qualitative functions, a model whose parameters (especially the use of the *ṭhekā*, and the tempo) are highly variable. Seen from this point of view, the relationship of *tāl*'s various features and functions becomes clearer.

Example 5.15 illustrates a little of the complexity of the relationships between the different aspects of *tāl*: (*a*) the *ṭhekā* generates the accentual hierarchy; (*b*) the clap pattern indicates the quantitative (durational) structure; and (*c*) the *ṭhekā* may assume the clap pattern's time-measuring function. As the parameters of rhythmic organization are altered, for instance by the use of extreme tempi or by

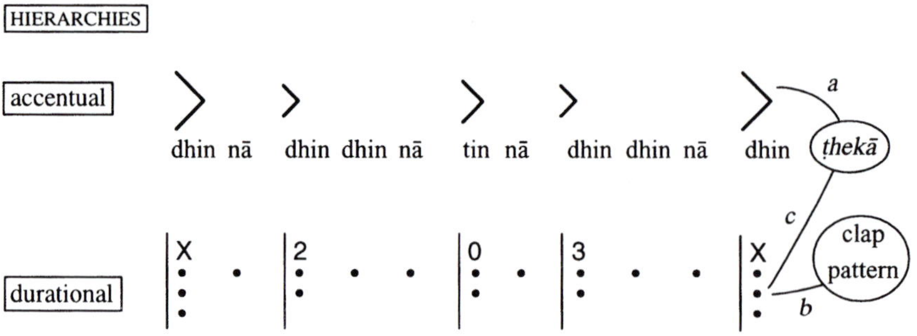

Example 5.15 An illustration of the relationship between *ṭhekā* and clap pattern, and the unified model of metric organization

varying the use of the *ṭhekā*, this affects the relationship between the different aspects of rhythmic organization. For example in melismatic *baṛā khyāl* where the accentual pattern of the *tāl* is of little or no importance and the clap pattern even less so, the *ṭhekā* changes in function. Rather than generating a characteristic accentual pattern to complement the clap pattern's time-measurement function, it actually replaces the clap pattern in this respect: an accentual pattern becomes transformed at slow tempo into a sequence of audible clues to the progress of the *tāl* cycle. If, on the other hand, the *ṭhekā* is barely used and the rhythmic organization reverts to the essentially quantitative 'syllabic' model (as in most *dhrupad*, and some instrumental music), then the upper stratum of the model as depicted in Example 5.15 becomes redundant.

6

Lay: tempo and rhythmic density

6.1 The concept of *lay* in Hindustānī music

6.1.1 Definition and usage of the term

Lay is one of the most important rhythmic concepts in Indian music. It has long been recognized as the principle which regulates musical time; it has also been appreciated that *lay* is partly responsible for the aesthetic character of music.[1] *Lay* is a difficult concept, however, because its meaning and significance have changed substantially over history. It is an ancient concept which may be only imperfectly applicable to modern music, and from this fact arises considerable ambiguity in meaning.

The concept of *lay* is one which has developed and expanded over the course of time to the point where it could be considered an equivalent of the English term 'rhythm' in almost all of that word's diverse senses. The original meaning of '*lay*' is, however, the duration or time-span between two beats.[2] Derived from this is the concept of 'tempo' since the tempo of a piece of music is determined by the time-spans between beats (taking 'beat' as a point in time marked by an action, in accordance with the ancient Indian theory). When Indian musicians speak of a 'good sense of *lay*', they mean an ability to generate rhythmic variations while retaining awareness of *tāl* and control of tempo.

Loosely interpreted then, a 'good sense of *lay*' is simply a 'good sense of rhythm'; hence the apparent equivalence of the terms *lay* and rhythm and Powers's comment, '*Laya* is extended to cover the semantic field of "rhythm and tempo" in the same way that "rhythm" in the West covers a semantic field comprising "rhythm and metre"' (1980 : 118). There appears to be some ambiguity as to what we mean by *lay*—whether *lay* primarily refers to the perceived rate of the metric structure, or to the rate of rhythmic events (rhythmic density), or indeed to the ratio between the two. In fact, it can mean any of these things, but the sense is usually clear from the context.

Lay as tempo Three tempo categories are traditionally recognized in Indian music, namely *vilambit*, *madhya*, and *drut* (slow, medium, and fast). Since in

[1] Ranade and Chavan cite the Viṣṇudharamorttara Purāṇā, which correlates *lay* to *ras* (aesthetic essence) (1976 : 3). This is also noted by Danielou (1957 : 70).

[2] See Rowell (1988*a* : 145), Chaudhary (1997 : 28). This sense is explicitly referred to by Deva when he writes that 'The flow of time has first to be calibrated. This calibration is what is called the *laya* or tempo. For, if the unit of calibration is small we feel the passage of time as quick; this is the drut . . .' (1981 : 268–9).

modern times the range of performance tempi has increased considerably at both extremes, it is helpful to add two further categories (*ati-vilambit* and *ati-drut*); some also find occasion to define intermediate categories (*madhya-vilambit* and *madhya-drut*), giving a total of seven notional bands (see Table 6.1).

Table 6.1 Tempo (*lay*) designators for Hindustānī music

lay	tempo
ati-vilambit	very slow
vilambit	slow
(*madhya-vilambit*)	(medium-slow)
madhya	medium
(*madhya-drut*)	(medium-fast)
drut	fast
ati-drut	very fast

In this way *lay* may translate the Western concept of tempo, the perceived rate of pulsation of a piece of music. Within the Indian context, however, there is some ambiguity over whether *lay* in this sense refers exclusively to the rate of succession of the *tāl*, or whether it is also dependent on surface rhythmic density. Indeed, the latter meaning is clearly intended when musicians speak of 'increasing the *lay*', not only when increasing the tempo, but also when increasing the rhythmic density by subdividing the pulse in generating surface rhythm.

Lay as the ratio of rhythmic density to tempo Several terms are employed by musicians to refer to the ratio of rhythmic density to tempo (cf. *laykārī*, Chapter 10). Terminology is diverse and often confusing, but some of the more common terms are given in Table 6.2 (for more on this topic see Chapter 10).

Moreover, since there is a clear affinity between '*lay* ratios' sharing a common factor in the numerator (e.g. between 3 : 2, 3 : 1, and 6 : 1), other sets of terms group these levels, as in Table 6.3. The terms in the first column all derive from

Table 6.2 Terms describing *lay* as the ratio of rhythmic density to tempo (*lay* ratio)

lay	rhythmic density: tempo (metric pulse)
barābar (*lay*)	1 : 1
deṛh (*deṛhī lay*)	3 : 2
dugun (*dugunī lay*)	2 : 1
tigun (*tigunī lay*)	3 : 1
caugun	4 : 1
pāñcgun	5 : 1
chegun	6 : 1
sātgun	7 : 1
āṭhgun	8 : 1

Table 6.3 Terms for *lay* reflecting the categorization of lay ratio by numerator, with equivalent '*jāti*' terms

lay	*jāti*	no. in groups
āṛī lay	*tryaśra jāti*	3 (3 : 2, 3 : 1, 6 : 1, etc.)
	caturaśra jāti	4 (2 : 1, 4 : 1, 8 : 1, etc.)
kuāṛī lay	*khaṇḍa jāti*	5 (5 : 4, 5 : 2, 5 : 1, etc.)
viāṛī lay	*miśra jāti*	7 (7 : 4, 7 : 2, 7 : 1)
	saṅkīrṇa jāti	9 (very rare)

the modifier *āṛī* ('crooked'); the '*jāti*' (lit. 'class') terms are used particularly in South India but also by some Hindustānī musicians. This list is not exhaustive, since the terminology is not standardized across the tradition as a whole; moreover some of the terms given in Table 6.3 have other interpretations. In order to consider the *lay* characteristics of the various genres of Hindustānī music, and tempo variation in performance practice, it will be necessary to use any or all of these terms—for tempo (as in Table 6.1), the ratio of rhythmic density: tempo (Table 6.2) and the categorization of such ratios (Table 6.3).

6.1.2 Tempo and metrical structure

Tempo is usually understood to be a function not of surface rhythm,[3] but of the underlying beat or metrical structure. Consistent with this approach, the measure of tempo generally adopted in North Indian music is the rate of succession of the basic time unit, the *mātrā*. However, in practice, the *mātrā* is not always the most appropriate measure of tempo. The assumed function of the *mātrā* as the tactus—the highest metrically significant pulse level—is in many cases shifted to some other pulse level ($\frac{1}{2}$ or $\frac{1}{4}$ *mātrā* divisions, or groups of 2, 3, or 4 *mātrās*) depending on the tempo. As a result, *mātrā* rates are not strictly comparable as tempo measurements.

The *mātrā* was originally a standard and notionally invariable time unit in Indian music:[4] *tāls* were composed of various time units (the *laghu*, *guru*, *druta*, etc.), which were reckoned as fractions or multiples of the *mātrā*. Hence the ratio between the time units employed in a particular pattern and a globally fixed time unit (the *mātrā*) functioned as a practical measure of tempo. From being a fixed

[3] See however Kolinski (1959), who regards it as just that. His idea that for comparison between cultures, rhythmic densities form a more objective measure than a subjectively defined 'beat' has considerable advantages; it is not, however, so useful for discussion of a single music culture, especially one (such as North Indian music) with sophisticated indigenous rhythmic concepts.

[4] The term *mātrā* is defined in the Nāṭyaśāstra (pre-5th cent.) as the time of five *nimeṣas* (lit. 'blinking of the eye') (NS 31.3, cited in Nijenhuis 1970 : 324). The Saṅgītaratnākara (13th cent.) defines the *mātrā* as the time taken to pronounce five short syllables (SR 5.16, cited in Gautam 1977 : 341). Gautam estimates the *mātrā* as 1.2 sec., giving a *mātrā* rate of 50 MM. Rowell's estimate on the same basis is 60–72 MM (1988*a* : 150). I find these figures a little low; my own trials, using 5 short Sanskrit syllables, yielded figures of 0.67–0.94 sec., which would give *mātrā* rates of *c*.70–90 MM.

time unit, as Indian art music evolved the *mātrā* became increasingly flexible, so that ultimately the duration of the *mātrā*, rather than the combination of various time units, became the measure of tempo.

The *mātrā* has latterly become a flexible measure of time: nowadays the *mātrās* of the fastest North Indian music are less than 0.1 sec. long; in the slowest they are over 5 sec. in duration. This means that tempo measurements based on *mātrā* rates vary from less than 12 MM to over 600 MM (in fact, rates at least as high as 720 MM can be heard): however, since at the slowest tempi the *mātrās* are consistently subdivided to provide the effective pulse of the music, and at the fastest rates the *mātrās* are perceptually grouped for the same reason, these measurements provide an exaggerated impression of the range of perceived tempi. Sachs had difficulty accepting a ratio of 1 : 8 between the slowest and fastest performance tempi (1953 : 32): a ratio of 1 : 60 (12 : 720 MM) is possible for rhythmic densities, but certainly not for perceived rates of *metric* progression.

Clearly, in some cases *tāl* structures have become temporally distorted, to the extent that the metric functions of *tāl*'s various structural levels change or are abandoned altogether, and measures of tempo must take this into consideration. The *tāl* system essentially provides three metrically significant pulse levels, the *mātrā*, *vibhāg*, and *āvart*. The manipulation of the *tāl* structures to permit both very slow and very fast tempi means that other metrical levels come into play, and the three basic levels may shift or diminish in metric importance. This must be taken into account when reckoning the effective tempo of a piece of music. Moreover, if surface rhythm is to be interpreted with respect to the *tāl* structure, these changes in performance practice mean that it is often more meaningful to consider the surface rhythm with respect to a metric level other than the *mātrā*.

Although this concept of *lay* as the ratio between rhythmic density and a constant metric pulse rate has its roots in ancient and medieval practice (i.e. when the *mātrā* was an arbitrary and invariable time unit, tempo was defined as the rate of its subdivision), it now has to compete with the concept of *lay* as metric pulse rate itself. Similarly, the notion of acceleration as an increase in the rate of subdivision of the metric pulse (*laykārī*, see Chapter 10) has to compete with the practice of gradual acceleration of the metric structure, and as a result the former concept has diminished in importance.

6.1.3 Determining the effective pulse rate

Selecting a pulse level to serve as a measure of tempo may remain difficult. Having in principle allowed a level other than the *mātrā* in this role, as a necessary response to changes in practice, such an acceptance nonetheless involves subjective decisions which may be problematic. Lerdahl and Jackendoff, who tried to determine such pulse rates (their 'tactus') in Western tonal music, found that it was frequently impossible to choose objectively between two pulse levels (usually in the ratio 2 : 1). In Hindustānī music, if two such pulse rates are present and one of them is regarded by generally accepted theory as the *mātrā*, we should have no hesitation in selecting that level as primary; if not then the decision might be somewhat arbitrary.

The type of metric pattern illustrated in Example 4.3, with three basic levels (*āvart*, *vibhāg*, and *mātrā*) and occasionally an extra intermediate level (such as the half-*āvart*), will be the predominant one at a tempo range of *c*.30–180 MM (*mātrā* 0.33–2 secs.). In this case, tempo is determined by the *mātrā* rate. In *ati-vilambit lay*, the $\frac{1}{2}$ or $\frac{1}{4}$ *mātrā* subdivision may replace the *mātrā* in function; in *drut* and *ati-drut lays* the 2- or 4-*mātrā* level (which is in many cases the *vibhāg* division) takes on this function. The metrical significance of the *vibhāg* level varies with *tāl* and context, as does that of other intermediate levels such as the half-cycle division which reflects the symmetrical *tālī/khālī* division of many *ṭhekās*. I will now illustrate these points using metric dot notation.

Not just one, but several levels of pulse (or recurrence), may be determined in any piece of metrically bound (*nibaddh*) music. These range from the surface rhythmic density down to the rate of recurrence of the *tāl* cycle, with a number of significant intermediate levels. The basic principle of Indian metric organization remains, despite numerous changes in performance practice over the centuries, that surface rhythmic patterns overlie the consistent metric structure determined by the *tāl*. Neither the fact that in some cases (in melismatic styles), the relationship between surface rhythm and *tāl* structure is apparently loose, nor the hypothesis that the function of those structures has been considerably distorted by their expansion or compression, invalidates this principal model.

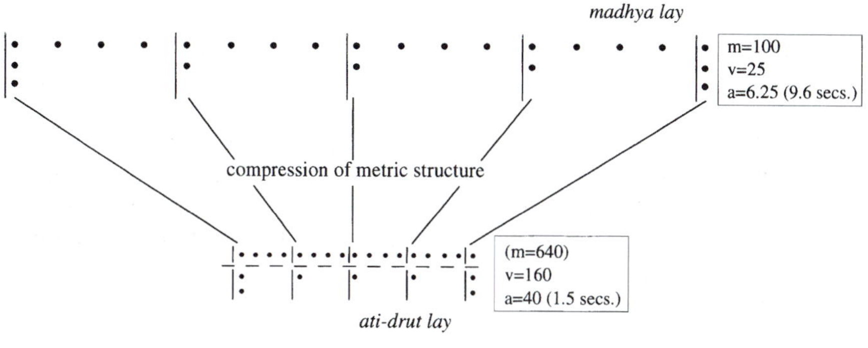

Example 6.1 An illustration of the compression of *tāl* structure at very fast tempo

Examples 6.1 and 6.2 illustrate both the basic model, and the effect of its distortion by extreme shifts in tempo. Example 6.1 illustrates how, when the metric structure is compressed at very fast tempi, the listener counts the *vibhāg* as the 'beat', giving a tempo shift up to (in this example) 160 MM, rather than 640 MM (the higher rhythmic density in *ati-drut lay* would be significant in further influencing the listener's perception of speed but not 'tempo' in its strict sense as the rate of metric progression).

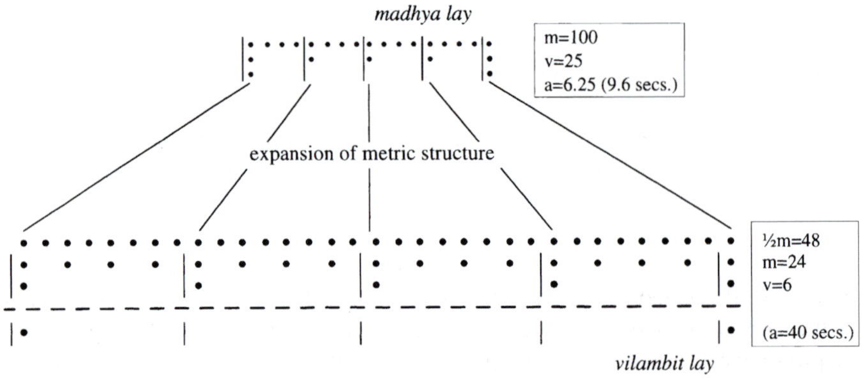

Example 6.2 An illustration of the expansion of *tāl* structure at very slow tempo

As for the converse phenomenon, Example 6.2 shows how, when the metric structure is expanded at slow tempi, the listener counts the half-*mātrā* pulse as the 'beat', giving a tempo shift down in my hypothetical example to 48 MM, rather than 24 MM. Comparing the three illustrations (of *tīntāl* in *madhya lay*, *ati-drut lay*, and *vilambit lay*), we can see how the difference in *mātrā* rate (of 24 MM in *vilambit lay* to 100 MM in *madhya lay* to 640 MM in *ati-drut lay*), compares with the difference in effective tempi (48 MM in *vilambit lay* to 100 MM in *madhya lay* to 160 MM in *ati-drut lay*). This illustrates my hypothesis that the effective tempo range in Hindustānī music is much less than it would appear from measurements of *mātrā* rates. One does come across indications of the fact that musicians have taken this on board: *ektāl* may be referred to as a *tāl* of 24 or 48 beats, rather than the standard 12 (see e.g. Bhowmick 1975 : 40), and *kaharvā* is often quoted as comprising 4 *mātrās* rather than 8 (see e.g. Ratanjankar 1967 : 121). However, such designations have not become standardized or even consistently used; it may even be that the trend is now in the opposite direction, to standardizing the number of *mātrās* designated for each *tāl* while releasing the concept of *mātrā* from its functional significance.

6.2 The measurement of *lay*

6.2.1 Determining *lay* (tempo and rhythmic density)

In most cases the appropriate measure of tempo will remain the *mātrā* rate, because musically literate listeners, not to mention performers, will interpret the *mātrā* as the primary pulse whenever this is practicable. In certain cases where a listener not educated in the music system might be inclined to take the $\frac{1}{2}$- or 2-*mātrā* pulse as primary, the knowledgeable listener will resist this; this factor makes a wide range of perceived tempi possible. However, at extreme tempi such an adjustment of perceived pulse is unavoidable, and our understanding of both metric structure and tempo must take account of this.

One other phenomenon complicates matters further. In 'complex' *tāls* such as *rūpak* (3 + 2 + 2) and *jhaptāl* (2 + 3 + 2 + 3), as the tempo increases so the pulse level (at which listeners would tap their feet) shifts from the *mātrā* to the *vibhāg*, giving an irregular (non-isochronous) pulse. Although it could be argued that at very high tempi an *average* value for this pulse would be a reasonable measure, the *mātrā* rate will be retained below as the basis of tempo measurements.

Another level must be taken into consideration, to supplement our understanding of perceived tempo, namely the rhythmic density.[5] Rhythmic density is the measure of the speed of articulation, and relates to the speed of the performers' physical movement. In this context, density effectively means speed, and is as much an indicator of tempo as is the metric pulse rate (see Kolinski 1959).

It is appropriate in a study of this repertoire to use the rate of metrical movement as the principal measure of tempo, taking rhythmic density as a secondary indicator. *Average* rhythmic densities of surface patterns are of relatively limited use (although they may be useful in music of melismatic style, where accurate determination of articulation points can be difficult), especially where it is possible to study the composition of surface patterns and their relationship to those underlying structures. In many cases the *maximum* density, and an appreciation of the relationship between this value and the primary metric pulse (which may stand in a simple mathematical proportion, e.g. 3 : 2 or 4 : 1) are of greater significance.

Another factor which needs to be considered (although perhaps not strictly speaking an indicator of *lay*) is the length of the *āvart*. The *tāl* cycle is the largest regularly repeating time unit; moreover the first beat (*sam*) is highly significant structurally, as it frequently marks the coming together of the rhythmic streams of soloist and accompanist, and the resolution point for rhythmic tension. Since two pieces with the same metric tempo and rhythmic density but in different *tāls* may have very different cycle lengths, this is of considerable significance for the metric structure of the music. In fact, since very slow *khyāl tāls*, almost without exception, display a considerable degree of subdivision of the *mātrā*, the effect of slowing the *tāl* down is much more marked on the cycle length than it is on the effective metric tempo.

As I will argue below, *tāl* functions are altered in very slow tempo pieces, principally because the cycles become too long to be directly perceived as single entities. In the same way, metric structure is affected since a long *āvart* (up to 60 seconds or more) cannot be considered a metric pulse level, rather it may be regarded as a higher-level organizational unit. Thus the principal measure of *lay* or tempo will be (*a*) the *mātrā* rate, except where this rate has clearly been displaced in function by (*b*) another metric pulse level. In addition to this, I will consider (*c*) rhythmic density, and (*d*) the relationship between density and tempo (*lay* ratio); and (*e*) the cycle length.

[5] Several authors have pointed to the importance of *predictability* of events in the perception of tempo (see e.g. Dowling and Harwood 1986 : 182), yet this is beyond the scope of this study.

Before I present measurements from performance, I should put these measurements (and in particular those of tempo) in context. David Epstein's discussion, in which he cites several earlier authors, suggests that something in the region of 37–40 MM falls at the very bottom end of the range of recognized tempi in Western music, with maxima a little over 300 MM (the highest figure he cites is 376 MM, Epstein 1995 : 109–17). According to George Houle, 'the beat becomes too slow around MM 40, and too fast around MM 130–35 . . . The *tactus* [in the seventeenth century] was near the center of this range, since the body's resting pulse generally corresponds to MM 60–80' (1987 : 5). Walther Dürr and Walter Gerstenberg too suggest that a pulse rate felt as moderate is that of the human heartbeat, 60–80 MM; less than 60 is perceived as slow, more than 80 as fast (1980 : 806). Rebecca Stewart suggests a mean for *madhya lay* (medium tempo) of 90 MM, apparently based on an estimate of 80–90 MM for the heartbeat (1974 : 81.)[6] Curt Sachs rejected the idea of a basis for tempo in the heartbeat, suggesting instead 'the regular stride of a man walking leisurely' as the physiological basis. His figure is nevertheless consistent with those above, '76–80 M.M.'. His figures for the overall range of tempi stretch from 32 to only 132 MM (1953 : 32–3). Jay Dowling and Dane Harwood claim that evidence of any physiological basis is unconvincing: however, citing psychological research, they state that: 'Though the evidence is often weak, it points in the direction of a natural pace for psychological events of 1.3 to 1.7 per second (i.e . . . between 80 and 100 beats/min). This agrees roughly with the intuitions of musicians regarding a moderate tempo . . . ' (1986 : 182).

Whatever the physiological and/or psychological basis, it seems reasonable to take the range of 60–100 MM as a rough guide to what may be felt as a 'moderate' tempo. The lowest recognized tempi seem to be somewhere in the range 32–40 MM. There appear to be two main schools of thought on the maxima: one finds tempi above c. 130 MM (*mātrā* $<$ 0.46 sec.) to be very fast, while the other allows figures well over 300 MM (*mātrā* $<$ 0.2 sec.). I tend to agree with the former, and regard the latter as credible for rhythmic density rather than for the rate of metric succession.

6.2.2 *Lay* in performance

The following observations are based on measurements of over 100 performances, including examples of all the principal genres of Hindustānī *rāg* music. Cycle lengths were measured to an accuracy of at least $\pm$0.1 sec.:[7] These

[6] Cf. G. H. Ranade: 'In the normal condition it (the heartbeat) is between 80 and 90 beats per minute. So the ancients used to adopt this natural unit of Laya as their standard. In our everyday language we may call it a standard *Matra*' (Ranade 1961 : 122).

[7] Measurements were made in the first instance with a 1/100 sec. stopwatch; later measurements were made with a computer-based timer, which gave readings of comparable accuracy. I estimate the error in readings at $\pm$0.1 sec., reducible to $\pm$0.05 sec. in some cases where measurements were repeated up to 3 times and averaged.

time-span measurements were converted to *mātrā* rates using a computer spreadsheet application, which I also used to calculate changes in tempo from cycle to cycle (expressed as a percentage, see 'acceleration' in Table 6.4), and to plot graphs of tempo against cycle. An example of the procedure is given below; Table 6.4 is part of a spreadsheet generated from one such performance, and the corresponding tempo chart is given here as Example 6.3.

TABLE 6.4 Detail of a spreadsheet showing measurements of cycle lengths

	duration (secs.)				
cycle	I	II	average	tempo (MM)	acceleration (%)
ālāp	2′03.22	2′03.09	2′03.15		
1	30.02	30.01	30.02	32.0	
2	28.68	28.64	28.66	33.5	5
3	27.72	27.83	27.78	34.6	3
4	27.62	27.52	27.57	34.8	1
5	27.27	27.24	27.26	35.2	1
6	26.96	27.02	26.99	35.6	1
7	26.10	26.02	26.06	36.8	4
8	26.06	26.09	26.08	36.8	0
9	25.68	25.66	25.67	37.4	2
10	25.89	25.88	25.89	37.1	−1
11	25.53	25.60	25.57	37.6	1
12	25.10	25.09	25.10	38.3	2
(and so on)					

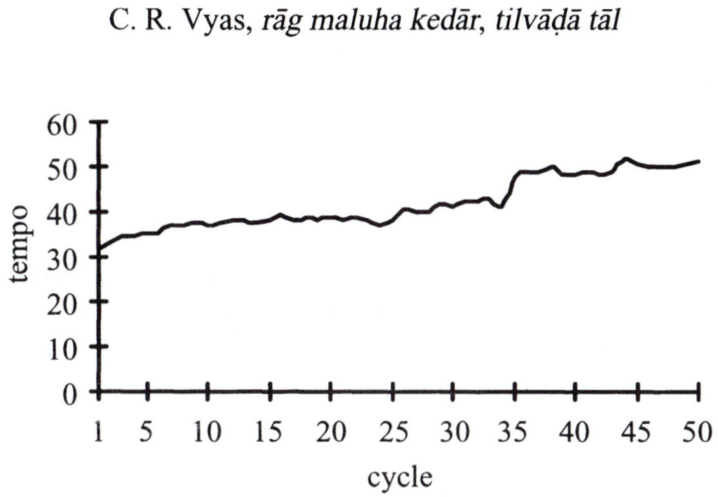

EXAMPLE 6.3 A graph of tempo plotted against cycle, generated from the spreadsheet illustrated in Table 6.4

Table 6.5 Tempo ranges for common Hindustānī *tals*

tāl	vocal genres				instrumental
	mātrās	*khyāl/ṭappā*	*tarānā/ṭhumrī/dādrā*	*dhrupad/dhamār/sādrā*	*gat* (*sitār/ sarod* unless stated)
jhūmrā	14 (28/56)	12.7–39	—	—	—
ektāl (*vil.*)	12 (24/48)	10.4–42	—	—	—
tilvāḍā	16 (32)	21–51	—	—	—
tīntāl (*vil.*)	16 (32)	25–60	—	—	32–105
cautāl	12	—	—	39–125 (*dhrupad*)	56–77 (*bīn*)
dhamār	14	—	—	54–128 (*dhamār*)	107–29
jhaptāl	10	38–50 (*vilam.*) 52–69 (*madhya*)	—	55–104 (*sādrā*)	89-165
rūpak	7	29–33 (*vilam.*) 83–108 (*madhya*)	97–113 (*ṭhumrī*)	—	86–181
tīntāl (*madhya*)	16	130–174	—	—	99–174
tīntāl (*sitārkhānī*)	16	60–92 (*ṭappā*)	118–129 (*ṭhumrī*)	—	96–140
dīpcandī/ cāñcar	14/16 (7/8)	—	77–90 (*ṭhumrī*)	—	202–232 (*bānsurī*)
kaharvā	8 (4)	—	130–160 (*ṭhumrī*)	—	165–187 (*sitār*) 389–480 (*bānsurī*)
dādrā	6 (3)	—	56–76 (*dādrā*)	—	245–327
sūltāl	10 (5)	—	—	224–411 (*dhrupad*)	—
ektāl (*drut*)	12 (6/3)	217–301	174–427 (*tarānā*)	—	281–600
tīntāl (*drut*)	16 (8/4)	169–300	189–313 (*tarānā*) 302–500 (*ṭhumrī laggī*)	—	234–738

Tempo Table 6.5[8] gives maximum and minimum tempo (*mātrā* rate) figures for the most common Hindustānī *tāls*, abstracted from measurements such as those illustrated in Table 6.4 and Example 6.3. The tempo ranges are distributed through several columns to allow comparison of the same *tāl* in different genres. Each set of figures is compiled from a number of different performances, and does not imply that each performance utilizes all or even most of the possible tempo range.

The following observations may be made in connection with these figures (and the measurements from which they are derived). First, the measured range in *mātrā* rate in these examples is from 10.4 MM to about 730 MM. The perceived range in tempo is however much less than this. Taking the lower end first, all the examples in this sample below 21 MM showed consistent subdivision in the *ṭhekā*, suggesting a basic pulse rate 2 or 4 times that indicated. For instance, the slowest example in terms of *mātrā* rate[9] had a clearly defined pulse at 4 times the *mātrā* rate (i.e. at least 42.8 MM).

In my subjective experience, pulse rates of below about 30 MM (i.e. *mātrā* > 2 secs. in duration) feel extremely slow. Some singers manage to go considerably below this without consistently subdividing the pulse, but the minimum possible is probably around 20 MM (*mātrā* = 3 secs.). The only exception to this I have found was a *baṛā khyāl* recording of Amir Khan, in which the *mātrā* rate drops to 12.7 MM (*mātrā* = 4.7 secs.) without subdivision.[10] This is a remarkable performance since the *ṭhekā* is virtually impossible to perceive as regularly pulsed, let alone metrical. This effect is compounded by the use of a version of *jhūmrā*'s *ṭhekā* which has no stroke on *mātrās* 2 or 9 (the strokes are displaced to the half-way points in these *mātrās*, see Example 6.4), giving a pulse which is in any case irregular with a maximum time-span between *tablā* strokes of up to 7 secs. (This recording is also remarkable in other ways, as will be shown in Example 6.10.)

jhūmrā tāl: 14 *mātrās*, 3+4+3+4

X	2	0	3	X
dhā –dhā trkt	dhin dhin dhāge trkt	tin –tā trkt	dhin dhin dhāge trkt	dhā

|←→|

4.5-7 secs.

EXAMPLE **6.4** In Amir Khan's performance of *rāg mārvā* in *jhūmrā tāl*, pauses between *tablā* strokes reach up to c.7 secs. (Audio Example 2 features the first two cycles of this performance; the longest gap between the main strokes here is just under 5 secs.)

Thus rates of 30 MM, maybe as low as 20 MM, are perceivable as consistent pulses. At the other end of the scale lies *ati-drut lay* (very fast tempo): some

8 Figures in parentheses indicate the number of metric pulses, where the *mātrā* rate is too fast or too slow to function as a primary pulse. Spaces marked '—' are not applicable, i.e. these *tāls* are not generally used in these genres.

9 Pandit Jasraj, *rāg miyān kī toḍī, khyāl* in *vilambit ektāl* (Swarashree PJ0001).

10 Ameer Khan, *rāg mārvā, khyāl* in *vilambit jhūmrā tāl* (EMI EALP1253).

instrumental *tīntāl* performances go well over 600 MM (*mātrā* < 0.1 sec.) in the concluding *jhālā* sections (in fact, up to around 730 MM; *mātrā* $= 0.082$ sec.). Yet there is a straightforward case to be made for considering the metric structure of such pieces as a 4 'beat' cycle, where each beat or pulse is located on the *vibhāg* divisions (see Example 6.1 above). The *mātrā* rate itself is not metrically significant, but is best understood as a surface rhythm level at a *lay* ratio of 4:1 against the (*vibhāg*) pulse rate. This would give an effective pulse rate of at most 730/4, i.e. 182 MM (time-span $\sim$ 0.33 sec.). This pulse level is close to the maximum possible before consistent grouping necessarily comes into effect. This maximum would be, by my subjective estimate, between 180 and 210 MM (time-spans = 0.28–0.33 sec.).

If perceived pulse rates in Hindustānī music vary, as this suggests, between approximately 20 and 200 MM, covering the range from very slow to very fast, this still suggests a wide range of performance tempi, according to the estimates cited above. I believe that this is because factors peculiar to North Indian music make a wider range of tempi practicable, in particular the use of familiar metric structures which may be manipulated for use over a wide range of tempi.

Table 6.6 presents the data of Table 6.5 in three rough tempo bands—*vilambit*, *madhya*, and *drut lays*. Anything more precise, or involving the possible seven bands cited in Table 6.1, would exaggerate the consistency with which these terms are used.[11] Tempi in instrumental music are in most cases significantly higher than those in vocal music, and their ranges are consequently given separately.

Table 6.6 Tempo ranges for Hindustānī vocal and instrumental music (MM)

genre	*vilambit lay*	*madhya lay*	*drut lay*
vocal	10.4–60	40–175	170–500
instrumental	30–105	85–190	230–740

Rhythmic density Maximum rhythmic densities (figures which treat gaps as rhythmic events, rather than averaging out the density of only the articulated notes or syllables), are useful in medium and fast tempo syllabic music, in which the relationship between surface rhythm and *tāl* is clear—they may be worked out as follows;

- highest *lay* ratio sustained × tempo = maximum rhythmic density (*bols*/min.)

In the fastest instrumental music, these figures reach levels of over 700 *bols*/min.; they are somewhat lower in vocal music, rarely over 400 *bols*/min.,[12] due to a lower physical limit on the speed of articulation. For the earlier stages of performances, where rhythmic densities are lower and *lay* ratios not clearly

[11] See however Stewart (1974:81).

[12] The fastest measured in these examples is approx. 640 *bols*/min., briefly achieved in a *dhamār* performance by Bidur Mallik; this is exceptional however.

established, average rhythmic densities may be calculated, using either of the following formulae:

- no. of *bols* in cycle × 60 ÷ length of cycle = av. rhythmic density (*bols*/min.)
- no. of *bols* × tempo (MM) ÷ no. of *mātrās* = av. rhythmic density (*bols*/min.)

Examples of this kind of figure are given in Tables 11.3/4 and Examples 11.7/8.

Cycle length Cycle lengths vary from around 1.5 secs. in *ati-drut tīntāl* to over 65 secs. in *ati-vilambit jhūmrā tāl* and *ektāl*. I have suggested that the use of very long cycles has a significant effect on rhythmic organization, since cycles of over 65 seconds are—according to psychological research—far too long to be perceived as single entities or Gestalts (see Chapter 3). If we accept this position, it follows that patterns lasting 60 seconds or more will not generally be experienced as metrical entities; at the very least, we can assert that patterns lasting this long will be experienced in a significantly different way to those lasting only a few seconds, since their recognition as patterns must rely on a degree of memory and conscious conception not necessary for shorter patterns. This factor may explain why very slow *tāls* are often said to be lacking in metric character.

6.2.3 Variation of tempo in performance

Hindustānī music shows a wide variety of practices concerning the variation of tempo in the course of performance, a much greater variety, in fact, than is generally assumed. As Rebecca Stewart appreciated, rather than maintaining a constant tempo for the metrical structure, with only the surface rhythm accelerating—which was previously assumed to be the ideal—many genres had come to embrace the concept of acceleration in performance (1974 : 396–8). Stephen Slawek has also touched on this issue, with reference to Ravi Shankar's *sitār* performances (1987 : 196–7, 209–12).[13]

My research, however, has revealed a tremendous diversity of performance practice embracing constancy of tempo, gradual and stepwise acceleration, deceleration (very occasionally), and combinations of the above. Many changes in tempo are conscious and deliberate, some are certainly unconscious, and inevitably accidents and errors in performance also play their part. Some features are characteristic of genre, some of *gharānā* style, others show a high degree of individuality. The basic findings of this research are illustrated below with some examples.[14]

1. **Constancy of tempo**, although not as common as often assumed, does nevertheless occur. It is most likely to be a feature of entire performances of *vilambit khyāl* or *ṭhumrī*,[15] while stable tempi are also maintained for significant

[13] See also Manuel (1989).
[14] Illustrations of variation in rhythmic density are found in Chapters 10 and 11.
[15] Excluding *laggī* sections.

stretches of instrumental *vilambit-* or *madhya lay gats*. It is most rare in *dhrupad-dhamār*, perhaps surprisingly since these genres are often considered representative, to a considerable degree, of an earlier stage in the development of Hindustānī music. The lack of constant tempo in *dhrupad* in practice is due to the high degree of interaction between soloist and drummer, which seems inevitably to create a tendency to accelerate. In *khyāl*, by way of contrast, there is much less interaction between the two, and consequently the stability of tempo is almost entirely dependent on the *tablā* player. Example 6.5 illustrates constant tempo in a typical *vilambit khyāl* performance.

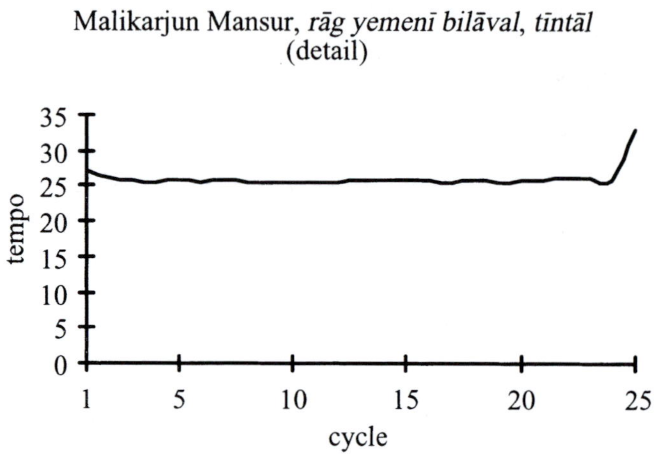

Example 6.5 Detail of tempo chart from a *vilambit khyāl* performance, showing almost constant tempo

2. **Acceleration** can be categorized as follows:
(*a*) Gradual and slight, and perhaps unintentional, as in Example 6.6.[16]

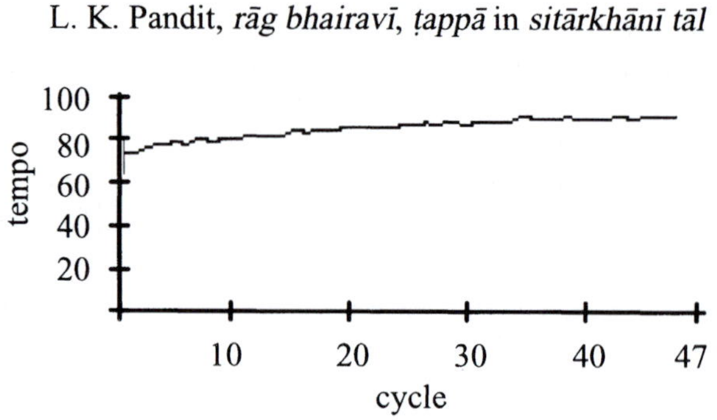

Example 6.6 Tempo chart of a *ṭappā* performance, showing gradual acceleration

[16] Acceleration in this case is from 76–91 MM, i.e. approx. 20%.

(*b*) Gradual but significant; resulting in increased tension and excitement. This is the norm in *dhrupad-dhamār*, and in instrumental *madhya lay*- and *drut gats* (Example 6.7).[17]

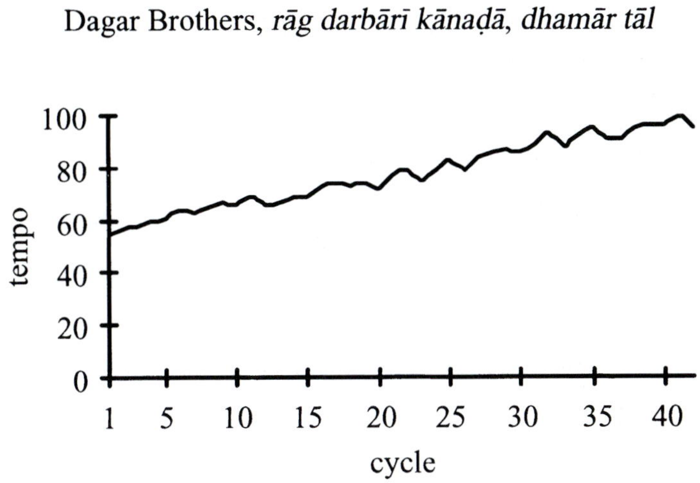

Example 6.7 Tempo chart of a *dhamār* performance, showing a gradual but significant acceleration

(*c*) Stepwise; a conscious acceleration at a particular point in the performance, for example in *khyāl* or instrumental *gat* if a faster tempo is required for *tāns* than for *vistār*. In some cases this involves tempo as much as doubling, a characteristic of *khyāls* in *vilambit lay* (especially *tīntāl*) which effectively thus move up from *vilambit* to *madhya lay* (Example 6.8).[18]

(*d*) Temporary; for example to serve the needs of a *tablā* solo (Example 6.9).[19]

3. **Deceleration** is almost unknown, and may usually be interpreted as one of the following:

(*a*) Winding down at the end of a performance,

(*b*) A return to the desired tempo after a temporary acceleration; for example, after a *tablā* solo (see Example 6.9).

(*c*) Adjustment between statement of a *khyāl bandiś* and the *vistār* phase; many singers apparently find that the *vistār* (melodic development) requires a slower tempo than that necessary for the composition (see Example 6.5, c. 1–3).

(*d*) Accidental or in error.

(*e*) Gradual and significant; a kind of 'intensification of languor'. Although very rare, this is exemplified by Amir Khan's recording of *rāg mārvā* in *jhūmrā*

17 Acceleration in this case is from 54–96 MM, i.e. 77%.

18 The steps in this case are 31–41 MM and 45–55 MM, accelerations of 32% and 22% respectively. The most celebrated example of stepwise acceleration is the change to the *laggī* section in *ṭhumrī*, which also generally involves a change of *tāl*. See Manuel (1989: 118–21).

19 Peaks mark *tablā* solos, while the underlying trend is of only slight acceleration.

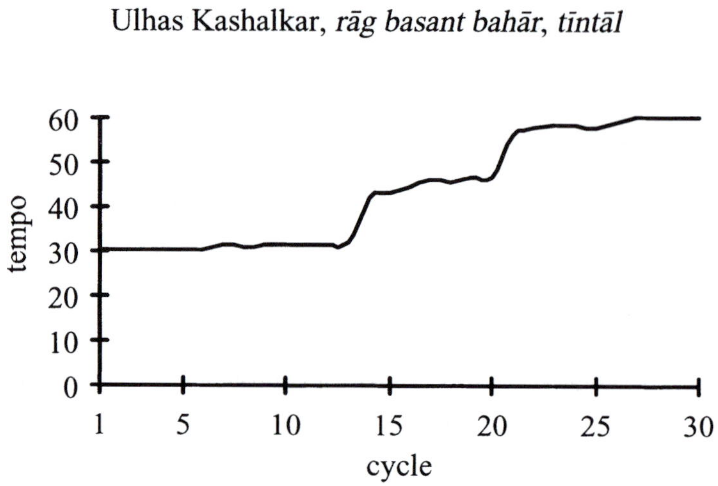

Example 6.8 Tempo chart of a *baṛā khyāl* performance in *tīntāl*, showing two clear stepped increases in tempo

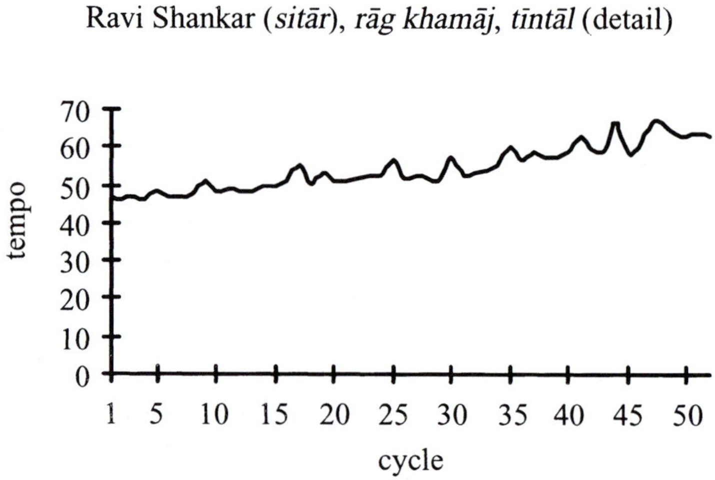

Example 6.9 Tempo chart from a *vilambit gat* performance on *sitār*

tāl, as described above. This performance decelerates considerably before reaching a plateau at around 13 MM (Example 6.10). This example reaffirms that *tāl* structures show radically different characteristics—in this case deceleration—when a metric tempo of below about 20 MM is used without consistent subdivision of the *mātrā* pulse. It also illustrates a more general point, that when musical structures are altered, changes in any one parameter (in this case tempo) cause knock-on effects in other parameters.

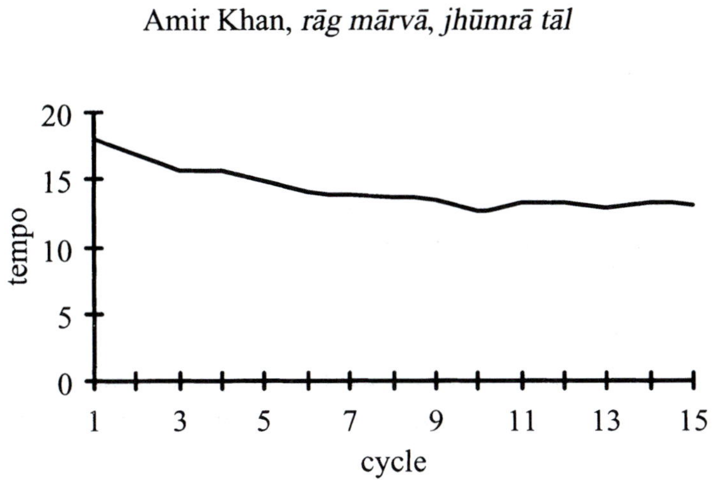

Example 6.10 Tempo chart of a *baṛā khyāl* performance by Amir Khan, showing significant deceleration

6.3 Summary

1. Tempo in Hindustānī music is usually understood as the rate of succession of the metric structure, the *tāl*, expressed as the *mātrā* rate. The Indian term *lay* refers either to 'tempo' in this sense, to rhythmic density or to the ratio between rhythmic density and tempo (*lay* ratio).

2. *Mātrā* rate is not the only useful measure of tempo however, because the extension of the tempo range at both extremes has caused the function of *tāls* to be modified at both very slow and very fast tempi. In these cases some other metric pulse level may be a more significant measure of tempo than the *mātrā* rate. The range of *mātrā* rates in Hindustānī music is at least 11–730 MM, that of effective tempo about 20–200 MM.

3. Rhythmic density is another important indicator of tempo, to be considered alongside pulse rate. In fact, the ratio between these two rates is often highly significant (see 1, above). The maximum rhythmic density possible in instrumental music is at least 730 *bols*/min.,[20] but is somewhat less in vocal music (usually around 400 *bols*/min., but very occasionally 600 *bols*/min. or higher).

4. *Lay*—both tempo (*mātrā* rate) and rhythmic density—tends to be higher in instrumental than in vocal music.

5. Tempi (*mātrā* rates) show a wide variety of patterns in performance embracing constancy, gradual and stepwise acceleration, and in special

[20] Considerably higher levels (c. 1400 *bols*/min.) may be reached in a *santūr* (dulcimer) performance, since both hands may be used to strike the instrument alternately. See Example 10.17.

circumstances deceleration. These patterns clearly relate to other aspects of performance practice.

These findings illustrate once again that there is considerably more diversity in Hindustānī rhythm than could possibly be imagined from the conventional *tāl* theory. This diversity is clearly evident in measurements of tempo and surface rhythmic density rates, in patterns of tempo variation and in the functioning of metric structures, as demonstrated above: it is also true of almost every other variable of rhythmic structure and organization in Hindustānī music.

The importance of drum use and accompaniment style is confirmed by the difference between Example 6.5 (constant tempo, made possible by *tablā ṭhekā* accompaniment), and Example 6.7 (acceleration of tempo due to interactive *pakhāvaj* accompaniment). The interdependence of the various rhythmic parameters is clear.

More specifically, they supply empirical confirmation of several points made in the theoretical exposition of Chapter 4. The extremely wide range of *mātrā* rates demonstrates that the 'ideal' syllabic model of metric organization outlined in Chapter 4 has been considerably modified in many genres; often the *mātrā* cannot function as the primary pulse rate ('tactus'), due to inescapable psychological constraints. The same modifications in rhythmic organization are suggested by the ambiguity of the concept of *lay*, which reflects the fact that the conceptual structure of which it originally formed an integral part has been dramatically altered.

7

Performance practice and rhythm in Hindustānī music

7.1 Introduction

Rhythm in North Indian music is generated by the application of a variety of idiomatic processes or techniques of development, either precomposed or (more commonly) realized in extemporized performance. Rhythm is generated at a local level, although shaped by a sense of progression both within improvised 'episodes'—within which particular musical ideas are stated and developed, and which must lead back to the fixed composition—and more loosely, over the performance as a whole. Any formal scheme which may be identified by means of synchronic analysis implies not so much an overall structural plan, as general tendencies in the performance process—typically of episodically organized development, expansion, increase, and intensification.

While formal structure is not fixed in the sense of much Western art music, a more loosely conceived sense of progression and 'good organization' is valued in *rāg* performance. I am concerned in this and the following three chapters with the relationship between performance practice in this sense (and the wider aesthetic context) and rhythmic patterns actually produced in performance. Since surface rhythm is generated by means of idiomatic techniques and processes, it may profitably be analysed in terms of those techniques, on which large-scale structure, local surface rhythm, and *laykārī* (including rhythmic variation *per se*) are dependent.

My presentation at this stage will be quite general. There are too many variables in North Indian music—formal, technical, and stylistic—to allow a comprehensive study of the rhythmic features of all its genres, forms, and styles in a single volume. A general analysis of the principal rhythmic and formal parameters of North Indian music, however, is possible, if it is based on the ideas or assumptions shared by all genres and styles of Hindustānī music. These assumptions include the clear structuring of performance as 'fixed composition + extemporized development', the episodic organization of that development, and the general tendencies to increase *lay* (tempo and/or rhythmic density), expand and vary material, and intensify affect. With reference to the factors of rhythmic organization introduced above, and to issues which may be identified as particularly important rhythmically (such as text use and distribution, and preference for syllabic or melismatic rhythmic styles), I will sketch out below an analytical approach to surface rhythm which may be applied to all the genres and styles of North Indian *rāg* music.

7.1.1 Elements of performance and their organization

In any musical performance in this tradition a number of basic elements may be identified, within whose context local processes and techniques are carried out. Any performance of *rāg* music may be said to contain any or all of the following three primary elements, combined in a number of ways.

- Exposition of the *rāg* (*ālāp, ālapti, baṛhat, vistār*).[1]
- A fixed composition, synthesizing *rāg*, *tāl*, and text or instrumental stroke patterns (*bandiś, cīz, gat*).[2]
- Improvised development; either specifically focused on the use of the composition text, or more generally melodic and rhythmic variation based on the *rāg* and set within the *tāl* (*upaj, bol bāṇṭ, bol banāo, toḍā, tān, laykārī* etc.).[3]

The schemata in Table 7.1 illustrate three of the many possible methods of combining these primary elements. 'A' represents the most common pattern of *dhrupad* performance (some *khyāl* styles too follow this plan); 'B' gives the most common *vilambit khyāl* scheme, and 'C' similarly for *ṭhumrī*. In 'A', *rāg* development, the *bandiś*, and textual/rhythmic development follow each other in sequence. In 'B' the exposition of the *rāg* follows the *bandiś*, and may merge into other forms of development. In 'C' the *rāg* is not developed methodically, but melodic possibilities are explored in the context of expressive development of the text.

These primary elements (*rāg* exposition, *bandiś*, improvised development) may thus be combined in different ways. A simple progression, '*rāg* development—*bandiś*—rhythmic development', applies only to certain genres (in particular, *dhrupad* and *dhrupad*-based instrumental forms), while the incorporation of *rāg* development into the post-*bandiś* development phase makes analysis of performance practice in other genres (especially *vilambit khyāl*) more complicated.

A concentration in performance on *rāg* development may override both rhythmic and textual factors (as in unaccompanied *ālāp*, and some *vilambit khyāl vistār*); other forms of melodic development occur in the ornamental

[1] *Ālāp* (lit. 'conversation', but see Rowell 1992 : 239 for a discussion of the term's significance) refers to the exposition of the *rāg*, either in metred or (more usually) in unmetred music. *Baṛhat* (lit. 'increase, extension') and *vistār* (lit. 'spread') usually refer to this process within *nibaddh* (metred) sections.

[2] *Bandiś* (lit. 'structure, pattern') refers to any composition, but particularly vocal compositions; *cīz* (lit. 'article, item') is used for *khyāl* compositions in particular; *gat* (lit. '(way of) going, moving') describes idiomatic instrumental compositions (i.e. those not based on vocal pieces).

[3] *Upaj* (lit. 'produce, product') is a term for post-*bandiś* development, used especially for *dhrupad*. The other terms are explained in the text below. Deshpande, who uses the term in the context of *khyāl*, translates *upaj* as 'derivative phrase' (1987 : 31).

Table 7.1 Three possible schemes for the organization of performance in North Indian classical music

	anibaddh (no *tāl*)	*nibaddh* (*tāl* bound)	
A	*ālāp, joṛ* (*rāg* development)	*bandiś* (fixed composition)	*bol bāṇṭ* (rhythmic development of *bandiś* text)
B	(none)	*bandiś*	*vistār* (rhythmically quasi-free *rāg* development, with and/or without words) and *tāns* (fast runs or flourishes)
C	(none)	*bandiś*	*bol banāo* (melismatic ornamentation of *bandiś* text)

melismatic flourishes of *bol banāo* (particularly in *ṭhumrī*), or in the context of fast, and often rhythmically exciting *tāns* (in *khyāl* and instrumental *gat* forms). In *bol bāṇṭ*, text is broken up into semantic chunks, which are sung in different rhythmic combinations to melodic material already developed; in this case the emphasis lies on the rhythmic-cum-textual development.

The next section (§7.2) is concerned with the rhythmic organization of *anibaddh* sections such as *ālāp* and *joṛ*; the final part of this chapter (§7.3) introduces general issues of performance practice in *nibaddh* forms which are amplified and illustrated in following chapters.

7.2 *Ālāp*: unmetred (*anibaddh*) forms

The rhythmic structure of *ālāp*, the unmetred exposition of the *rāg*, is a fascinating but extremely challenging subject. Very little work has been published to date: in fact, a couple of recent studies by Richard Widdess (1994, 1995) and a few comments by Wim van der Meer (1980) and Sandeep Bagchee (1998) comprise virtually the entire literature on the subject. While Indian musicians and musicologists have developed sophisticated theories over the centuries to explain and codify the practice of *tāl*, little has been written on the rhythmic organization of *ālāp*; whatever comes before the establishment of *tāl* in a performance is classed as *anibaddh* (unbound), and described in English as rhythmically 'free'.

The reasons for this are not too hard to find. From a performer's perspective, *ālāp*—the unmetred, literally 'unbound' section of a performance, is the movement in which the performer is free to explore the intricacies of melodic structure without the constraint of *tāl* or lexical text (in *dhrupad ālāp*, performers may use non-lexical syllables such as tā, nā, re, and nom to aid articulation, for which reason it is sometimes called *nom-tom ālāp*). The idea of examining the rhythmic structure of supposedly arhythmical music appears to be counter-intuitive, with the result that it has seldom been attempted.

Not only that, but as I have argued elsewhere (Clayton 1996) the avoidance of analysis of 'free rhythm' forms is not restricted to India but is the norm in both Western music theory and ethnomusicology. Theories of rhythm in the West, as in India, assume the existence of metrical frameworks, and despite the slowly developing interest in free rhythm in ethnomusicology (see e.g. Frigyesi 1993) theorists are still stumbling in the dark in their attempts to develop research strategies to explain the rhythmic organization of forms such as *ālāp*.

Extended unaccompanied *ālāp* is most common in *dhrupad* and instrumental genres, although it is also performed by some *khyāl* singers, and most *khyāl* performances begin with at least a few phrases, adding up to at least a minute or two of unaccompanied introduction to the *rāg*. Most performers divide *ālāp* into a number of stages: at the simplest level three stages are identified as *vilambit*, *madhya*, and *drut* (slow, medium, and fast). Instrumental unmetred sections too are often described in three parts, as *ālāp-joṛ-jhālā*, where *joṛ* is the equivalent of *madhya ālāp*, and *jhālā* refers to a fast unaccompanied section in which melody notes are interspersed with rapid patterns played on the *cikārī* (punctuating) strings of the *sitār* or *sarod*. (*Jhālā* is in fact a distinct, and optional, phase of development: some instrumentalists prefer to simply accelerate their *joṛ* until a climax is reached.) Some performers describe *ālāp* as being divided into many more sections than three; however, in these cases the distinctions seem on the whole to be made on the basis of melodic features (range to be explored in each section, for instance) rather than rhythmic factors.

Again, the conscious organizing principle of *ālāp* seems to be one of process, whereby (i) the structure and character of the *rāg* is gradually revealed, or unfolded, without regard to any rhythmic constraint (*vilambit ālāp*, or simply *ālāp*); (ii) that structure is explored in performance with a regular pulse and over a wider melodic range (*joṛ*, *madhya ālāp*); and (iii) that pulse is gradually accelerated until a climax is reached (*jhālā*, *drut ālāp*).

These processes of revelation and intensification may be conceptualized differently by different performers. The process of gradual manifestation of the *rāg* may perhaps be regarded as a metaphorical re-enactment of the cosmic process of the crystallization of form from formless matter (see Rowell 1992 : 242–3); for others the process is more one of evocation, whereby the *rāg*—which is pre-existent and always latent—is temporarily manifested in a form audible to human ears; even for those of a less metaphysical bent, the performance of *ālāp* is a delicate process involving not simply the presentation of melodic materials, but the evocation of the distinctive mood of which the *rāg* is itself capable.

Ālāp proper, or *vilambit ālāp*, refers to a stage in which the rhythm is not only unmetred, but also appears to lack a pulse; the relative durations of the notes seem to be determined entirely by the structure of the *rāg* rather than by any rhythmic principle. The only point of the (*vilambit*) *ālāp* which is clearly pulsed is the *mukhṛā*, a short cadential phrase used to mark the end of sections.

In *joṛ* (or *madhya ālāp*) a pulse is clearly present, although such music is not considered to be 'in *tāl*'. The final stage, *drut ālāp* or *jhālā*, retains this pulse and accelerates towards a climax; in instrumental *jhālā*, melody notes are typically interspersed with strokes on the high drone or punctuating strings (*cikārī*), and in *drut ālāp* in *dhrupad*, melody notes are usually repeated several times each (see Example 7.1).[4]

instrumental	*ālāp*	*joṛ*	*jhālā*
vocal (*dhrupad*)	*vilambit ālāp*	*madhya ālāp*	*drut ālāp*
	mostly 'unpulsed'	pulsed, but not in *tāl*	

EXAMPLE **7.1** The usual tripartite structure of *dhrupad* or instrumental *ālāp*

The category 'without *tāl*' (*anibaddh*) includes different types of musical rhythm, varying in degree of pulsation and speed of articulation. Moreover, the general tendencies noted in earlier chapters—that performances tend to increase in speed and rhythmic definition—also apply to this phase, which moves from apparently unpulsed and free, to pulsed at medium tempo, to pulsed at high tempo and density. Study of these portions of performance should tell us a great deal about rhythmic organization, free rhythm, and the relationship between Indian and Western rhythmic concepts.

It appears at first sight that, just as *tāl* is a concept closely related to metre, varieties of North Indian music without *tāl* represent different kinds of 'free rhythm'; that which is completely free (*ālāp* proper), and that which is pulsed but unmetred (*joṛ*, *jhālā*). Before reaching such a conclusion, however, it is worth looking at both these assumptions a little more closely.

7.2.1 *Ālāp*: pulsed or unpulsed?

Theoretical perspectives The rhythmic structure of *ālāp* was studied by Richard Widdess in collaboration with *dhrupad* singer Ritwik Sanyal (1994). Widdess, reporting the views of his informant, throws considerable doubt on the premiss that *ālāp* is ever, in fact, unpulsed.

> Sanyal asserted that there is always a pulse in his mind throughout ālāp, and that this is regular and consistent apart from a gradual acceleration. In slow ālāp it may be concealed by the slow tempo and by the placing of pitches and melodic/rhythmic events off the pulse rather than on it, but it becomes explicit in the mukhṛā. (Widdess 1994 : 65)

These findings have been questioned by some other theorists, and some musicians deny the existence of pulse in slow *ālāp*. Widdess and Sanyal's

[4] Speed of articulation, and thus rhythmic density, increases with time (from left to right).

collaborative analysis of the latter's *ālāp* is however highly convincing, and demonstrates that (for some performers at least) slow *ālāp* merely *appears* to be unpulsed, while in fact it is organized around a consistent pulse; in other words that a pulse is present in the performer's mind, but is not perceived by most listeners. Seen in these terms, the processes outlined above would be regarded not as a move from unpulsed to pulsed music, but from an unmanifested to a manifested pulse.

Widdess's findings substantiate the brief remarks of van der Meer on the subject.

> In all parts of music there is a pulsation which is *laya*. It need be stressed that even in the slowest parts of Indian music (including *ālāpa*...) there is an idea of proper timing in which phrases are built and in which justice must be done to the duration of notes according to the rules of the rāga. The masters create a compelling unity of the rāga through this *laya* even if it is hardly perceivable to the layman... the artist has syncopes and rubato at his disposal to hide the pulsation which could otherwise damage the melodic purity. (1980 : 6)

Their observations are supported and extended by Bagchee:

> A notion of proper timing, which the development of the *rāga* has to follow and maintain in terms of the prescribed duration for each note, is laid down in these rules of the *ālāp*. Failure to do so would lead to the *rāga* degenerating into meaningless sounds. In the portion of music which is accompanied by a percussion instrument, this timing or pulsation becomes manifest... (1998 : 71)

> The first section, the *vilambit ālāp*, is the most essential as it comes closest to pure melody and allows the intricacies of the *rāga* to be shown in detail. Although the entire *ālāp* is without rhythmic accompaniment, it is not strictly speaking a-rhythmic as there is a time element inherent in its unfolding which is marked by the singing of the notes. (1998 : 96)

These comments combine an impression of objective observation (if rather imprecisely expressed) with a subtle suggestion that *ālāp* must be rhythmically ordered since that which is unordered is by definition meaningless. As Widdess has pointed out (1995 : 83) we need to take care in evaluating such statements in view of the high status generally accorded to rhythmic regulation and time measurement in Indian music theory. Nonetheless, these comments should not be dismissed and their perspective is clearly worth further investigation.

Widdess's findings on *ālāp* actually have considerable significance for the study of free rhythm in general, particularly if they can be shown to apply more widely. The possibility has been established that music can be founded on a consistent pulse, and yet nevertheless appear to be completely unpulsed, and this opens the question whether music is ever performed, in fact, completely without reference to pulsation. Psychological research certainly points to the role of rhythmic regularity, and hence pulsation, in aiding both motor co-ordination and memory. This would perhaps suggest that human beings are predisposed to perceive and/or generate pulsation, and that this tendency helps to determine the fact that a very large proportion of music, if not all, is at some level organized around a pulse. According to this hypothesis, the apparent absence of pulse is all the more significant, even if interpreted as an auditory illusion caused by 'the slow tempo and by the placing of pitches and melodic/rhythmic events off the pulse rather than on it'.

William Condon's studies of the correlations between speech and body motion suggest, moreover, that we may expect to find even more complex organization than that determined by a simple but concealed pulse. Basing his remarks on detailed and extensive sound-film analysis, he suggests that: 'speech and body motion are precisely synchronized across multiple levels in the normal speaker, suggesting that they are the product of a unitary neuroelectric process. This speech/body motion hierarchical organization can also be interpreted as wave-like, since it exhibits characteristic periodicities' (1985 : 131).

These periodicities, which he speculates may be correlated to different species of brain waves, range from c. $\frac{1}{15}$ sec. (the mean length of a phoneme) to around 1 second (that of an utterance), arranged in a nested hierarchical order. 'Metaphorically, it is as if the [human] organism were constantly generating an integrated, multilevel wave hierarchy that behavior necessarily follows. All behavior appears to be integrated together as a function of a basic, organized rhythm hierarchy' (1985 : 132).

Condon has not demonstrated, of course, that such hierarchical organization need be perceptible in unmetred music. However, it may be worth pursuing a search for such organization, testing the hypothesis that *ālāp* may be organized:

(*a*) with reference to a pulse which is largely concealed, and which may moreover be somewhat intermittent or irregular. This (hypothetical) pulse is manifested during the cadential patterns at the end of development episodes; and/or

(*b*) under the control of a hierarchical organization, whose nested levels extend from the *vilambit ālāp* section as a whole down to single episodes, to simple melodic gestures and perhaps to periodicities inherent in the ornamentation of each note or gesture.

If so, it should not be surprising if such rhythm is difficult to remember or to describe, given the important role played by metre in the cognition of rhythmic structure (see Eric Clarke 1987 : 233). This would also accord with Jeffrey Pressing's intuition that music may exhibit organization intermediate between metrical and non-metrical—in other words, without the clear sense of periodic organization but nevertheless exhibiting some degree of recurrence (1993 : 111).

Ideas concerning the importance of hierarchical time organization (in, for instance, speech and music) go back at least to K. S. Lashley (e.g. 1951), whose ideas have inspired later theories of James Martin (1972) and Mari Riess Jones (e.g. Jones and Yee 1993). Martin suggested that 'sequences of sounds, speech or otherwise, that are rhythmic will possess hierarchic organization, that is, a coherent internal structure...' (1972 : 488), and went on to hypothesize that rhythmic patterning, with its implicit hierarchical organization, facilitates anticipation—which in turn facilitates 'attention cycling' between input (in our case sound) and processing. Jones builds on this idea with her own theory of attentional periodicity, suggesting that a listener's attention is in itself inherently periodic, and that these attentional rhythms 'synchronize with auditory events': 'The primary attentional vehicle involves internal rhythms whose synchronous operations permit . . . allocations of attentional energy to parts of the environment, thus subtly tethering a listener to his or her surroundings' (1993 : 80).

Jones is concerned primarily with time hierarchies and the synchronization of attentional periodicities to those of sound stimuli—which has obvious significance for the cognition of metre. What, though, does this theory imply for apparently unmetred music? Jones's theory of attentional periodicity would indicate that the listener is predisposed to synchronize internal periodicities to recurrent patterns in music: where this is not possible the musical stimulus will be harder to learn or remember. In the case of *ālāp* the absence of metre is clearly a conscious choice—it may be that the significance of this choice is that by denying the listener anticipation (the latter may have an idea what is likely to happen, but not when) the soloist insists on concentration on the present stimulus.

An example of instrumental *ālāp* Although a thorough analysis of *ālāp*, in all its manifestations and phases, is beyond the scope of this study, even a brief look at a single example should be enough to focus discussion of these issues, and to illustrate both the difficulties and possibilities of the study of *ālāp* in rhythmic structure. The extract illustrated in Example 7.2 is taken from the beginning (it comprises roughly the first minute) of a performance of *ālāp* in *rāg bilāskhānī toḍī* by the *sarod* player Amjad Ali Khan. The extract is typical of the early stages of *ālāp* in that the music cannot be heard as metrical, nor even (so far as I know) as regularly pulsed. It seems to comprise a series of phrases (each comprising several notes or gestures) extending from the drone note Sa down to the flattened sixth degree (komal Dha) in the lower octave and up to the flattened third (komal Ga), both of which are important notes in this *rāg*. Almost every note or phrase is preceded by a short sharp stroke on the high punctuating strings (*cikārī*). While transcription of the melodic development presents few problems, the indication of rhythm seems to be an almost intractable problem.

I have arranged my Example 7.2 around a waveform display of this extract, which is shown here with a horizontal time scale above.[5] Below the waveform I have transcribed the melody into *sargam* notation (s = 1, r = 2♭, g = 3♭, m = 4, d = 6♭, n = 7♭), using an exclamation mark to indicate the *cikārī* strokes. Below the *sargam* notation I have sketched dynamic outlines for what I interpret as three phrases within this short extract: this interpretation is based on the idea that a return of the melody to Sa marks the end of a passage of *rāg*

[5] This display was generated in ProTools on a Macintosh computer: only one of the two stereo tracks is shown in order to save space.

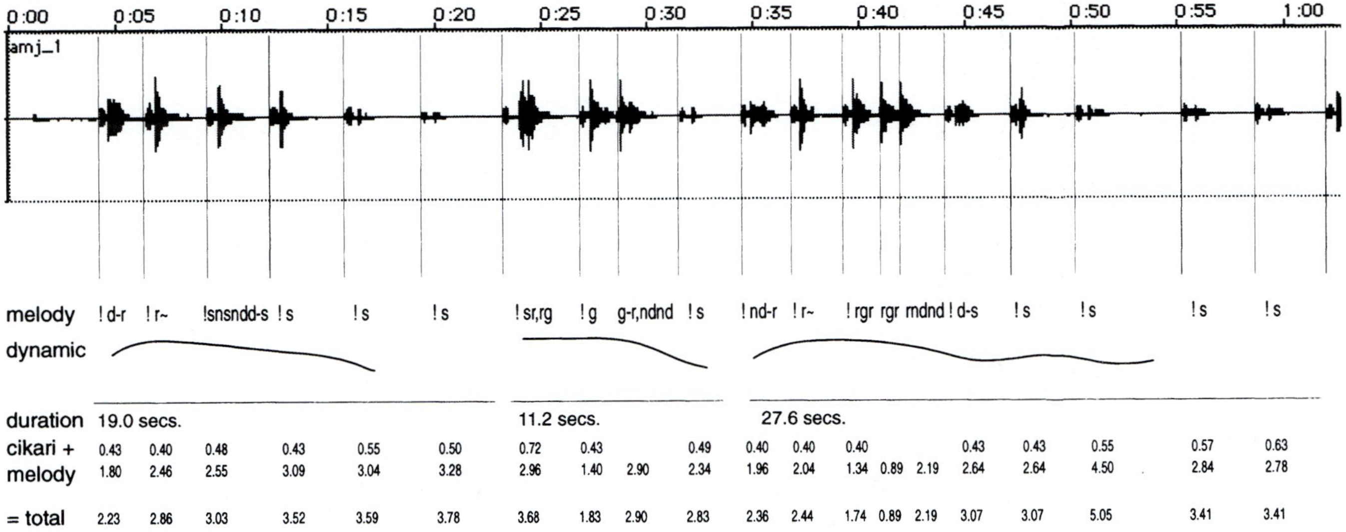

Example 7.2 Amjad Ali Khan, *ālāp* in *rāg bilāskhānī toḍī*, extract (Audio Example 3)

development: the outlines were produced by tracing the peaks of each gesture over the three phrases. The outlines suggest to me that each phrase reaches a peak early on, gradually falling off towards the end: I believe that the modulation of dynamic level works together with the return to Sa to mark off phrases within the *ālāp*.

The vertical lines superimposed on Example 7.2 mark the extent of each note or note cluster, from the onset of one *cikārī* stroke to that of the following *cikārī* stroke. The bottom rows consist of timings of each of these time-spans, produced by adding together the durations of the *cikārī* stroke and the main note. What these seem to show is that the time-spans taken up by notes or gestures varies between 0.9 sec. and a fraction over 5 seconds. Moreover, shorter durations seem to occur during periods of intense melodic activity, while the repeated Sa's at the end of phrases extend from 3 up to 5 seconds—although some of the melodic gestures too can extend up to and beyond 3 seconds, these tend to contain a considerable amount of melodic information, in contrast to the repeated Sa's which convey very little.

My interpretation of these figures is that they bear out the significance of the perceptual present, and its normal limit of 2–3 seconds. By separating the repeated Sa's with durations of over 3 seconds, the artist ensures that any emerging sense of pulse or rhythmic organization built up in the melodic episodes is dissipated. The relatively long durations of the Sa's also reinforces the division into phrases suggested by the melodic structure and dynamic modulation. Close listening to each melodic gesture reveals that in several cases some sense of pulse or oscillation may indeed be perceived within the gesture itself, yet the overall arrangement, dominated by clear strokes separated by irregular and long durations, means that the extract as a whole is extremely unlikely to be perceived as pulsed, and the soloist has in effect succeeded in directing most listeners' attention to the melodic structure and detail.

This leaves a few questions still to be asked, for instance concerning the perceptual role of the *cikārī* strokes. I perceive the *cikārī* as a kind of 'upbeat' preparing for the main stroke. In fact, in some *sarod* performances this *cikārī* stroke can be felt (and counted) as the last beat of a four-beat pattern, although that is not the case in this extract: it may, however, be interpreted as an 'upbeat' occurring within a very flexible period.

The intriguing possibility remains, perhaps, that the artist himself may have a regular pulsation in mind which he is concealing, consciously or unconsciously, from the listener. Even if this were the case, however—as Widdess and Sanyal demonstrated for some *dhrupad* performance—I do not believe this would invalidate the points outlined above, but rather add an extra dimension to them. I would summarize these, inevitably tentative, findings, as follows:

1. As the melodic development of *ālāp* seems inevitably to be made up of a series of notes or gestures arranged into longer phrases or episodes, timing seems to play a role (alongside melodic information and dynamic modulation) in marking phrase boundaries.

2. *Ālāp* seems to be organized on a number of temporal levels, from the division of the entire *ālāp* into three major phases down to the sort of phrases investigated here (10–30 secs.), made up of individual notes, gestures, or events (1–5 secs.) each of which may comprise distinct phases and exhibit rhythmic oscillation at the micro-level.

3. The 2–3 second extent of the perceptual present seems to match the normal extent of the gesture in slow *ālāp*; the use of longer durations at the end of phrases may be interpreted as a deliberate marking of boundaries and breaking up of any emergent pulse.

4. While the possibility remains that a fairly regular pulse underlies the production of this music, whether or not the performer is conscious of such a pulse, this does not alter the fact that such a pulse is extremely unlikely to be perceived in this kind of *ālāp*.

7.2.2 *Joṛ*: metred or unmetred?

Since the identity of *tāl* with metre, and the consequent description of *ālāp* as free rhythm, are rarely considered or questioned, *joṛ* (and its vocal equivalent, the *madhya ālāp* of *dhrupad*) is—perhaps rather carelessly—grouped with 'unmetred' forms. In fact, all *joṛ* has a regular pulse, and most is organized around a simple 2, 4, or 8-beat pattern: in effect, it has two pulse levels and therefore fulfils at least Lerdahl and Jackendoff's basic conditions for metre. Of course *joṛ* of this kind cannot be said to have *tāl*, since it is not organized by any authorized metric cycle. Moreover, since it is not set to a *tāl* and usually not accompanied, the metre may be inconsistent. Beats may be dropped from or added to the binary scheme, the musician may change temporarily to a 3, 5, or 7-beat pattern, or take a break in singing or playing without retaining the binary 'metre' in his mind. This irregularity is no more notable than in many other musics which are considered metrical, yet it is very irregular by the standards of *tāl*.

In some cases the metre of *joṛ* can become more elaborate. Some musicians take, for example, two 4-beat patterns to be one integral unit. This is true of sitārist Deepak Choudhury, who claims to keep such a structure in mind when playing *joṛ*, and encourages his students to 'count time' for his *joṛ*, marking the 4-beat patterns with an alternation of claps and waves (*tālī* and *khālī*). Several other modern musicians, including Pandit Ravi Shankar, have played *joṛ* in a strict 8-beat *tāl*-like pattern, accompanied by a *pakhāvaj* or a *kharaj* (bass) *tablā*: this is said to be a traditional practice.[6]

As in the case of slow *ālāp*, a full consideration of this subject is beyond the scope of this study, but nevertheless a look at a brief episode (from the same performance by Amjad Ali Khan) should prove a useful exercise. The extract illustrated in Example 7.3 is from early in the *joṛ* phase of this performance. The

[6] Deepak Choudhury (personal communication). Some *dhrupad* singers also adopt this practice, while *bīn* (stick zither) players sometimes have their *pakhāvaj* (barrel-drum) accompanist play the 12-*mātrā cautāl* during the *joṛ* section (Richard Widdess, personal communication).

extract is clearly based around a steady pulse, although the artist confuses this sense of pulsation occasionally by shifting his *cikārī* strokes from the 'off-beat' onto the pulse. I therefore transcribed it into simple rhythmic notation with melody indicated once again in *sargam*.

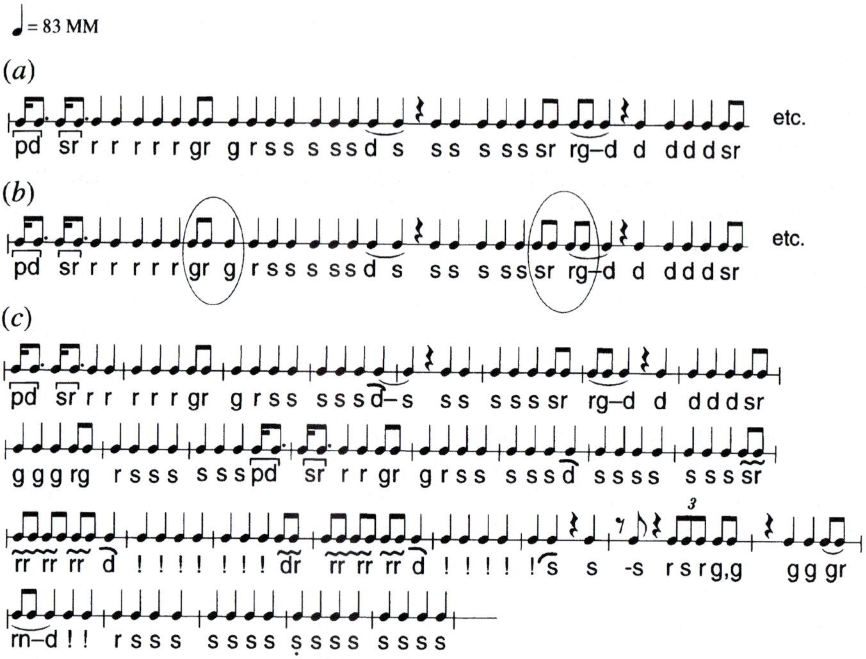

⌐	*mīṇḍ* (slide)	~	*gamak* (shake)
⌐¬	*kṛntan* (hammer-on)	!	*cikārī*

Example 7.3 Amjad Ali Khan, *joṛ* in *rāg bilāskhānī toḍī*, extract (Audio Example 4)

In the first instance I was not conscious of any regular grouping of these pulses, and made a simple transcription as in Example 7.3*a*. I became conscious however that the doubling of certain strokes (e.g. the eighth beat of Ex. 7.3*a*) seemed in many cases to indicate upbeats (anacruses): this is, in fact, quite consistent with the practice of Hindustānī music in other respects, where an increase in rhythmic density is often used to increase the sense of anacrusis and/or cadence (Example 7.3*b*). Taking each pair of quavers (or the first of each sequence) as an upbeat, it can be seen quite easily how this would be consistent with a 4-beat pattern, with the sole exception of the initial group. I therefore added bar-lines to indicate such a grouping, and found that such a scheme could readily be felt as a possible 4-beat metrical arrangement, as in Example 7.3*c* (albeit not, perhaps, the only such possible). Intrigued by the possibility

I checked back from the beginning of this episode to the final cadence of the slow *ālāp*, and found that a regular and uninterrupted 4-beat pattern could be counted from that point through to the end of this passage (despite an intervening period during which Amjad Ali Khan had to retune his instrument).

This recognition of a 4-beat pattern is consistent with the accounts of many musicians and students of *rāg* music, and I have no doubt that it is a significant factor in the organization of this episode, almost certainly consciously. (In fact, it may be that some higher, or lower level metrical organization is at work which I have not detected, such as a grouping of two fours to make an 8-beat metre.) This does not, however, alter the fact that the 4-beat pattern is not immediately obvious, at least on first listening. Again, there may be detectable reasons for this. A notable feature of this extract is that the melodic development seems to be padded out with a considerable amount of apparently redundant material, in the form of repeated notes (particularly Sa) and *cikārī* strokes. One effect of this is to emphasize the repeated note (in which sense it is not strictly speaking melodically redundant). Another effect is to break up any sense of '4-ness'. Looking at the timings, the average duration of a pulse (notated here as a crotchet) is about 0.73 seconds; the most common numbers of repetitions of the Sa are between 5 and 7, giving durations of approximately 3.5 to 5 seconds, remarkably close to those encountered in the slow *ālāp* when the same artist breaks up any emerging sense of pulse. It seems that the effect of the repeated Sa's here may be similar, breaking up the sense of a 4-beat pattern and stopping it from taking hold in the listener's mind. The disorienting switch of the *cikārī* stroke from 'off-beat' onto the main beat and back onto the off-beat (in my Example 7.3*c*, line 3) surely has a similar effect, as does the syncopated pattern towards the end of the episode.

What seems to be happening here is that Amjad Ali Khan is using a concealed metrical organization, rather as Ritwik Sanyal uses a concealed pulse (Widdess 1994). The extract can be shown to be organized around a 4-beat metre (or at least, such a pattern seems to be a possible metrical interpretation; I would not present it with such confidence if it were not for the large body of anecdotal evidence that musicians do indeed use such implicit metrical patterns in performing *joṛ*). Yet the metre is not at all obvious, and seems almost to be deliberately concealed from the listener. I would suggest that the significance of this finding goes beyond the rather limited question of whether or not *joṛ* is metrical, and suggests that we may in many other cases ask too narrow questions about metre. Perhaps in this, as in many other cases of music analysis (in Western music as well as in ethnomusicological studies), we should be less satisfied with the question 'What is the metre of this piece of music?', and more prepared to ask 'How (and why) does this piece of music manipulate listeners' disposition to recognize certain kinds of metrical patterns in music?' The most obvious (although perhaps not the only) answer to the 'why' question in this case may be that the listener's attention should be focused on the melodic dimension of *ālāp* (hence the breaking up of the sense of pulse); while in *joṛ* a sense of pulse and movement is added but the listener should not focus on metrical organization (hence the concealment of that organization).

7.3 *Bandiś* and development: metred (*nibaddh*) forms

The *bandiś* (composition) is the key to the *nibaddh* section of a *rāg* performance. This fixed composition is generally stated as soon as the *tāl* is introduced, and a part of it is subsequently used as a refrain between episodes of improvised development; furthermore the development frequently employs, transforms, or builds on, material introduced in the *bandiś*. Whatever follows the *bandiś*, in what may be termed the 'development phase', must be seen in the context of the concerns of the music tradition as a whole—*rāg* exposition, rhythmic and textual development (or variation of stroke patterns in instrumental music)—and of the particular genre and style.

What makes analysis of development phases particularly difficult is that in practice, techniques and processes are not always clearly distinguished. Techniques are often not clearly defined, nor are they always separated in performance, especially in the stylistically eclectic genre of *khyāl*. Moreover, each *gharānā* or individual style has distinct development techniques, as well as particular ways of describing them. The terms employed by one musician may adequately describe his own music, but remain inappropriate for that of another artist. The tradition as a whole is in fact rather heterogeneous, and extreme care needs to be taken in applying any terms universally.

It is certainly possible to define a limited number of development techniques of importance in Hindustānī music (*bol bāṇṭ*, *bol banāo*, *tān*, etc.), but in truth the stylistic diversity ensures that however they are defined, much music will defy categorization. In any North Indian music, a number of basic processes may continue simultaneously, such as *rāg* development, text manipulation, acceleration, and other forms of intensification. These different processes may come together in particular definable combinations in particular contexts, but the mix of elements is immensely variable. My intention here and in Chapter 9 is to identify certain important parameters by which the music of any genre or style may be characterized in rhythmic analysis.

7.3.1 Development techniques and their resolution into rhythmic parameters

By resolving any improvised development into a number of rhythmic parameters, we may avoid a great deal of terminological confusion. In terms of development techniques (and before considering rhythm as such), the principal variables will be as follows:

- Articulation: singers may use the composition text; *ākār* (or other vowels); or a variety of other syllables such as *sargam*, *nom-tom* and *tarānā*.[7]
- Text syllable (or instrumental stroke) usage: the usage of the text in development may involve either division and recombination of the text; expression of the text using the melodic/rhythmic variation and ornamentation; or the use of text syllables as a vehicle for *rāg* development. In instrumental *gat* forms, strokes may be used in a number of ways, involving mainly either the imitation of any of the techniques of text use, or division and recombination according to the logic of *tāl* structure, melodic pattern or *laykārī*.
- *Rāg*: treatment may focus on repetition or embellishment of previously developed material, the introduction of new material, or the expansion of melodic range.

Moving into the rhythmic domain as such, the basic parameters are:

- *Tāl* and *lay*
- Rhythmic style (on a continuum from syllabic to melismatic), and the mode of rhythmic organization (see Chapter 4).
- *Laykārī* (use of rhythmic variation techniques, see Chapter 10).

These are some of the most important factors which may be identified in post-*bandiś* development. Certain logical combinations of these parameters are frequently observed: for instance, *dhrupad bol bāṇṭ* may be described as a synthesis of (1) articulation using text only, (2) development of that text by division and recombination (*bāṇṭ*), (3) repetition of previously developed melodic material, (4) the use of one of a limited number of *tāls*, typically *cautāl*, (5) moderate tempo, (6) syllabic rhythmic style, with a high degree of correlation between surface rhythm and *tāl*, and (7) the use of various idiomatic *laykārī* techniques.

In this case, the type of development is defined by the use of the text (*bol bāṇṭ* = 'distribution of the words'), but associations of *lay*, rhythmic style, and so on are assumed. The rhythmic parameters listed above are all more or less logically determined, in that they either establish a suitable environment for this type of text-based development process (e.g. the tempo), or are dependent on that process (the syllabic rhythmic style, and use of idiomatic *laykārī* techniques).

Several other techniques or processes are similarly defined—by text use in particular—such as *bol banāo*, *bol ālāp* (introduction to the *rāg*, sung to the text syllables), or *nom-tom ālāp* (ditto, sung to '*nom-tom*' syllables). Other types of development are defined by their rhythmic aspect, for example *tān* (fast, virtuosic run[8]). In each of these cases, association with other parameters is less fixed than in the case of *dhrupad bol bāṇṭ*, and one finds considerable

[7] *Ākār* is the use of the vowel 'ā'; sargam are solfège syllables (Sa, Re, Ga, Ma, Pa, Dha, Ni); *nom-tom* are particular syllables used in *ālāp* (tā, nā, re, num etc.); *tarānā* is a vocal genre using particular non-lexical syllables (tā, dere, dīm, nā, etc.).

[8] From an ancient musical term referring to pentatonic and hexatonic derivatives of seven-note scales; see Rowell 1992: 160–2. The closest modern Hindī word is *tānnā*, 'to stretch, to spread' (Chaturvedi and Tiwari 1986: 285).

overlaps between the surface rhythm produced by different types of development technique.

7.3.2 Performance processes

Episodic organization of development One principle shared by performers of the various genres is the episodic organization of performance. In virtually all North Indian music, all or part of the fixed composition is used as a refrain, between passages of improvised development. In some genres, especially instrumental *gats*, these refrains accompany percussion solos.

Thus the statement of the *bandiś* is followed by an episode of improvised development, then a refrain comprising part of the *bandiś*, then more development, the refrain again and so on;[9] this is true regardless of the genre, style or type of development employed. This structure may be illustrated schematically as in Example 7.4. This episodic structure is a key concept in the rhythmic organization of North Indian music; it is associated with the extemporary nature of the performance process, and is a constant factor, no matter how various the contents of development episodes may be.

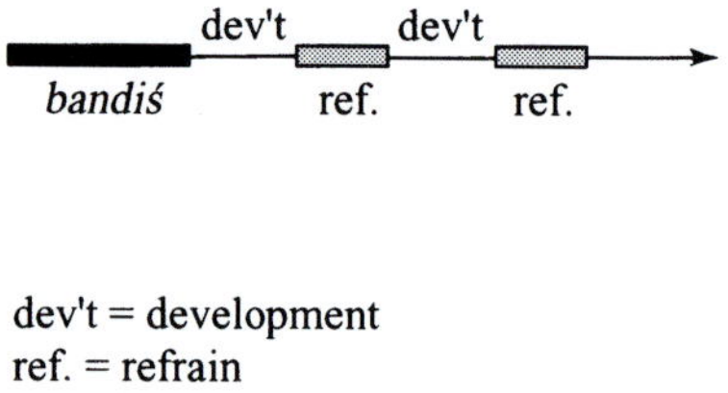

Example 7.4 An illustration of the episodic organization of Hindustānī music performance

Acceleration Another principle common to most North Indian music is a tendency to increase the *lay*, which can be regarded as an aspect of the more general tendency to intensification in North Indian *rāg* performance. If episodic organization is the key to local level structure, then acceleration is the most obvious factor which creates a sense of progression in the performance as a whole. This acceleration may occur in the metric tempo, rhythmic density, or both. It is a tendency which reaffirms the primacy of process over structure in Indian music: without it, we might expect a balance between acceleration and deceleration, and between increase and decrease in dynamic level, as in Western art music. Acceleration is the key to one of the principal processes in Indian music—the transition from unmetred or loosely metred, melismatic, and slow tempo melodic development to metred, syllabic, and fast tempo rhythmic development.[10]

[9] What I have termed 'episodes (of improvised development)' and 'refrains', Wade refers to as 'events' between 'demarcation points' (1984*b*: 40–1).

[10] Cf. Wade's 'multifaceted progression' (1984*b*: 41). She raises several of the issues discussed in this chapter; episodic organization (although she uses different terms for the same concept),

The various development techniques used in North Indian music tend to be ordered by this general rule of increasing *lay*. Thus *ālāp* will generally precede *bol bāṇṭ*, which will precede *tāns*. Rules of this kind are not universally adhered to, and indeed several very distinguished singers have been famous for their lack of such logical organization (*vyavasthā*).[11] Nevertheless, such 'good organization' is widely regarded as a desirable attribute. Issues of technique and style, as well as those of structure and form, are thus inseparable from those of process: performance process is the key to understanding large-scale structure, as it is to understanding local level rhythm.

These ideas—of the place of the *bandiś*, the use of various development techniques (and the possibility of resolving them in analysis into rhythmic parameters), episodic structure and acceleration—are illustrated in Examples 7.5 and 7.6 in formal schemes taken from actual performances in two different genres of North Indian music. The first (Example 7.5) is taken from a *dhrupad* performance,[12] the second (Example 7.6) a *khyāl*;[13] they illustrate the performances' progression (including acceleration) and the variety of development techniques (and the interrelationships of these factors).

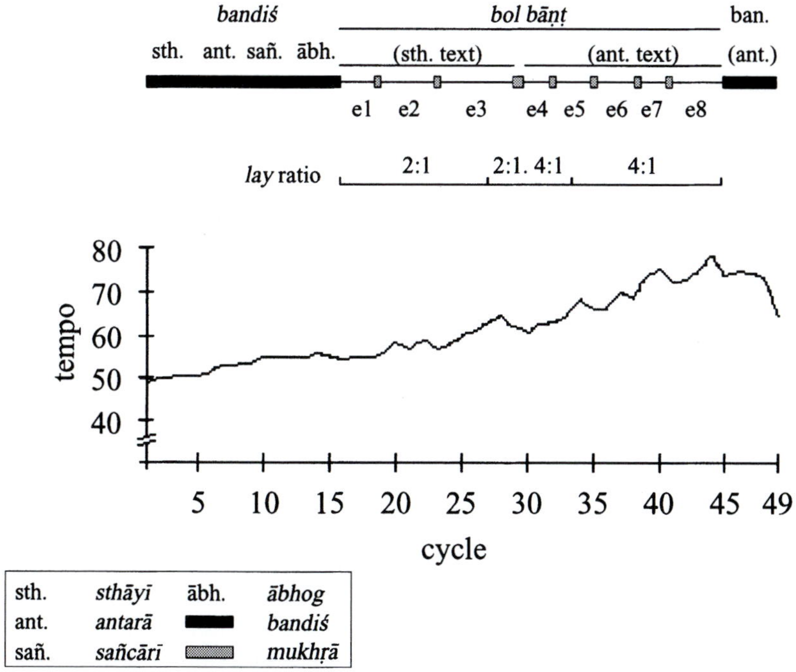

Example 7.5 The formal scheme of a *dhrupad* performance by the Dagar Brothers

[11] See, for instance, Deshpande's discussion of Bade Ghulam Ali Khan's singing style (1987: 56–8).

[12] By the Dagar Brothers, of *rāg jaijaivantī* in *cautāl*.

[13] By Veena Sahasrabuddhe, of *rāg śrī* in *rūpak tāl*.

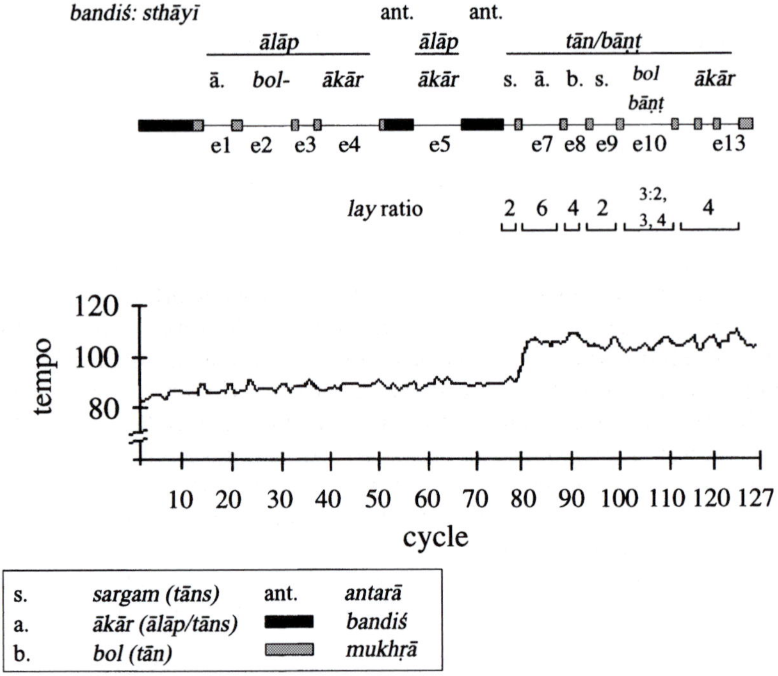

Example 7.6 The formal scheme of a *khyāl* performance by Veena Sahasrabuddhe

episodic structure, *lay* ratio, and tempo (and hence acceleration). At the bottom in each case is a chart of tempo against cycle (roughly speaking tempo against time), which shows how the *dhrupad* gradually accelerates from 50 MM to a little over 70 MM, while the *khyāl* remains relatively stable apart from one clearly intentional acceleration around cycle 80 (Example 7.6). Above the tempo chart I have indicated the *lay* ratio (ratio of density to tempo) for those parts of the performance for which this is clearly defined (the whole of the improvisation in the case of the *dhrupad*; the latter part only in the *khyāl*).

The diagrams in the upper part of these Examples indicate the formal organization of the performances: in the case of the *dhrupad* a statement of the 4-section composition is followed by *bol bāṇṭ* improvised on the text of first the *sthāyī* (episodes 1 to 3) and then the *antarā* (episodes 4 to 8); in the *khyāl* the *sthāyī* only is stated at the beginning, the first 5 episodes feature a combination of different kinds of *ālāp*, with two statements of the composition's *antara* towards the end; episodes 6 to 13 feature a wide variety of different techniques performed at different *lay* ratios. Although these two performances differ in many respects, the key concepts outlined above—the '*bandiś* + development' pattern, episodic structure and acceleration—are illustrated clearly in both cases. The *dhrupad* (Ex. 7.5) is more simply and clearly organized, since only one development technique is employed in the metered section. The relationship between tempo variation and performance process should be clear in both cases.

7.3.3 The percussion accompaniment

All *nibaddh* music is accompanied by drums: *dhrupad, dhamār*, and *sādrā* by the barrel drum *pakhāvaj*, and all other genres by the drum pair *tablā*. This accompaniment plays a crucial role in the rhythmic organization of modern North Indian music, in that it can articulate the metrical framework which forms one level of this structure. (The drum pattern should not however be confused with that metrical framework, which is essentially a conceptual construct.) The drum accompaniment is not only an essential element of rhythmic organization in *nibaddh* forms, it may also influence surface rhythm, and must therefore be taken into consideration in several contexts. There are a number of styles of accompaniment however, and the mode of accompaniment may have an important influence on the rhythmic patterns produced by the soloist. The principal modes of accompaniment are the following;

• Accompaniment by *ṭhekā*: the drummer plays a version of the *tāl*'s *ṭhekā* (i.e. a pattern similar to those listed in Example 5.1, but elaborated to varying degrees depending largely on the tempo), and does so with little or no variation between cycles. In this case the soloist may rely on the drummer for audible cues to keep him in time; at medium and fast tempi the use of a repeated *ṭhekā* enhances the accentual pattern of the *tāl* structure, and the *ṭhekā*'s accentual pattern may directly influence surface rhythm.

This type of accompaniment is the most common for *khyāl* and *ṭhumrī* performance, but may be heard at some point in most performances, in all genres. In some cases, particularly where the *ṭhekā* accompaniment is being used in instrumental *gat* forms, the *tablā* player bases his accompaniment on the *ṭhekā*, but varies the *bol* pattern noticeably between cycles, and interpolates new material (for example, repeating the soloist's rhythmic phrases or variations thereon) into the basic pattern.

• *Sāth saṅgat*: the accompanist departs from the *ṭhekā*, and plays *sāth saṅgat* ('synchronized accompaniment') in which he imitates the rhythm of the soloist with a minimal time delay, occasionally even anticipating him. This type of accompaniment is particularly important in *dhrupad-dhamār*, and is therefore associated with the *pakhāvaj*. It is also known as *laṛant* ('fighting', see Kippen 1988 : 102 and Bhowmick 1975 : 39).

• Accompaniment with drum solo: the drummer plays virtuosic pieces, either drawn from the solo repertoire (e.g. the *pakhāvaj*'s '*parans*') or improvised. This type of accompaniment is especially popular in *dhrupad-dhamār*, where *parans* are often played to accompany all or part of the statement of the *bandiś*. In instrumental *gats*, *tablā* solos (usually accompanied by the first line of the *gat*) are interpolated between episodes of melodic improvisation;[14] brief *tablā* solos are also heard occasionally in *choṭā khyāl*.

In the case of *ṭhekā* accompaniment, the accentual pattern of the drum line may influence the surface rhythm. This is not the case with other types of accompaniment, which tend to favour the quantitative aspect of rhythmic organization, and features of syllabic rhythmic style such as *laykārī*. Thus the type of accompaniment affects rhythmic style and mode of rhythmic organization.

[14] This style of accompaniment was popularized in instrumental music by Ravi Shankar in particular (see Kippen 1988 : 104).

8

The *bandiś*

8.1 The place and importance of the *bandiś*

The fixed composition, called either *bandiś* or *cīz* in vocal genres and either *bandiś* or *gat* in instrumental genres,[1] holds a position of central importance in North Indian *rāg* performance. The vocal *bandiś* is essentially a song—a text set to *rāg* and *tāl*—which exists both as a piece of music in its own right, and as the basis of further musical development. In instrumental music the composition is either an imitation or adaptation of such a vocal *bandiś*, or a piece based instead on idiomatic stroke patterns, in which case it is called a *gat* (the term *bandiś* is used in the discussion which follows to cover all kinds of compositions).

The *bandiś* may be studied in terms both of its own structural parameters, and also of the material which it provides for development. Since the material of the *bandiś* acts as the basis of subsequent development, study of the structural parameters of *bandiśes* effectively gives an indication of the rhythmic organization and style of the performance as a whole.

The *bandiś* usually opens the *nibaddh* stage of the performance; sometimes the complete *bandiś* is stated at this point, although one or more sections may be reserved until later (for instance the *antarā*, generally the second section, featuring a melodic movement into the upper tetrachord, is often not sung or played until the upper Sa has been established in the *vistār* portion of a *khyāl* or *vilambit gat*). In some styles all or part of the *bandiś* may also be repeated towards the end of the performance. Moreover, either all or part of the first section (*sthāyī*) is used as a refrain between episodes of improvised development (the first line of the *antarā* is also sometimes used in this way).

The *bandiś* may itself constitute a large part of the performance: moreover it is used as the basis of much improvised development. Rhythmically, its structure (and the variability of that structure) give important clues as to the rhythmic style of the performance, and of the genre to which it belongs.

The principal structural parameters of the *bandiś* which I will consider are the following:

- *tāl* and *lay*.
- length: the number of sections and lines.

[1] In instrumental music, '*bandiś*' is used especially for adaptations of vocal compositions.

- melodic rhythm: its correlation with the *tāl* structure (commetric and contrametric patterns, the use of syncopation and of the *mukhṛā* or anacrusis); and the influence of verse metre.
- variability of the *bandiś*.

Of these factors, *tāl* and *lay* are easily determined in each case; the rest of this chapter is concerned with the other parameters in turn.

8.1.1 The length of the *bandiś*

There is considerable variability in *bandiś* length. *Bandiśes* are composed of between two and four sections (*dhātu, aṇg*) of which at least two are usually performed, named *sthāyī* and *antarā*.[2] The *sthāyī* is the first section, using the first line of text: all or part of the *sthāyī* is used as a refrain between episodes of development. The *antarā* is often the second (and contrasting) section, and generally has a higher melodic range than the *sthāyī*. All or part of the *antarā* may also be used as a refrain in some circumstances, especially where improvised development is based on the *antarā* text or is concentrated in the upper end of the melodic range. Many compositions use only these two sections, *sthāyī* and *antarā*, although in some cases additional sections are included.

Dhrupad bandiśes generally consist of a total of four sections or *dhātus*, called *sthāyī, antarā, sañcārī*, and *ābhog*, although often in practice only the first two of these are sung. Another type of extension is found in instrumental *gat* forms in particular, where an extra section may be interpolated between *sthāyī* and *antarā*, often of lower tessitura, called *mañjhā*.[3] In *ṭhumrī bandiśes*, middle sections (where present) are called *madhya* (*madhya* is in fact synonymous with *mañjhā*, meaning 'middle').[4]

This gives three basic patterns, as follows:

- *sthāyī-antarā*: most genres
- *sthāyī-antarā-sañcārī-ābhog*: *dhrupad*, *sādrā* only
- *sthāyī-mañjhā/madhya-antarā*: instrumental *gat*, *ṭhumrī* only

Each section may consist of one or two text lines (and exceptionally more), and extend to between one and four *tāl* cycles in all (in short *tāl* cycles, one text

[2] In fact, since *antarā* sections are sometimes not performed, or are rhythmically indistinguishable from the improvisation which precedes and follows (especially in *khyāl* and *vilambit gat* performance), the compositions may in such circumstances fairly be termed single section *bandiśes*. *Sthāyī* = lit. 'permanent, constant', *antarā* = lit. 'intermediate'.

[3] Dick points out that early (i.e. early 19th-cent.) *razākhānī gats* consisted of two sections corresponding to the modern *sthāyī-mañjhā*, not *sthāyī-antarā*, and that the addition of the *antarā* is probably due to the influence of vocal forms; he also suggests *masītkhānī gats' mañjhā* lines may be created by 'triple repetition of the first sub-bar' of the *sthāyī* (1984 : 394). Hamilton claims that the *mañjhā* is effectively the renamed second line of the *sthāyī* in *masītkhānī gats* (1989 : 76). Similarly the *dhrupad sañcārī* and *ābhog* were originally one section, named simply *ābhog* (see Widdess 1981*a* : 163; Srivastav 1980 : 49); in fact they are still usually performed without interruption, effectively as one long section.

[4] See Manuel (1989 : 105).

line may cover two cycles; otherwise generally one line occupies one cycle). Sections tend to be longer in *dhrupad bandiśes*, although sections of two or more lines are also encountered in *khyāl* and other genres. To give an impression of the variability of these parameters, Table 8.1 compares data from 10 performances in a variety of genres.

These figures are based on particular performances, and I will therefore not generalize too much from the precise numbers. Each is nonetheless typical of its genre to a degree, and in this respect they illustrate some of the points made above. The longest *bandiśes* are those used in the *dhrupad* and *sādrā* examples (the latter is effectively in '*dhrupad*' style); not surprisingly therefore the statement of the *bandiś* takes up a greater proportion of the performance in *dhrupad, dhamār*, and *sādrā* than in any other genre. Overall the text was employed for the highest proportion of the performance in these genres and in the *ṭhumrī*, and for the lowest proportion of time in the *baṛā khyāl*. These are some of the clearest differences between the genres, expressed in a quantified manner.

Table 8.1 A comparison of the length and proportion of total performance of the *bandiś*, in a sample of ten recordings of various Hindustānī genres

				bandiś length			
artist	genre/ form	*tāl*	*lay* (MM)	no. of sections	no. of lines	no. of cycles	% of perf.
Dagar Brothers	*dhrupad*	*cautāl*	49–79	4	12	12	40 + 60*
Bidur Mallik	*dhamār*	*dhamār*	60–80	2	4	5†	40 + 60*
K. G. Ginde	*sādrā*	*jhaptāl*	90–104	4	16	16	50 + 50*
Pandit Jasraj	*baṛā khyāl*	*ektāl*	10.7–11.8	2	2	2	8
Veena Sahasrabuddhe	*khyāl*	*rūpak*	83–108	2	4	8‡	15
Bhimsen Joshi	*choṭā khyāl*	*drut tīntāl*	258–302	2	4	4	30
Munawar Ali Khan	*ṭhumrī*	*pañjābī tīntāl*	118–130	2	4	4	80§
Ravi Shankar	*masītkhānī gat (sitār)*	*vilambit tīntāl*	46–81	3	3	3	15
Nikhil Banerjee	*madhya lay gat (sitār)*	*jhaptāl*	113–165	2	2	2	4
Amjad Ali Khan	*razākhānī gat (sarod)*	*drut tīntāl*	265–722	2	5	5	11

* the first figure refers to *bandiś* statement, and the remainder *bol bāṇṭ* using the *bandiś* text.
† In this performance the second text line covers two cycles, and all others only one cycle.
‡ This *rūpak tāl khyāl* performance is the only one of this sample in which each line covers two cycles.
§ Including *bol banāo*.

8.2 Rhythmic structure of vocal *bandiśes*

It is usually possible to determine the rhythmic structure of a *bandiś*, based on the grouping implicit in the melodic rhythm, and on the distribution of text syllables and words. (This may vary somewhat from line to line, and section to section, but for the purposes of the present discussion I will concentrate on first lines, since these are by far the most significant in terms of the performance as a whole.) This structure may be derived entirely from the *tāl* structure and divisions (so, for example, a *jhaptāl bandiś* may have its melodic rhythm grouped according to the 2 + 3 + 2 + 3 division of the *tāl*). This is not necessarily the case, however, either because the melodic rhythm runs contrary to the *tāl* divisions, or because a portion of the *bandiś* called the *mukhṛā* precedes the *sam*, forming an anacrusis.[5]

Contrametric *bandiś* structures—those in which the melodic rhythm forms a syncopated rhythm against the *tāl* divisions—are particularly common in *dhrupad*. In the majority of *cautāl bandiśes*, the melodic rhythm falls into four groups of three *mātrās* each, often (but not necessarily) with word breaks between each of these groups.[6] Example 8.1 is an illustration of such a rhythmic pattern in a *dhrupad bandiś* as sung by the younger Dagar Brothers in *rāg jaijaivantī*. *Dhamār bandiśes* typically fall into groups of 4 + 3 + 4 + 3 *mātrās*, with the first group of 4 *mātrās* functioning as an anacrusis (*mukhṛā*). Example 8.2 illustrates the first line of a *bandiś* of this type, as sung by Bidur Mallik in *rāg jaijaivantī*.

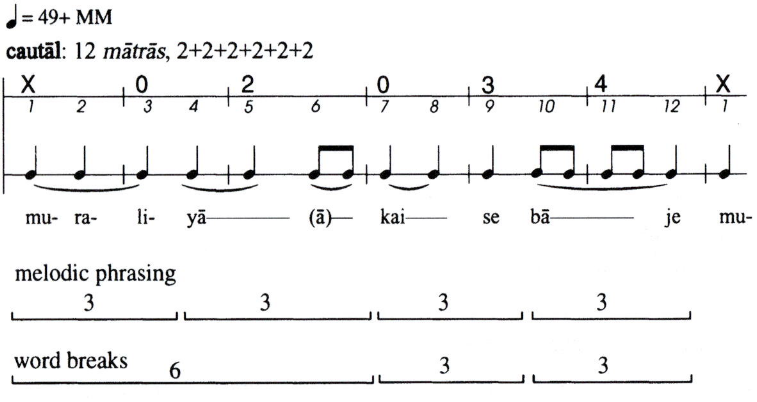

text: muraliyā kaise bāje

Example 8.1 The rhythmic structure of the first line of a *dhrupad bandiś*, as sung by the Dagar Brothers in *rāg jaijaivantī*, *cautāl* (Audio Example 5)

[5] The *mukhṛā* may be defined either as the anacrusis, or as the anacrusis plus *sam*. The former is more common in instrumental music, the latter in vocal performance.

[6] See below; also Widdess (1981*a*: 137).

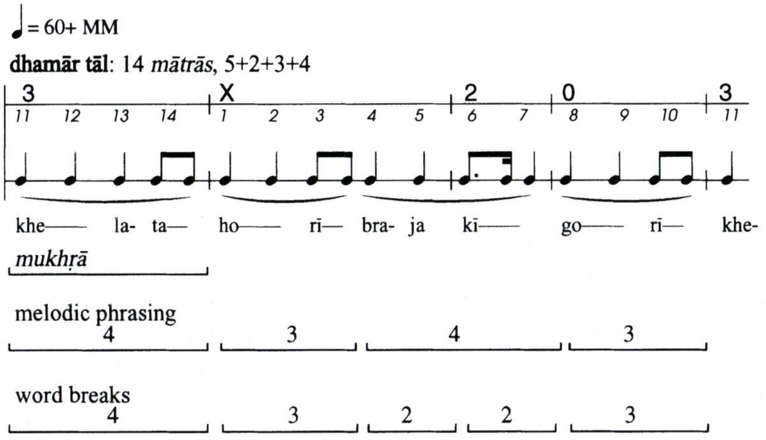

text: khelata horī braja kī gorī

Example 8.2 The rhythmic structure of the first line of a *dhamār bandiś*, as sung by Bidur Mallik in *rāg jaijaivantī, dhamār tāl* (Audio Example 6)

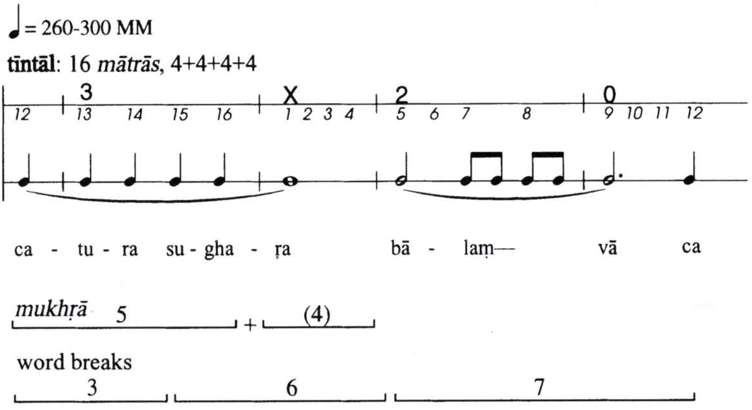

text: catura sughaṛa bālamvā (balamvā)

Example 8.3 The rhythmic structure of the first line of a *choṭā khyāl bandiś*, as sung by Bhimsen Joshi in *rāg durgā, tīntāl* (Audio Example 7 features this line sung several times with small variations)

The use of a *mukhṛā* is in fact common in most genres, and particularly so in *khyāl*;[7] Example 8.3 illustrates the first line of a simple *choṭā khyāl bandiś*, performed by Bhimsen Joshi in *rāg durgā*. There are several differences between

[7] *Khyāl bandiśes* which do not have a *mukhṛā* as such, use the whole first line as a refrain.

this example and the *dhrupad* and *dhamār bandiśes* illustrated in Examples 8.1 and 8.2. For instance, the word breaks in this case appear to play no role in determining or supporting rhythmic structure; the text syllables are also more unevenly distributed, and hence the rhythmic style is less syllabic. The structure falls into two halves; the first half, comprising the *mukhṛā* plus the long note on *sam,* being balanced by the second half (*mātrās* 5–11). The central pillar of the *bandiś* is therefore the *mukhṛā*, and the remaining structure is worked around this—something typical of many, perhaps most, *choṭā khyāls*.

Example 8.4 illustrates three of many other possible rhythmic structures of *choṭā khyāl bandiśes* in *tīntāl*. Of these three (*a*) has a shorter *mukhṛā*, of only 3

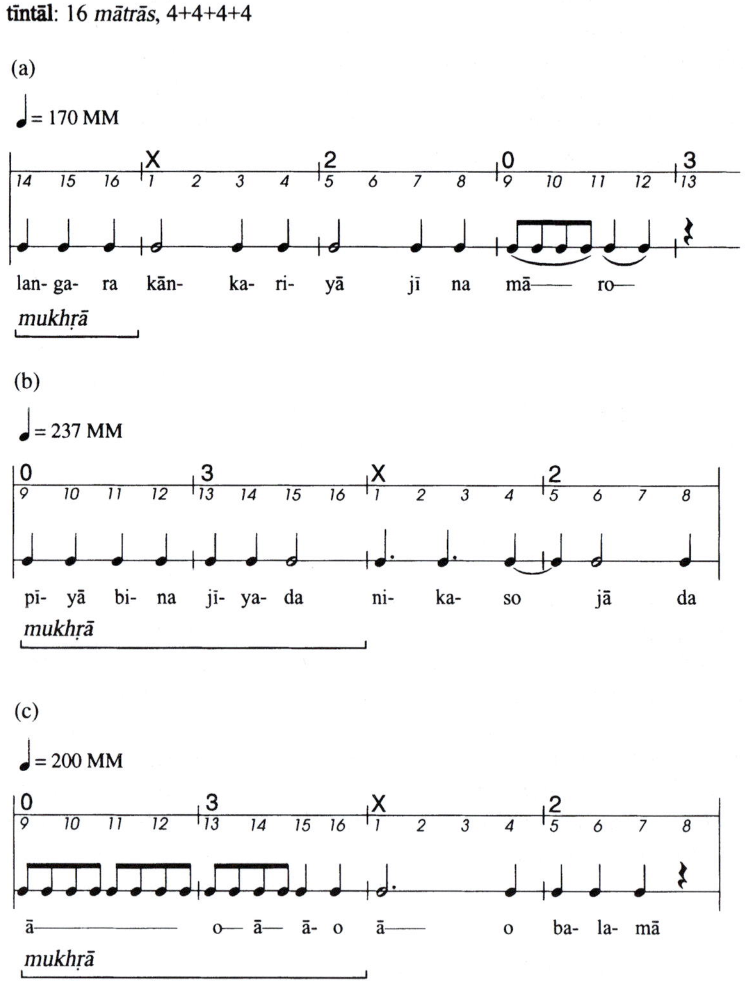

Example 8.4 Three *choṭā khyāl bandiśes* in *tīntāl* (*sthāyī* only) (These extracts can be heard as Audio Examples 8, 9, and 10 respectively)

mātrās (for a number of variants of this line, see Example 8.23 below); (*b*) begins from the mid-point of the cycle (*khālī*), giving an 8-*mātrā mukhṛā*; and (*c*) also begins from *khālī*, but incorporates a *tān*-like melisma on the word 'āo' (come!). *Choṭā khyāls* may then come in a variety of forms, and performers are free to experiment with new variants: it would be fair to say, however, that a construction with a 5-*mātrā mukhṛā* (such as that illustrated in Example 8.3) is particularly common.

The importance of the *mukhṛā* evident in these *choṭā khyāl bandiśes* is even more noticeable in slow tempo *khyāls*. Example 8.5, from a recording by Malikarjun Mansur in *rāg yemenī bilāval*, shows how in *baṛā khyāls*, considerable melismatic embellishment is incorporated into *mukhṛā*-based structures showing an underlying similarity to those of many *choṭā khyāls*. In comparing this example with those in Examples 8.3 and 8.4 we can see how the *mukhṛā* (and in some cases the phrase immediately preceding the *mukhṛā* proper) is particularly dense in text syllables, while the sense of repose on the *sam* is marked by a longer note (with or without melisma).

These few examples have illustrated something of the variety of *bandiś* structures in the principal vocal forms. The most important rhythmic parameters are melodic grouping and text distribution, the relationship of the *bandiś* rhythm to *tāl* structure, the use or absence of a *mukhṛā*, and the rhythmic style. There appear to be a number of more or less clear correlations between different structural features and wider rhythmic parameters. On the one hand, genres which favour more syllabic, rhythm-oriented styles tend to use *bandiśes* which take up a greater part of the performance, and which have a clearly defined rhythmic structure and relatively even text distribution. More melismatic styles, on the other hand, favour *bandiśes* of fewer lines and sections, whose text is relatively concentrated in the *mukhṛā*.

Other features such as the use of *tāl*-derived as opposed to contrametric rhythmic patterns, and the employment of the *mukhṛā*, are not so easy to tie in with these features. Unquestionably contrametric structures (as opposed to *tāl*-derived structures distorted by syncopation and rubato) are indicative of rhythmically focused, syllabic music, yet they are not an essential component of the same (while *cautāl dhrupad bandiśes* are often set as an apparently contrametric 3 3 3 3, as above, a grouping of 4 4 2 2 which does not overlap the *tāl* divisions is also possible, particularly in '*dhrupad*' *bandiśes* played on the *bīn*). The *mukhṛā* is an essential feature of *vilambit khyāls*, where it has a key role in performance practice: in many other genres it is optional, but it remains a common feature in most. The common use of the *mukhṛā* (anacrusis) is not surprising, given the widespread preference for iambic, anacrustic, and cadential features in Indian rhythm.

8.2.1 Verse metre and text distribution

Bandiś texts are generally composed in either modern standard Hindī (Khaṛī Bolī), or one of the literary 'dialects' (such as Braj Bhāṣā and Avadhī); a few

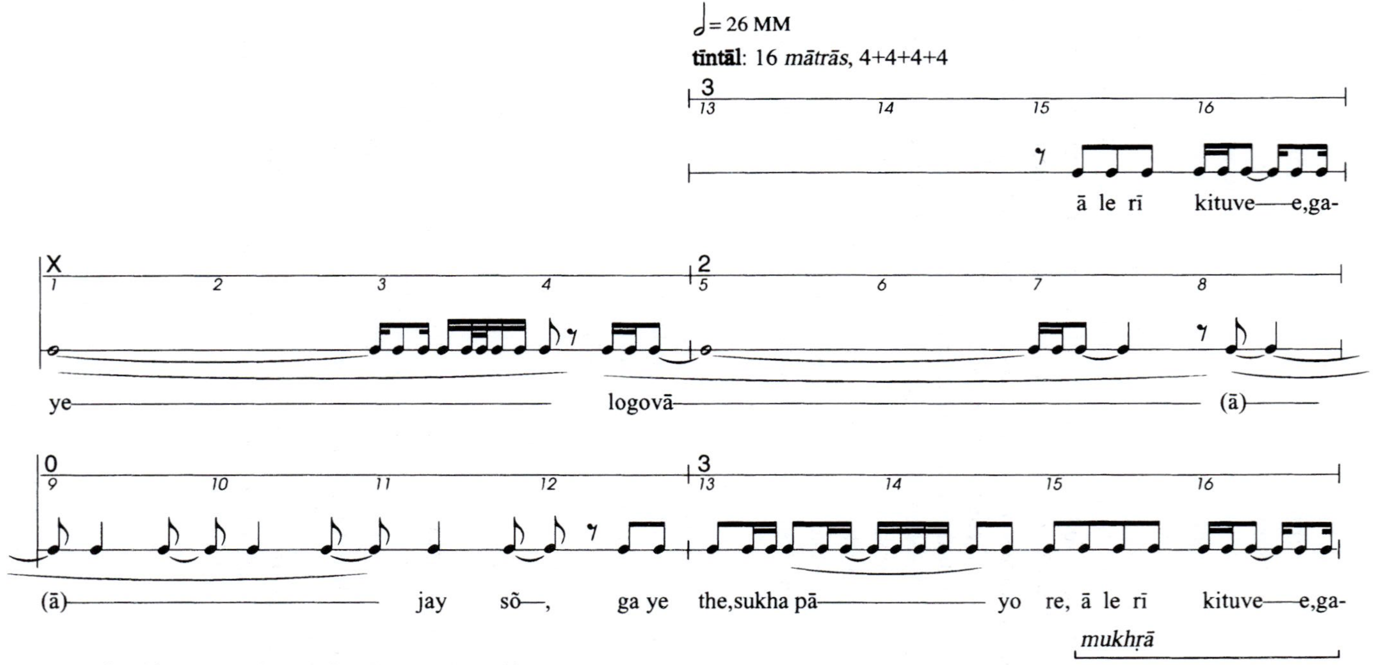

text: ālerī kituve gaye logovā jay sõ gaye the sukha pāyo re

Example 8.5 The rhythmic structure of the first line of a *baṛā khyāl bandiś*, as sung by Malikarjun Mansur in *rāg yemenī bilāval*, *tīntāl* (Audio Example 11 features this line; note that the first *mukhṛā*, sung before the entry of the *tablā*, is somewhat extended)

compositions may also be encountered in modern Indian languages other than Hindī, and even in Sanskrit. Prosody in Indian languages is a vast topic, but in general we may say that verse metres can be based on the quantity and/or the arrangement of syllables. Each text syllable (*akṣara*) is classified as either *laghu* ('short, light') or *guru* ('long, heavy'),[8] and verse metres are defined either (i) according to the arrangement of *laghu* and *guru akṣaras*, or (ii) according to the total number of *akṣaras*, or (iii) according to the sum total of the metric quantities of the *akṣaras* in each line. In the latter case, a *laghu akṣara* counts as 1 *mātrā*, and a *guru* as 2 *mātrās*. Scansion is usually reckoned in groups of syllables called *gaṇa* ('foot').[9] A variety of verse metres may be encountered in *bandiś* texts, although in many cases the metre is imperfectly realized (due perhaps to inaccuracies in transmission). In fact many *bandiś* texts, probably the majority, are not recognizably set in any verse metre.[10]

In Rupert Snell's study of musical settings of devotional Braj Bhāṣā texts and their performance, he found that 'The metres of the CP [Caurāsī Pada] for the most part show a close correlation to *tāla* structure' (1983 : 354), and his work illustrates this relationship with examples transcribed from performance (1983, 1991*a*). Although the temple tradition studied by Snell lies outside the range of my work, it is nonetheless relevant here since it is closely related to the classical *dhrupad-dhamār* style, and indeed many of the devotional texts may be heard in both contexts. Moreover, parallels may be found between the ways in which text is set in these two types of music.

Snell transcribes a text in the *vinaya* metre (12 + 12 + 12 + 8 *mātrās*), sung in the 12 *mātrā cautāl*. The first line is sung in the rhythm illustrated in Example 8.6. In effect, each long syllable (*guru*, marked –) occupies two *mātrās* of the *tāl* cycle, and each short syllable (*laghu*, marked ◡) one *mātrā*; the correlation of verse metre to *tāl* could not be more exact. Not all *cautāl dhrupads* are composed in this metre—many others are described as *ghanākṣarī* in which all syllables are pronounced 'short', and lines typically comprise 16 + 15 syllables arranged 8/8// 8/7//, and others still are free verse '*pads*'[11]—yet some of the features of this piece are nevertheless observable. For instance the *dhrupad* transcribed in Example 8.1 above shows one important similarity with the piece in Example 8.6, in that the melodic rhythm falls into groups of 3 *mātrās*, and in 3 out of the 4 groups no syllable falls on the second *mātrā* of the group.[12]

The *dhrupad bandiś* whose first line is transcribed in Example 8.7 does not share the metre of Snell's *Caurāsī Pada* text (Example 8.6), and the correlation of

[8] In general, syllables containing the vowels *ā, ī, ū, e, ai, o*, or *au* are considered long (*guru*). Those containing the remaining vowels (*a, i, u, ṛ*) are short (*laghu*) unless followed by a conjunct consonant (*kt, sp, tr*, etc.), *anusvara* (nasalization representing in effect a conjunct consonant, i.e. *ñj, nt*, etc.), or *visarga* (ḥ) (Snell 1991*b* : 19).

[9] See Snell (1983 : 369, 377; 1991*b* : 20 ff.) and Chandola (1988 : 81).

[10] Cf. Delvoye: 'most of the *dhrupadas* available in printed editions have a rather loose metrical structure' (1983 : 90). See also Snell (1983 : 376).

[11] A *pad* is a 'hymn'; the term is often used to describe verses of loose metrical structure.

[12] Cf. Widdess (1993).

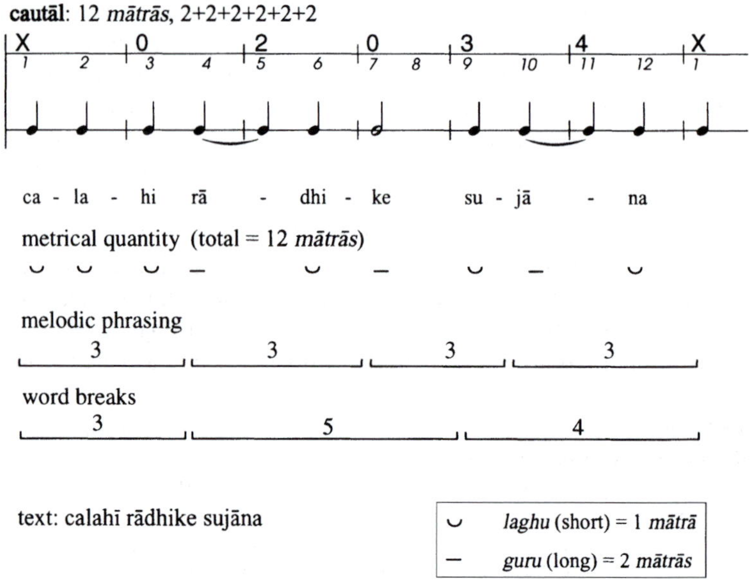

EXAMPLE 8.6 An illustration of the correlation of melodic rhythm and verse metre; from a *dhrupad* performance

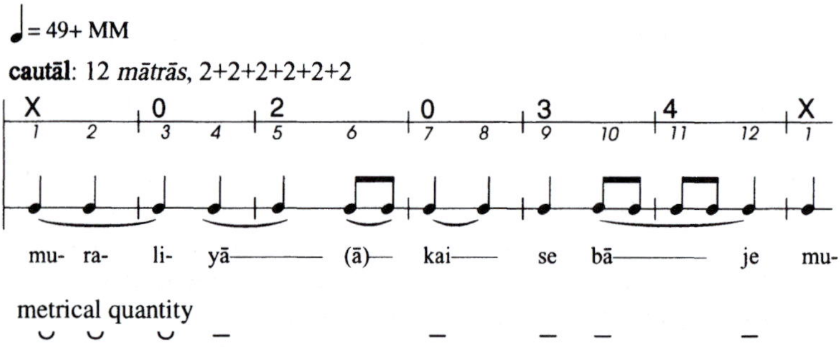

EXAMPLE 8.7 An illustration of the lack of correlation of melodic rhythm and verse metre; from a *dhrupad* performance (cf. Ex. 8.1)

text syllable quantity with musical duration is not nearly as simple.[13] (Actually, metrical quantity appears to be irrelevant here, as this is an 8-syllable *ghaṇākṣarī* line; the second half of the line nonetheless mimics the typical *guru-laghu* arrangement referred to above.) The preference for $(2 + 1) \times 4$ groupings in *cautāl* settings of *dhrupad* texts— as exemplified here—may, however, be an instance of indirect influence of verse metre on musical rhythm (either the *vinaya* metre

[13] For examples of *dhrupad* texts which are based on *guru-laghu* groups see the first line of the *bandiś* transcribed in Widdess (1981*a*: 174), or that discussed by Chandola (1988: 56–7).

above, or others based for example on repetition of *guru-laghu* groups; see Snell 1991*b* : 26–7). In other words, the melodic grouping determined by a typical verse metre (Example 8.6) is imitated even in the case of texts not set in that metre.[14]

A somewhat different situation is illustrated in the *dhamār bandiś* whose first line is transcribed in Example 8.2. In this case the text is composed in a regular metre, but this metre does not correspond to the *tāl*. Each line of text consists of 16 *mātrās*, yet the text is set in the 14 *mātrā dhamār tāl*. In the first line (Example 8.8), the metre has been accommodated within the typical *dhamār bandiś* pattern of 4 + 3 + 4 + 3, with the first group constituting a *mukhṛā* (as in the *cautāl* examples above, the groups of three are split 2 + 1 with no syllable falling on the 2nd *mātrā* of the group). The text syllable to *tāl* correlation is as close as could be accomplished in setting a 16-*mātrā* verse metre in a 14-*mātrā tāl*.[15]

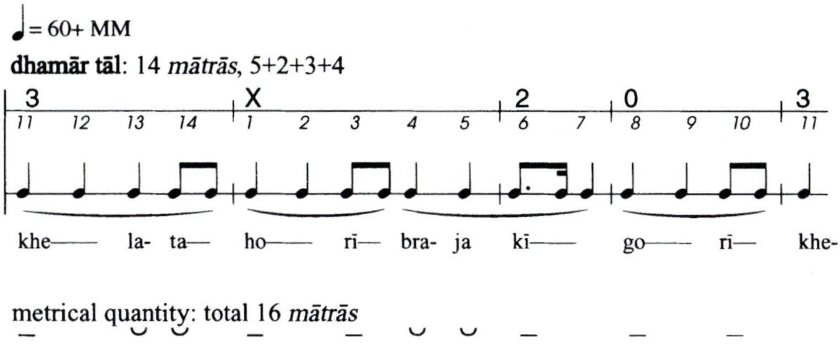

Example 8.8 An illustration of the setting of a 16-*mātrā* text line in *dhamār tāl*

These examples illustrate that in the syllabic settings of *dhrupad* and *dhamār* texts, some influence of poetic metre may be identified, albeit generally without a one-to-one correlation between text syllable length and musical duration. This influence is less than that observed in the temple tradition described by Snell, and may be indicative of the fact that in classical music the demands of musical structure override poetic considerations, whereas in temple singing the music is regarded primarily as a vehicle for expression of the text.

In other vocal genres such as *khyāl* and *ṭhumrī*, the musical considerations are yet more dominant, and the influence of verse metre is in most cases negligible. This is evident in the *choṭā khyāl* transcribed above in Example 8.3. In this example the text syllables are concentrated in the 5-*mātrā mukhṛā*. The verse is free of metrical restrictions, and the musical setting is not determined by syllabic quantity; the syllable of longest duration is the metrically short '*ṛa*' which falls on *sam* (see Example 8.9).

[14] Chaudhary also discusses the phenomenon of either using 3-syllable groups (*trikala*) or extending syllables (*karṣaṇa*) to produce long + short patterns in *dhrupad bandiśes* (1997 : 425–6). She speculates that it may have originated in order to make *tigun laykārī* (rhythmic variations in triple speed) easier; whether or not this is part of the cause, it is certainly an effect.

[15] This phenomenon is also noted by Chaudhary (1997 : 432–3).

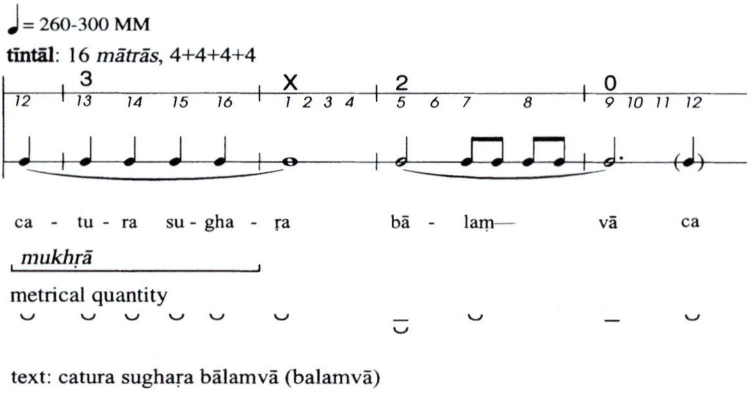

EXAMPLE **8.9** An illustration of the setting of a metrically free *khyāl bandiś*

Overall then, verse metre is not a major factor in determining the melodic rhythm of *bandiśes* in most genres. This lack of correlation between verse metre and *tāl* in most *khyāl bandiśes* is confirmed by the fact that the same text may often be set in more than one *tāl* (see for instance Wade 1984*a*: 14, 24 ff., and with respect to *ṭhumrīs* Manuel 1989 : 109–10). Some such influence may nonetheless be discerned in the settings of texts in music of syllabic rhythmic style, particularly *dhrupad-dhamār*. Another fact noticeable here is that breaks in melodic rhythm do not always correspond with word breaks. This suggests that the text is often made to fit an essentially predetermined melodic rhythm, rather than the melodic rhythm being derived from the metre. In *khyāl* the distribution of text syllables over the cycle is a significant factor; the concentration of text in the *mukhṛā* in Example 8.9 is typical of the genre, and is also observable—on a grander scale—in the *baṛā khyāl* illustrated in Example 8.5.

8.3 Rhythmic structure in instrumental *gats*

Instrumental compositions may be imitations or adaptations of vocal *bandiśes* (and this applies particularly to the repertoires of blown or bowed instruments such as the *bānsurī* and *sāraṅgī*), or else idiomatic pieces based on stroke patterns, called *gats*. Most *sitār* and *sarod* compositions may be classified as *gats*; in these pieces the stroke pattern is assigned a role analogous to the text of the vocal *bandiś*. Although there are only two main strokes or *bols* (da, the inward stroke on a *sitār* or the downward on a *sarod*; and ra, the outward or upward stroke), the patterns actually played (and recited) can be surprisingly complex. (The combined syllable diri (dir) is used to represent da followed by ra, usually at a faster speed than that prevailing for the single da or ra strokes; the same combination played so fast that the first sounds like an ornament to the second is spoken 'dra', and 'dotted' rhythms tend to come out as 'da -r'.

Most instrumental *gats* feature *mukhṛās*, and distribute the *bols* fairly evenly over the *tāl* cycle. The structures are therefore similar in principle to *dhamār* or *dhrupad bandiśes* which feature *mukhṛās*, or to the more syllabic *khyāls*. *Gats* may be divided into three classes according to tempo, as follows;

- *vilambit gats*; the overwhelming majority of which are in *tīntāl*, and based on the '*masītkhānī*' stroke pattern.
- *madhya lay gats*; which may be played in a number of *tāls* (e.g. *jhaptāl, rūpak tāl, tīntāl*), with a variety of possible structures.
- *drut gats*; most of which are in *tīntāl* or *ektāl*, many of the former based on the so-called '*razākhānī*' pattern.

These and other *gat* patterns are described below, and elsewhere by Allyn Miner (1993 : 180 ff.) and by Stephen Slawek (1987 : 54 ff.).

8.3.1 *Vilambit gats*

Most *vilambit gats* can be described as *masītkhānī gats*. The basic *masītkhānī* pattern has a 5-*mātrā mukhṛā*, and consists of a repeated 8-*mātrā* stroke sequence, as illustrated in Example 8.10. The strokes here are employed in ways comparable to the use of text syllables in the vocal *bandiśes* above. At medium tempi the settings are syllabic, with 'da' and 'ra' long and 'diri' short; at slower tempi melisma (*mīṇḍ*) is interpolated between strokes, in a manner comparable to the *vilambit khyāl* in Example 8.5.

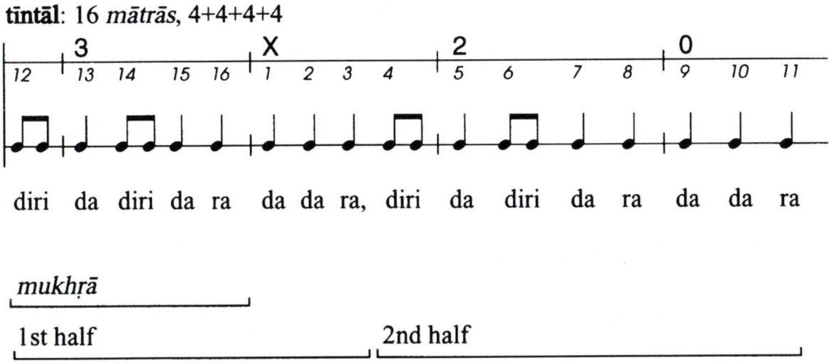

Example 8.10 The basic *masītkhānī gat* stroke pattern, in *tīntāl*

Although simple *masītkhānī gats* are played, following the standard *bol* pattern illustrated in Example 8.10 exactly, some elaboration is also common. Example 8.11 illustrates the *sthāyī* section of a *masītkhānī gat* which features some variation to the basic *bol* pattern in the *mukhṛā*. This example is quite typical in that the elaboration occurs principally (here, solely) in the form of additional strokes in the *mukhṛā* portion. The relationship between this kind of embellishment and the relatively high density of syllables in *khyāl mukhṛās* is noteworthy: as in *khyāl*, the effect here is to enhance the sense of repose—of the

Example 8.11 (Audio 12)

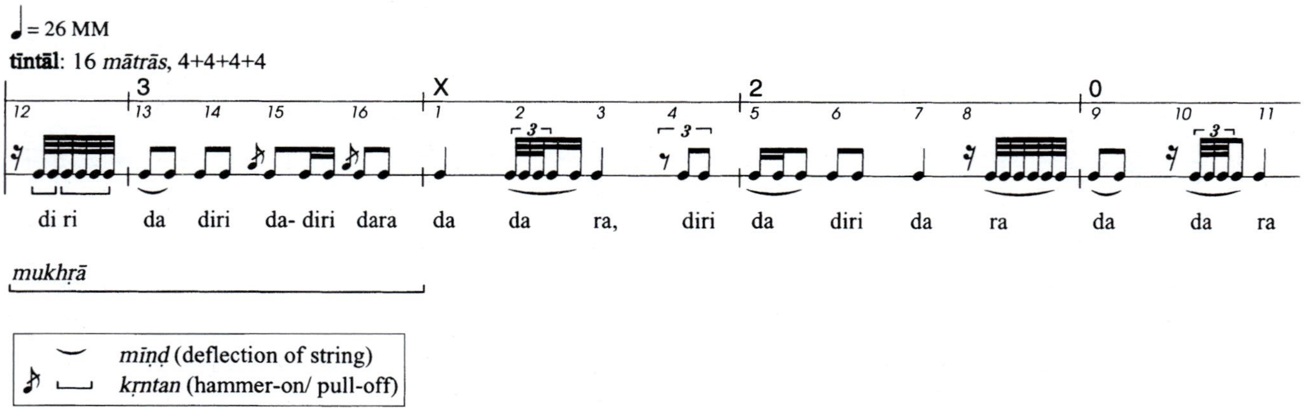

Example 8.11 A *vilambit gat* as played by Ravi Shankar (*sitār*) in *rāg gauḍ sāraṅg*, *tīntāl* (Audio Example 12)

release of tension—coinciding with the *sam*. Although the effect is similar, however, the process is somewhat different. In *vilambit gats*, the *mukhṛā* tends to be more highly embellished, whereas in *khyāl*, the anacrustic effect is preserved at low tempi by compressing the *mukhṛā* into (usually) between 1 and 2 *mātrās,* thus retaining a high rhythmic density. The *mukhrā* can be compressed in this way if the overall structure of the *bandiś* is of limited importance; in the *masītkhānī gat* this overall structure must be retained, therefore the anacrustic effect is preserved by embellishment rather than compression. The most stable parts of the pattern are *mātrās* 1–3, which usually emphasize a rest-tone (*viśrānti sthān*) of the *rāg*, thus highlighting the tension-relaxation alternation generated by the *gat* structure (see Example 8.12).

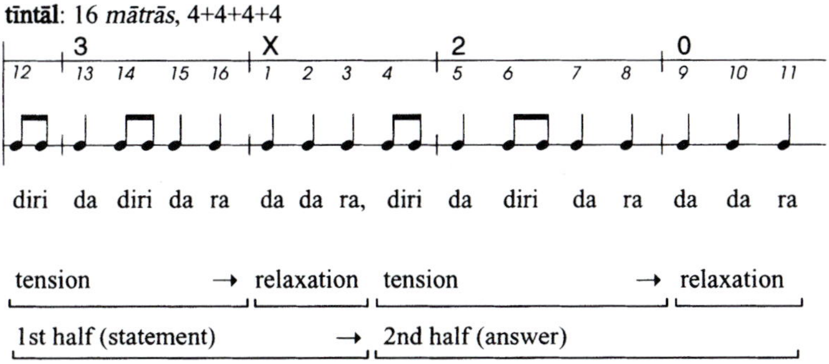

Example 8.12 An illustration of the binary alternation of tension and relaxation on two levels in the *masītkhānī gat* structure

The *masītkhānī gat* pattern realizes binary oppositions on two levels (see Example 8.12), besides featuring an anacrusis (the *mukhṛā*); it also overlaps the *tāl* structure, increasing the cadential and anacrustic propulsion towards *sam* (see Example 8.13 and Chapter 5). It is little wonder, given that it embodies so

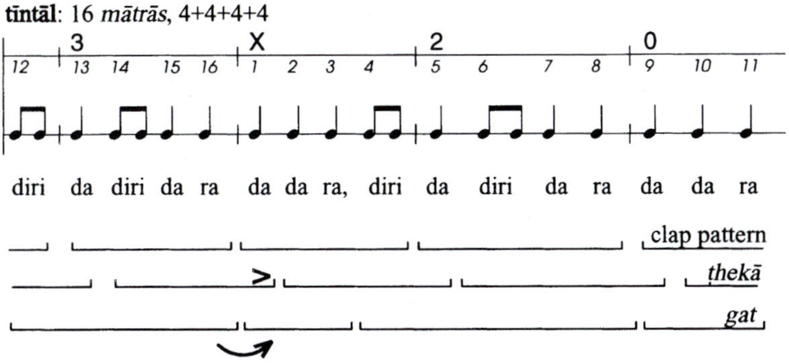

Example 8.13 Three overlapping structural divisions for the *masītkhānī gat*

many important principles of Indian rhythm, that this *gat* has achieved such predominance in the instrumental repertoire.

8.3.2 *Madhya lay gats*

Madhya lay (medium tempo) *gats* use a variety of patterns—with or without *mukhṛā*, syncopated or entirely commetric. In fact, since instrumental medium-tempo compositions are sometimes based on *khyāl bandiśes*, this is easily the most diverse area of the instrumental repertoire. The simplest varieties of *madhya lay gats* are based on *bol* patterns which express the divisional structure of the *tāl*.[16] For example, *jhaptāl gats* may be based on variants of the simplest expression of a 2 + 3 + 2 + 3 structure, as in Example 8.14.

jhaptāl: 10 *mātrās*, 2+3+2+3

X		2			0		3			X
da	ra	da	ra	da	da	ra	da	ra	da	da

Example 8.14 A simple *bol* pattern for a *jhaptāl gat*

The basic rule, as illustrated here, is that the 'da' stroke should fall on the accented beat (in this context, the first *mātrā* of each *vibhāg*).[17] This prototypical pattern is usually modified by one or both of the following processes; *bols* may be varied by doubling either 'da' or 'ra' to 'diri', and/or the final group of three *mātrās* may be divided into two equal segments. The bol for this $1\frac{1}{2}+1\frac{1}{2}$ group is usually 'da ra da ra', distributed in either of two ways (Example 8.15). There appears to be a functional equivalence between these two distributions (which applies in all *tāls* with similar 3-*mātrā* groups); they are completely interchangeable, and the rhythm actually heard is often somewhere between the two.

da – ra da – ra
da ra da ra

Example 8.15 Two methods of distributing the *bol* 'da ra da ra' over 3 *mātrās*

Space does not allow me to describe every variety of *madhya lay gat*, any more than it allows discussion of every type of *khyāl bandiś*, but a couple of examples are given below. The *gats* in Examples 8.16 and 8.17 both include *mukhṛās* of $2\frac{1}{2}$ *mātrās*: 8.16, set in *rūpak tāl*, extends over two cycles, whereas 8.17, in *jhaptāl*,

[16] Slawek quotes the well-known *sitārist* Lalmani Misra 'A common feature of the *kūṭ-bāj gat*-s [i.e. non-*tīntāl gats*] is that their *mizrāb-bol* patterns are usually governed by the divisions of the *tāl* in which they are composed' (1987:67). (The *mizrāb* is the wire plectrum with which the *sitār* is plucked.)

[17] In some cases accented strokes are played on the *sitār* using a technique called *ṭhoṅk* (lit. 'hammer'), where the 'da' is substituted by a 'ra' stroke in which the *mizrāb* (plectrum) follows through to clip the soundboard and *taraf* (sympathetic strings). In this case the *bol* would still be recited as 'da' however, and likewise would be transcribed in this work as 'da'.

lasts only for a single cycle. This type of *gat* seems to illustrate the influence of *khyāl bandiśes* on *madhya lay gats*.

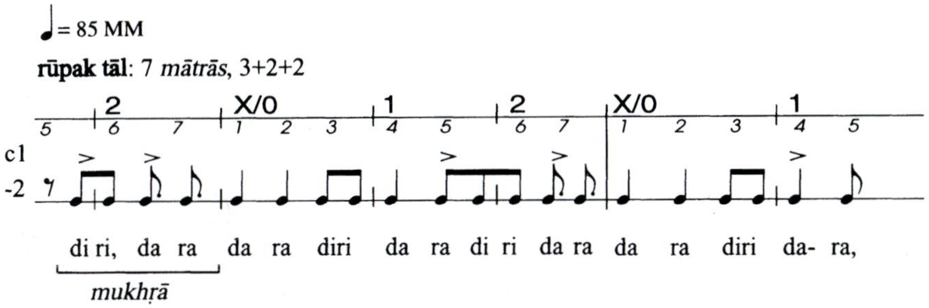

Example 8.16 A *madhya lay gat* as played by Deepak Choudhury (*sitār*) in *rāg tilak kāmod*, *rūpak tāl* (Audio Example 13)

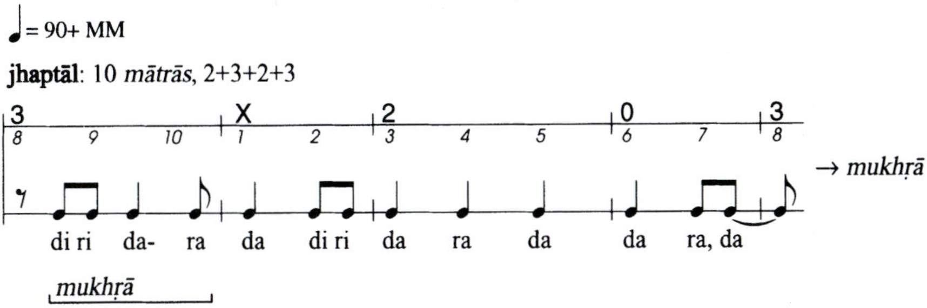

Example 8.17 A basic *bol* pattern for a *mukhṛā*-based *gat* as played by Deepak Choudhury in *rāg pūriyā*, *jhaptāl* (Audio Example 14 features this line played as an accompaniment to a *tablā* solo)

8.3.3 *Drut gats*

Drut gats also exist in a variety of different forms. One of the most common is the *tīntāl 'razākhānī' gat*, which starts from the 7th *mātrā* (and thus has a 10-*mātrā mukhṛā*). The basic *razākhānī* pattern is commonly taught as in Example 8.18. In practice this pattern may be varied considerably; Example 8.19 (from a

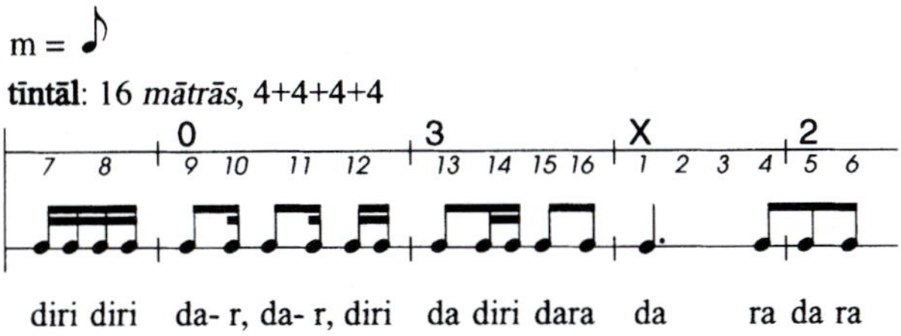

Example 8.18 The basic *razākhānī gat* stroke pattern, in *tīntāl*

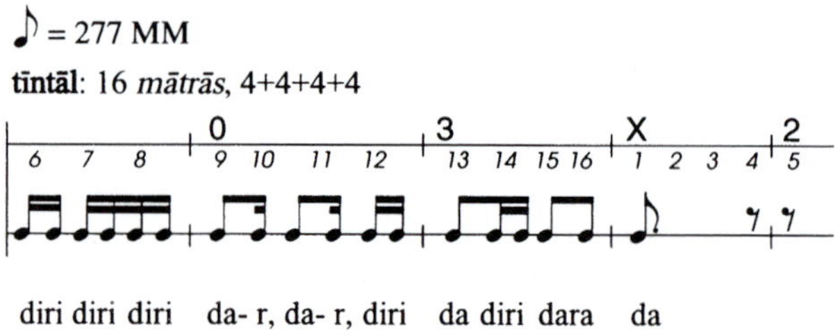

Example 8.19 The first line of a *razākhānī gat* as played by Amjad Ali Khan (*sarod*) in *rāg nandkauns*, *tīntāl* (Audio Example 15)

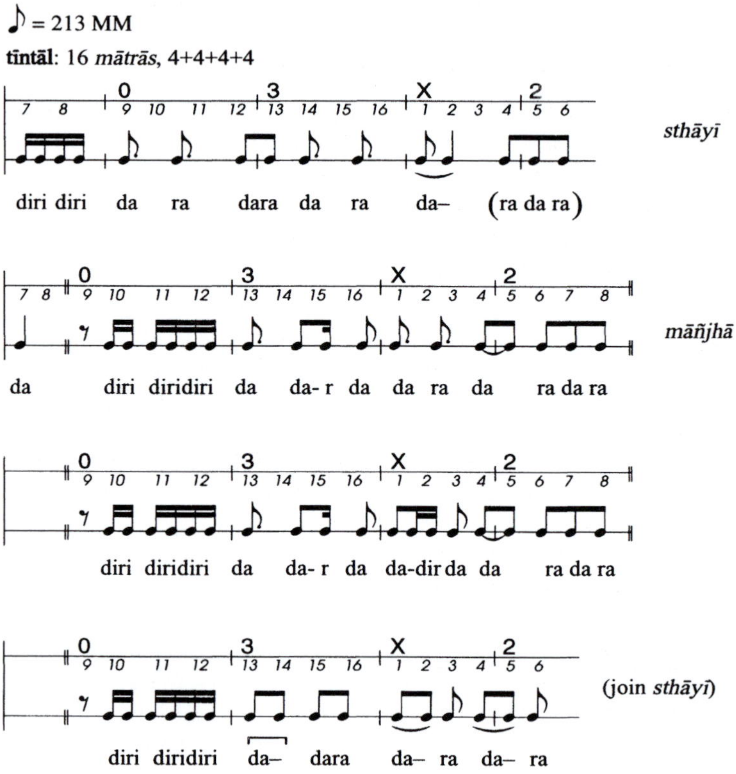

Example 8.20 The first two sections of a *razākhānī gat* as played by Manilal Nag (*sitār*) in *rāg jogkauns*, *tīntāl* (Audio Example 16 includes the *sthāyī* played three times, leading into the *mañjhā* and back to the *sthāyī*)

recording of *rāg nandkauns* by Amjad Ali Khan) illustrates a variant *razākhānī* pattern, in which the *mukhṛā* starts one *mātrā* earlier than the 'basic' pattern, and the part following *sam* is simplified to a single stroke. Another variant of the *razākhānī gat* is illustrated in Example 8.20, which is transcribed from a recording by Manilal Nag (*sitār*) of *rāg jogkauns*. In this case the traditional 10-beat *mukhṛā* is preserved, but the *vibhāg* immediately before *sam* is somewhat simplified. Many other variations may be encountered: artists evidently feel free to compose new variants to suit the particular *rāg* which they are playing.

Not all *drut gats* are *razākhānī gats*, although in practice the name is often used indiscriminately. Instrumentalists have created *drut gats* with an enormous variety of patterns—again, *sam* to *sam* or using *mukhṛās* of different lengths, essentially based on *bol* patterns but often incorporating a variety of left-hand, ornamental techniques (especially in the case of the *sitār*).

8.4 Further issues in *bandiś* structure

8.4.1 *Mukhṛās* in vocal and instrumental *bandiśes*

As I have shown, the *mukhṛā* is an extremely common feature of compositions in Hindustānī music, albeit not a universal one. The *mukhṛā* performs various tasks, helping the performer to generate a sense of upbeat resolving on the *sam*, as well as providing the option of a shorter refrain than the full line. The few examples I have been able to cite above have included *mukhṛās* of 8 *mātrās* (from *khālī* in *tīntāl*), 7, 5, 4, and 3 as well as 10 and 11 *mātrā mukhṛās* in fast *gats*.

Without wishing to over-generalize, it does appear that a particularly common species of *mukhṛā* provides a kind of 'double anacrusis', in the form of a short fragment which prepares the way for a longer portion which eventually leads to *sam*. It is notable for instance that a similarity exists between the *mukhṛās* of the *masītkhānī* and *razākhānī gats* (illustrated in Examples 8.10 and 8.18), and the *khyāl* illustrated in Example 8.3. The *masītkhānī* pattern uses a 5-*mātrā mukhṛā*, as does this *khyāl*, while the *razākhānī gat*, which is played at a faster tempo, has a 10 *mātrā* anacrusis. The relationship between the three is illustrated in Example 8.21.

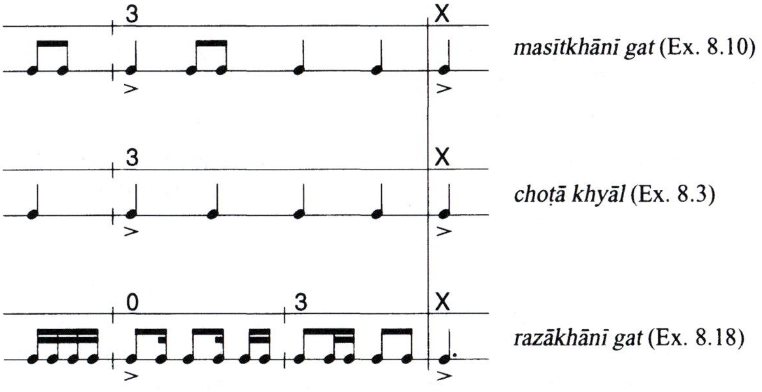

Example 8.21 A comparison of *mukhṛās* from compositions in three different genres

In each of these three instances a strong accent is felt on *sam*, and a weaker accent is generally felt four beats previously as well. This suggests that the first of the five *mātrās* (or the first two of ten in the latter case) acts as a mini-anacrusis, preparing for the next 4 (or 8).[18] It is not possible to say where this feature originated, but it does seem that in genres where the *mukhṛā* plays an important role in performance practice, a preference for five-beat patterns (divided $1+4$) is frequently observed.[19]

A related phenomenon may also be observed in *vilambit khyāl bandiśes*, where the *mukhṛā* generally retains a relatively high rhythmic density, and is compressed into a smaller portion of the *tāl* cycle. Two *vilambit khyāl mukhṛās* are illustrated in Example 8.22. The first is $1\frac{3}{4}$ *mātrās* long and the second, only $1\frac{3}{8}$ *mātrās*. *Vilambit khyāl mukhṛās* often occupy between one and two *mātrās*: the first part may prepare for the last full *mātrā*, in a manner similar to the five-beat patterns illustrated in Example 8.21.

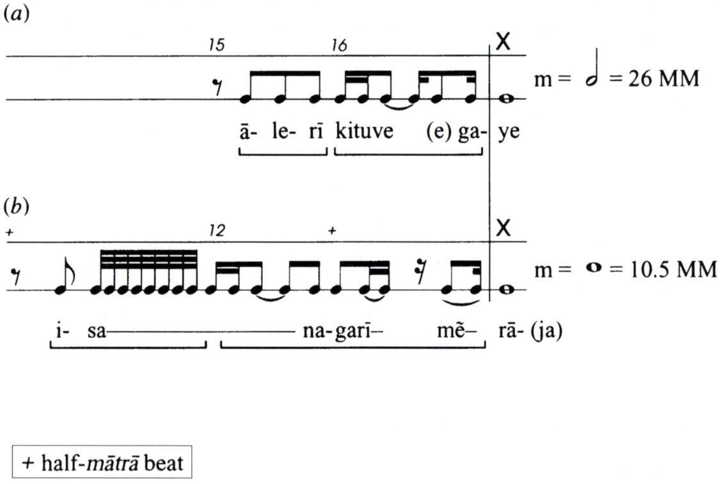

Example 8.22 A comparison of *mukhṛās* from two *vilambit khyāl bandiśes* (These can be heard as Audio Examples 17 and 18 respectively)

8.4.2 A note on the *antarā* and variation of structure between lines

My discussion up until now has concentrated mainly on *sthāyī* sections, since the *sthāyī* (and the first line in particular) is almost invariably the most prominent part of the *bandiś*. The *sthāyī* is generally repeated many times in a single performance, whereas the *antarā* and other sections are rarely heard more than once or twice. *Antarās* may however be analysed with reference to the same parameters employed above. A number of factors are noticeable in the compar-

[18] A view suggested to me by sitārist Deepak Choudhury (personal communication).

[19] A number of *dhrupads* also feature 5-*mātrā mukhṛās* (see the examples in Widdess 1981*a*: 162).

ison of *sthāyī* and *antarā* sections, since on occasions they do not share the same structure, and are in fact designed so as to be complementary or even contrasting.

In *dhrupad* and *dhamār bandiśes, antarā* sections generally follow the same structural principles as *sthāyīs,* although they may be distinct in detail. For instance if the melodic grouping of the first line is 3 3 3 3 (in *cautāl*), then subsequent lines (including the *antarā*) may either follow the same pattern, or change to 4 4 4 (or to some other division such as 2 4 3 3).

A more striking distinction may often be observed between the structural parameters of *khyāl sthāyīs* and *antarās.* Whereas almost all *sthāyīs* have *mukhṛās, antarās* may have either no *mukhṛā*, or a *mukhṛā* of different construction to that of the *sthāyī.* (Similarly, although some *dhrupad sthāyīs* have *mukhṛās,* the *antarās* generally do not.) *Khyāl antarās* also tend to have more syllables than those of *sthāyīs* sections, and the rhythmic style is consequently often more syllabic (although there is considerable variation in this respect between *khyāl* styles).[20] In *vilambit khyāl* the *antarā* is often not sung through, at least not in the form of a continuous setting of the *antarā* text line. What happens more often is that the *antarā* text is introduced into the improvised *bol ālāp*, as the melodic development reaches the upper Sa.

In *masītkhānī gats,* the *antarā* (and *mañjhā*) sections are based on the same stroke pattern as the *sthāyī. Drut gats,* in contrast, often use different patterns for each section (and often for each line) of the composition. Sometimes—as with *choṭā khyāl bandiśes*—these omit or modify the *mukhṛā.* Another distinction between *vilambit* and *drut gats* is that *vilambit gat antarās* are often improvised, whereas in *drut gats* they are generally pre-composed. To some extent therefore, the distinction between *choṭā* and *baṛā khyāl antarās* is matched by an analogous difference between those of *drut* and *vilambit gats.*

8.4.3 Variation of the *bandiś* structure

In most performances some degree of variation of the *bandiś* may be observed. Since the *bandiś* may therefore be slightly different on each repetition, it is often impossible to determine exactly what the true or basic form of the composition is. Although it is common for *bandiśes* to be notated, such notations do not specify a high level of detail, either melodic or rhythmic, and few musicians would regard notated versions as definitive.

Variations in performance may be primarily melodic (substituting alternative melodic movement, without changing text and rhythm), or rhythmic but superficial (e.g. slight variations in rubato or ornamentation, or the displacement of syllables off the beat). It is not uncommon, however, for other rhythmic parameters to change too; text distribution for example, or rhythmic density in instrumental *gats* where double strokes may be substituted for single.

[20] See Wade (1984*a*: 19). A similar point is made with respect to *madhya* and *antarā* sections of *ṭhumrī bandiśes* by Manuel (1989: 121).

Example 8.23 extends the example given above as 8.4*a*, the *khyāl* in *rāg toḍī* performed by Shruti Sadolikar, to show how the composition is deliberately varied. It is often impossible in such cases to separate tolerance of variation in composition structure from conscious manipulation of that structure: this example clearly moves into the latter, but it is not clear at what point. Here, Sadolikar's first 5 versions of the *bandiś* all feature a 3-*mātrā mukhṛā* and a relatively long note for the syllable 'kān-' on or just after *sam*. The remainder of the structure, not to mention details of melody, seem remarkably pliable.

Example 8.23 Variation of the *bandiś* in a performance of *rāg miyān kī toḍī* (*khyāl* in *tīntāl*), by Shruti Sadolikar (Audio Example 19)

Example 8.24 is an example from a *sitār* performance by Deepak Choudhury of *rāg bāgeśrī* in *jhaptāl*. This extract covers the first four cycles of a performance; it is fairly typical of medium tempo *gats* in performance. It consists of a *sthāyī* section in basically two parts—a single fixed line (c. 1–3) and a semi-improvised second line (or *mañjhā*, c. 4, repeated without variation in c. 5). This *gat* contains many variations, both melodic and rhythmic, so that it would be problematic to objectively determine an archetypal form on which the variations are based.

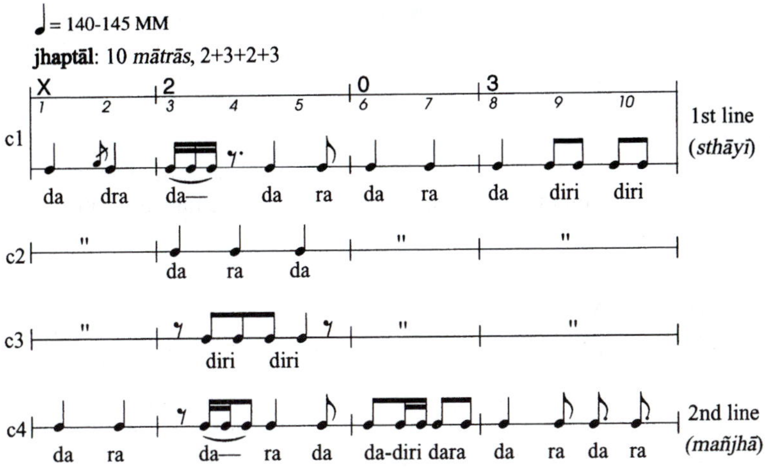

Example 8.24 A rhythmic transcription of a *madhya lay gat*, as performed by Deepak Choudhury in *rāg bāgeśrī, jhaptāl* (Audio Example 20)

In truth the form of such *gats* is somewhat fluid, as it is with many *khyāls*. The type and distribution of variations are in fact just as important in this context as the underlying structure. In Example 8.24, the rhythm in the second *vibhāg* is particularly susceptible to variation—that which is furthest from the *mukhṛā* in fact. Similarly in the *khyāl* in Example 8.23, the variations seem to indicate the importance of the *mukhṛā* and of the relative stability associated with *sam*; it seems less important exactly how the remainder of the syllables are distributed in the cycle. It seems more profitable to note this fact than to attempt to determine which version is 'correct'.

Despite the rhythmic variations, the basic structure of the *jhaptāl gat* in Example 8.24 is extremely simple, and these patterns must be seen as a selection from the infinite number of possible variations. The structure is based on the *tāl*'s 2 + 3 + 2 + 3 division, and there is no syncopation across these *vibhāg* divisions. It is therefore possible, and instructive, to consider the patterns as 2- and 3-*mātrā* 'modules'. These *bol* patterns are all variants of the basic 'da ra' and 'da ra da' patterns, derived according to one or more of the following processes.

- Syncopation (within the *vibhāg*); the displacement of strokes by half a *mātrā* (i.e. onto 'off-beats').
- Stroke doubling; 'da' or 'ra' become 'diri'. If redoubled, the stroke 'da ra' may become 'da-diri dara', performed in the same time.
- Splitting the group of 3 into halves (hemiola). 'da ra da' becomes 'da ra, da ra' (c. 4).

Analysing variation—what is varied (and what is constant), how much it is changed and in what ways—can reveal a good deal about the essential rhythmic structure of the *bandiś*, and the performer's style.

8.5 Summary

The *bandiś* plays an important role in the performance practice of North Indian *rāg* music. It constitutes a substantial proportion of the performance itself, besides providing material for the development that follows, and may be analysed with respect to a number of rhythmically significant parameters. These include *tāl*, *lay*, the length of the *bandiś*, the rhythmic structure as determined by melodic rhythm, variability of that structure, and text distribution. It is possible in principle to map correlations between these parameters, and between the *bandiś* structure as a whole and the variables of rhythmic style and organization.

Some of the most important observations made and illustrated in this chapter concern the implications of the rhythmic structure of compositions. The *mukhṛā* in particular is telling in a number of respects: the fact that *mukhṛās* often have a high rhythmic density relative to the remainder of *bandiśes* (something preserved and even enhanced by a variety of means in compositions which have been slowed down over time), together with the prevalence of 'double anacrusis' type *mukhṛās* strongly suggest the importance of the *mukhṛā* as preparation for the repose which is brought by the *sam*. The importance of these aspects for structure are emphasized further when patterns of variation are analysed, and it becomes clear that the parts of compositions around *sam* are relatively stable.

9

Development techniques and processes

9.1 Introduction

A rough distinction may be drawn in the post-*bandiś* phase of performance, between development with a strong rhythmic and/or textual component and that which focuses overwhelmingly on the presentation, variation, and embellishment of melodic material. The most important techniques are classified in this way in Table 9.1. Although it is not always possible clearly to distinguish between these categories, the latter, *rāg*-oriented development (*ālāp, vistār*) generally features a highly melismatic style, and a far less clearly defined *tāl*-surface rhythm relationship than other types of improvisation.

Analysis of melismatic *rāg* development must therefore employ a different set of premises from that of rhythm-oriented development. The latter may reasonably be analysed in terms of syllabic organization, *laykārī* techniques, and the relationship between surface rhythm and *tāl*. *Rāg*-oriented development has different terms of reference: here questions of rhythmic organization focus on the methods by which musicians achieve an impression of free rhythm while retaining awareness of the *tāl*, and on transitions from 'free rhythm' to the relatively syllabic *mukhṛā* refrain, and back again.

There is a degree of overlap and mutual influence between even these two broad categories; *rāg* development in apparently free rhythm may elide with a cadential (and more syllabic) *tihāī*, or overtly rhythmic development may incorporate elements of melisma and rubato. Even the most syllabic, rhythmic passages may be organized melodically so that the melodic range is gradually extended as it is in an *ālāp*. Indeed the term *vistār* (lit. 'expansion'), which I have used primarily to refer to *ālāp*-like *rāg* development in *nibaddh* sections, is sometimes used as a general term for all post-*bandiś* development. These

Table 9.1 Examples of terminology for stages in post-*bandiś* development

categories	vocal	instrumental
rāg-oriented	*ālāp* *bol ālāp* *bahlavā*	*vistār/baṛhat*
text/rhythm-oriented	*bol banāo* *bol bāṇṭ* *tān*	 *toḍā* *tān*

qualifications notwithstanding, I will apply the distinction between *rāg*-oriented (melismatic) and rhythm and/or text-oriented (syllabic) development in the following sections.

9.2 *Rāg*-oriented development

9.2.1 Vocal performance

In much *khyāl* singing (and *khyāl*-based instrumental styles), a more or less systematic *rāg* development can be heard within the *tāl*-bound section, akin to the unmetred *ālāp* of *dhrupad* and *dhrupad*-based instrumental styles. This *rāg* development (called *vistār*, *ālāp*, *ālapti*, or *baṛhat)* focuses on the expansion and variation of melodic material, and rhythmic constraints are subjugated to melodic considerations. Rhythm is not always clearly defined and nor is the *tāl*-surface rhythm relationship, so that *laykārī* as such has no relevance. Vocalists use '*ā*' or other vowels (called *ākār*), or else use text syllables in a melismatic fashion. Since the articulation points of notes are consequently often unclear, especially those falling within a melisma, it can be extremely difficult to analyse rhythm in 'syllabic' terms.

However, in a more general sense, these episodes can be seen in the context of the *tāl* and the various performance processes. The main parameters in analysis would be: the starting point of the episode; the duration of the episode (and the duration of individual phrases); the introduction of the *mukhṛā* and the attendant shift to a more syllabic rhythmic style; and the text distribution (in *bol ālāp*). Although the impression of free rhythm is often created, even the most melismatic *vistār* is rarely if ever completely 'uncoupled' from the *tāl*, although different singers show wide variation in the manner and degree of *tāl*-surface rhythm correlation. In most cases, some form of rhythmic organization may be traced, but a 'rhythmic' transcription is not always appropriate, and may not be necessary in order to understand the processes involved in performance.

Detailed rhythmic transcriptions may in many cases suggest a rhythmic complexity which is illusory—if (for instance) the salient fact about the articulation of a syllable is that it occurred shortly after a particular beat, rather than whether the delay is best indicated by a quaver, semiquaver, or dotted-quaver rest. Such transcriptions may nevertheless be useful, especially where they incorporate indications of text use. Example 9.1 is a rhythmic transcription of a portion of development from a *vilambit khyāl* performance, by Malikarjun Mansur in *rāg yemenī bilāval.*

This example is typical of much *vistār* in *baṛā khyāl* in that it blends melismatic *ālāp* with more syllabic fragments. The singer uses the *sthāyī* text throughout; the use of text in this instance is at some points comparable to that of *bol bāṇṭ* (see the example in Example 9.5 below), in others it is highly melismatic (this would be called *bol ālāp*). In fact, since the three longest melismas are sung to the vowel

text: ālerī kituve gaye logovā una (jay) sõ gaye the sukha pāyo re

bol ālāp: (ga)ye logovā

ālerī kituve gaye logovā una sõ gaye the sukha pāyo

ālerī,

ālerī kituve gaye

mukhṛā

Example 9.1 A rhythmic transcription of a portion of development, from a *khyāl* performance by Malikarjun Mansur of *rāg yemenī bilāval* in *tīntāl* (Audio Example 21 features this extract; the second singer Rajshekhar Mansur's contribution is not included in the transcription) '*ā*' (m. 3–4, 6–8, 14–15), there is little to distinguish these passages from *ākār ālāp*. Overall, this would generally be described simply as a passage of *bol ālāp*.

It is significant that the words '*logovā*' and '*ālerī*', which are treated melismatically in the first half of the cycle, both finish at the end of their respective *vibhāgs*. The fact that the episode seems to be structured in accordance with the *tāl* divisions suggests that the artist organized even this melismatic *ālāp* with a clear awareness of the *tāl*. This hypothesis is confirmed by other factors: displacement of syllables $\frac{1}{6}$- or $\frac{1}{8}$-*mātrā* off the beat occurs consistently in the early part of the *vibhāg*, and the syllables held for the longest time occur in mid-*vibhāg*.

A second example of *bol ālāp* is given in a schematic form as Example 9.2, which is an extract from a *khyāl* performance by Pandit Jasraj in *rāg miyān kī toḍī*. In Example 9.2 the tempo is considerably slower than in Ex. 9.1, giving a cycle of 69.6 secs. (12 *mātrās* of approximately 5.8 secs. each) in comparison with 38.4 secs. in Example 9.1. The structure of the episode is similar nonetheless: the longest pauses occur early in the first and second *vibhāgs* (just after *mātrās* 1 and 5), suggesting that the *vibhāg* division guides the artist's improvisation; phrases typically extend for upwards of 5 sec., up to a maximum of around 10 sec.—in my Example 9.1, most phrases range from 6 to 7 seconds in duration. In both

m = 10.4 MM

ektāl: 12 *mātrās*, 2+2+2+2+2+2

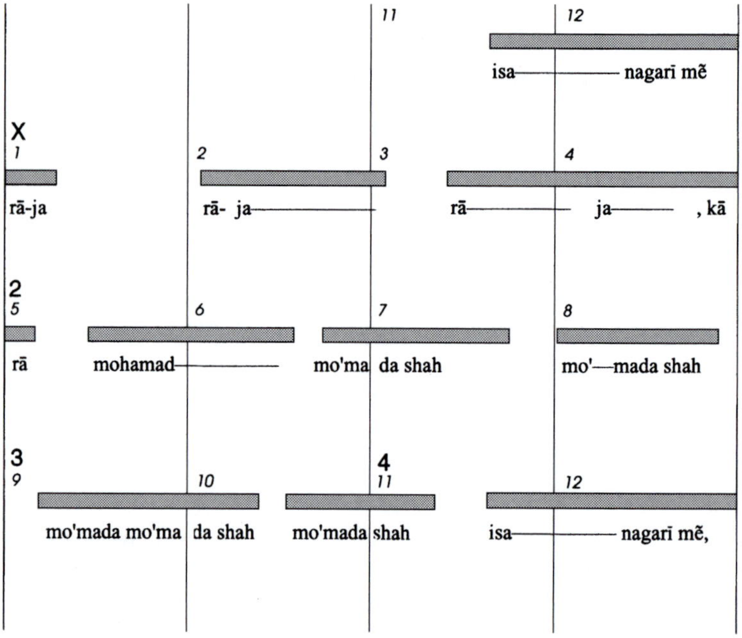

Example 9.2 A graphic representation of one cycle of *bol ālāp*, from a *khyāl* performance by Pandit Jasraj of *rāg miyān kī toḍī* in *ektāl* (Audio Example 22)

TABLE 9.2 Phrase lengths for two extracts of *bol ālāp*

Example 9.1		Example 9.2	
phrase	duration (secs.)	phrase	duration (secs.)
ālerī kituve gaye	**4.3**	**isa nagarī mẽ rāja**	**9.3**
(rest)	1.1	(rest)	5.0
logovā	**6.7**	**rāja**	**5.7**
	2.9		1.6
ālerī	**6.9**	**rāja karā**	**9.9**
	0.5		3.0
kituve gaye, logovā	**6.4**	**Mohammad**	**5.7**
	0.2		0.9
una sõ, gaye the	**2.2**	**Mohammad Shah**	**5.6**
	0.4		1.7
sukha pāyo, ālerī	**6.3**	**Mohammad Shah**	**5.3**
ālerī kituve gaye	**4.3**		1.3
		Mohammad Mohammad Shah	**7.9**
			1.0
		Mohammad Shah	**3.4**
			1.8
		isa nagarī mẽ rāja	**9.3**

Examples the density of text syllables gradually increases over the cycle. The *mukhṛā* in Example 9.2 is much more extended, however, around 8 seconds as against c. 2.7 secs. in Example 9.1. Table 9.2 compares phrase lengths for these two excerpts.

Aesthetically, the *khyāl* singer's art is often conceived in terms of achieving an apparently seamless flow of melody and rhythm, away from the *sam*, stretching out over the *tāl* cycle and flowing back effortlessly into the *mukhṛā*. This is how *khyāl* singer Veena Sahasrabuddhe expresses this intent.

The phrases used while improvising on a bandish must match the form and tempo of that bandish. The more the form and laya of the alaps matches those of the mukhra, the more seamless and perfect the avartan will appear. We are not talking here about simply starting the mukhra at the right point in the avartan so that sam is met. The perfect avartan maintains a close relation between the swaras and phrases of the alaps on the one hand and the progress of the theka on the other hand, so that the listener can feel the mukhra and sam coming. The end point appears so natural, so logical, that the listener is moved to giving out an immediate expression to her joy. This logic of relating to the tala bears the technical name amad.[1] (Sahasrabuddhe 1999 : 16)

It is possible to see some of the means by which this is achieved in my two examples: the division of the development into clear sections coinciding (more or

[1] *Āmad* (lit. 'approach, arrival') is also used as a technical term in drumming and *kathak* dance, where it describes an item of repertoire.

less) with the *tāl āvarts*; the careful balancing of melisma with sustained notes, and the gradual increase in density towards the end of the cycle in order to effect the transition into the *mukhṛā* (*āmad*), are all aspects of improvisation technique in *khyāl*. Although these brief examples of rhythmic analysis of music which is often taken to be free-rhythmic cannot hope to do justice to the variety and complexity of *khyāl vistār*, they nevertheless illustrate some important issues in analysis of *rāg*-oriented development. It is clear that analysis of text use and rhythmic style helps substantially in clarifying rhythmic organization.

9.2.2 Instrumental performance

Instrumental performance can be roughly divided into strictly *khyāl*-based forms and those built on *gats*. The former category includes principally the repertoires of the *bānsurī* (flute) and *sāraṅgī* (fiddle), instruments capable of considerable sustain, and (particularly in the case of the *sāraṅgī*) unlimited facility for pitch modulation, enabling them to replicate vocal performance to a considerable degree. The latter category includes principally the plucked string instruments *sitār* and *sarod*, and the hammered dulcimer *santūr*. Due to the high status of vocal performance in India, however, even on these instruments performers (with the help of instrument makers) go to considerable lengths to replicate vocal ornaments and glissandi. Many refer to this style of playing as the *gāyakī* (lit. 'vocal') style, in contrast to the less prestigious *gatkārī* (i.e. *gat*-based) style.

Although instrumentalists have been influenced by features of all the major vocal genres, one of the most pervasive manifestations of this is the attempted replication of *khyāl*-style *vistār*. Consequently it is not surprising that there are stylistic similarities between the early development episodes of a *vilambit gat* and those of a *baṛā khyāl*. There are also notable differences however, necessarily so given the relatively weak sustain of plucked instruments in comparison with the voice, and the distinct structures of the compositions (the fixed stroke patterns of the *gat*, as against the more loosely arranged text of the *khyāl*).

Example 9.3 illustrates a typical example of *vistār* from a *vilambit gat* performance by Deepak Choudhury in *rāg bhaṭiyār*.[2] This *vistār* may be interpreted as the interpolation of melismatic features into a fundamentally syllabic framework. A sense (an illusion perhaps) of free rhythm is created at times, through a combination of melisma, rubato, and syncopation. The example includes the first four cycles of the performance; the last two of these conclude with *tihāīs* (triple repetitions; see Chapter 10).

Despite the illusion of free rhythm, the artist remains aware of the *tāl* at all times, and rhythmic analysis reveals a clear structural foundation in a large proportion of *gat vistār*—a foundation on the *bol* pattern of the *gat* itself, or on the *tāl* structure. In the case of brief passages where such an underlying

[2] Slawek too makes the distinction between *rāg*-oriented and *laykārī*-oriented development (1987: e.g. 198).

Example 9.3 An extract of *gat sthāyī* and *vistār* from a performance of a *tīntāl vilambit gat* in *rāg bhaṭiyār* by Deepak Choudhury (Audio Example 23)

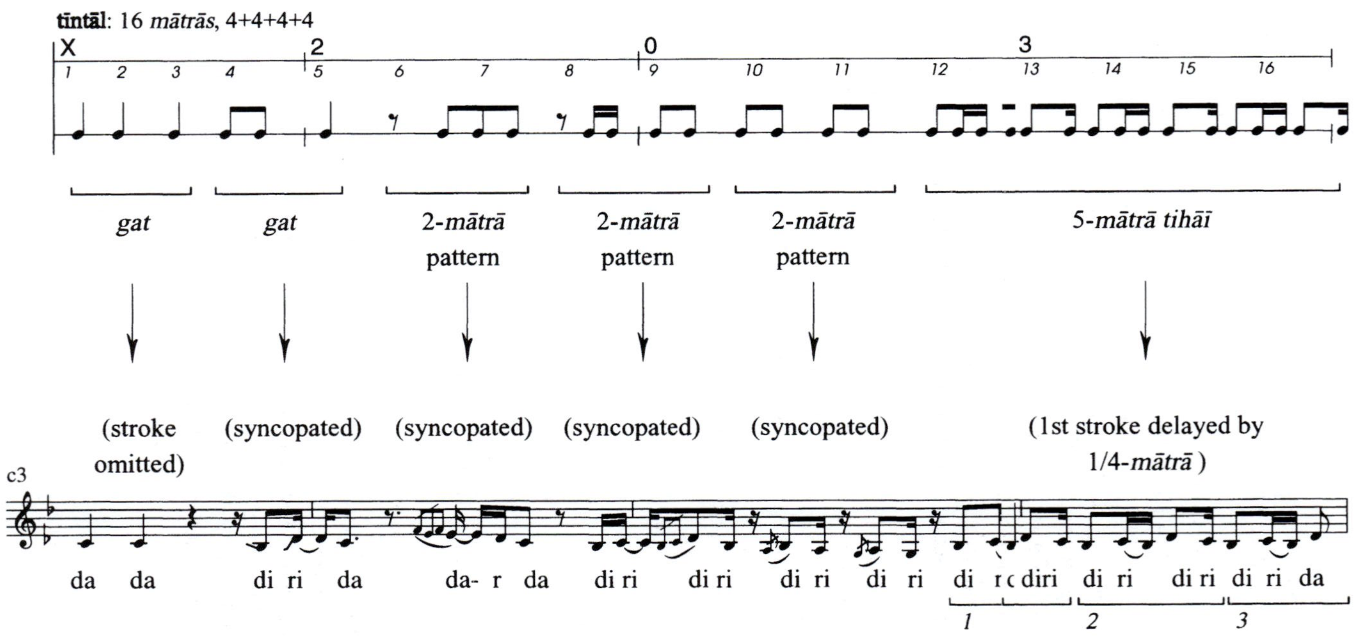

Example 9.4 An illustration of the derivation of the surface rhythm in *vistār* from *gat* and *tāl* structures

foundation cannot be clearly established, the most likely explanation is that the performer has freed himself temporarily from the restraint of the *tāl*, relying on either cues from the *ṭhekā* or his own 'instinct' to guide him back to *sam*. By instinct, I mean that with the experience of many years playing these *gats*, it is possible to develop a kind of dual perception of the music, following both *tāl* structure and improvisation simultaneously, while appearing to keep the latter free of the controlling metric structure. This facility is developed from an early stage in training, by means of counting exercises and a strict insistence on keeping a steady *lay* in practice; the ability to play in apparently free rhythm while retaining awareness of the *tāl* is its logical development.

My analysis of a single line from Example 9.3 is illustrated in Example 9.4. The rhythm of the first five *mātrās* is derived from the *gat* itself, and the last five *mātrās* are filled with a *tihāī*. The remaining six *mātrās* in the middle of the cycle (m.6–11) can be seen to be derived as syncopated variants of a set of three 2-*mātrā* patterns.

It is clear how important the *gat*'s *bol* pattern is, underlying a great deal of the subsequent development. Once firmly established, the *bol* pattern remains always in the performer's mind, both generating rhythmic structure and assisting time-keeping. A rigorously phonetic transcription[3] of such music would look extremely complex. However, once the principal structural features are recognized (cadential patterns, references to the *gat*'s *bol* pattern, *tihāīs* and so on), the underlying rhythmic structure is greatly clarified. Furthermore, on analysis of the *bol* patterns, it becomes clear that much of the apparently complex rhythm is generated by means of simple distortions (roughly speaking, rubato and syncopation)[4] of patterns derived according to syllabic principles from the *gat* and/or *tāl* structures.

9.3 Rhythm and/or text-oriented development

9.3.1 Vocal performance

In most genres other than *khyāl* (and indeed in some *khyāl* too), *ālāp* is either considered unnecessary or has already been completed in previous sections; thus most development is focused on text and/or rhythm. The melodic material of the *rāg* is of course ever-present, and on occasions rhythmic or textual variations may be combined with melodic development or embellishment, but where deliberate techniques of rhythmic and/or textual development are identified, we may justifiably focus on these in rhythmic analysis.

[3] The term 'phonetic' is used here in the same sense as by Hood (1971 : 55 ff.), denoting the indication of the maximum amount of rhythmic and melodic detail in a transcription.

[4] The term 'rubato' is used here in the sense suggested by Scholes; 'that type of flexibility which consists of a *"give and take" within a limited unit of the time-scheme*' (1991 : 894). Cf. the same author's definition of 'syncopation'; 'a displacement of either the beat or the normal accent of a piece of music' (1991 : 1002).

A wide variety of *laykārī* (rhythmic play) techniques may be identified, which will be dealt with in Chapter 10: this section will consider development techniques which focus on aspects of the variation of text or instrumental stroke patterns. It is the application of these techniques or processes that directly generates much rhythmic interest, besides providing a context for more explicitly rhythmic play. The most important categories are outlined here:

- breaking the text (generally into semantic units), in order to generate new rhythmic combinations; *bol bāṇṭ*.[5]
- expressive melodic development or melismatic elaboration employing the text; *bol banāo*.[6]
- fast runs (i.e. sequences of notes of equal rhythmic quantity at high rhythmic density), sung to text syllables; *bol tān*.
- imitation of any of these techniques, substituting *sargam* (solfège), *tarānā* syllables, or vowels for text syllables (*sargam tān*, *ākār tān*, etc.).

There are clearly overlaps between these different approaches to the text, and between each of them and the more *rāg*-oriented *bol ālāp*. The most obvious overlaps are between *bol ālāp* and *bol banāo*, and between *bol bāṇṭ* and *bol tān*. It is not always possible to objectively distinguish *rāg* development sung to text syllables (*bol ālāp*), from textual development using melismatic ornamentation (*bol banāo*); similarly at high rhythmic density *bol bāṇṭ* may resemble *bol tāns*. Although performers may have no doubt which term should be applied to their own singing, no single set of terms is consistently applied across the tradition as a whole.

If it is clear which process is intended, this is often because certain techniques are identified with particular genres. For example in *dhrupad*, improvised development (*upaj*) may be assigned to the *bol bāṇṭ* category, since *dhrupad* development is exclusively identified with that process—terms such as *tān* would never be used in this context. In modern *ṭhumrī* the primary process is *bol banāo*,[7] and terms such as *bāṇṭ* or *tān* would rarely if ever be used. In *choṭā khyāl* on the other hand, the text is rarely employed outside the *bandiś*, and *tāns* (especially *ākār tāns*) predominate.

Khyāl remains the most eclectic of North Indian vocal genres, and may use and combine any of the techniques described above (depending on the particular style and the *lay*). In analysis of *khyāl* it is often difficult for an observer to know exactly which terms best define the development style, but nevertheless an appreciation of these technical categories is invaluable.

The examples that follow illustrate the techniques described above. The first illustrates *bol bāṇṭ* in a *sādrā* performance (effectively a *jhaptāl dhrupad*); the second *ṭhumrī bol banāo*, and the third a succession of techniques (*sargam*-,

[5] Cf. Srivastav (1980 : 52).

[6] *Banāo*, as Manuel points out, has a range of meanings from 'formation' through to 'decoration' or 'embellishment' (1989 : 131-2).

[7] See Manuel (1989 : 105 ff.).

ākār-, and *bol tāns*) from a single *khyāl* performance. First the *bol bāṇṭ*; Example 9.5 shows how *dhrupad* singers repeat lines, phrases, or individual words of the *bandiś* text in *bol bāṇṭ*. The music is particularly syllabic, and illustrates how the surface rhythm is determined to a large extent by the use of the text. The episode, which is from K. G. Ginde's recording of *rāg khaṭ*, ends with a *tihāī*, in c. 37.

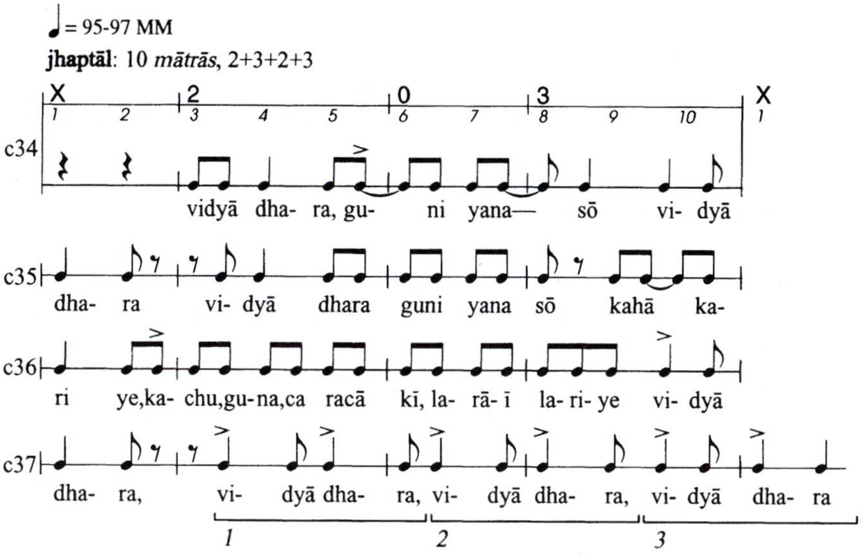

text: vidyādhara guniyana sō kahā kariye, kachu guna caracā kī larāī lariye

bol bāṇṭ: vidyādhara guniyana sō,
vidyādhara,
vidyādhara guniyana sō kahā kariye, kachu guna caracā kī larāī lariye
vidyādhara,
(vidyādhara) x 3

Example 9.5 A rhythmic transcription of a passage of *bol bāṇṭ*, from a *sādrā* performance by K. G. Ginde of *rāg khaṭ* in *jhaptāl* (Audio Example 24)

Example 9.6 illustrates a fragment of *ṭhumrī bol banāo*, from a performance by Munawar Ali Khan and Raza Ali Khan. Here too phrases and lines of text are repeated: however in contrast to the *dhrupad bol bāṇṭ*, the focus is on the melismatic ornamentation of that text. The setting is therefore not syllabic, and the surface rhythm is freer and not determined directly by the sung text.

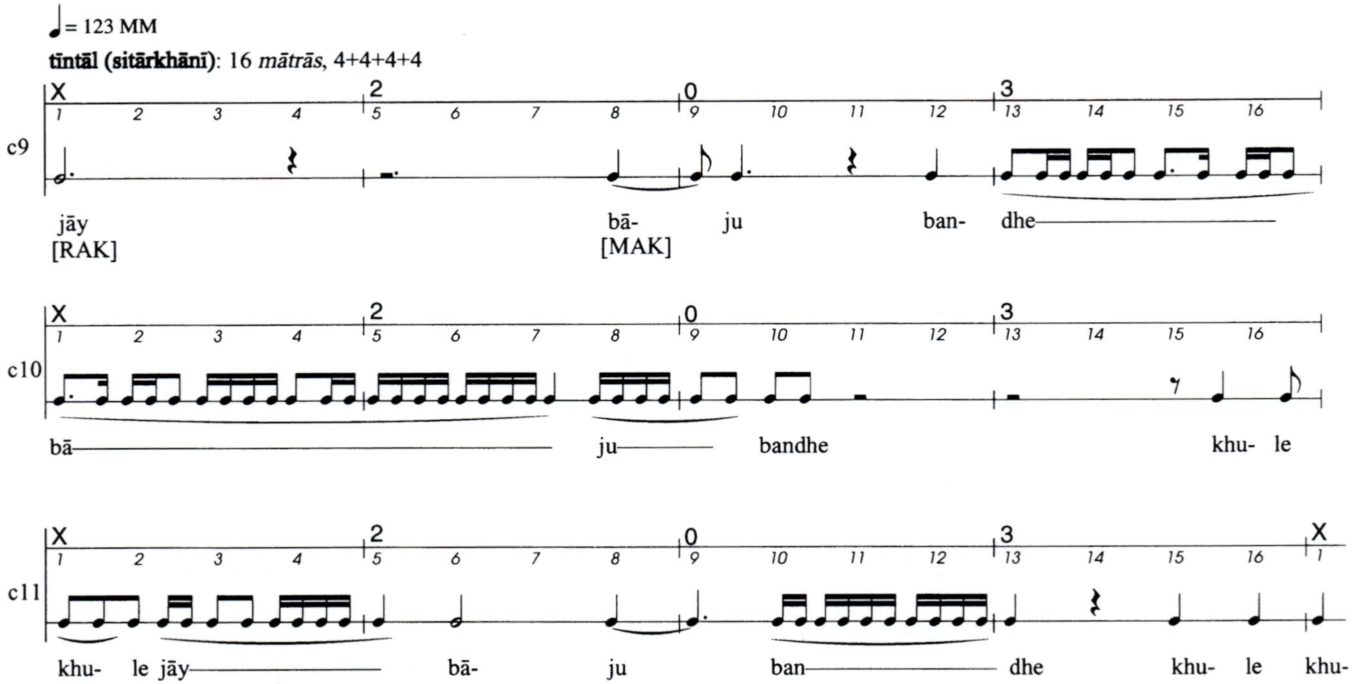

[MAK] Munawar Ali Khan
[RAK] Raza Ali Khan

text: bāju bandhe khule khule jāy
bol banāo: bāju bandhe
bāju bandhe khule khule jāy

EXAMPLE 9.6 A rhythmic transcription of a passage of *bol banāo*, from a *ṭhumrī* performance by Munawar Ali Khan of *rāg bhairavī* in *sitārkhānī tāl* (Audio Example 25 features this extract, followed by a little more from the performance)

Example 9.7 is taken from a medium tempo *khyāl* performance by Veena Sahasrabuddhe in *rāg śrī*. This example illustrates the varied nature of post-*vistār* development in much *khyāl*, especially at medium tempo. A *sargam tān* links, via the *mukhṛā*, to a restatement of the *bandiś sthāyī* (c. 76–80). This is followed by a sequence of short, fast *ākār tāns* (c. 83–5), then a longer and slightly slower *bol tān* (c. 86–7). The *bol tān* lies, in terms of rhythmic style, between the syllabic *bol bāṇṭ* and the melismatic *bol banāo*.

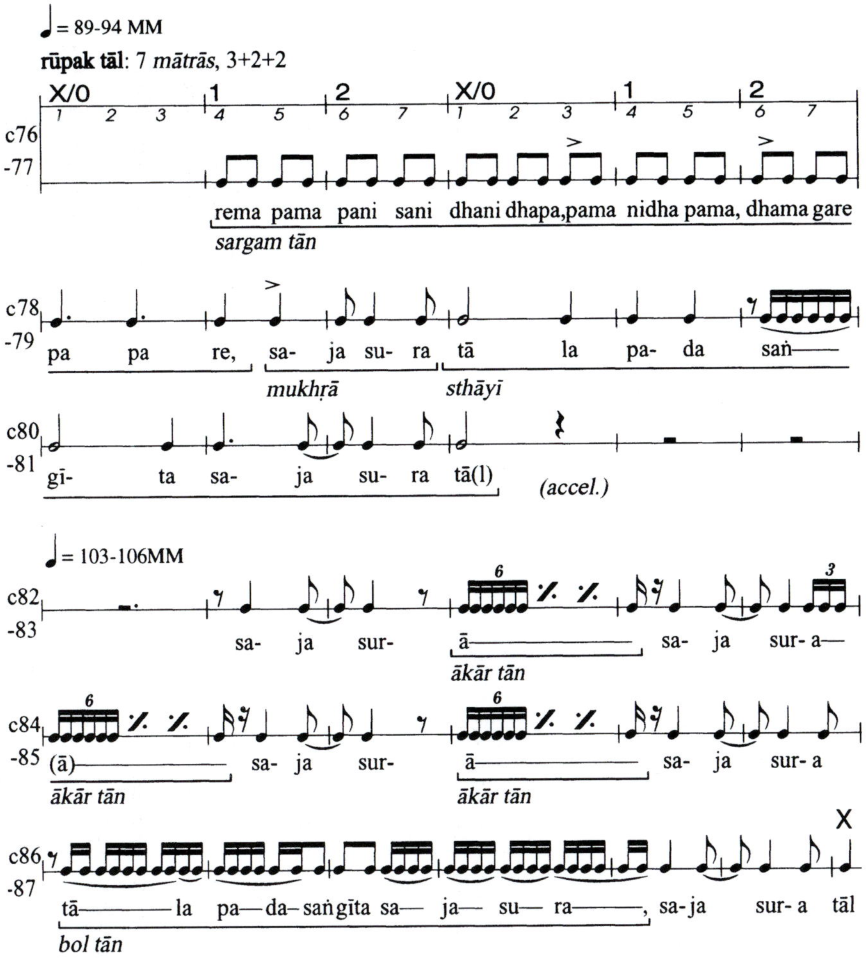

Example 9.7 A rhythmic transcription of a passage of development from a *khyāl* performance by Veena Sahasrabuddhe of *rāg śrī* in *rūpak tāl*, featuring *sargam-*, *ākār-* and *bol tāns* (Audio Example 26)

These three examples illustrate some of the most important post-*vistār* development techniques in vocal music. They are relatively clear-cut illustrations of these techniques; it is not feasible to demonstrate here the variability of their application, the overlaps between and blending of the techniques, or indeed the differences between various singing styles.

The point clarified by the comparison between Examples 9.5–9.7 is that development in vocal genres is largely defined by two parameters—text use and rhythmic style. Any piece of singing uses either the text, *ākār*, *sargam*, *nom-tom*, or other syllables to articulate the melody; the rhythmic style largely determines whether the development may be described as *ālāp*, *bāṇṭ*, *banāo*, or *tān*. This rhythmic style itself is determined by a number of factors, of which the most important is the relation of text (or other) syllable to the articulation of notes, which lies on a syllabic-melismatic continuum. Other factors such as rubato, syncopation, and so on are unlikely to affect the definition of techniques in this context.

Moreover, since unlike text use, rhythmic style cannot be easily and objectively described, the definitions of these categories (*bāṇṭ*, *tān*, etc.) vary between musicians, as do the distinctions between categories. This also confirms that definitions of development techniques cause as many problems as they solve in analysis, and although it is important to be aware of these categories, one must also be prepared to resolve development techniques into rhythmic parameters.

9.3.2 Instrumental performance

Instrumental development techniques can be even harder to define, without the information provided by the text use. They may also be defined by rhythmic style, however, and by a number of other factors. Many types of vocal technique may be imitated on instruments; in the case of plucked instruments, *bols* (strokes) replace the text syllables in function. The terms *bol bāṇṭ*, *bol banāo*, and *bol tān* are not generally used for instrumental music: however in instrumental *gats* a process somewhat analogous to *bol bāṇṭ* occurs, in which the material of the *gat* is broken up, rearranged and developed (called *toḍā*). Fast runs are called *tāns*, in instrumental as in vocal music.

One important difference between vocal and instrumental development is that neither can the latter be defined by text use, nor is it either generated or limited by that factor. Thus the logic of instrumental development tends to be more explicitly the logic of rhythmic variation *per se*. Moreover rhythmic techniques such as stroke doubling are more easily effected, since the soloist does not have to find text syllables with which to articulate the new notes thus generated.

Again, instrumentalists display a great variety of rhythmic patterns, which are perhaps even harder to classify than those of vocal performance, given the absence of textual clues. Two terms which are widely used, however, are *toḍā*, referring to passages combining single and double strokes, and *tān*, fast runs based on the model of *khyāl* performance. Example 9.8, which is from a performance by Deepak Choudhury in *rāg bāgeśrī*, illustrates a typical combination of *toḍā* with a *tihāī*, set in *jhaptāl*.

The *tihāī*

is of a common type in which the accented stroke of the pattern (the third) falls on *khālī* in the first repetition, and on *sam* in the third.

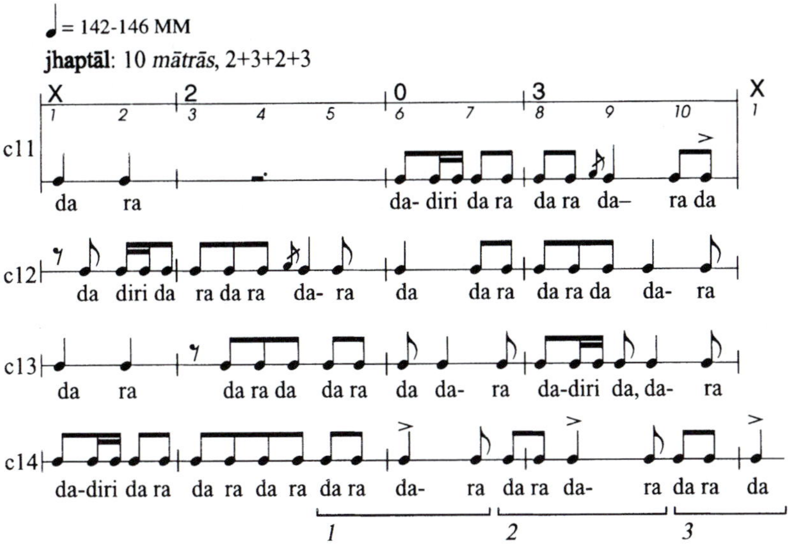

Example 9.8 An extract from a performance by Deepak Choudhury of *rāg bāgeśrī* in *jhaptāl* (Audio Example 27)

Audio tracks 28 and 29 illustrate the use of *tāns* in instrumental performance. Track 28 is taken from a performance by Amjad Ali Khan in *rāg brindābanī sāraṅg, vilambit tīntāl*; track 29 is extracted from a *sitār* performance of *rāg pūriyā kalyāṇ* in *drut tīntāl* by Budhaditya Mukherjee.

9.4 Summary

A loose distinction between *rāg*-oriented and rhythm-and/or text-oriented development is useful in discussing improvised development, since these two categories must be analysed with different terms of reference. However, in practice this notional boundary is often crossed, particularly in *khyāl* performance. In the latter category (rhythmic/textual development), a number of development techniques may be recognized, although once again the boundaries between them are not clear and one must frequently have recourse to analysis of rhythmic parameters. The main categories of development in vocal music are illustrated in Table 9.1: *ālāp*, the quasi-free rhythm exposition of the *rāg*; *bol banāo* and *bol bāṇṭ*, both defined as operations carried out on the text; and *tāns* of various kinds. The specific techniques used, and their progression, depends on genre and individual style.

Development in instrumental *gats* is generally underpinned by the syllabic structure of the composition. In *rāg* development, which may be intended as an imitation or adaptation of *khyāl vistār*, this structure is concealed by the use of melismatic ornamentation and syncopation, but nevertheless detectable. *Toḍā* describes a style of improvisation which exploits the rhythmic possibilities of simple stroke combinations, while *tāns* are faster runs based on the *khyāl* model. These stages are also illustrated in Table 9.1. *Vilambit gat* development tends to progress from melismatic *vistār* to *tāns*, in some traditions (such as that of the Maihar *gharānā*) making this transition through a gradual increase in the number of strokes per *mātrā* (*lay* ratio; as described in the following chapter).[8]

[8] This type of progression is referred to as *śṛnkhalā* or *silsilā* (lit. 'chain, sequence') (Slawek 1987 : 73).

10

Laykārī: rhythmic variation

10.1 The concept of *laykārī*

Any technique intended to vary or develop rhythm (as opposed to a technique of textual or melodic variation which indirectly determines rhythm), may be thought of as an aspect of '*laykārī*'—a word which has, like the related term *lay*, a variety of senses. The term *laykārī* is derived from *lay*, which (to summarize the discussion in Chapter 6) meant originally the space or rest between beats, and has come to mean both tempo and rhythmic density, and by extension become the closest equivalent of the English term 'rhythm'.

Laykārī has a similar, if not greater, semantic range. It means primarily either (*a*) the variation (usually increase) of *lay* ratio, or (*b*) the distortion of, or deviation from a steady beat (i.e. syncopation or rubato); both these senses derive from the roots *lay* + *kārī* ('doing, work').[1] By extension from these senses, *laykārī* describes (*c*) any technique dependent on or derived from the division of the *tāl* and variation of the speed level (i.e. cross-rhythmic accenting, permutation of rhythmic groups, and so on); and hence (*d*) rhythmic variation in general (this sense is analogous to the more general sense of *lay* itself).

Laykārī is an aspect of performance process in development, and should be understood in that context. Moreover since acceleration (of rhythmic density at least) is an important aspect of performance practice, *laykārī* as rhythmic variation is often dependent on the process of *laykārī* as increase in rhythmic density. Most aspects of *laykārī* are thus dependent at least conceptually on the idea of a *tāl* performed at steady tempo. *Laykārī* is not an alteration in the rate of succession of the *tāl*; one of its most important aspects is, on the contrary, the stepwise increase in rhythmic density relative to the *tāl*'s notionally stable tempo.

Belonging to the same conceptual apparatus is the idea that notes are dependent on syllables; and that those syllables may in principle be added, subtracted, multiplied, or permutated within the *tāl*'s metric framework. There is therefore a clear association between the division-based *laykārī* techniques I will describe below and syllabic style. These ideas may be traced back a long way in Indian musicological thought; they may also be demonstrated in much of the modern North Indian music discussed in this book. Although not all North Indian music operates according to these principles, division-based *laykārī* techniques are

[1] *Kārī* is defined as 'a suffix denoting performance of an act or a doer' (Chaturvedi and Tiwari 1986 : 132), or as 'doing, making, performing work' (McGregor 1993 : 192).

used in many genres, especially in *dhrupad-dhamār*, instrumental *gat,* and solo percussion and *kathak* dance repertoires. Many of the techniques described below are in fact more typical of South Indian than they are of Hindustānī music. They are however used increasingly in the latter, especially in modern instrumental styles, as North Indian musicians incorporate techniques from South India and from solo percussion repertoires (and thus perhaps indirectly from *kathak* dance).

In considering the various *laykārī* techniques, it is worth bearing in mind that the application of these techniques is constrained by absolute rhythmic density. *Laykārī* techniques are used to create interest in different ways in different contexts, depending on the rhythmic density. At low densities, interest is created by the combination of *bols*, by rhythmic variety, ornamentation, syncopation, and rubato. At higher densities, this is effected by speed itself, and by placement of accents (including cross-rhythmic accenting). Thus while *laykārī* may be understood in some cases as a process of acceleration, taking the music from low to high rhythmic densities, the techniques employed vary according to the stage reached within that progression.

The most important *laykārī* concepts involve, in brief:

- 'Divisive *laykārī*'; i.e. the variation of *lay* ratio,
- Rhythmic grouping and patterning,
- Ordering and manipulation of rhythmic groups; including repetition, permutation (*prastār*[2]), and 'shape' (*yati*[3]),
- Cadential techniques; especially varieties of *tihāī* (triple repetition).

10.2 Divisive *laykārī*: definition and variation of *lay* ratio

The most common usage of the term *laykārī* is to denote any type of rhythmic play involving a change in rhythmic density or *lay* ratio (thus for example, the density of notes may increase from 2 per *mātrā* to 3 per *mātrā*, the *lay* ratio from 2 : 1 to 3 : 1). Surface rhythm in North Indian music's most syllabic styles is dependent on a further division of the highest metrically significant level ('tactus' or 'beat')—typically the *mātrā*, but often a 4, 2, $\frac{1}{2}$ or $\frac{1}{4}$ *mātrā* pulse. The most common levels of division of this beat lie between 1 : 1 and 8 : 1 (although they may exceed this in exceptional circumstances). The range of divisions is limited by practical considerations—for example rhythmic density rarely exceeds 400 *bols*/min. in vocal music or 720 *bols*/min. in instrumental, due to physical limitations—and the choice of division depends partly on the degree of rhythmic complexity intended by the artist.

Such procedures may be considered from a number of different perspectives. First, the change in speed level (this level or ratio is itself often referred to as 'the *laykārī*' or 'the *lay*', but I have called it '*lay* ratio' in this work) implies a focus on

[2] Lit. 'spreading, extent'. [3] Lit. 'restraint, caesura'.

the rhythmic aspect of development, and tends to be accompanied by one or more rhythmic manipulation techniques; secondly it may be considered in the context of the widespread tendency to acceleration in Hindustānī music performance practice.

Thus the process of increasing the *lay* ratio by steps, with respect to a relatively stable tempo, not only constitutes rhythmic variation in itself; it is also one method of achieving the required increase in rhythmic density, and may provide the link between low density and high density development techniques. Thus, for example, in Maihar *gharānā* instrumental style the development of the *vilambit gat* generally includes a passage of stepped increases in *lay* ratio, which effectively links the low density, melismatic *vistār* with the high density, syllabic *tāns*.

The 'supra-metric' pulse level, generated by division of the *mātrā* and forming the basis of surface rhythm in *laykārī*, may be represented in dot notation form by a row of dots placed above the grid representing the metric structure, as in Example 10.1.

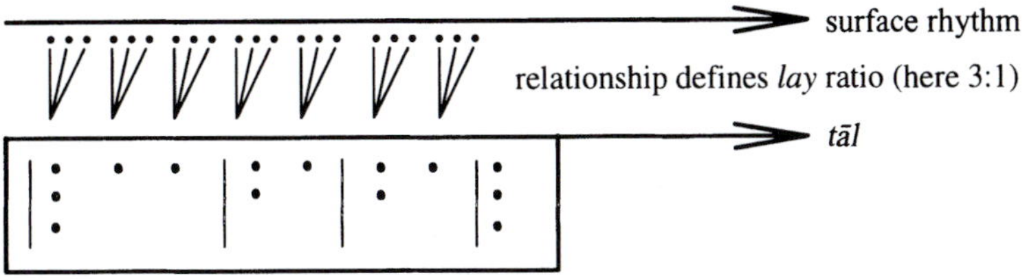

Example 10.1 An illustration of the relationship between *tāl* and surface rhythm in 'divisive *laykārī*'

10.2.1 Terminology

The terminology of *laykārī* is diverse, and can work in one of two ways. First, *laykārī* may be defined simply by the rate of subdivision of the beat, as in Table 10.1, column 2 (Gottlieb uses the term 'darja of lay', i.e. levels of *lay*, for these different divisions; see 1977 : 45). Most of these terms are everyday Hindī words for double, triple, and so on: '*dugun*', for example means double. In most cases '*dugun*' implies playing 2 notes per *mātrā*, although in fact *dugun* can mean one or more of three things: either 2 pulses per *mātrā*; 2 pulses per beat; or double the preceding density. These may amount to the same thing, but where they do not there is some potential for confusion.

Another way of reckoning *laykārī* is more qualitative, and involves classification of the rate of subdivision into multiples or fractions of either 3, 4, 5, 7, or 9;[4] this avoids the problem of confusion over the identity of the 'beat'. This quality

[4] Note that although a group of six may be regarded as the sum as two 3s, and eight of two 4s, nine belongs to a separate category, subdivided 4 + 5 (i.e. a grouping of three 3s would be regarded as a deviation from the norm).

is called the *jāti* (lit. 'class'), and there are five recognized *jātis*; *tryśara* or *tiśra* (division into multiples or fractions of 3), *caturaśra* (of 4), *khaṇḍa* (of 5), *miśra* (of 7), and *saṅkīrṇa* (of 9). This system of terminology is more common in South Indian music, but is also sometimes employed in the North Indian tradition. There is also a third way of naming *laykārīs,* according to a principle related to that of *jāti.* Here any binary subdivision is *barābar*, ternary subdivisions are *āṛ* (or *āṛī lay*[5]), quintal subdivisions are *kuāṛ* (*-ī lay*) and septimal *viāṛ* (*-ī lay*).[6] These terminologies are compared in Table 10.1.[7]

A *laykārī* may also have yet another type of designation, if the rhythmic pattern corresponds to the *chand* (accentual pattern) of another *tāl.* For instance, playing *jhaptāl* style phrases (grouped 2 3 2 3) against a *tīntāl* framework is called '*jhaptāl chand*', and similarly *ektāl*, *rūpak*, *dīpcandī*, and *dhamār chands* are recognized.[8]

TABLE 10.1 Three types of terminology describing division of the *tāl* in *laykārī*

	Laykārī terminology		
lay ratio	relative speed	*lay*	*jāti*
1:2	*thāh*	*barābar*	
3:4	*paunegun*	*āṛ*	*tiśra*
1:1	*ekgun,* thāh*	*barābar*	
5:4	*savāgun, savāī*	*kuāṛ*	*khaṇḍa*
3:2	*deṛhgun, deṛhī*	*āṛ*	*tiśra*
7:4	*paunedugun*	*viāṛ*	*miśra*
2:1	*dugun*	*barābar*	*caturaśra*
5:2	*aṛhāīgun*	*kuāṛ*	*khaṇḍa*
3:1	*tigun*	*āṛ*	*tiśra*
7:2	*sāṛhetigun*	*viāṛ*	*miśra*
4:1	*caugun*	*barābar*	*caturaśra*
5:1	*pāñcgun*	*kuāṛ*	*khaṇḍa*
6:1	*chegun*	*āṛ*	*tiśra*
7:1	*sātgun*	*viāṛ*	*miśra*
8:1	*āṭhgun*	*barābar*	*caturaśra*
9:1	*naugun*		*saṅkīrṇa*
12:1	*bārahgun*	(*mahā-*)*āṛ*	*tiśra*

* '*Ekgun*' according to Gottlieb: Srivastav gives *thāh* (lit. depth) for this category (1980 : 51).

[5] Some musicians take *āṛī lay* to mean, not 'triplet rhythm', but uneven rhythm without a simple mathematical relationship with the *tāl.* See Gottlieb (1977 : 204), and *viṣam*, below.

[6] Literally, *barābar* = 'even', *āṛ (āṛā)* = 'oblique', *ku-*= 'deficient', *vi-*= 'intensified' (Chaturvedi and Tiwari 1986).

[7] Gottlieb clarifies much of the terminological confusion. A similar chart appears in his work (1977 : 45).

[8] Kippen quotes Ustad Afaq Hussain, *tablā* player of the Lucknow *bāj*, giving four *chand* categories; *jhaptāl chand* (1, 2, or 4 *mātrās* into 5 parts), *dādrā chand* (into 6 parts), *rūpak chand* (7 parts) and *kaharvā chand* (8 parts) (1988 : 169–70). See also Ghosh (1968 : 66).

Not only are these sets of terminologies used, but so too are a handful of other terms. Thus a quintal division (*khaṇḍa jāti*) may be called '*jhampak*', and a septimal division (*miśra jāti*) '*jhūlnā*'.[9] The *Pañjāb tablā bāj* call one type of division into 7s '*gīt aṅg*',[10] while the Banaras *bāj* have yet more terms; Kishan Maharaj apparently uses '*kuāṛ*' for divisions of 9, in which case '*savāī*' is used in its place for 5s. Other Banaras terms include *baṛtha* for the division into 9s and *padma āṛ* or *divya saṅkīrṇa* for 11s.[11] Gottlieb also gives the following; *mahā-kuāṛ* (10 : 1) and *mahā-viāṛ* (14 : 1) (1977 : 44). Even *laykārīs* not listed here may be attempted, 5 : 3, 7 : 5, and so on, but they are so rare as not to warrant specific designations.

10.2.2 Usage

Divisive *laykārī* has an important role in acceleration and performance process in general, in several genres. These include *dhrupad, dhamār*, the more syllabic *khyāl* styles, instrumental *gat*, solo *tablā*, and *pakhāvaj* and *kathak* dance. Although overall, a wide variety of levels may be employed, in any single performance it is rare that one hears more than three or four different levels (e.g. 2 : 1, 3 : 1, and 4 : 1; or 2 : 1, 4 : 1, 6 : 1, and 8 : 1). Divisions into 5 or 7 parts (*khaṇḍa* and *miśra jātis*) are somewhat rare,[12] and those into 9 (*saṅkīrṇa jāti*) exceedingly so. The use of five or more levels in one performance is also somewhat unusual, although more common in instrumental than vocal music.

The performance schemes illustrated in Examples 10.2 and 10.3 highlight passages of divisive *laykārī*, and the different levels employed. The first (10.2) is taken from a *dhamār* performance by Bidur Mallik, and illustrates how the divisive *laykārī* is used to accelerate the rhythmic density dramatically against a relatively stable tempo. A similar process is illustrated in the *vilambit gat* performance illustrated in Example 10.3, which is from a recording by Ravi Shankar. The *lay* ratio increases from 6 : 1 to 12 : 1 while the tempo remains stable, then falls to a typical level of 8 : 1 for *tāns*, allowing the tempo itself to increase in the latter part of the performance.

[9] These terms from *dhrupad* singer Nimai Chand Boral, via Widdess (personal communication); *jhūlnā* is also mentioned in Gottlieb (1977 : 42). Note the phonetic similarity and possible etymological connection between the terms *jhampak* and *jhaptāl* (also sometimes *jhāṃptāl*), and between *jhūlnā* and *jhūmrā*.

[10] The *Pañjāb bāj* recognizes 2 different styles of *miśra jāti* (septuplet) rhythms; *gīt aṅg*, where one *mātrā* is divided into 7 equal parts with no *bakra* cross-rhythms, and *dīpcandī chand*, where the groups of 7 create cross-rhythms when set against groups of 4 or 8 *mātrās* (Gottlieb 1977 : 62, 82).

[11] See Gottlieb (1977 : 42–3).

[12] The use of *laykārīs* employing divisions of 5 and 7 particularly, has in some cases been influenced by the South Indian practice called '*gati (bheda)*' and '*naḍai svara*'. This is particularly true in the case of Maihar *gharānā* instrumental styles. Marcie Frishman writes of South Indian music 'The term gati or naḍai indicates the pulsing, ie. the number of mātrās in each akshara of an avart. There are five varieties of gati' (1985 : 12). (Note the different usage of terms in Karnatak music, where '*akṣara*' is the equivalent of the Hindustānī '*mātrā*', which is used here for the supra-metric pulse; North Indian music has no generally accepted term for the latter.) Cf. L. Shankar (1974 : 90), Brown (1965 : 13) and Sambamoorthy (1964 : 100).

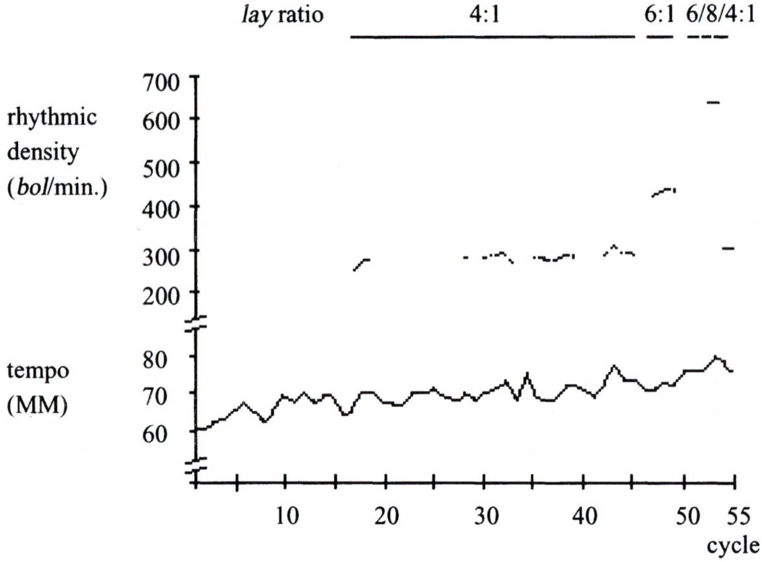

Example 10.2 An illustration of the role of 'divisive' *laykārī* in accelerating rhythmic density, from a *dhamār* performance by Bidur Mallik of *rāg jaijaivantī* in *dhamār tāl*

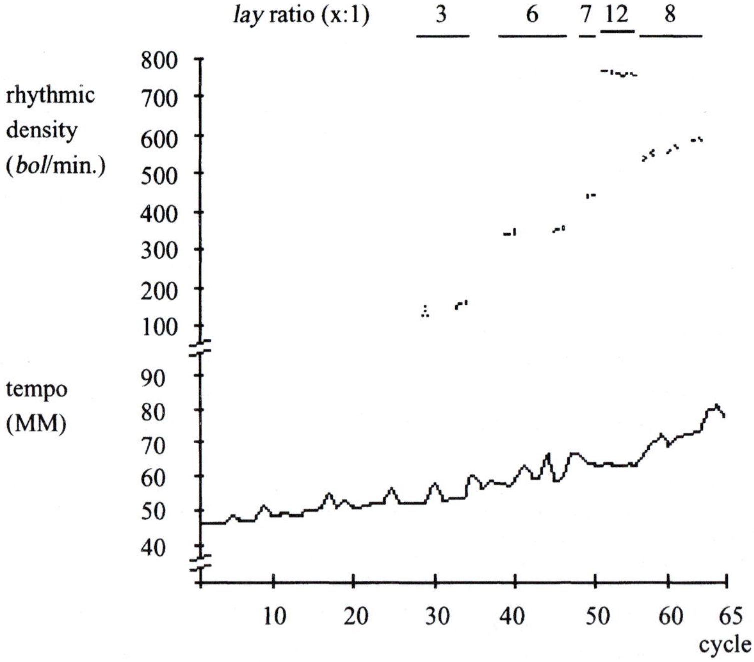

Example 10.3 An illustration of the role of 'divisive' *laykārī* in accelerating rhythmic density, from a *sitār vilambit gat* performance by Ravi Shankar of *rāg khamāj* in *tīntāl*

10.2.3 *Lay bāṇṭ*

Lay bāṇṭ is a special technique involving diminution of the *bandiś* to double, triple, and/or quadruple speed within an unchanging *tāl* structure.[13] It is extremely rare in practice, since it is really appropriate only to the syllabic *bandiś* structures encountered in *dhrupad*, yet the most famous *dhrupad* performers (namely the Dagar family) regard *lay bāṇṭ* as too contrived a technique to use in performance.[14] *Lay baṇṭ* is nevertheless heard on occasions, particularly in the singing of Darbhanga style *dhrupad* singers such as Bidur Mallik.

10.2.4 Rhythmic patterns and grouping structure

Techniques involving repetition and permutation are a common feature of *laykārī*, and these are all dependent on the establishment and recognition of rhythmic groups, patterns, and phrases.[15] All surface rhythm patterns may be analysed in terms of their grouping and phrase structure and the relationship of this to the metric framework. In the case of *laykārī* techniques, grouping structure is particularly amenable to analysis, particularly since this structure has generally been consciously generated by the performer with reference to the *tāl*.

The study of rhythmic patterns has always presented a problem in Western musicology, where the urge to devise a system enabling reduction of all rhythm to a finite number of primary patterns (analogous to the Greek system of poetic feet) has remained unfulfilled.[16] It is similarly inappropriate to attempt to devise such a classificatory system for Hindustānī music. Even if one were to limit oneself to rhythm built up of simple syllabic blocks whose place in the metric scheme is unambiguously defined, such a classification would be at best irrelevant to the real musical processes involved, since rhythm is rarely if ever conceived as a string of durable patterns.

In this context it is most profitable to look first at how and why rhythmic groups are formed, taking as a starting point the undifferentiated stream of pulses generated by the division of the *tāl*; then at how these groups may be combined into larger groups or phrases; and finally how the stream of pulses may be broken up by either rests or sustained notes on the one hand, or by further subdivision on the other, to produce more complex rhythmic patterns.

[13] Comparable to the South Indian technique of *trikāla(m)*, playing compositions or phrases at three speed levels. See L. Shankar (1974 : 98), Brown (1965 : 14), and Widdess (1977).

[14] Ritwik Sanyal (personal communication).

[15] The term 'group' is used here to refer to patterns of notes of equal length—usually 2, 3, or 4—which may be combined or transformed into longer and/or more complex 'phrases'.

[16] The best known of such attempts, which actually employed this Greek system of prosody, was that of Cooper and Meyer (1960). Many subsequent writers have criticized their method: see e.g. Lerdahl and Jackendoff (1983 : 26–7) and Kolinski (1973 : 495). As Yeston wrote more than 20 years ago, 'A theoretical basis for determining a finite number of primary rhythmic patterns such that any other design must be an aggregate of two or more of these patterns has never been adequately specified' (1976 : 12).

An assumption underlying my analytical approach is therefore that rhythmic patterns composed of notes or syllables of different lengths are best analysed not as the sum of different note values, but rather as the result of transformation of an undifferentiated rhythmic stream (by, for instance, doubling or omitting notes).

Western notation implies a succession of notes of various relative durations; Indian *sargam* notation is less precise rhythmically, and generally defines only the articulation point of a syllable, and the number of *mātrās* elapsing before the next such articulation. This reflects the fact that whether a note is prolonged or followed by rest is of secondary importance: the point at which the syllable is initiated (and therefore is related to the metric structure), is primary, and the rest or sustain which follows can be regarded as the non-articulation of the following pulse.[17]

Once a *lay* ratio has been decided—say 3 : 1—the next stage of rhythmic transformation is the definition of rhythmic groups. The human cognitive tendency to group subjectively any sequence of rhythmic impulses is well known, and that tendency is even greater when these impulses have been generated by division of *mātrās*; the conceptual organization of pulses into groups coinciding with the *mātrās* is a simple matter, and this forms in practice a kind of 'default' grouping structure in *laykārī* (Example 10.4).

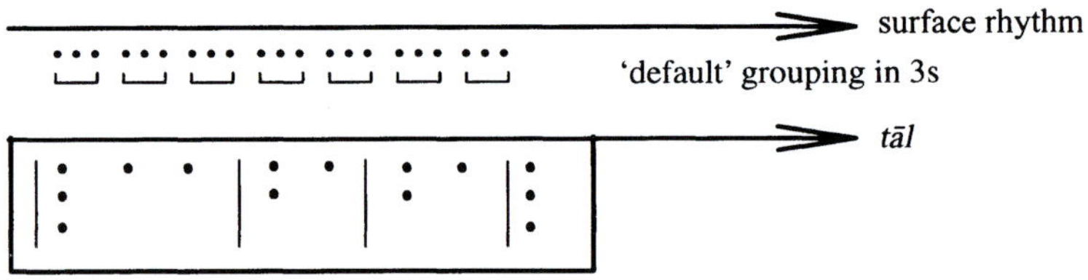

Example 10.4 An illustration of a 'default' grouping pattern for surface rhythm pulses in divisive *laykārī*

With grouping determined by the *mātrā* divisions (patterns derived in this way are described as *sīdhā*, lit. 'straight'), the place of dynamic accents in defining grouping structure is minimal, although they may be used to emphasize the fact that grouping follows the *mātrā* division. Accenting does play a far more important role in defining grouping where that grouping runs contrary to the *mātrā* division (called *vakra* or *bakra*, lit. 'crooked'): in this case the first element of each group is emphasized.[18] Thus if the 'default' grouping in 3s of the *tigun*

[17] Cf. Frishman on South Indian music 'A *kārvai* is a rest or a gap, also thought of as an unspoken syllable' (1985 : 15).

[18] This again seems to be determined by psychological factors: Mursell writes that when an accent is produced by intensity, it is perceived at the beginning of a 'unit group' (1937 : 172). He goes on to contrast dynamic with durational accents, where the lengthened note is perceived at the end of the group (many of my examples include just such a durational accent at the end of a group or phrase).

example (Ex. 10.4) is to be disrupted, this is conveyed either by dynamic accents (Example 10.5),[19] by word breaks or by melodic grouping.

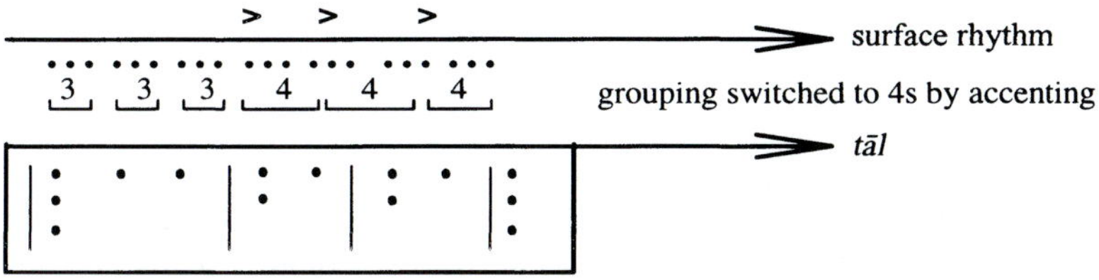

Example 10.5 An illustration of *bakra* (syncopated or contra-metric) grouping of surface rhythm pulses in divisive *laykārī*

In *laykārī* which employs division into 5, 7, or 9 parts, a subdivision of these pulses into 2 + 3, 3 + 4 (or 3 + 2 + 2), or 4 + 5 (or 4 + 2 + 3) respectively is implied by the *jāti* classification. Thus there is a strong tendency to subdivide a group of 5 into an iambic 2 + 3, with (where necessary, i.e. in contrametric patterns) a strong accent on the first and a weaker accent on the third pulse of the group. The subdivision may be reversed (i.e. to 3 + 2), but only for special effect, the iambic variety being much more common (Table 10.2).[20]

Table 10.2 *Jāti* groupings, and their implicit iambic subdivisions

no. in group	classification	subdivided
3	*tiśra jāti*	–
4	*caturaśra jāti*	(2 + 2)
5	*khaṇḍa jāti*	2 + 3
7	*miśra jāti*	3 + 4 (3 + 2 + 2)
9	*saṅkīrṇa jāti*	4 + 5 (4 + 2 + 3)

This suggests that any stream of rhythmic impulses will tend to be broken down ultimately into groups of 2, 3, or 4, although larger (subdivided) groups such as 5, 7, and 9 are also recognized. The tendency to subdivide seems to be partly dependent on speed; thus a 4-pulse group is acceptable at high speed, but slowed down it will tend to be divided into 2 + 2. This in turn suggests a two-tier organization; 2, 3, and 4-pulse units are added together to form longer 'phrases', and conversely larger groups are broken down into smaller subgroups of 2, 3, and 4 pulses. Example 10.6 illustrates just such a two-tier grouping structure.

[19] This process is recognized explicitly in South Indian music—see the examples given by L. Shankar (1974: 91 ff.).

[20] This preference for iambic patterns also applies to many *tāl* structures; for example *jhaptāl*'s 10 *mātrās* are grouped 2 + 3 + 2 + 3, not 3 + 2 + 3 + 2. This is not universally true: an example of the converse situation is found in Korean traditional music, where 'the lines of the melodic instruments invariably divide the quintuple meter into a group if three plus a group of two...' (Lee 1981: 121).

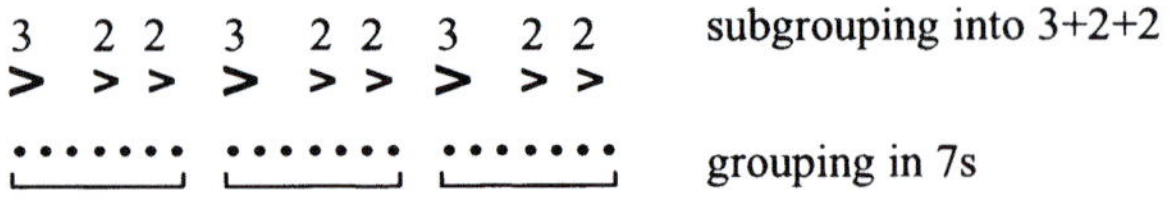

Example 10.6 An illustration of the subdivision of 7-pulse groups into a pattern of 3 + 2 + 2, generating a two-tier grouping structure

An interesting factor emerges in these cases: where a particular grouping structure is repeated, and that grouping is itself organized into a two-level hierarchical structure, the organization of surface rhythmic groups is in effect quasi-metric, and seems to follow principles shared with the structures of the *tāls* themselves, such as that of iambic subdivision. The logical implication of this is that it is possible for a *tablā* player actually to play the *ṭhekā* of one *tāl* within another *tāl*, simply by choosing the appropriate *laykārī* division. This is indeed something practised by many *tablā* players; moreover the use of repeated grouping patterns such as 3 + 2 + 2 or 2 + 3 + 2 + 3 in *laykārī* is referred to in the *tablā* repertoire as playing in a particular *chand*, and this *chand* is identified with the *tāl* which shares this grouping structure (see above).

10.3 Generation and variation of rhythmic patterns

Playing at any given *lay* ratio, a soloist has the option of playing phrases of any length within the cycle, divided by rests (unarticulated pulses) of any length; he may play a simple rhythmic pattern, consisting of notes of equal length; or he may leave some pulses unarticulated and/or subdivide others; he may play in groups according to the *mātrā* subdivision (*sīdhā*), or use means including dynamic accents to indicate a different grouping structure (*vakra*). Some possibilities which may be encountered in *tigun* (3 : 1) are illustrated in Example 10.7. Of these examples, (*a*) demonstrates a simple 'triplet' rhythm generated at 3 : 1 (*sīdhā*); (*b*) alters this grouping with a dynamic accent (*vakra*); (*c*) modifies the original pattern by means of further subdivision; and (*d*) sustains a note, leaving a pulse unarticulated.

Example 10.8 shows some of these processes at work in a piece of *khyāl bol bāṇṭ* in *tigun*, from a performance by Veena Sahasrabuddhe in *rāg śrī*. A grouping in 3s is adopted at the start, in each case with two syllables sung on the first and third of the group (in this instance the second pulse of the group is articulated with the vowel of the preceding syllable). This grouping shifts to the *vakra* 2 + 2 + 2 (from c. 106, m. 5); the concluding *tihāī* is sung in the original 2 + 1 grouping, but with the first note held rather than rearticulated with the vowel sound.

Example 10.9 again illustrates how a division of the *mātrā* is used as the basis of further manipulation, this time in a *dhrupad* performance by the Dagar Brothers. This episode appears to start in *caugun* (4 : 1), but settles down to

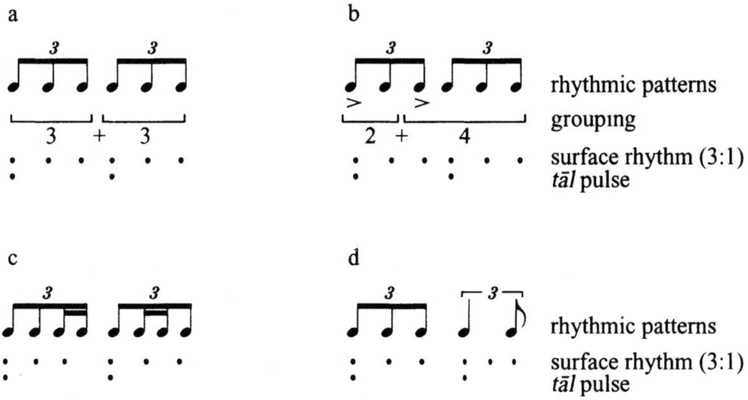

EXAMPLE 10.7 Various rhythmic patterns generated from a surface rhythm pulse at 3 : 1 (*tigun*)

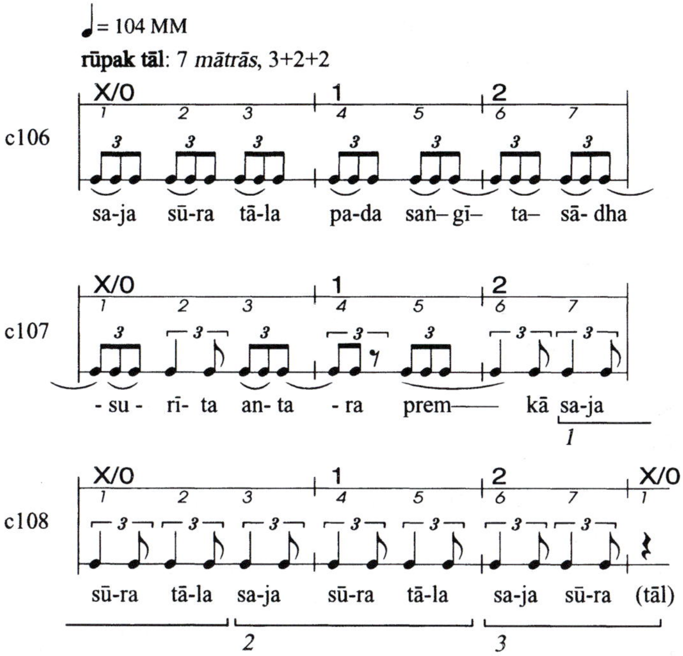

EXAMPLE 10.8 An illustration of *bol bāṇṭ* in *tigun*; from a *khyāl* performance by Veena Sahasrabuddhe of *rāg śrī* in *rūpak tāl* (Audio Example 30)

dugun (2 : 1) with occasional pulses subdivided. Besides this subdivision, frequent use is made of syncopation, indicated both by the dynamic accents and the word breaks. The integration of textual and rhythmic process in *dhrupad bol bāṇṭ* is apparent here.

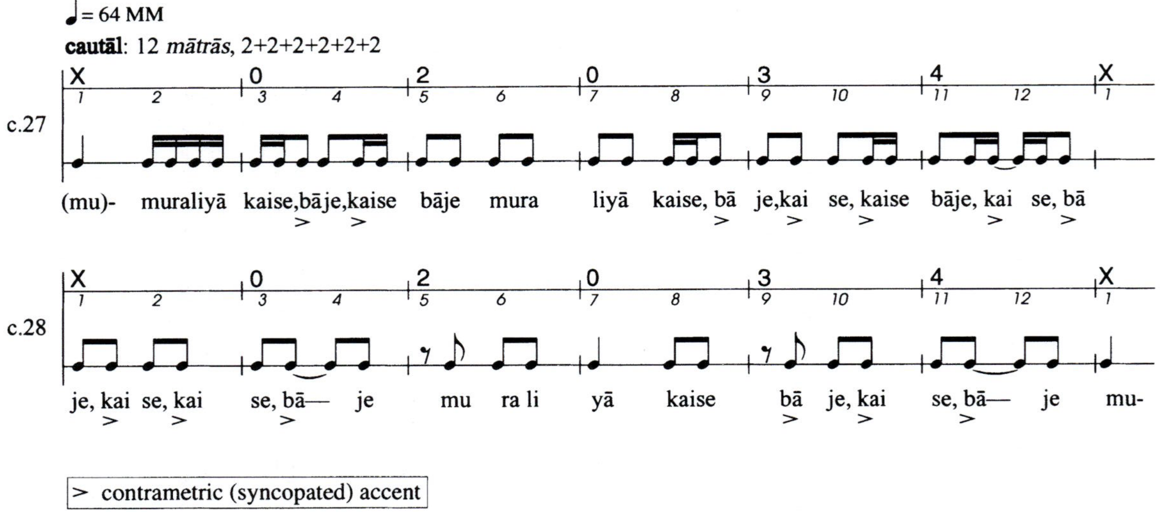

Example 10.9 An illustration of *bol bāṇṭ*. From a *dhrupad* performance by the Dagar Brothers of *rāg jaijaivantī* in *cautāl* (Audio Example 31)

Example 10.10 illustrates similar processes in an instrumental performance, in this case a *santūr* performance by Shiv Kumar Sharma. In this extract Sharma plays a simple 8-beat pattern (*a*), but these 8 'beats' occupy only 5 *mātrās* of the *tāl* (thus establishing the extremely rare *lay* ratio of 8 : 5). He varies this further by interpolating *tāns* in the first half of the cycle, retaining this ratio (*b*); and finally brings the passage of improvisation to a close by switching back to a 4 : 1 *lay* ratio and finishing with a *tihāī*. While this episode is unusually complex for instrumental performance (let alone vocal), this demonstrates the type and level of rhythmic complexity the system facilitates for the most accomplished performers.

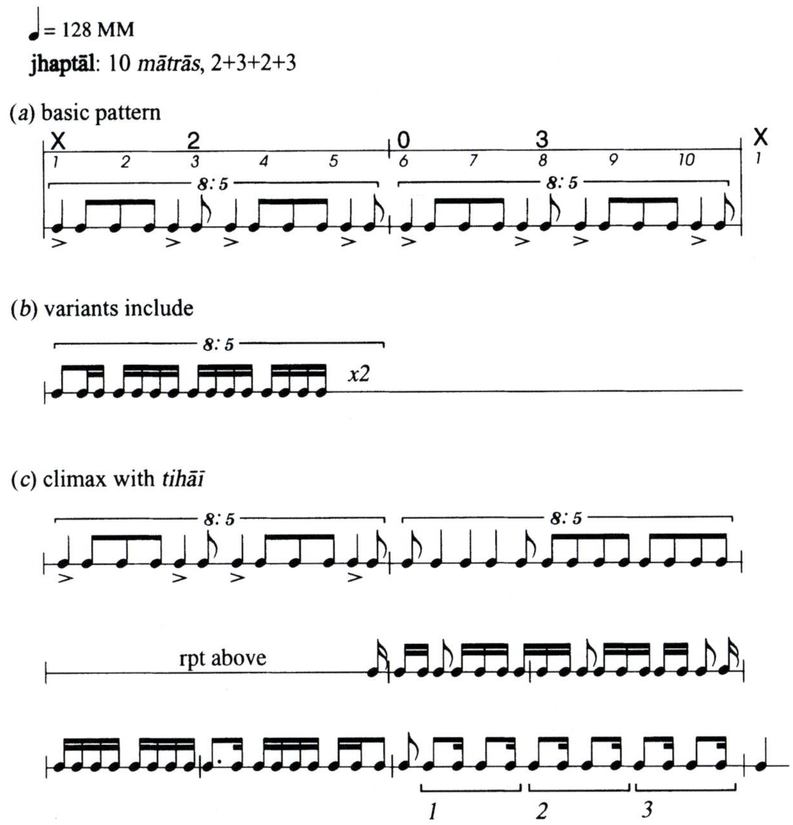

Example 10.10 An example of *laykārī*. From a performance by Shiv Kumar Sharma (*santūr*) in *rāg miān kī malhār*, *jhaptāl* (Audio Example 32)

10.3.1 Variation and development

In performance, rhythmic ideas may be varied and developed in a number of ways. For instance, having introduced a particular rhythmic pattern, the artist can carry out one of several operations on it, as illustrated in Example 10.11. Most of the principles of repetition (with or without expansion, contraction, change of *lay* or change to the off-beat) and rearrangement illustrated here have been explained above or are self-explanatory.[21] The last of these, *yati*, is less obvious, and deserves a short explanation.

10.3.2 *Yati*

Yati is an organizational concept, more familiar in South Indian music but nevertheless applied in some circumstances in the North Indian tradition. *Yati* is a principle according to which rhythmic phrases or other formal elements may be combined; for example with elements all of equal length, or arranged short–long–short, or in some other arrangement. In South Indian music the concept applies mainly to rhythmic phrases of different lengths (or to the classification of *tāl*, see Subramaniam 1995 : 73–5); in North Indian percussion repertoires it applies as commonly to phrases of different *lay*. A list of the six *yatis* according to South Indian tradition is given here as Table 10.3.[22]

These six classes of *yati* provide a tool for describing the arrangements of rhythmic phrases in South Indian music.[23] Two North Indian writers who have mentioned *yati* in the context of solo percussion repertoires are Pagaldas (1967 : 10–12) and Alkutkar (*c.*1960 : 10–11). Both define *yati* as the organization of phrases of a different *lay*, rather than length (the latter, according to Chaudhary, was the original meaning of the term; 1997 : 142–3); both give five classes, omitting *viṣama* (which is presumably redundant for their prescriptive purposes). The list in Table 10.4 is taken from Alkutkar.

Perhaps because North Indian music features fewer pre-composed rhythmic variations than South Indian, the place of *yati* in Hindustānī music is very limited. However it does have a place in the percussion repertoire, and also in

Table 10.3 Six classes of *yati*, interpreted as the organization of phrases of different length

yati	literal meaning	musical meaning
sama	equal	all elements equal length
viṣama	unequal	irregular arrangement of elements
gopuccha	cow's tail	elements arranged long to short
srotovaha	river	elements arranged short to long
mridaṅga	barrel drum	elements arranged short–long–short
ḍamaru	hourglass drum	elements arranged long–short–long

[21] Kippen lists the following 'methods of rearrangement' (for Lucknow *bāj tablā*): permutation of *bols*, substitution of *bols*, repetition of phrases, and introduction of gaps (1985 : 411 ff.).

[22] See Frishman 1985 : 13; Subramaniam 1995 : 73–5; and Sambamoorthy 1964 : 107 ff. *Yati* is one of the *tāla dasa prāṇa*, the 'ten vital breaths of tāl', often cited by South Indian theorists.

[23] See e.g. Wade (1984*b* : 42) and Brown (1965 : 14).

- repeat phrase (with or without change of melody or text)
- repeat the phrase with rhythmic variation (e.g. extended or reduced) (e.g. strokes doubled)
- repeat the phrase at different *lay* ratio
- repeat, changing the relationship with the *tāl* (e.g. shifting whole pattern to off-beat)
- repeat three times to produce a *tihāī*
- *prastār*: rearrange elements of phrase (e.g. change grouping of 322 to 223)
- arrange rhythmic groups according to principles of *yati*

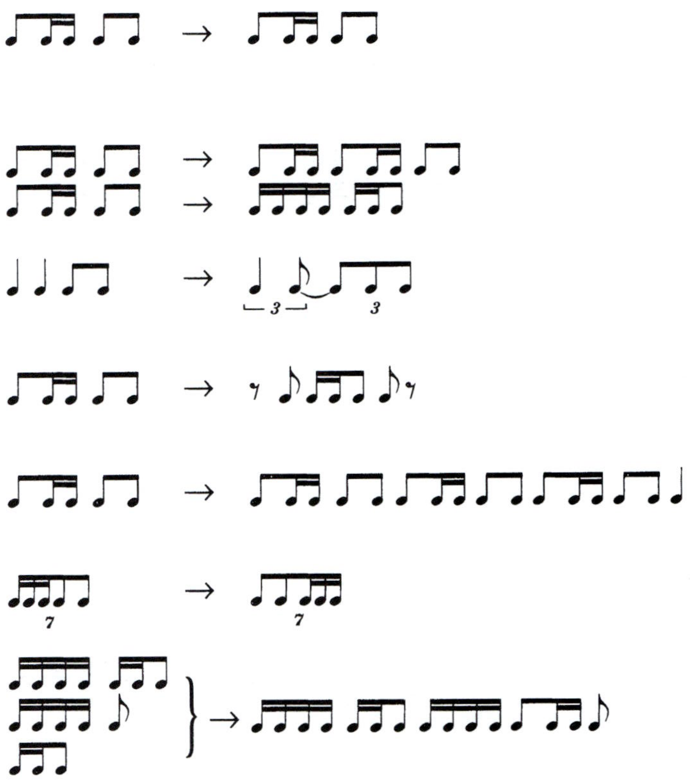

EXAMPLE **10.11** Examples of some of the most common processes by which rhythmic patterns are modified

Table 10.4 Five classes of *yati*, interpreted as the organization of phrases of different speed

yati	literal meaning	musical meaning
samā	equal	elements of equal *lay*
*śrotovahā**	river	elements arranged *vilambit* to *drut* (slow to fast)
mṛdaṅg	barrel drum	elements arranged *drut-vilambit-drut*
pipīlikā	ant	elements arranged *vilambit-drut-madhya*
gopucchā	cow's tail	elements arranged *drut-vilambit*

* Given as '*śrotogatā*' in Pagaldas (1967 : 10–12).

instrumental music to some extent, probably as a result of influence from South India and/or solo drumming. Example 10.12 is an example of this type, in which a simple phrase is played at *lay* ratios of 4 : 1, 3 : 1, and 2 : 1 against the *mātrā* pulse.

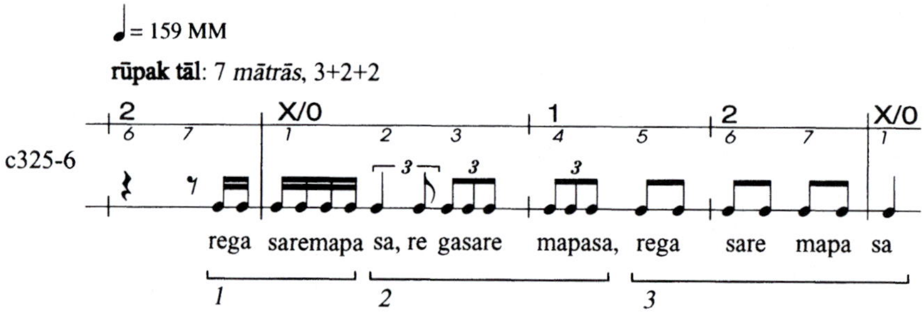

Example 10.12 An example of '*gopucchā yati*' (phrases arranged fast to slow), from a *madhya lay gat* performance by Deepak Choudhury of *rāg tilak kāmod* in *rūpak tāl* (Audio Example 33 illustrates three successive *tihāis*, of which this example is the last)

10.3.3 Cadential techniques

Since development in *nibaddh* forms is organized into episodes punctuated by refrains, cadential patterns often provide a link from improvised development back to the refrain. (They also—in melismatic styles—often help to re-establish the relationship of surface rhythm with the *tāl*.) A cadential pattern is in effect an anacrusis, which prepares the listener for the structurally important beat which follows. This may be achieved in a number of ways, for instance by an increased use of contrametric accents before *sam* (see e.g. Example 10.9, c. 28, m. 9–12). In some styles, performers simply use the *mukhṛā* as a cadence, and either end their improvisation before the *mukhṛā*, or perhaps elide with its start. Often, however, specialized cadential techniques are employed. The most common of these involve phrases played three times, which are called *tihāīs* (lit. 'one-third').[24]

[24] Also called *tīyā*.

10.3.4 *Tihāī*

A *tihāī* is a rhythmic phrase[25] played a total of three times, constructed so as to end on or just before a structurally important point in the *tāl* cycle (usually on *sam* or just before the *mukhṛā*). The *tihāī* in its simplest form is an exact triple repetition of melodic, textual, and rhythmic material. It is not uncommon in practice however, for one or more of these parameters to be varied (including the rhythmic group itself in improvised *tihāīs*, as the artist strives to ensure that the pattern will end at the correct point).

There is no limit to the length or complexity of a *tihāī*; for example they are used in different *lay* ratios, and may employ syncopation (a common variety features a shift of accents to the off-beat for the second element, returning to the beat on the third). The use or absence of rests between elements is also a factor—*tihāīs* with no rest between elements are called *bedam* (lit. 'without a breath'), those with rests are *damdār* (lit. 'with a breath'). The only limits are those imposed by the norms of performance practice of particular genres and styles, and particular musicians' technical facility.

Tihāīs are common in more syllabic styles, but a syllabic rhythmic style does not necessarily imply widespread use of *tihāīs*; for instance, many *dhrupad* singers use the *tihāī* quite sparingly. The *tihāī* is a common feature of percussion solos and of *kathak* dance: it is also particularly common in *horī dhamār*, some *dhrupad*, *khyāl*, and *tarānā* styles, and many instrumental *gat* styles.[26] A simple *tihāī* from a *sādrā* performance by K. G. Ginde is illustrated in Example 10.13; Example 10.14 features an almost identical instrumental *tihāī* from a performance by Nikhil Banerjee (*sitār*) in *rāg megh*.

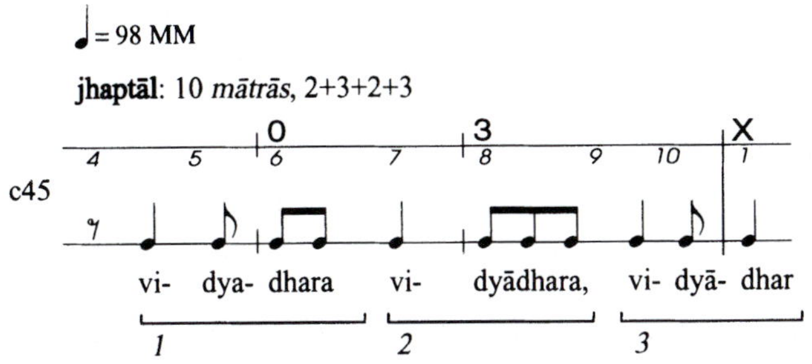

EXAMPLE **10.13** A simple *tihāī* in *jhaptāl*, from a *sādrā* performance by K. G. Ginde of *rāg khaṭ* (Audio Example 34)

Tihāīs need not end on *sam*: Example 10.15 illustrates an example of improvisation in *pāñcgun* (5 : 1) concluded by a *tihāī* timed to elide with the *mukhṛā*. In this piece, *mātrās* 3–11 inclusive are in *pāñcgun*, of which m. 3–6 are in straight

[25] The phrase is called a *pallā* in the *tablā* repertoire; see Gottlieb (1977 : 63). Nijenhuis reports the use of the term *mohra* in this sense (1974 : 60).

[26] *Tihāīs* are also used in South Indian music, where they are called *morā*.

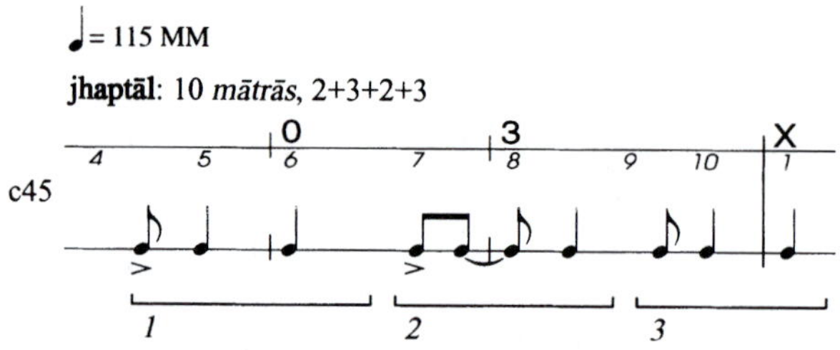

Example 10.14 A simple *tihāī* in *jhaptāl*, from a *sitār* performance by Nikhil Banerjee of *rāg megh* (Audio Example 35)

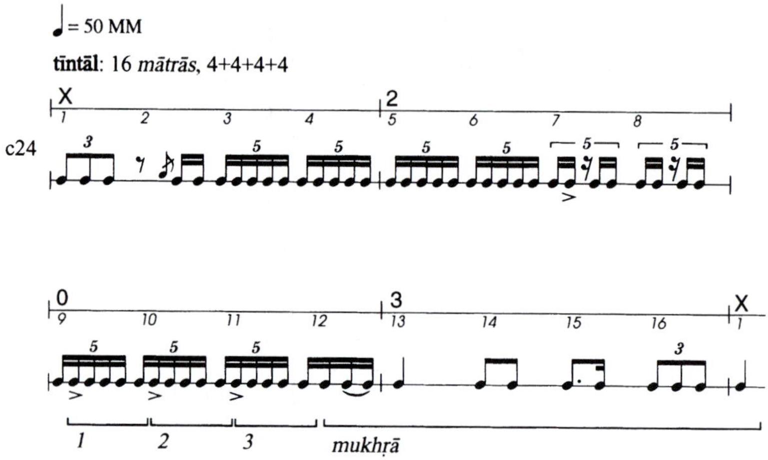

Example 10.15 An extract of improvised development from a *tīntāl vilambit gat* in *rāg bhairavī* by Deepak Choudhury (Audio Example 36)

5 : 1 (*sīdhā*), with the basic or 'default' 2 + 3 subdivision. This pattern is then disturbed in m. 7–8 by cross-rhythmic accents, and m. 9–11 comprise a *tihāī*. The *tihāī* is made up of a simple five-note phrase, which elides with the *mukhṛā*. (Other examples of *tihāīs* have already been introduced in Examples 9.3, 9.5, 9.8, 10.8, and 10.10.)

10.3.5 *Cakkardār* and *nauhār tihāīs*

The *cakkardār* (lit. 'circular, round-about') *tihāī* is a special variety, popular in the *kathak* and *tablā* repertoires, in which each element is itself composed of a short *tihāī*, usually preceded by a short introductory phrase. The *tihāī* of each of the first two elements finishes either before or after *sam*, so that only the third lands on *sam*.[27] *Tihāīs* of this type may also be referred to as *nauhār*, since they

[27] Cf. Gottlieb; 'the phrase lengths do not correspond with the divisions of the time-cycle' (1977 : 51). See also Brown (1965).

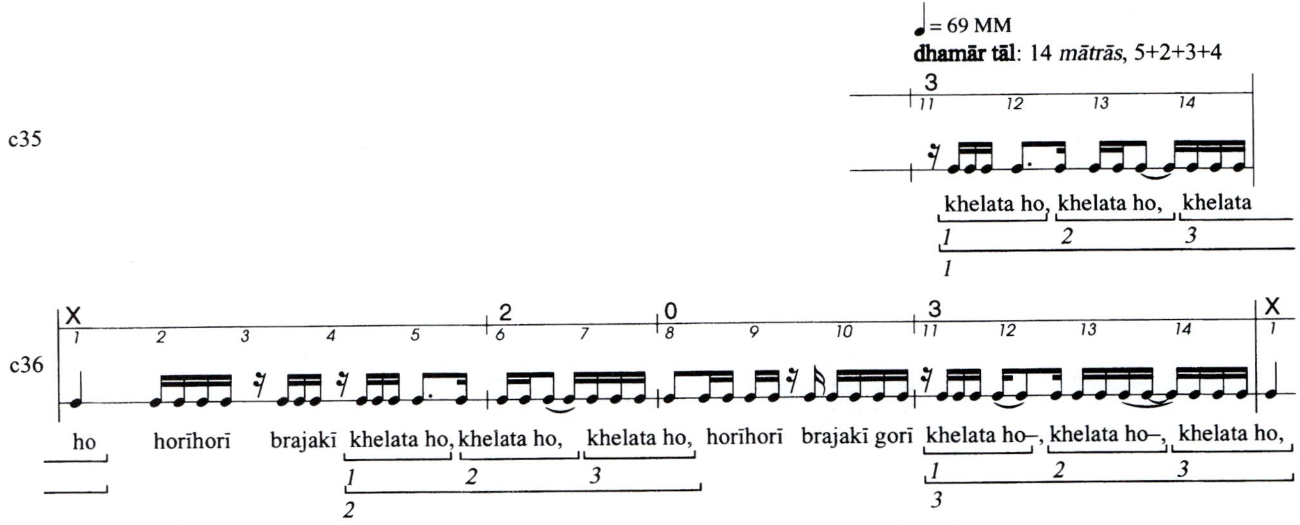

Example 10.16 A *nauhār tihāī*, from a *dhamār* performance by Bidur Mallik of *rāg jaijaivantī* in *dhamār tāl* (Audio Example 37)

have a total of nine (*nau*) short *tihāī* elements.[28] Example 10.16 illustrates a *nauhār tihāī* from a *dhamār* performance by Bidur Mallik.

Many modern instrumentalists use particularly elaborate forms of *tihāī* to end performances; one such, as played by Shiv Kumar Sharma on the *santūr*, is illustrated in Example 10.17. It begins with a long descending pattern repeated three times, before the *cakkardār tihāī* proper begins. Each element of the *cakkardār* consists of a *tihāī* plus a short rest: furthermore each of these short *tihāīs* contains a triple repetition on high Sa, making a total of 27 (3 × 3 × 3) sas.

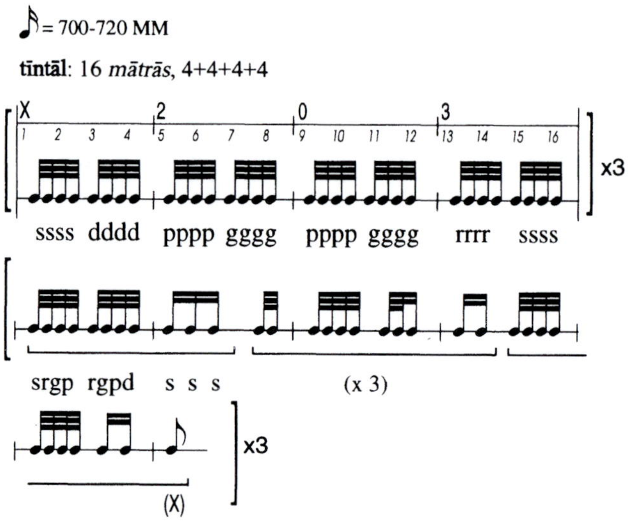

Example 10.17 A concluding *tihāī* from a *drut gat* performance by Shiv Kumar Sharma (*santūr*) of *rāg bhūpāl toḍī* in *drut tīntāl* (Audio Example 38)

10.3.6 *Sam* and *viṣam* in *laykārī*

In most *laykārī*, the soloist's aim is to end a development episode either by returning to the *mukhṛā* of the *bandiś*, or by reaching a cadence on *sam*. Some musicians however, use a technique called *viṣam*, in which improvisations end deliberately just before or just after *sam*.[29] Those ending before *sam* are described as *anāgat*, and those which overshoot are *atīt*.[30] The technique is particularly appropriate to *dhrupad* or *dhamār* accompanied by '*sāth saṅgat*', where singer and *pakhāvaj* player both improvise simultaneously. In this case the

[28] Cf. the *tablā*'s '*nau Dhā*' (nine Dha) *tihāī*; Gottlieb (1977 : 63).

[29] This information on *viṣam* is from the *dhrupad* singer Ritwik Sanyal (personal commmunication); the terms *atīt* and *anāgat* are confirmed in this sense by Roychoudhury (1975 : 2). Gottlieb uses the term *viṣam* for irregular (non-binary) divisions of the *tāl* (1977 : 42); see also *viṣam yati* above; while Danielou uses the same word to refer to the mid-point in the *tāl* cycle (1968 : 67).

[30] Cf. Gottlieb (1977 : 148), Chaudhary (1997 : 144–5). In South Indian music, these same terms are used to describe the starting points of compositions, when they begin either before or after the start of the cycle. See L. Shankar (1974 : 18) and Frishman (1985 : 13).

singer may use *viṣam* in order to throw his accompanist off the *tāl*, in a spirit of friendly competition. Some instrumentalists too use this technique, in deliberately constructing *tihāīs* to end off-*sam*. Example 10.18, from a performance by Deepak Choudhury of *rāg tilak kāmod* in *rūpak tāl*, illustrates a variety of '*anāgat*' *tihāī*, which ends immediately before *sam*.

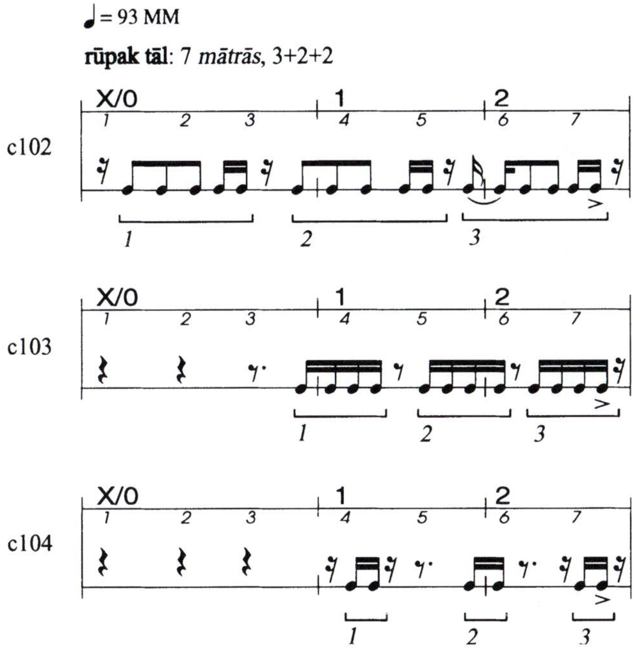

Example 10.18 An extract from a performance by Deepak Choudhury of *rāg tilak kāmod* in *rūpak tāl* (Audio Example 39)

10.4 Usage of *laykārī* techniques

There clearly exists a wealth of rhythmic variation techniques in North Indian music: these are not and cannot, however, be employed purely at the whim of the artist, but are associated with the aesthetic norms of genre and style, and must be consistent with development technique, *tāl* and *lay*. In practice, most performances only use a limited selection of the *laykārī* techniques available to the tradition as a whole.

The more syllabic styles tend to use more *laykārī* than melismatic styles (i.e. *dhrupad*, *dhamār*, medium-fast *khyāl* and *tarānā* use these techniques more than slow *khyāl* and *ṭhumrī*); and in general instrumental *gat* forms, being less limited by the employment of text, use the most *laykārī* of all. At the other end of the spectrum, some *vilambit khyāl* and *ṭhumrī* barely uses any techniques which could be described as *laykārī*.

In vocal genres which do allow extensive use of *laykārī*, usage is largely dependent on that of the development techniques described in Chapter 9. For example in *dhrupad* and *dhamār bol bāṇṭ* a number of techniques may be accommodated: shifts in *lay* ratio (including in some cases *lay bāṇṭ*) contributing to overall acceleration; rhythmic grouping (here grouping is partly dependent on text distribution) and a limited amount of *prastār*, plus *tihāīs* and *viṣam*.

Thus a variety of techniques may be used, but in practice (especially in *dhrupad*), such techniques will be used only where text allows. The balance is slightly different in *dhamār* than in *dhrupad*, and the playful spirit of *horī dhamār* encourages the greater use of *tihāīs* (as in Example 10.16 above). In *tarānā* the singer does not have the same limitations of text use, and can in theory use the full range of *laykārī* techniques: in practice however, many singers perform *tarānā* exactly like *choṭā khyāl*, alternating the *bandiś* with *ākār tāns* and introducing little rhythmic play. *Khyāl* performance may lie anywhere on a continuum from virtually no *laykārī*, to a use of *laykārī* comparable with *dhrupad* or instrumental *gat* performance.

As we have seen, in instrumental forms the stroke patterns replace text in function to a considerable extent. Stroke patterns may be manipulated much more freely than text, without semantic limitations: as a result, most modern instrumental *gat* styles (in particular those of Maihar *gharānā* musicians), have exploited *laykārī* to a degree impossible for vocalists to emulate. Instrumentalists have borrowed from the percussion (and, perhaps indirectly, *kathak* dance) repertoires, and from South Indian music, to extend the rhythmic vocabulary of North Indian music: techniques introduced in this way may include the *cakkardār* and *nauhār tihāīs*, *prastār* and *yati*, and to some extent the application of divisive *laykārī* (and certainly its *jāti* terminology).

Examples 10.19 and 10.20 illustrate the usage of various *laykārī* techniques in performance. The first (10.19) is taken from a medium tempo *khyāl* performance by Veena Sahasrabuddhe (cf. Example 7.6), the second (10.20) from a *vilambit gat* played on *sitār* by Ravi Shankar. Both are performances which use somewhat more *laykārī* than average for their genres, although not so much as to be considered atypical. It is easier (largely because of the distinctions in text use) to break Veena Sahasrabuddhe's *khyāl* performance down into clear stages than Ravi Shankar's *sitār gat*, which seems gradually to shift from *vistār* to *laykārī* and finally to *tāns*. This is typical of the two genres, as is the much greater use of *tihāīs* in the *sitār* recital—which, not surprisingly, occur almost entirely in the *laykārī* and *tān* sections—than in the *khyāl*, where only two *tihāīs* are used in the entire performance. The higher numbers in the *lay* ratios in the *sitār* performance reflect the lower metric tempo of the *vilambit gat*.

10.4.1 *Laykārī* in improvisation

It is difficult to be more precise about the techniques which may be used in any particular genre; quite apart from variables of *tāl* and *lay*, there are differences

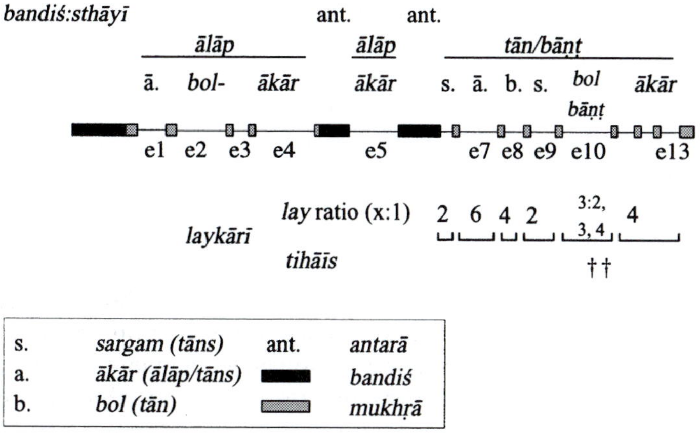

Example 10.19 Performance scheme of a *khyāl* performance by Veena Sahasrabuddhe of *rāg śrī* in *rūpak tāl*, illustrating usage of *laykārī* techniques (cf. Ex. 7.6)

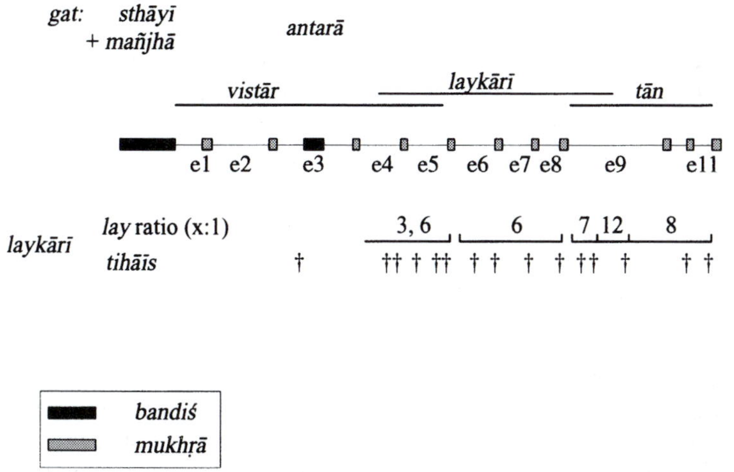

Example 10.20 Performance scheme of a *sitār vilambit gat* performance by Ravi Shankar of *rāg khamāj* in *tīntāl*, illustrating usage of *laykārī* techniques

in melodic and textual material which may limit rhythmic play, and considerable stylistic diversity between performers. There are, however, further issues to be addressed regarding *laykārī* in the context of performance practice. These concern the structure of improvised episodes (starting and ending points, ways of dividing the *tāl*, cadences and returns to the *mukhṛā* or *sam*), and the use of computation in generating rhythmic variations.

Various possibilities are available for structuring each episode of improvisation. As for starting points, a new improvisation may begin at any point in the cycle, since before the introduction of a new episode, the statement of the previous refrain may in practice end at any point in the cycle (although episodes tend to end shortly after *sam*); and this may be followed by a pause of any length.

At the end of the episode the artist has more restraints. In most contexts he will link back to the refrain, by ending his improvisation (perhaps with a *tihāī*) either on *sam*, or shortly before the starting point of the *mukhṛā*. Thus the latter part of an improvised episode is often concentrated on the composition of a suitable *tihāī*, with which to rejoin the refrain. This is particularly true of *laykārī* in instrumental *gats*; in *dhrupad* the situation is similar but the cadence is less likely to involve a *tihāī*.

Each episode may be subdivided by other cadential patterns into 'sub-episodes'; these are less likely to involve the *mukhṛā* and more likely to extend to *sam* (in *dhrupad*, sometimes deliberately over- or undershooting; see *viṣam* above). Within each sub-episode the artist has the option of treating the *tāl* cycles in one of several ways, for instance;

- Developing rhythmic ideas according to their own logic—or the logic of text distribution—relying on his ability to recognize the place reached in the cycle and readjust to the *tāl*.
- Constructing rhythmic variations with the *tāl* cycle in mind, i.e. multiplying the number of *mātrās* (of the whole cycle, or those remaining in the cycle) by the *lay* ratio, in order to find the maximum number of syllables; then devising rhythmic patterns to fill the available space.
- As above, but constructing variations to fill each *vibhāg* in turn rather than the cycle as a whole.

10.4.2 Computation in *laykārī*

The second and third possibilities here imply the use of some form of computation in order to exploit the rhythmic possibilities of *laykārī*. This is more apparent in the construction of *tihāīs*, where the length of the overall pattern is important, since it must end in a particular place. In theory it is possible to compute the necessary length for the basic element of a *tihāī* ending on *sam*, as follows:

no. of *mātrās* remaining until *sam* × *lay* ratio = total number of pulses
(total no. of pulses + 1) ÷ 3 = no. of pulses in basic *tihāī* element

These two stages of computation will calculate the length of a pattern which, if played 3 times, will end with its final syllable or stroke on *sam*. For example if a musician wants to fill five *mātrās* at a *lay* ratio of *caugun* (4 : 1), with a *tihāī* to end on *sam*, he may calculate;

5 *mātrās* @ 4 : 1 = 20 pulses
$(20 + 1) \div 3 = 7$ pulses in each *tihāī* element

Therefore, a 7-pulse pattern, without a gap between repetitions (*bedam*) will end on *sam*, after five *mātrās* in *caugun*, on its third statement. This computation is illustrated graphically in Example 10.21, with an example of a possible *tihāī*. While this type of computation may be carried out in performance (or prepared in advance, i.e. pre-composed), more often than not musicians either apply patterns with which they are familiar—stock patterns, so to speak—or adjust or modify those familiar patterns in some way. The possibilities of computation and the manipulation of stock patterns are illustrated in a tradition of *tablā* solo performance, in which members of the audience may request the artist to play a particular type of composition—stipulating, for example, the length of a *tihāī*. This is called a *farmāiś* (commission), and pieces composed in this way are called *farmāiśī*. See Kippen (1988 : 101), Gottlieb (1977 : 127).

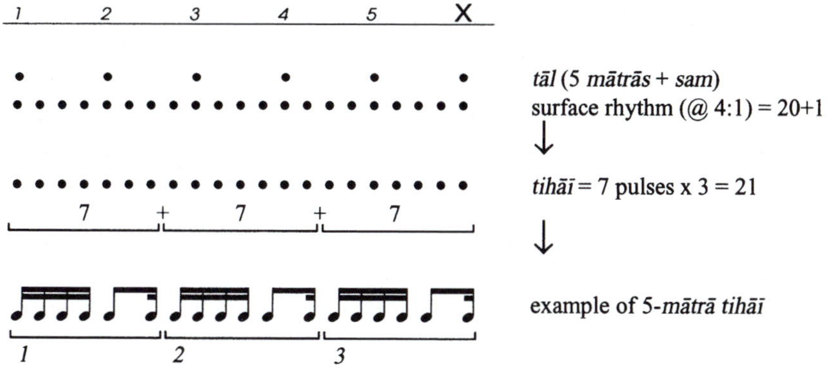

Example 10.21 The use of computation in generating a 5-*mātrā tihāī* at *caugun*

Musicians who are trained in styles which employ *laykārī* techniques a great deal, learn a large number of composed patterns for *tihāīs* from their masters, and hear many more. An experienced improviser of *tihāīs* would not therefore have to make the computation above, since he would know instinctively (i.e. through learning, practice, and experience), a variety of 5-*mātrā tihāī* patterns. He could to use the knowledge that a 7-pulse pattern works out as a 5-*mātrā tihāī* in *caugun* as the starting point of further variation (such as playing a familiar 5-*mātrā* pattern over 6 *mātrās*, using two $\frac{1}{2}$ *mātrā* rests between repetitions). This type of variation and adaptation is more typical of *laykārī* in practice than more complicated models of computation: the computation generates the pattern, but that does not mean that a musician actually has to do the mathematics on each occasion.

10.5 Summary

The term *laykārī* has a range of meanings; it is most commonly taken to signify the use of one or more rhythmic variation techniques, and describes music in which rhythmic play is a major component. As we have seen in earlier chapters however, this concept is also associated with a particular 'syllabic' model of rhythmic organization, in which *laykārī* defines the relationship between *tāl* and surface rhythm. In this context acceleration is effected by an increase in the ratio between surface rhythmic density and tempo—the '*lay* ratio'—and hence *laykārī* is also closely associated with this acceleration process.

The most common type of *laykārī* involves a conceptual and practical division of the *tāl*, which generates a supra-metric pulse level. Surface rhythmic patterns are created by further manipulation of this pulse level; such manipulation involves either variation of the grouping patterns which are inferred on the basis of the *tāl*'s basic pulse level, by means including dynamic accents; further subdivision of this pulse (e.g. stroke doubling); or sustaining notes and/or leaving rests. The rhythmic patterns generated by means of these processes may be repeated, varied, and/or organized according to principles such as *prastār* (permutation), and *yati* ('shape').

Cadential patterns play an important role in performance practice, associated with the improvisatory nature of development and its episodic structure; they form, therefore, an important component of *laykārī*. The most common cadential type is the *tihāī*, which is based on the principle of triple repetition (a rhythmic phrase is stated a total of three times, ending on or just before a structurally important beat). The *tihāī* has many forms in practice, ranging from the simple to the highly complex. Finally, usage of *laykārī* techniques is inseparable from performance practice in general—for instance acceleration is associated with increase in *lay* ratio, episodic structure with cadential patterns, and text use with the generation of rhythmic patterns.

11

A case study in rhythmic analysis: instrumental *vilambit* and *madhya lay gats* in the repertoire of Deepak Choudhury (Maihar Gharānā)

11.1 Introduction

I will now apply the principles and theories outlined thus far in a case study, not only in order to back up my theoretical speculations with a more concrete example, but also to show how such analysis can shed light on issues of wider significance. I would like to suggest not only that it is possible to characterize a specific repertoire in considerable detail in terms of its rhythmic parameters; more importantly, that analysis can throw considerable light on issues of great importance to theorists and historians of Indian music, including the historical development of Hindustānī music and the relationships between the various genres and styles.

Oral tradition, of course, has a lot to say about these issues and others, and that tradition is often the most reliable, or even the only source of information. However, oral tradition (perhaps I should speak of traditions in the plural, since musicians are often at odds with each other, particularly over issues of history and authenticity) also has its limitations. To take but one example, the historical development of instrumental *gat* forms and their relationship to vocal forms is an issue of considerable importance to historians of Indian music. Most instrumentalists have something to say about the subject, yet their testimony is almost invariably affected by the high status accorded to the voice in Indian musical tradition. Since the human voice is the pre-eminent musical instrument in India, and instrumental music derives its own prestige, such as it is, largely from the understanding that a solo instrument (such as the *sitār*) is essentially a surrogate for the voice, instrumentalists are naturally inclined to stress the vocal elements (*gāyakī*) in their repertoires and play down the idiomatic instrumental elements (*gatkārī*).

I don't mean this to sound unduly cynical—without a doubt vocal models have indeed been amongst the most important sources of instrumental repertoire—merely to make the point that a historical investigation needs to find ways of complementing the evidence of the oral tradition. This is not, of course, the only such issue on which light could be shed by rhythmic analysis: but my intention in this chapter is not to exploit every possibility for rhythmic analysis but rather to show by means of a single case study a little of what might be possible.

11.2 The case study

This case study will concentrate on two important types of instrumental composition or *gat*, as performed by an eminent sitārist.[1] The artist in question is Deepak Choudhury (hereafter referred to as 'DC'), a senior disciple of Pandit Ravi Shankar and hence a representative of the Maihar *gharānā*,[2] and my teacher since 1985.

The compositional forms under scrutiny are the *madhya lay gat* and the *vilambit gat*. In DC's repertoire *madhya lay* ('medium tempo') *gats* are mostly set in *tāls* with structures which may be described as 'complex' or 'irregular' (cf. §4.3). They are performed immediately after a full *ālāp*. *Vilambit* ('slow') *gats* are set in the quadratic *tīntāl*, and performed without an extended *ālāp*. The performer's view, as expressed to me, is essentially that the logic behind the performance of these two *gat* forms in the repertoire of Maihar *gharānā* artists, is that a complete concert performance should ideally comprise items derived from all three major *gāyakīs* or vocal styles, namely *dhrupad*, *khyāl*, and *ṭhumrī*. Each of the *gats* under consideration is supposedly modelled on, or at least analogous to, important stages in vocal performances in the genres *dhrupad* and *khyāl*.

This three-part principle was established by Ustad Allauddin Khan (d. 1972), the founder of the Maihar *gharānā*, who built on earlier instrumental *gat* forms in so doing. The *vilambit gat* was developed using an extant form, the *masītkhānī gat* (Chapter 8). The *masītkhānī gat* was originally (i.e. from the eighteenth or early nineteenth century) performed at a moderate tempo; it was subsequently slowed down, and elements of *khyāl gāyakī* incorporated.[3] The type of *madhya lay gat* described here was created more recently, probably within this century; the inspiration for this was the perceived need to create a medium tempo form to complement the *ālāp*, thus completing the '*dhrupad aṅg*'[4] (*dhrupad* component).

The first segment of a *sitār* recital by DC generally consists of *ālāp*, *joṛ*, and a medium-tempo composition (the *madhya lay gat*). This sequence is derived from

[1] This chapter is based on an article published in the *British Journal of Ethnomusicology* (Clayton 1993*b*).

[2] For more background information on Maihar *gharānā sitār* style, see Slawek (1987).

[3] According to Slawek, Ravi Shankar credits this development to both Allauddin Khan and the sitārist Rameshwar Pathak (1987 : 19). A similar development took place at roughly the same time (probably within the first half of the 20th cent.) in the Imdadkhānī *sitār gharānā* (see Hamilton 1989 : 74, 175).

[4] The terms *dhrupad*, *khyāl*, and *ṭhumrī aṅg* are also mentioned by Slawek (1987 : 20).

Table 11.1 The division of Deepak Choudhury's *sitār* repertoire into three *aṅgs*

aṅg	instrumental forms	vocal 'models'
dhrupad aṅg	*a*. extended *ālāp-joṛ*	*dhrupad*-style *ālāp*
	b. *madhya lay gat* (medium tempo composition)	*dhrupad, dhamār*
	c. (optional *drut gat*, fast tempo composition)	(optional fast *dhrupad*)
khyāl aṅg	*a*. brief *ālāp* (optional)	*khyāl*-style *ālāp* (optional)
	b. *vilambit gat* (slow tempo composition)	*baṛā khyāl* (slow tempo *khyāl*)
	c. *drut gat* (fast tempo composition)	*choṭā khyāl* (fast tempo *khyāl*)
ṭhumrī aṅg	*a*. *dhun*	stylized folk tune; some *ṭhumrī* influence
	b. (optional *drut gat*)	

the vocal genre *dhrupad,* in which the major *rāg* development precedes the introduction of *tāl*. The second item comprises a combination of slow and fast tempo compositions, analogous to the *baṛā*- and *choṭā khyāl*, in which the main *rāg* development takes place within the context of the slow tempo *tāl*; finally a lighter item (*dhun*) is performed, usually based on folk melodies and preferably incorporating some influence from *ṭhumrī gāyakī*.[5] These relationships are set out in Table 11.1.

The clearest connection between the respective instrumental and vocal forms is that described above, and illustrated in Table 11.1; DC's *dhrupad aṅg* and *khyāl aṅg* imitate the large-scale organization of recitals in their respective 'parent' genres.[6] Thus the vocal models provide a rationale for the arrangement of different elements in DC's recitals, suggesting the appropriate performance order for the various instrumental forms.

If the performer's view is confirmed by analysis, one would expect to find a clear distinction between the performance style of the *madhya lay* and *vilambit gats,* and indications that the differences are not derived simply from the different tempi, but determined in some way by analogies with *dhrupad* and *baṛā khyāl*. One would expect to observe distinctions in one or more of the following areas: the use of particular *tāls*; the rhythmic structure of the *gats*; the techniques used in the improvised development; the ranges and patterns of change of both tempo and rhythmic density; and the style of drum accompaniment. The approach of the study described here was to look at each of these areas in turn. My intention was to abstract rhythmic profiles of each *gat* type,

[5] The relationship between *dhun* and *ṭhumrī* is discussed by Slawek (1987 : 21–2).

[6] Although in practice a variety of sequences may be used, for *khyāl* recitals in particular, the best-known archetype is arguably the one given in Table 11.1. Like DC's *khyāl aṅg*, many *khyāl* performances begin with a brief *ālāp* (similar in style to that of *dhrupad*, but shorter and less thorough).

incorporating the most important rhythmic parameters, and then to compare these profiles, both with each other, and with those of vocal genres.

The analytical techniques employed in this study combined appraisal of the *sitār* performance—on the basis of a knowledge of Maihar *gharānā* technique and style—with an empirical analytical approach. The principal methods employed were therefore:

(*a*) Analysis of the *tāl* structure, taking into account both *ṭhekā* and clap pattern.

(*b*) Determination of the rhythmic structure of the *gat*, based on *bol* (stroke) patterns, and its relationship to *tāl* structure.

(*c*) Analysis of the rhythmic structure of improvised passages (again, by means of reference to *bol* patterns), and correlation of these structures with those of the *gat* and/or of the *tāl* itself. This included recognition of idiomatic rhythmic techniques, such as various types of *tihāīs* (triple repetitions), and analysis of their application, as well as consideration of the preferred rhythmic style. Rhythmic style is characterized in terms of two archetypes, named 'syllabic' and 'melismatic'.

(*d*) Measurement of *lay*, in both its aspects as metric tempo and rhythmic density, with consideration for the relationship between the two (*lay* ratio). *Lay* charts were used to clarify patterns of acceleration, and these were correlated with formal schemes of the performances studied, to illustrate the relationship between changes in tempo and those in development technique.

(*e*) Analysis of the style of percussion accompaniment.

For this case study I analysed a representative selection of 6 *madhya lay gat* and 5 *vilambit gat* performances by DC, comprising both concert and commercial recordings. This study concentrated on each of the areas listed above in turn, and also correlated the different parameters in order to build up a picture of rhythmic styles.

11.3 Results

The results of these investigations are many and complex; those relevant to the specific questions under consideration are summarized below in six sections (*tāl* structure; *gat* structure; development procedures; *lay*; accompaniment style; and the correlation of rhythmic parameters), together with observations on their significance.

11.3.1 *Tāl* structure

There is a clear distinction between the types of *tāl* employed in the two *gat* types. In *madhya lay gats*, DC uses a variety of *tāls* which are composed of *vibhāgs* of different lengths (e.g. 2 + 3 + 2 + 3 or 4 + 4 + 3). The most important of these, according to DC himself, are the six listed in Example 11.1.[7] In contrast, all *vilambit gats* are set in *tīntāl*, in which all sections are the same length (4 + 4 + 4 + 4), as illustrated in Example 11.2.

rūpak tāl: 7 *mātrās*, 3+2+2

X/0	1	2	X/0
tin tā trkt	dhin nā	dhin nā	tin

matta tāl: 9 *mātrās*, 2+3+4

X 0	2 3 0	4 5 6 0	X
dhā ghira	naka ghira naka	tiṭa kata gadi gana	dhā

jhaptāl: 10 *mātrās*, 2+3+2+3

X	2	0	3	X
dhin nā	dhin dhin nā	tin nā	dhin dhin nā	dhin

savārī tāl (cārtāl kī savārī): 11 *mātrās*, 4+4+3

X	0	2 (3)	X
dhī trkt dhin nā	tū nā kat tā	dhīdhī nā,dhī dhīnā	dhī

dhamār tāl: 14 *mātrās*, 5+2+3+4

X	2	0	3	X
ka dhi ta dhi ta	dhā –	ge ti ṭa	ti ṭa tā –	ka

pañcam savārī tāl: 15 *mātrās*, 4+4+4+3

X	2	0	3 (4)	X
dhī nā dhīdhī kat	dhīdhī nā,dhīdhīnā tin--tra	tinnā trkt tinnā kattā	dhīdhī nā,dhī dhīnā	dhā

EXAMPLE **11.1** *Tāls* used in Deepak Choudhury's '*dhrupad aṅg*' *madhya lay gats*

tīntāl: 16 *mātrās*, 4+4+4+4

X	2	0	3	X
dhā dhin dhin dhā	dhā dhin dhin dhā	dhā tin tin tā	tā dhin dhin dhā	dhā

EXAMPLE **11.2** *Tīntāl*

There are therefore clear distinctions here between many *tāls* (in the *madhya lay gat*) and one *tāl* (in the *vilambit gat*), and between 'complex' and largely asymmetrical structures on the one hand, and a regular and symmetrical pattern on the other. The six main *tāls* used in DC's *madhya lay gat* appear to have been selected to fulfil a requirement for rhythmic complexity and diversity; there is also a (possibly significant) preference for a final *vibhāg* of 3 *mātrās* (also evident

[7] DC also occasionally performs *madhya lay gats* in a *tāl* of 13 *mātrās* (*jay tāl*), and in $\frac{1}{2}$-*mātrā tāls* (e.g. $9\frac{1}{2}$, split $4 + 4 + 1\frac{1}{2}$). The *ṭhekās* given here for *matta*, *savārī*, and *pañcam savārī tāls* are from *tablā* player Arup Chattopadhyay (personal communication).

in an alternative clap pattern for *matta tāl*, 4 + 2 + 3 rather than 2 + 3 + 4). Neither of these factors applies to the *vilambit gat*, which is always set in *tīntāl*.

The selection of *tāls* does not however present a clear picture of influence from vocal genres. The greater emphasis on rhythm in DC's *madhya lay gat* is clearly evident in the greater variety and complexity of the *tāls* used, and this reflects a greater emphasis on rhythm in *dhrupad* than in *khyāl* (although, in the case of the vocal genres this emphasis is not similarly reflected in a greater variety of *tāls* used for *dhrupad*). Of the *tāls* of DC's *madhya lay gat*, *jhaptāl*, *dhamār tāl*, occasionally *matta tāl* and even *rūpak tāl* may be used for *dhrupad*, and the two *savārī tāls* for the associated genre of solo *pakhāvaj* (barrel drum) performance: however, the main *dhrupad tāl*, the 12-*mātrā cautāl*, is conspicuous by its absence from this list. On the other hand although *tīntāl* is employed for *khyāls*, so too are other *tāls* (e.g. *jhūmrā tāl*, *ektāl*) which are not used for *vilambit gats*. Moreover, clear distinctions between the types of *tāl* structures employed, such as those noted above, are not observed between *dhrupad* and *khyāl*. Overall therefore, evidence for the influence of vocal genres on instrumental forms in *tāl* use is limited.

11.3.2 *Gat* structure

In both *gat* types, the fixed compositions appear to be based on idiomatic *sitār* patterns; however, they are organized according to slightly different rhythmic principles. *Vilambit gats* are almost invariably based on modified versions of the *masītkhānī gat* form, with a stereotypical *bol* pattern incorporating a 5-*mātrā mukhṛā*. This pattern was apparently created by the *sitārist* Masit Khan in the eighteenth century,[8] and therefore pre-dates the influence of *baṛā khyāl* on instrumental *gats*, which took place largely in the twentieth century (see Example 11.39). (Indeed the *masītkhānī gat* dates from a period before the fashion for very slow *khyāl* performance had been established. There may have been a connection between *khyāl* and the *masītkhānī gat* at this stage (see Slawek 1987 : 17), but it is not directly relevant to this discussion.)

Most of DC's *madhya lay gats* are based on the *tāl* structure itself, employing relatively simple *bol* patterns and generally with no overlap or syncopation across the *vibhāg* divisions, and show a preference for hemiola where the final *vibhāg* contains 3 *mātrās*; *rūpak tāl gats* are more likely to be syncopated, and usually have lines of two *tāl* cycles. DC has however developed a new type of *gat* in recent years which incorporates a $2\frac{1}{2}$-*mātrā mukhṛā*—thus apparently transferring a feature of the *vilambit gat* to the *madhya lay gat*. Examples of these *gat* structures are given in Example 11.4, in *jhaptāl*.

All the *gat* types illustrated in Examples 11.3 and 11.4 are clearly idiomatic instrumental forms; in the absence of text syllables, it is the patterns of strokes (*bols*) which form the basis of their rhythmic organization. The basic pattern of

[8] See Dick (1984 : 394), Miner (1990 : 34–5).

tīntāl: 16 *mātrās*, 4+4+4+4

(*a*)

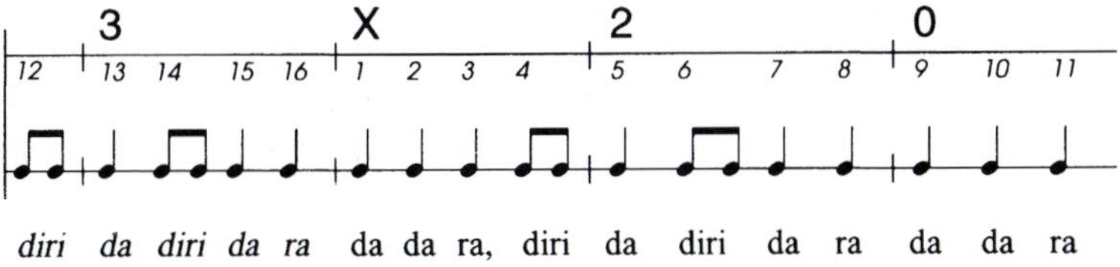

(*b*)

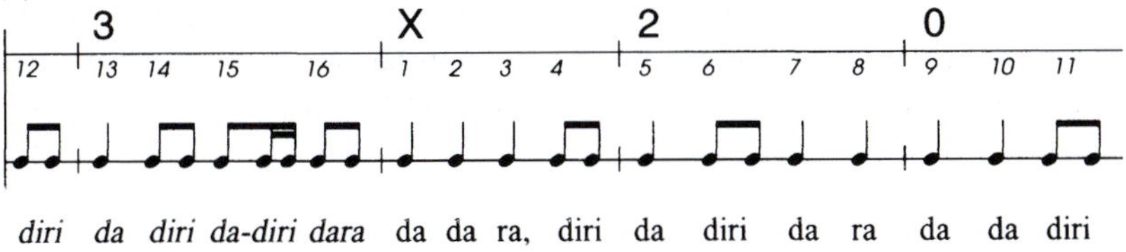

EXAMPLE **11.3** Examples of *bol* sequences for simple and elaborated *masītkhānī gats*

jhaptāl: 10 *mātrās*, 2+3+2+3

(*a*) a typical *sam-to-sam* pattern

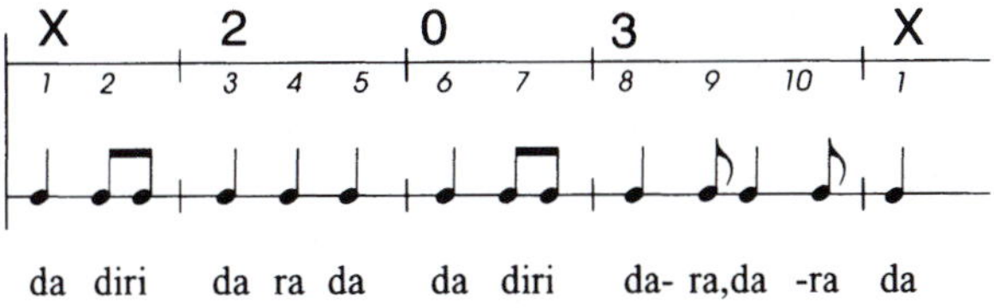

(*b*) a *mukhṛā*-type pattern

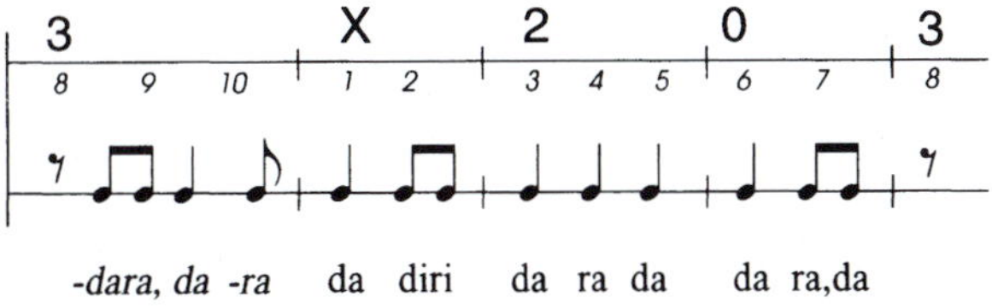

EXAMPLE **11.4** Two *bol* patterns for *sitār gats* in *jhaptāl* (10 *mātrās*)

the *vilambit gat* has been retained over some two centuries, and the decrease in performance tempo over this period has been compensated for by an elaboration of the basic pattern, which is particularly prominent in the *mukhṛā* (see Example 11.3*b* which is taken from a *vilambit gat* performed by DC).[9] Patterns for *madhya lay gats* are of more recent origin, and are clearly based in the first instance on the structure of the *tāls*. These have tended to crystallize into archetypal patterns, such as those cited above (Example 11.4).

If the influence of vocal genres were to be felt, certain features of the '*dhrupad aṅg*' *gats* might be expected to provide a connection with the typical *dhrupad* practice of setting *cautāl* compositions with a textual/melodic grouping of 3 + 3 + 3 + 3 against a *tāl* structure of 4 + 4 + 2 + 2 (see Chapter 8). This is not the case—evidently, the influence of *dhrupad* does not extend into this type of contrametrical composition structure (indeed, DC does not use *cautāl* at all for *madhya lay gats*). In *baṛā khyāl* compositions, the most prominent aspect of the rhythmic structure is the *mukhṛā*, which is a feature also observed in the *vilambit gat*. However, since almost all fast tempo *khyāls*, and many *dhrupads* and *ṭhumrīs*, also feature *mukhṛās*, we must be careful not to read too much into this feature. The use of the *mukhṛā* does not necessarily imply the influence of *baṛā khyāl*, especially as the *masītkhānī gat* pattern appears to pre-date that influence. Another difference between *baṛā khyāl* and the *vilambit gat* is in the adjustment of the *mukhṛā* to slow tempi; in *baṛā khyāl* as a general rule, the slower the tempo the fewer *mātrās* the *mukhṛā* takes up. In the *vilambit gat* the *mukhṛā* always takes up 5 *mātrās*; the slower the tempo, the more elaborated the pattern becomes.

The structures of the *gats* themselves confirm their histories: the *vilambit gat* developed through adaptation of an earlier form, while the *madhya lay gat* was composed relatively recently on the basis of the *tāl* structure, and is at an earlier stage in its development. Once again therefore, evidence for the influence of vocal genres is less than overwhelming, although the analysis has been productive in other ways.

11.3.3 Development procedures

In both *gat* types, a rough distinction may be drawn between development techniques and procedures that are suited to a low rhythmic density and immediately follow the statement of the *gat sthāyī* (first section), and those that are suited to higher rhythmic densities and are therefore employed towards the end of the performance—although in practice no clear division is made. Since in the *khyāl aṅg*, *rāg* development occurs within the metred section, the melismatic *vistār*[10] has an important place in the early stages of DC's *vilambit gat*

[9] This example is transcribed from a *vilambit gat* by DC in *rāg jaunpurī*; there are many other possibilities.

[10] *Vistār* is used in both a general sense, meaning 'expansion' or 'development' and—as here—in a more specific sense to refer to *rāg* exposition in melismatic style.

development. At a comparable stage in the *madhya lay gat*, the technique employed by DC, loosely termed '*toḍā*', involves the generation of new rhythmic and melodic combinations based on material already introduced.[11] The *vilambit gat vistār* is comparable to the *vistār* in some styles of *baṛā khyāl*; the *toḍā* of medium tempo compositions is, arguably, similarly analogous to the *bol bāṇṭ* ('text division') procedures typical of *dhrupad* performance.

At a later stage and at faster tempi, however, *ekharā tāns* (fast runs with one note per stroke) are performed in both *gats*. In *vilambit gats* the normal '*lay* ratio' for *tāns* is 8 : 1, with occasional bursts of up to 12 : 1. In *madhya lay gats* the normal *lay* ratio for *tāns* is 4 : 1, with some extra-fast passages of 6 : 1 or even 8 : 1. This reflects the preference for fast *tāns* in *sitār* performances of all *gat* types; in vocal music they occur principally in *khyāl*.

The transition from *vistār* or *toḍā* through to *tāns* is smoothly effected in both cases, by means of a progression through various intermediate *lay* ratios—this progression is a notable feature of Maihar *gharānā* style. In *vilambit gats* the progression from the point at which this ratio becomes clear (it is not in the early stages of *vistār*) may be 4 : 1-(5 : 1)-6 : 1-(7 : 1)-8 : 1;[12] in *madhya lay gats* it would be 2 : 1-(5 : 2)-3 : 1-(7 : 2)-4 : 1 against a metric tempo twice as high as that of the *vilambit gat*. In both cases these levels are used in a more systematic way than in either *khyāl* or *dhrupad* performance, and in fact such use is largely the result of influence from solo percussion repertoires and from South Indian music. The process of stepwise acceleration is an important feature of DC's performance style, usually described as an aspect of *laykārī*.

Other aspects of development technique may be considered, in addition to the preference for *toḍā* (emphasis on rhythm and stroke patterns, syllabic in style) or *vistār* (emphasis on melody and fluid continuity, melismatic in style), or the common use of *tāns* and of South Indian-influenced '*laykārī*' (stepwise acceleration). In any *gat* form, following the initial statement of the *gat* itself (usually in fact following the *sthāyī* or first section only), the improvised development is organized into 'episodes' separated by refrains which consist of repeated statements of the first line of the *gat sthāyī*.[13]

Episodes of development may start from any point and in many different ways; a pattern is more discernible in the way in which improvised episodes end, and link back to the *gat* refrain. In all cases this transition from improvisation episode to fixed refrain is effected as smoothly as possible. In the *vilambit gat*, both *vistār* and *tāns* link back either to the *sam* or to the start of the *mukhṛā*. In a large proportion of cases this link involves a *tihāī* calculated to end on *sam* or before the *mukhṛā*, or to elide with the start of the *mukhṛā*. *Tihāīs* are also

[11] *Toḍā*, like *vistār*, has a range of senses. Specifically it refers to development based on stereotypical *bol* patterns which combine single and double strokes; more generally to any development in a syllabic style (as here). In DC's *madhya lay gat*, *toḍā* refers to the generation of new rhythmic combinations, using melodic material already introduced in the foregoing *ālāp*. There is a considerable degree of overlap between the usage of the terms *toḍā*, *vistār* and *baṛhat*.

[12] *Lay* ratios in parentheses are optional.

[13] Or in some circumstances the first line of the final section, the *antarā*.

common in the *madhya lay gat*. In the case of simple *gats* which run *sam*-to-*sam* (see Example 11.4*a*), they generally end on *sam* itself; where the *gat* includes a *mukhṛā* (Example 11.4*b*) they more often conclude just before the *mukhṛā* begins.[14]

The use of potentially complex rhythmic techniques such as *tihāīs* may suggest *dhrupad* influence, since there is generally more emphasis on rhythmic virtuosity in *dhrupad* than in *khyāl* performance. However a comparison with *dhrupad* performance reveals that, as with the technique of stepwise acceleration ('*lay-kārī*'), the *tihāī* is employed far more in both *gat* styles than it is in *dhrupad*. This suggests that the main inspiration for this high usage of *tihāīs* in *sitār gats* also lies elsewhere. The most probable sources are the repertoires of the drums *pakhāvaj* and *tablā*, of the *kathak* dance and even possibly of South Indian music; in all these cases *tihāīs* are used extensively.

Study of development procedures in these two types of *gat* thus provides evidence for the influence of the vocal models (in the distinction between techniques and styles of *toḍā* and *vistār*); for mutual influence (in the use of *tāns*, a *khyāl* feature, in the *madhya lay gat*); and for influence from other sources (the use of *laykārī*, and of *tihāīs*). Although the evidence for the modelling on vocal forms is modest, the analysis once again highlights a number of other interesting issues.

11.3.4 *Lay*

Analysis of *lay* includes measurement of tempo (and characterization of patterns of variation), calculation of rhythmic density, and recognition of the relationship between the two. First, tempo ranges of *madhya lay gats* are considerably higher than those of *vilambit gats*, with maxima approximately double, as Table 11.2 shows. Measurements for rhythmic density are perhaps more interesting. In the early stages of the improvised development (immediately following the statement of the *gat sthāyī*), a calculation based on the number of *bols* (strokes) in each cycle[15] reveals that the average *bol* density is much lower in *vilambit* than in *madhya lay gats* (in fact, it is approximately half). This confirms that the rhythmic style of the former is more melismatic, as described above: one would expect that a more melismatic style would use fewer strokes per minute.

By the second half of the performance however, rhythmic density levels are almost identical.[16] The reason for this is that while the technique and rhythmic style of the performance are quite different in the early stages of the

[14] *Tablā* player Bikram Ghosh describes this style of improvisation—ending just before the *mukhṛā* begins—as the '*muqām*' style (personal communication). *Muqām* means 'halting place'.

[15] i.e. number of *bols* in cycle $\div$ length of cycle (in secs.) $\times$ 60 = average *bol* density.

[16] At this stage maximum rhythmic densities were calculated by multiplying the metric tempo by the *lay* ratio (i.e. if *tāns* were performed with a *lay* ratio of 8 : 1 at a tempo of 60 MM, the maximum rhythmic density would be calculated as $60 \times 8 = 480$ *bols*/min.).

Table 11.2 Tempo ranges for *vilambit* and *madhya lay gats*, as performed by Deepak Choudhury

composition type	range of tempo (MM)
vilambit gat	32–92
madhya lay gat	85–180

development, in the latter stages they are basically the same; fast *tāns* are performed. Figures taken from one example of each *gat* type are given in Table 11.3.

Table 11.3 *Lay* measurements for two *gat* performances by Deepak Choudhury

lay indicator	*rāg bhaṭiyār* *vilambit gat, tīntāl*	*rāg pūriyā* *madhya lay gat, jhaptāl*
tempo	43–82 MM	89–160 MM
average rhythmic density (initial development)	67–90 *bols*/min.	110–185 *bols*/min.
maximum rhythmic density (*tāns*)	290–656 *bols*/min.	294–640 *bols*/min.

This pattern is not found in the vocal genres, since *tāns* are exclusive to *khyāl*. In the later stages of a performance, rhythmic densities are higher in most *khyāl* performances than in *dhrupad*, whereas they are very similar in the two *gat* forms.

Acceleration patterns for the two *gat* types are remarkably similar; in the earlier part of the performance rhythmic density increases over a more or less constant tempo, in the latter the tempo increases by a number of significant, and clearly deliberate, increments. Patterns of tempo change are illustrated in Examples 11.5 and 11.6 with respect to two typical performances, one for each *gat* type.[17] The patterns for *vilambit* and *madhya lay gats* are very similar to each other; they are derived from neither *dhrupad* nor *khyāl*, although they are certainly more similar to those of *khyāl* performances. Analysis of sample performances suggests that tempo in *dhrupad* performances does generally accelerate significantly, although never by clear and deliberate increments (see Chapter 6). *Khyāl* performances often retain very steady metric tempi for long periods, but do often include stepped increases in tempo as well. This indicator gives useful corroborating evidence of the similarities in performance practice between the two *gat* types. Overall the results of the analysis of *lay* support the earlier findings—that is, that while there are some indications of the influence of vocal forms, a number of other factors are equally important.

[17] The greater fluctuation in this chart (compared to Ex. 11.5) is caused by the greater sampling rate, since the error in timings is proportionally higher for the shorter and faster *tāl* cycles of the *madhya lay gat*.

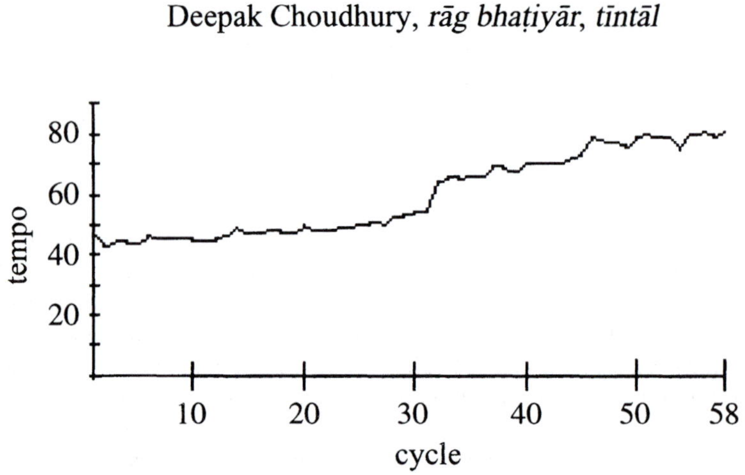

Example 11.5 *Lay* (metric tempo) chart for a *vilambit gat* performance of *rāg bhaṭiyār* in *tīntāl*, by Deepak Choudhury

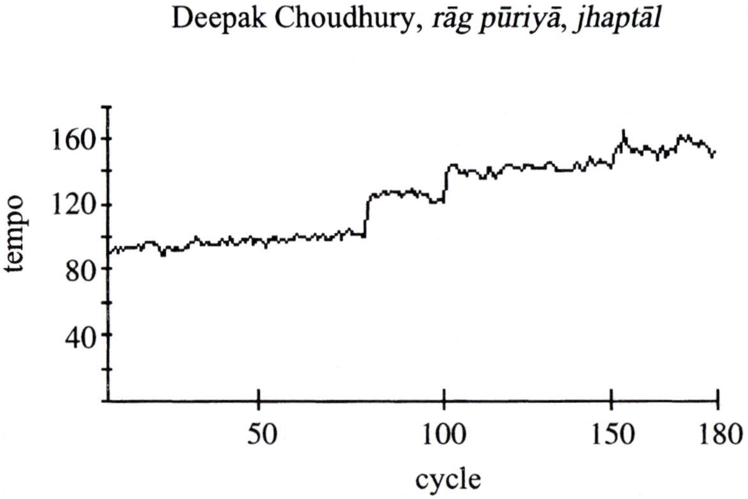

Example 11.6 *Lay* (metric tempo) chart for a *madhya lay gat* performance of *rāg pūriyā* in *jhaptāl*, by Deepak Choudhury

11.3.5 Accompaniment style

The style of *tablā* accompaniment is almost identical in DC's *madhya lay* and *vilambit gats*. The *tablā* plays the *ṭhekā* in an elaborated form throughout, except when playing solos to the accompaniment of the *gat sthāyī* played as a refrain. This accompaniment style is similar to that of *khyāl*, in which the *ṭhekā* is used for a very high proportion of the performance, but with a greater allowance for *tablā* solos. The only concession to *dhrupad* style accompaniment (as played on the *pakhāvaj*) is in a brief episode of *sāth saṅgat* ('synchronized accompaniment') with which DC's *madhya lay gat* performances are usually concluded. This feature is almost certainly included in order to imitate *dhrupad* practice.[18]

11.3.6 Correlation of rhythmic parameters

So far this discussion has focused on five distinct areas; *tāl* use and structure; *gat* structure; development technique and style; *lay* (tempo and rhythmic density), and the style of percussion accompaniment. Although it is convenient and effective to divide the analysis according to rhythmic parameters in this way, it must be emphasized that all these factors must necessarily be interdependent; and a change in one would be expected to have inevitable knock-on effects.

Connections between the parameters are many. The simplest way for some of these to be illustrated is graphically, as in Examples 11.7 and 11.8. Using tempo charts as the base line, a second trace has been added, using the calculations of rhythmic density described above. Aligned with these charts are lines illustrating the alternation of *gat*, improvised development and refrain in the *sitār* part, the stage of performance and techniques employed including *tihāīs*, and the *lay* ratio. In this way, both the overall progression and acceleration process, and the episodic performance structure are made clear; so too are changes in technique and *laykārī* correlated with the measured changes in *lay*. Two charts are given here, one from a *madhya lay gat* (Example 11.7) and the other a *vilambit gat* (Example 11.8).

These charts not only allow different rhythmic parameters to be correlated, they also graphically illustrate the similarities and differences between performance styles. Not only are patterns of tempo and rhythmic density increase rather similar (except that the rhythmic density in the *vilambit gat* starts lower, yet reaches the same maximum); so too is the episodic structure of the performance, in which *tablā* solos intersperse development episodes. In both cases the *sthāyī* only is stated at the beginning, and the *antarā* introduced after two episodes of development. Both performances start with one or two strokes per *mātrā* (a similar *lay* ratio), and both end with very similar rhythmic densities (but with different *lay* ratios). Both feature at least two significant accelerations by the soloist (and the *vilambit gat* performance has several others due to the *tablā* player accelerating for his solo interludes). Both also last approximately the same time, although this is slightly misleading since *vilambit gat* performances tend on the whole to be a little longer than *madhya lay gats*.

The differences are found in the more melismatic style of the *vilambit gat* (illustrated here through the lower rhythmic densities in the early part of the

[18] Some musicians believe that the selection of *tablā bols* in *madhya lay gat* accompaniment is, or should be, limited to those derived from the *pakhāvaj*, but this lies beyond the scope of this chapter.

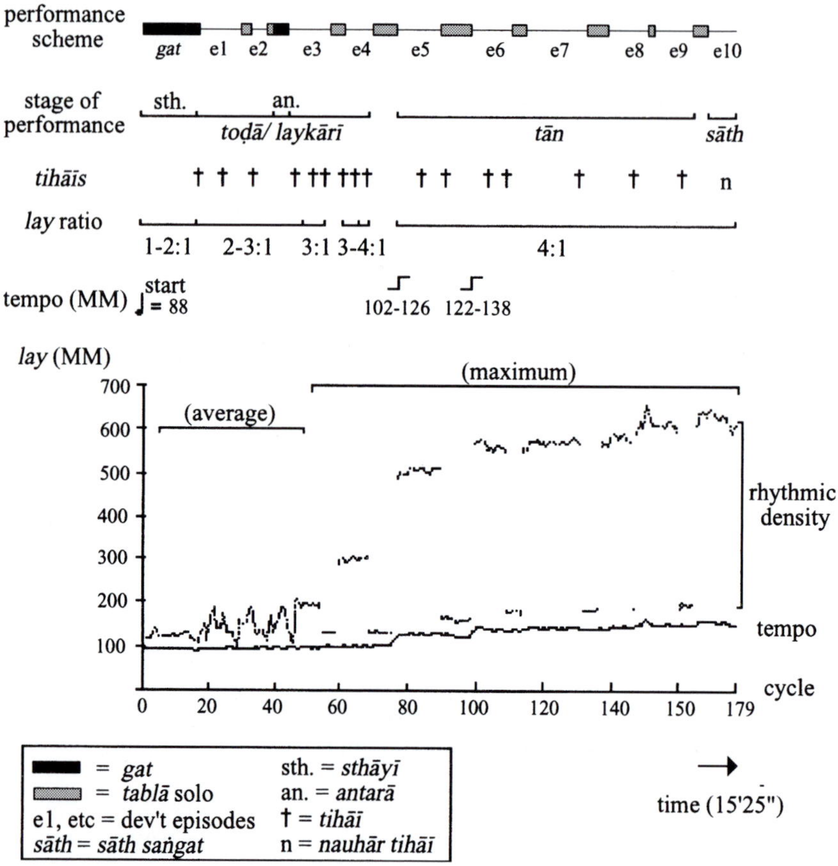

Example 11.7 A correlation of rhythmic features of a performance of a *madhya lay gat* in *rāg pūriyā* by Deepak Choudhury, in *jhaptāl*

performance), and the greater number of *lay* ratios employed here (due to the need to shift from a lower rhythmic density than the *madhya lay gat* to the same maximum). Surprisingly, given the otherwise greater emphasis on rhythm in the *madhya lay gat*, of these two examples the *vilambit gat* actually employs more *tihāīs* than the *madhya lay gat*. One possible explanation for this is that the cycle of *jhaptāl* in the latter performance is so short (c. 4–6.5 secs.) that *tihāīs* must either be very short, or they must cover more than one cycle, as does the ending *nauhār tihāī*. In the cycle of *vilambit tīntāl* on the other hand, there is enough time (12–22 secs.) for a substantial *tihāī* leading to either the *mukhṛā* or *sam*, and this partly explains the high number counted. Therefore the comparison between the charts points to considerable similarity between the performance styles, besides confirming the significant difference in approach at the early stages of the development.

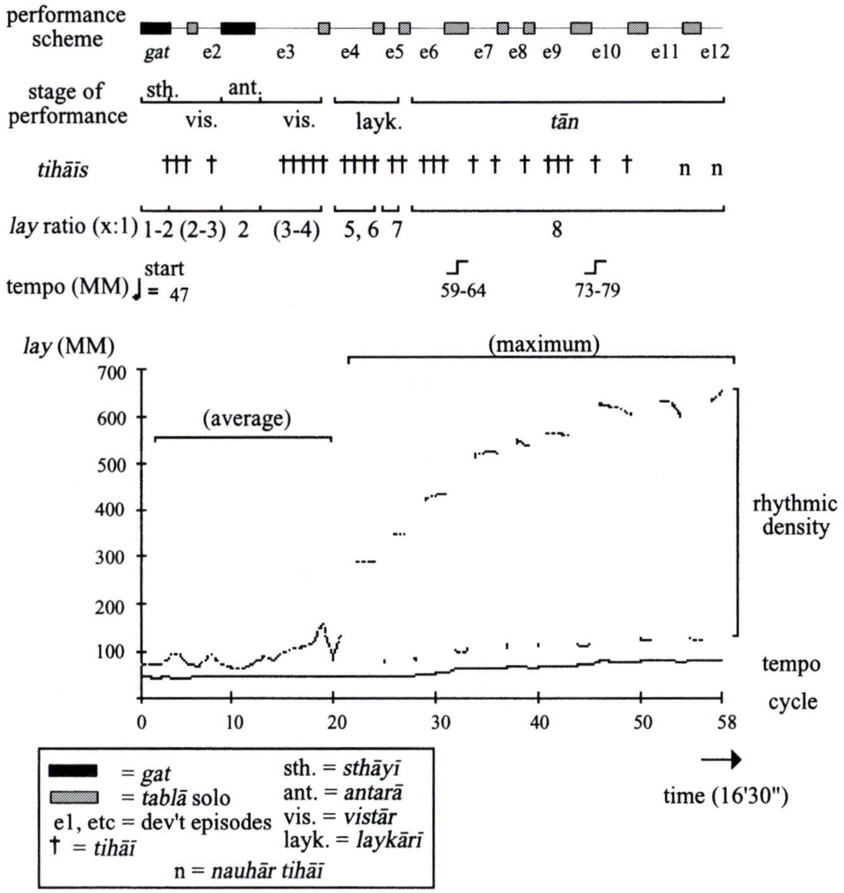

Example 11.8 A correlation of rhythmic features of a performance of a *vilambit gat* in *rāg bhaṭiyār* by Deepak Choudhury, in *tīntāl*

A number of features are illustrated clearly in both charts. These include the association of the first significant increase in tempo with the switch to *tāns* (in the case of the *vilambit gat* in Example 11.8, the acceleration actually follows the first burst of 8 : 1 *tāns*), the use of a stepwise increase in *lay* ratio to raise the rhythmic density to a suitable level for fast *tāns*, and the episodic structure common to both performances. Useful as these charts are however, they cannot illustrate all the important rhythmic parameters, nor can they illustrate connections with vocal genres. In order to compare a wider range of rhythmic parameters—not only *madhya lay* versus *vilambit gat*, but also each of these versus its vocal 'model', the most important parameters are set out in Table 11.4.

In this chart the comparison may be made between the four columns, and it is clear that in several respects the *gat* forms do appear to correlate with their

Table 11.4 A comparison of rhythmic parameters between *dhrupad*, *baṛā khyāl*, and Deepak Choudhury's *madhya lay gat* and *vilambit gat*

1 genre	*dhrupad (dhamār)*	*madhya lay gat (dhrupad aṅg)*	*vilambit gat (khyāl aṅg)*	*baṛā khyāl*
2 vocal influence	n/a	said to be analogous to *dhrupad*	said to be analogous to *baṛā khyāl*	n/a
3 performance context	follows full *ālāp*: sometimes precedes fast *dhrupad*	follows full *ālāp-joṛ*: sometimes precedes *drut gat*	follows *aochār* (brief *ālāp*): precedes *drut gat*	begins recital or follows brief *ālāp*: precedes *choṭā khyāl*
4 principal *tāls*	*cautāl* (4422), *jhaptāl* (2323), *dhamār tāl* (554)	*jhaptāl* (2323), *rūpak tāl* (322), *cārtāl kī savārī* (443), *pañcam savārī tāl* (4443), *matta tāl* (423), *dhamār tāl* (554)	*tīntāl* (4444)	*ektāl* (4422), *jhūmrā tāl* (3434), *tīntāl/tilvāḍā tāl* (4444)
5 *lay* (tempo)*	47–128 MM	85–180 MM	32–92 MM	10.7–60 MM
6 *lay* (average rhythmic density)†	n/a	110–185 *bols*/min.	67–90 *bols*/min.	n/a
7 *lay* (maximum rhythmic density)	up to 256 *bols*/min.	294–640 *bols*/min.	290–656 *bols*/min.	up to 378 *bols*/min.
8 *lay* (acceleration pattern)	most common: gradual acceleration. in some passages, tempo constant or with wide fluctuation.	starts stable, stepped acceleration around change to *tān* phase and one or more further increases.	(as *madhya lay gat*)	most common: constant, or gradual acceleration. stepped acceleration to *tāns* in some styles.
9 *lay* ratios used (those in parentheses optional)	most common: 2 : 1, (3 : 1), 4 : 1	2 : 1, 3 : 1, 4 : 1 (and occasionally 4 : 3, 5 : 2, 7 : 2, 6 : 1, 8 : 1)	3 : 1, 4 : 1, (5 : 1), 6 : 1, (7 : 1), 8 : 1, (12 : 1)	most common: 4 : 1, (6 : 1) and 8 : 1 against metric pulse (up to 32 : 1 against *mātrā*)

10 *bandiś* or *gat* structure	syllabic, cover whole cycle	syllabic, cover whole cycle	syllabic, cover whole cycle (with some melisma interpolated)	melismatic, except more syllabic *mukhṛā*
11	either *sam*-to-*sam* or with *mukhṛā*. *cautāl bandiśes* often with contra-metric setting	either *sam*-to-*sam*, or with $2\frac{1}{2}$ *mātrā mukhṛā*. most *tāl*-based, some syncopated	most based on modified *masītkhānī gat* (with 5 *mātrā mukhṛā*)	many styles use *bandiśes* with the only recognizable 'structure' in the *mukhṛā*, the remainder improvised
12 formal scheme of performance (development techniques)	1. *Bandiś* (composition) statement	1. *Gat (sthāyī)* statement	1. *Gat (sthāyī)* statement	1. *Bandiś* statement (usually *sthāyī* only)
13	2. Development (*upaj*); episodic	2. Development: episodic, with *tablā* solos accompanied by *sitār gat*	2. Development: episodic, with *tablā* solos accompanied by *sitār gat*	2. Development: episodic, with the *bandiś mukhṛā* as refrain
14	consists of *bol bāṇṭ*: syllabic, text-based rhythmic development	starts with syllabic rhythmic development (*toḍā, laykārī*). *gat antarā* follows	starts with *rāg* development (*vistār*); *gat antarā* follows	starts with melismatic *vistār* (*baṛhat, ālāp*); *bandiś antarā* usually follows once upper Sa reached
15	rhythmic density increases, but no *tāns*	*tāns* in 4 : 1 in latter part of performance	*tāns* in 8 : 1 in latter part of performance	fast *tāns* in latter part of performance
16	accompanied by combination of *ṭhekā*, *pakhāvaj* solo, and *sāth saṅgat*	ends with episode of *sāth saṅgat*	no *sāth saṅgat*	

* Figures refer to the sample of performances cited in the discography, unless otherwise stated.

† Average and maximum rhythmic densities are taken from the two *gat* performances illustrated in Table 11.3; those for vocal genres are based on the performances cited in the discography.

vocal 'models' (see rows 2, 3, 5, 14, and possibly 10, 15, and 16). However, in other cases the *gats* compare more closely with each other (see rows 7, 8, 9, 12, 13 and possibly 15), or demonstrate the influence of some other source (such as South Indian music), or in some cases present a situation too complicated to be summarized simply (rows 4 and 11). In this way the search for correlations with vocal music not only provides evidence of exactly that, but also of mutual influence between the *gat* forms, of the independent development of instrumental music, and of the influence from other sources on both *gats*.

11.4 Conclusions

The aim of the case study presented here was to investigate the view that these two *gat* forms are modelled on two analogous vocal forms. Differences in performance practice were recognized and analysed, with a view to determining whether they may be associated with the influence of vocal genres (and not simply due to, say, the differences in performance tempo). Evidence to support DC's contention on vocal influence included the difference in metric tempo, the presence of melismatic *vistār* in the *vilambit gat* and the relatively syllabic style of the *madhya lay gat*, and the *bol* density calculations which confirm the more melismatic style of the slow *gat*. The use of the *mukhṛā* in the *vilambit gat*, and the limited use of *sāth saṅgat* in the *madhya lay gat* accompaniment, may also be cited as possible evidence for the influence of vocal genres. However, the areas in which the vocal genres most clearly exert influence are in the large-scale organization (particularly in the fact that, as in *khyāl*, *rāg* development in the *khyāl aṅg* is concentrated in the metred section); and in a greater emphasis on rhythm in the *dhrupad aṅg* (although in several respects its realization is different from that in *dhrupad*).

Against this evidence, however, must be set the use of *tāns* in both genres (reflected in the near-identical maximum rhythmic densities), extensive use of *tihāīs* and of South Indian-influenced *laykārī* techniques, and a common accompaniment style. These factors, and others such as DC's recent introduction of *mukhṛās* into his *madhya lay gats*, suggest both the diversity of influences brought to bear on the *gat* forms, and a powerful tendency to mutual influence, illustrating the difficulty for a creative artist in limiting cross-fertilization between theoretically distinct forms.

It is clearly not the case that the *gats* are intended as literal imitations of the vocal genres. This is inevitable, since a number of factors would render imitations of vocal forms on the *sitār* less than satisfying. The loss of the text and its meaning might be felt to diminish the music, unless it were compensated for—as it is here by a greater rhythmic complexity in both *gat* forms. Moreover, and perhaps more importantly, the severe lack of sustain of the *sitār* relative to the voice means that this must be balanced by a higher rhythmic density;

consequently differences in rhythmic style between vocal and instrumental music are inevitable.

The development of the *vilambit* and *madhya lay gats* as part of the *khyāl* and *dhrupad aṅgs*, respectively, has succeeded in generating diversity and rhythmic interest in the Maihar *gharānā sitār* repertoire. However, each of the *gat* forms has continued to develop, and various forces are felt which continue to influence that development, of which three are particularly important: (1) the retention of certain elements which suggest the influence of the vocal forms (as initially envisaged perhaps); (2) the inevitable cross-fertilization of techniques and structural elements between *gats*; and (3) the adoption of elements from sources other than the two stated vocal genres. The later historical development of these *gats* may be understood to a great extent as the result of the interaction of these factors.

This study shows how investigation of the information available within the oral tradition can lead to a productive analysis. Although the main thrust of that tradition (at least in DC's interpretation)—that the difference in performance styles between the *gats* was due principally to their different origins in vocal forms—could only be partially confirmed, this undoubtedly remains an important factor. The investigation also brought to light other factors contributing to the complicated pattern of historical development of these *gats*, such as mutual influence between the different forms, and influence from other quarters such as the percussion repertoire and South Indian music. As had been hoped, rhythmic analysis proves to be a powerful tool in this kind of investigation.

12

North Indian rhythmic organization in cross-cultural perspective

12.1 Introduction

I suggested earlier that any study of rhythm in a specific repertoire ought to generate observations which contribute to the development of rhythmic theory in general. In this light, a number of questions present themselves immediately. Might it be possible, by pulling together data and analysis from many different music cultures, to develop generally applicable theories of rhythmic organization, according to which each individual system is shown to have certain fundamental features, explicable in general terms? Could each rhythmic system be described in terms of general parameters founded on psycho-physiological universals, with limits for each parameter determined locally? Or, on the contrary, is musical rhythm's boundless diversity beyond the reach of such general or comparative study?

These questions amount to more than idle speculation. If general and comparative study of rhythm is impractical (and many ethnomusicologists will assume it to be so, unless and until the contrary can be demonstrated) then how can we develop widely applicable definitions of basic rhythmic terms such as tempo, metre, and even rhythm itself, let alone of more sophisticated concepts such as syncopation, polyrhythm, and polymetre? And, without clearly defined concepts and terminology, how can comparative rhythmic analysis proceed? There are clearly dangers in simply employing Western terms and concepts in the rhythmic analysis and transcription of non-Western musics—not least that it is doubtful whether the current state of Western music theory can adequately describe even the greater part of Western tonal music itself—and if general theories cannot be developed these problems will continue to plague us.

With these issues in mind, I will now consider two interconnected issues—first, how does North Indian *tāl*, as described above, relate to metre in general; and secondly, how can a study of *ālāp* contribute to an understanding of the phenomenon of 'free rhythm' (and vice versa).

12.2 Metre and *tāl*

12.2.1 Six statements revisited

I proposed in Chapter 3 a set of six statements regarding musical metre, which I hoped would serve as points of comparison with North Indian music. They were as follows:

1. Much music (but not all) is organized with respect to a periodic and hierarchical temporal framework, in such a way that a cognitive representation of this framework may be generated in the mind of the listener. This organization and its representation are termed 'metre'.
2. Metre can be said to exist when two or more continuous streams of pulsation are perceived to interact; these streams are composed of time points (beats) separated by durations definable as multiples of a basic time unit. Time points which are perceived as beats on more than one level are 'stronger' than those which are beats on only one level; metre can thus be regarded as necessarily hierarchical.
3. Beats may be differentiated by stress and/or duration (i.e. they can be perceived as strong and weak, and/or long and short).
4. The relationship between metre and rhythm has two complementary aspects: metre is inferred (largely) on the basis of evidence presented by rhythm, while rhythm is interpreted in terms of its relationship to that metre.
5. The inference of metre is a complex phenomenon which is influenced by the musical experience and training of the listener, and more indirectly perhaps by his or her general experience and cultural background. Consequently both metric theory and practice are culturally determined to a great extent, although they are ultimately founded on the same psycho-physiological universals.
6. The cognition of metre appears to be dependent on one or more of the following factors: the extent of the perceptual present (determining that pulses are unlikely to be separated by more than 2–3 secs.); the function of short-term memory; and the ability to comprehend recurring patterns as single Gestalts which combine notions of stress and duration.

If one compares North Indian *tāl* with metre in this general sense, what can this tell us? Before answering this question, it is worth quickly reviewing the complexity and ambiguity of *tāl* as conceived by North Indian musicians. *Tāl* has two main aspects, one as an abstract temporal scheme manifested through clap patterns, the other as a repeated rhythmic pattern represented by a *ṭhekā*. Clap patterns manifest abstract temporal structures, defining the organization of a regular pulse into groups within a cycle. The history of theoretical speculation on *tāl* indicates that Indian musicians have long felt a clear conceptual separation between *tāl* (in this sense as an abstract temporal scheme) and rhythm.

However, use of the *ṭhekā* suggests that *tāl* is not a wholly abstract phenomenon, since *tāls* are associated with concrete rhythmic patterns which can be reproduced even outside their principal context. This suggests that in reality, a *tāl* may be simply a repeated rhythmic pattern with parameters of stress, timing, and timbre—a pattern perceived and remembered as a whole or Gestalt, perhaps in a 'figural' mode of rhythmic understanding. The importance of the concrete aspect of *tāl* (*tāl* as defined by stress patterns and their associated parameters), should not be obscured by the more abstract patterns outlined in theory.

Kolinski's Gestalt psychology-inspired concept of metre seems to apply to North Indian *tāl*, whether the latter is understood as abstract framework or even as a concrete rhythmic pattern. *Tāl* is a temporal framework acting as a background for rhythmic design, just as Kolinski described metre. Lerdahl and Jackendoff's theory of metre also seems to be applicable to *tāl*, which, as we have demonstrated, can easily be analysed in terms of their theory. The one significant allowance we have to make in so doing is for the possibility of the middle pulse level (the *vibhāg* or subsection) being irregular, as it is in *jhaptāl*—an example, perhaps, of Indian musical culture applying different 'well-formedness' rules for metre. Better still perhaps, adopting London's formulation—metre as a modular arrangement of beats rather than as the interaction of pulse levels—this problem might be avoided completely. *Tāl*-bound music is not only periodically organized, it is also structured hierarchically, and it is difficult to avoid the conclusion that *tāl* has a good deal in common with Western metre.

Comparing what we know about *tāl* with my six working statements on metre, we can make the following observations:

1. *Tāl* establishes a periodic and hierarchic temporal framework (a form of metre). We may reasonably assume that a cognitive representation of that framework may be constructed by a listener (depending, crucially, on that listener's knowledge and experience).

2. *Tāl*, like metre, can be described in terms of the interaction of two or more streams of pulsation (in fact, usually at least three). One of these pulse levels may, however, be composed of a sequence of unequal time intervals. Beats on more than one pulse level are structurally important and are marked by hand gestures.

3. Beats at the *mātrā* level are equal (categorically equivalent) in duration; some are marked as initiating *vibhāgs* by hand gestures, and/or drum stress and timbre. If we regard the *vibhāg* as a beat, *vibhāgs* may be differentiated by duration and/or stress.

4. As with metre, rhythm in Indian music is interpreted with respect to *tāl*. However, the inference of *tāl* is less subjective than that of metre in many other traditions, especially if the *tāl* structure is clearly illustrated by clap pattern and/or *ṭhekā*.

5. The inference of *tāl* by musically uneducated listeners, assuming it can be inferred, would be at least as complex as that of metre in any other music

tradition. In the case of musically educated listeners, however, it can involve relatively simple procedures—often simply the recognition of clap pattern and/or *ṭhekā*.

6. The evidence of *tāl* practice suggests that the perceptual present and/or short-term memory may have some significance, in that cycles longer than a few seconds tend not to be counted out with hand gestures, and rely instead on the cueing function of various *tablā* stroke combinations. However, the idea that the cycle or period should be limited to a few seconds is not borne out; Indian musicians seem happy so long as *mātrā* and perhaps *vibhāg* pulses are directly perceptible, leaving the *āvart* (cycle) to be consciously conceived with the aid of memory. Shorter patterns seem to be more amenable to direct, figural understanding, as one would expect.

It appears overall that North Indian *tāl* functions in many ways rather like metre in Western music, creating a periodic, hierarchic framework for rhythmic design. Perhaps the simplest way to state the relationship between *tāl* and metre is to say that metre is an important aspect of *tāl* (i.e. that *tāl* includes metre), but that *tāl* is also a broader concept, involving dimensions not encountered in other metric systems. It is reasonable therefore to describe *tāl* as a kind of metric system. If, however, we wish to make cross-cultural comparisons we must take care to compare like with like—much of the theoretical and conceptual paraphernalia of *tāl* are best compared only with similar constructions where these have developed in other cultures.

There are two important respects in which metre as generated by *tāl* differs from metre in tonal music—that it may have an irregular intermediate pulse level, and that it is usually determined absolutely objectively by convention. I have already described the former point as an instance of Indian music possibly applying different 'well-formedness rules' for metre than Western music. As for the latter, time signatures in Western music are determined by composers and generally remain fixed; nevertheless listeners are not obliged to interpret the metre of the performed music as written, and nor is their understanding or enjoyment of music always dependent on the 'correct' identification of metre—except perhaps in specific circumstances such as dances, where a particular motor response is expected.

In comparison with many other metric systems, *tāl* is peculiarly explicit—it is not simply an inherent quality of the music, to be inferred subjectively by the listener. If this were the case listeners might find two or more metric interpretations of a piece of music to be equally valid, an idea alien to most Indian musical thought. In Indian music it is not uncommon for a musician to be employed primarily or even exclusively to keep *tāl* (this applies to the *tablā* player himself in some genres of North Indian music). Singers count out the *tāl*, members of the audience join them, and there is no choice or subjectivity involved in metric interpretation. To say that a piece of music is 'in *tāl*' is thus more than to say it is metred, on two main counts:

1. *Tāl* is an explicit dimension of the music which must be established objectively and *unambiguously*.
2. Rhythm should be organized according to one or other *authorized* metrical pattern or *tāl*.

These conditions in turn reaffirm something of the values of Indian music culture. I suggested in Chapter 2 that *tāl* developed under the influence of music's relationship with religious ritual, and how that relationship dictated a stress on the importance of time measurement. The significance of this is confirmed by the importance of the unambiguous establishment of metre, and of the authorization of particular patterns.

12.2.2 *Tāl* and the general study of metre

As for what the study of North Indian *tāl* tells us about metre in general, perhaps the most important point is that it is possible to develop a theory of musical metre with cross-cultural applicability. There are enough points in common between the Western concept of metre, and the North Indian concept of *tāl*, for us to be able to extract those points and use them to help build a more general theory of metre; where elements of individual systems appear to be unique (as above), they may be recognized as such. Thus, at least in a small way, it is possible to move towards a generally applicable metric theory, within which specific examples are each regarded as special cases.

Were we to study different musics with a view to classifying rhythmic organization as either metric, periodic (i.e. based on repeating patterns but without accentual matrices, as suggested by Arom), or non-periodic, the systems of several other traditions would no doubt fall into the first category (such as, for instance, much music of the Middle East and South-East Asia). There is little doubt, also, that each would present unique features, while the shared nature of at least some of the aspects of metre described here would confirm the cross-cultural applicability of the concept.

More specifically, there are a number of areas in which a study of *tāl* may clarify issues in general studies of metre. First, it sheds light on the idea that the relationship between rhythm and metre is analogous to that between figure and ground in Gestalt psychology. At first sight North Indian music provides the clearest possible endorsement of this view, in that Indian musicians clearly separate rhythm and metre (*tāl*) conceptually; *tāl* is an abstract framework primarily constructed in the mind of the performer and represented by a clap pattern and/or a *ṭhekā* (from which it may in turn be reconstructed by a listener), while rhythm is understood and interpreted in the context of this framework.

There are some problems with this separation, however, which should be noted here. For instance, a *ṭhekā* is a rhythmic pattern used to represent or signify a *tāl* (and hence a metre)—since it performs this function, it comes to be identified with the *tāl*. Thus what signifies *tāl* comes to embody *tāl*, and there can in practice be no clear separation between the two levels. Thus both the separation of rhythm and *tāl* and the abstract nature of the latter may be compromised by the use of the *ṭhekā*. A similarly intimate relationship between rhythm and metre is found in many musics, to the extent that often a metre cannot be conceived as distinct from the rhythmic pattern which represents it; metre is therefore, paradoxically, both conceptually distinct from rhythm and an aspect of rhythm.

Secondly, this study confirms the crucial importance of tempo in the functioning of metre. Metre is formed by the interaction of pulse levels, and it is probable that particular pulse levels may be assigned certain functions in the cognitive representation of metre. Metres can be accelerated or decelerated, but if tempo is changed beyond certain limits then the functioning of the metre must be disturbed. The function of individual pulse levels, as I have shown, may change, and pulse levels may become obsolete in the cognition of metre, or new levels come into play. I have demonstrated this in North Indian music, and I have no reason to suppose that similar phenomena do not occur elsewhere.

A third area where the study of Indian music can assist development of a general theory of metre is in the important role of theory. North Indian music is a good example of a metric system which clearly could not exist in its present form, if it were not for the contribution of theory to the development of practice; nor could many of the metric structures employed in North Indian music be intuited by listeners who had no access to that same theory. Thus theory is not only something which describes *tāl*, it is part of the very fabric of *tāl* and cannot be dissociated from it. Theory plays a role in assisting the cognitive representation of complex structures, and creates possibilities for developments in practice.

12.3 Free rhythm and music without *tāl*

12.3.1 Free rhythm and *ālāp*

If the study of *tāl* should contribute to a general theory of metre, the same could be said of *ālāp* and so-called 'free rhythm'—in other words, the temporal organization of music without a clear metric structure. As I suggested in Chapter 7, there are numerous other musical styles around the world described as free rhythm, which appear to exhibit none of the qualities of metre (i.e. whose rhythmic organization is neither periodical nor hierarchical); such musical traditions have tended to be somewhat neglected in the literature of ethnomusicology, although interest in this field has increased in recent years.

My first task here is to clarify the sense in which I use the phrase 'free rhythm'. In the terms I have been using up to this point, 'free rhythm' complements not so much our narrow definition of metre, but a wider sense including both metre and other types of pulse-based periodic organization (such as that described by

Arom; for an extended discussion of this topic see Clayton 1996). A common-sense definition of 'free rhythm' as 'the rhythm of music without metre' would thus translate more precisely as the rhythm of music without pulse-based periodic organization—in other words, free rhythm may or may not have a simple pulse, but whenever this pulse is organized periodically, rhythm cannot be described as 'free'.

This definition of free rhythm may be clarified with reference to the graphic illustration in Example 12.1. All music has 'rhythm'; some but not all has a perceived pulse; of this 'pulsed' music some but not all has this pulse organized periodically; and some but not all forms of periodic organization may be described as 'metre'.[1] According to our definition, the term 'free rhythm' applies to the area shaded in the Example 12.1.

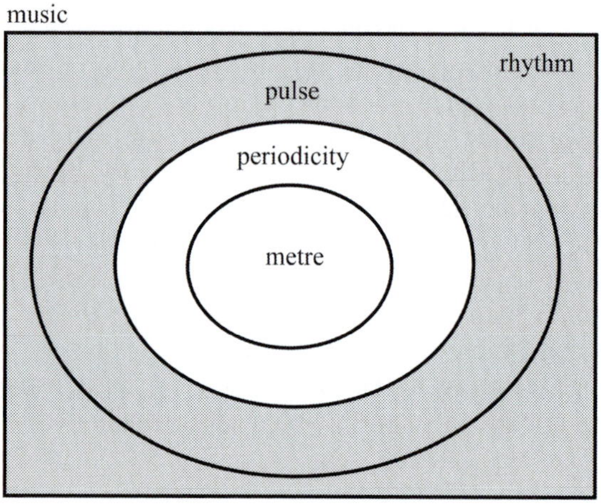

Example 12.1 The organization of rhythm in music. The shaded area is referred to as 'free rhythm'

12.3.2 Free rhythm and metre in music without *tāl*

I am not in a position to make sweeping generalizations about the organization of *ālāp* on the basis of only my own brief studies and those of Widdess (which to my knowledge are the only such analytical studies to date). These studies do, however, suggest a number of insights which deserve further investigation. Among these are the following:

1. That the well-known tendencies to subjective imposition of a pulse, and subjective grouping of a perceived pulse, in rhythm perception seem to have wider implications. In music such as the first stage of *ālāp*, where (it is generally

[1] Since almost nothing is known about the temporal organization of music without consistent pulse, it cannot be ruled out that some form of periodicity may be detected in such music. In this event, all subsequent references to 'periodicity' in this chapter should be read as 'pulse-based periodicity'.

affirmed) performers' and listeners' concentration should be on 'pure melody' without the 'distraction' of rhythm, it is actually rather hard to play or sing in such a way that no pulse is perceived. It seems likely that, in many cases at least, this is achieved by the performer actually keeping a pulse (in some cases, perhaps, unconsciously), but (*a*) making the pulse as slow as possible, and (*b*) using syncopations (i.e. playing off the beat) to the extent that the beat cannot be (or generally is not, at least) perceived. Pulse rates determined for *dhrupad ālāp* by Widdess, of around 1.65 secs. (1994 : 67), are close to the limits suggested by psychological research before 'pulses' begin to appear disconnected from one another. It may nevertheless be possible to sustain performance completely without pulse, concealed or not, for several minutes, if the durations between (potentially) rhythmic events is kept sufficiently high.

2. *Ālāp* seems to fluctuate between more or less 'pulsed' rhythm; as Widdess suggests, moments perceived as being particularly 'free' may be those of particular melodic significance or complexity, in other words exactly those moments when one would least want the 'distraction' of rhythmic regularity (1995 : 86).

3. Human beings may, as Condon suggests, tend to organize any activity according to a hierarchy of temporal levels, levels which may be related either to the frequency of particular brain-waves or to other cognitive or neurological functions. I would suggest that this tendency to organize activity hierarchically may typically extend beyond the kind of short durations considered by Condon.

The limited evidence of the example I presented in Chapter 7 may suggest that in rhythm at its slowest and most 'free', musical events, figures, or gestures tend to fall within a time-span of 2–3 seconds; longer gaps between the initiations of new gestures (up to 4 or 5 secs. perhaps) may be perceived as 'breaks' marking a higher hierarchical level—a sequence or phrase perhaps. These figures seem to be broadly similar, both in Widdess's examples where he does detect a pulse, and in mine where I do not. We do not have enough, or sufficiently detailed analyses to suggest mean or maximum durations for such sequences, but the evidence of my and Widdess's figures could be read as hinting at a range from around 10 secs. up to 20 secs. or even a little more. These temporally identifiable sequences seem to correlate with logical 'episodes' of melodic development, which are themselves organized into sections, and those sections into the greater sections of *vilambit*, *madhya*, and *drut ālāp* or *ālāp* and *joṛ*, which would typically last at least 10 minutes, and sometimes considerably longer.

4. In 'free rhythm' music in which text plays a role, I would expect the structure of the text (both phonetic and semantic perhaps) to be an important factor in controlling the temporal organization. Where text is not a factor, as in most *ālāp*, controlling factors seem to include physical constraints (such as the length of a breath, or the decay of the vibrations of a string); the logic of melodic development; and factors such as the limits of the perceptual present and short-term memory, and (perhaps) other cognitive or neurological functions.

I must reiterate that much of this is speculative, but it does nevertheless hint at what may be principles for the organization of rhythm which can operate either independently, or in conjunction with a pulse or metrical framework. These principles might be called gestural or figurative, and contribute to the 'grouping' structures which Lerdahl and Jackendoff insist on separating from metric hierarchies. If this can be demonstrated, then their position will be vindicated, and the commonplace assertion that 'metre organizes rhythm' may assume a greater significance. The frequent assertions that metre can and should be conceptually distinct from rhythm (although dependent on it), the two-level analyses of Lerdahl and Jackendoff, the Indian conceptual separation of *tāl* and rhythm, and Bamberger's suggestion of two modes of rhythmic understanding (figural and metric), all seem to me to point in the same direction. The suggestion that forms such as *ālāp* represent the situation where the metric level is either weak or absent, with grouping hierarchy only and rhythmic comprehension almost entirely figural, is—although not proven—an interesting one.

12.4 *Tāl*, metre, and free rhythm—a summary

It should be clear that in neither the case of *tāl* and metre, nor in that of *ālāp* and free rhythm are the two sets of categories identical. *Tāl*, although related to the concept of metre, is more specific and needs to be regarded as a special case within the latter's general category: consideration of the special qualities of *tāl* has helped clarify some of the qualities implied by the other term. There is some doubt whether all *ālāp* can be regarded as unpulsed 'free rhythm', while some if not all *joṛ* would certainly qualify, according to most definitions, as metred. Studies of *ālāp* and of the processes of gradual rhythmic and metric definition and acceleration can be used to shed light on general issues of 'free rhythm', and the boundaries between free rhythm and metre. Example 12.2 clarifies the relationship between Indian and Western categories with respect to the stages of *dhrupad* performance (and their instrumental equivalents).

instrumental	*ālāp*	*joṛ*	*jhālā*	*gat*
dhrupad	*vilambit ālāp*	*madhya ālāp*	*drut ālāp*	*bandiś*
Western	'free rhythm'	———	metre	———
Indian	———	no *tāl*	———	*tāl*

EXAMPLE **12.2** Four stages in complete performances of *dhrupad* and instrumental forms, described in terms of Western and Indian rhythmic categories

The subjectivity of rhythmic interpretation is once again a key point here. If metre is a quality inferred by the listener, then it is questionable whether any piece of music can be objectively said to be *in* a particular metre. Even in *rāg* music, a piece in *jhaptāl* will not always be *perceived* to be in a 10-beat metre—it is more than possible that a listener could fail to recognize this level of periodicity and hear the rhythm in relation to a simple pulse, or a binary alternation of pulses. Conversely, the music Arom suggests is not organized around a regular accentual matrix could still be heard as metrical by a listener who subjectively imposed such a framework.

Nevertheless, in many cases a particular metric interpretation is overwhelmingly more likely than any other (or none). This is all the more relevant when listeners—by listening, and particularly in the context of a social musical event—are effectively taught to interpret music in a particular way (as, for instance, where a particular style or piece of music has a dance associated with it). *Tāl* presents a special case in that a particular metric interpretation can generally be said to be 'correct' rather than simple 'more likely' or 'preferred': the listener who counts *tāl* differently does so incorrectly.

I will conclude this study with a number of general points which I find either emerge from or are confirmed by this study of North Indian *rāg* music.

1. The rhythmic organization of *rāg* music seems to me to reflect not so much a unique Indian approach to music-making (and hence a dichotomy with respect to Western music). I see *rāg* music as exploiting the same possibilities, and attempting to solve the same problems, as any other repertoire, but doing so in unique ways which produce rather distinctive sonic results.

2. I have argued against the position that rhythm simply reflects deeper structural patterns in culture, or that it 'represents' a particular world-view. Rather, I see such patterns, as revealed by ideological assumptions in other domains of culture, as having an impact on music which can be at times direct, but is more often rather indirect and contingent. I see music-making as part of a continuous process of our engagement with the world and with each other, and ideologies being constantly reinforced *and* challenged as part of that process.

3. The role of music theory in the evolution of music systems is often greatly underestimated. The example of metrical patterns in Hindustānī music which (I argue) could only have achieved their present form as the result of an interplay between practice and theory over several centuries, is a case in point. Theory does not simply describe, or for that matter prescribe practice: it has a considerable impact on the way people transform elements of repertoire which have been passed on to them, and therefore on the way repertoires change, often in ways which could not have been predicted.

4. If different rhythmic systems are to be described as different solutions to the same problems, or of different ways of working within the same parameters, then this begs the question of what those problems or parameters may be. The literature suggests many candidates, from the 'present' to various aspects of memory; from a cerebral clock to a natural and spontaneous pulse rate; the significance of breathing and heart rate or of natural walking pace; thresholds of

perception and general Gestalt tendencies. Any (or, indeed, all) of these, and other psycho-physiological factors may be significant in setting limits for rhythm. I must conclude, however, that theory in this area still has a considerable way to go.

5. The apparent paradox of metre—that it seems to be somehow independent of rhythm, and yet must be encoded in and decoded from rhythm—is as relevant to Indian music as it is to Western music. Although there has been some debate between those, such as Lerdahl and Jackendoff, who would apparently separate metre and grouping structure, and others such as Hasty who would reassert the dependence of metre on rhythm, part of the solution is surely the recognition that (at least) two hierarchical structures may be decoded from the same sonic information.

One of these is based on the recognition of pulse, and of its grouping (whether this is seen as the interaction of pulse levels or as a modular arrangement in which groups are not necessarily equal in duration), and may be termed metrical. The other is based on the (apparently) direct apprehension of musical Gestalts—notes, phrases, statements, gestures—and their hierarchical, quasi-semantic arrangement. These different types of hierarchy may be decoded from the same musical input, and not only that but they may be decoded simultaneously, and it would seem that the cognition of one type of hierarchy can influence the other—both together contribute to our sense of 'the rhythm' of a piece of music. Forms exist in which the perceived metric hierarchy is likely to be very weak or non-existent (so-called 'free rhythm'); other repertoires exist in which the two hierarchies coincide to such a degree that many would argue the distinction does not have any relevance.

6. It does seem that listeners are predisposed to discover both kinds of hierarchy, albeit perhaps with considerable individual and group differences in the ways that they do so. For instance, there appear to be cultural as well as individual differences in the priority given to various possible kinds of clues in the decoding of both kinds of hierarchy. A given piece of music does not simply have a given pair of hierarchies, metric and grouping. These hierarchies have to be inferred, and it seems that where, for instance, Indian musicians see the metric structure of a piece as being indicated by its drum pattern and (perhaps inaudible) hand gestures, others would be more inclined to infer metre from melodic structure and regard drum rhythms as decorative.

7. Besides these considerations, rhythm is one of the domains within which ideas of repetition, recurrence, change, variation, and development are worked out. I am not the first to note that in any musical performance, aspects of both recurrence and change may be observed (I find Jonathan Kramer's formulations of linearity and non-linearity particularly useful in this regard). A piece in which nothing recurs, and nothing is repeated, is a piece which is impossible to comprehend. We need to feel that 'the same' note recurred, the same chord, the same phrase or melody, the same rhythm or indeed the same beat of the metric pattern. Without sameness, without repetition, and without equivalence

classes, music cannot have (be assigned) structure and cannot make sense. Music, in fact, more than many other spheres of human activity, thrives on repetition.

At the same time, music depends on change, whether conceived as contrast or variation. For there to be a 'same' there also has to be a category 'not the same', for A to make sense there has to be a B with which to contrast it (and perhaps a C, D, and E). Even the simplest imaginable piece of music has a contrast between 'sounding' and 'not sounding' or between 'louder' and 'less loud'. I see the interplay between same and different, recurrence and change as inescapable in music, but of course different repertoires work with such basic principles in different ways, theories explain them in different ways, those theories engage with other spheres of discourse, and so on. Where the dominant ideology values change conceived as goal-oriented development, music theory is likely to find the same things in music; and perhaps, ultimately, musicians will practise what the theorists predicted. Where the dominant ideas accept recurrence as part of the natural order, music theorists will be more likely to conceive of metre as recurrence and cyclicity.

Both of these parallels have been drawn in the past, on the one hand between tonality and Enlightenment ideology in Europe, and on the other between cyclicity and the Hindu conception of time in India. Both analogies make sense, and both are almost certainly relevant factors in music history. The error that is frequently made is to deduce that therefore Western music is teleological and develops, while Indian music is cyclical and recurs. I would argue that such a dichotomy cannot exist, because whatever theory says, change and recurrence must continue to be aspects of both repertoires.

Similarly, there can be no dichotomy between form and process, although different ideologies may stress one or the other: form is what we remember, or consciously reconstruct, on the basis of a process of listening to music over a period of time. I would suggest that form is never as simply or neatly comprehended in the act of listening as an analytical chart can make it seem. Conversely, while Indian aesthetics may place more stress on the affect experienced at the moment of perception, as a result of the process of performing and listening, nevertheless memories and conceptions of 'the piece' or performance as a whole remain.

I do not see rhythm as a neatly bounded musical domain, to be extracted and analysed in isolation; rather, I see a concentration on rhythm as one of many possible routes into the study of music, a route which is particularly likely to yield certain kinds of insights. Focus on rhythm should encourage us to concentrate on the processes of music-making and listening, perception and cognition, on music as a temporal act, on the performative, and therefore the gestural, embodied, and spatial aspects of music. To return to the description with which I began this book, I see musical performance in India (and in general, for that matter) as a rich and many-layered gestural dance, in which musicians make statements, appeal, instruct, or plead, relate to others, express their physical and emotional beings and describe their environments. For music to make sense as music these gestures (and so on) have to be experienced *in time*, to mark duration and to impart a sense of regularity and recurrence. This, of course, has been the subject of this book.

Glossary of Indian musical terms

(K) indicates senses current in Karṇāṭak (South Indian) music but not North Indian

ābhog 4th and final section of a *dhrupad* composition
addhā a form of *tīntāl* (16 *mātrās*)
ādi a *tāl* of 8 or 16 *mātrās*
āḍā cautāl a *tāl* of 14 *mātrās*
adṛṣṭa phala 'unseen benefit'
ākār vocalization to the sound 'ā'
akṣar (1) syllable, (2) (K) beat
ālāp (1) unmetred introductory movement, (2) quasi-free rhythm passage in *khyāl*
ālapti see *ālāp*, sense (2)
āmad approach, arrival
anāgat concluding before *sam*
aṅg (1) subdivision of *tāl āvart*, (2) element of repertoire, (3) section of composition
anibaddh unmetred
antarā 2nd or 3rd section of a composition
aochār brief *ālāp* (esp. instrumental)
āṛ, āṛī lay based on division into 3
āṭhgun '8 times', i.e. with a maximum density 8 times the tempo
ati- very; very much
atīt concluding after *sam*
āvard, āvart, āvartan, āvṛtti cycle (of *tāl*)
bahlāvā 'diversion', a variety of *khyāl* improvisation
bāj playing style (used particularly of *tablā* players)
bakra contrametric, i.e. not following the divisions of the *tāl*
band bol *tablā* stroke without bass resonance
bandiś composition (esp. vocal)
bānsurī flute (transverse, bamboo)
baṛa great (used of slow-tempo *khyāl*)
barābar 'even', i.e. basic speed level (*lay* ratio)
bārahgun '12 times', i.e. with a maximum density 12 times the tempo
baṛhat development or improvisation, particularly that immediately following statement of a *bandiś*
baṛtha based on division into 9s (Banaras *tablā bāj*)
bāyā̃ left-hand drum of the *tablā*
bedam without a pause (used of *tihāīs*)
bhajan a kind of Hindu devotional song
bharī bol *tablā* stroke with bass resonance
bhāv emotion, affect
bīn a stick zither (also called *rudra vīṇā*)
bol (1) song text, (2) mnemonic syllables indicating instrumental strokes
bol ālāp *ālāp* employing song text (esp. *khyāl*)

bol banāo embellishment of song text (esp. *ṭhumrī*)
bol bāṇṭ (bā̃ṭ) manipulation of song text (*dhrupad*, *khyāl*)
bol tān *tān* sung to song text
brahma tāl a *tāl* of 14 *mātrās*
cakkardār extended *tihāī*, each of whose phrases itself includes a *tihāī*
cāñcar tāl a *tāl* of either 14 or 16 *mātrās*
Carnatic, Karṇāṭak South Indian (music)
caturaśra (jāti) based on division into 4s
cārtāl kī savārī a *tāl* of 11 *mātrās*
caugun '4 times', i.e. with a maximum density 4 times the tempo
cautāl, cārtāl a *tāl* of 12 *mātrās*
chand (1) poetic metre, (2) characteristic rhythm pattern associated with a *tāl*
chegun '6 times', i.e. with a maximum density 6 times the tempo
choṭā small (used of fast-tempo *khyāl*)
cikārī 'punctuating' strings, as on a *sarod* or *sitār*
cīz composition (esp. *khyāl*)
dādrā (1) a vocal genre, (2) a *tāl* of 6 beats
damdār with a pause (used of *tihāīs*)
ḍamaru (1) hourglass-shaped pellet drum; (2) a variety of *yati*
deṛhī, deṛhgun '1 $\frac{1}{2}$ times', i.e. with a maximum density 1 $\frac{1}{2}$ times the tempo (3 : 2)
dhātu part (section) of a composition
dhamār (1) a vocal genre, (2) a *tāl* of 14 *mātrās*
dhrupad a vocal genre
dhun instrumental composition based on folk tune or vocal *dādrā* composition
dīpcandī tāl a *tāl* of either 14 or 16 *mātrās*
divya saṅkīrṇa based on division into 11s (Banaras *tablā bāj*)
drut fast (tempo)
druta a time unit in the *mārgā tāla* system
dugun 'double', i.e. with a maximum density twice the tempo
ekgun 'single', i.e. with a maximum density equal to the tempo
ekharā tān *tān* comprising a chain of single notes (cf. *toḍā*)
ektāl a *tāl* of 12 beats
farmāiś, -ī commission, commissioned
gamak ornament, ornamentation (partic. oscillation)
gamak tān *tān* utilizing prominent shaking or oscillation
gaṇa foot, group of syllables
gāndharva (1) ancient Indian music, (2) celestial music
gat instrumental composition based on idiomatic stroke patterns
gati bheda (K) stepwise increase in *lay* ratio, cf. *naḍai svara*
gatkārī (of instrumental music) playing in an idiomatic style, i.e. not imitating vocal style
gāyakī (1) vocal style or genre, (2) instrumental music imitating vocal style
gharānā stylistic 'school' or tradition
ghazal a genre of romantic song
gīt a genre of light song
gīt aṅg a term for division into 7s (Pañjāb *tablā bāj*)
gopuccha, -ā a variety of *yati*

guru (1) teacher or preceptor, (2) heavy or long syllable, (3) a time unit in the *mārga tāla* system
havelī saṅgīt 'mansion music', devotional singing closely related to *dhrupad*
Hindustānī North Indian (music)
hori dhamār variety of *dhamār* sung during, and describing, the Holi festival
iqvāī tāl a variant of tīntāl (16 *mātrās*)
jāti 'class'; for application to *laykārī* see Chs. 6, 10
jhālā section of instrumental performance
jhampak a term for division into 5s
jhaptāl a *tāl* of 10 *mātrās*
jhūlnā a term for division into 7s
jhūmrā a *tāl* of 14 *mātrās*
joṛ section of instrumental performance
kaharvā tāl a *tāl* of 8 *mātrās*
kāl(a) time
kalpa age, aeon
kārvai (K) rest or gap
kathak North Indian classical dance genre
khālī (1) *tāl* beat marked by a wave, (2) *tablā* stroke without bass resonance
khaṇḍa (jāti) quintal, i.e. based on divisions into 5
kharaj (1) bass (e.g. *tablā*), (2) drone
khulī bol *tablā* stroke with bass resonance
khyāl a vocal genre
ku- deficient, defective
kuāṛ (-āṛī lay) based on division into 5s
laggī section of fast *tablā* improvisation, usually within *ṭhumrī* performance
laghu (1) light or short syllable, (2) a time unit in the *mārgā tāla* system
laṛant 'fighting' accompaniment, cf. *sāth saṅgat*
lay tempo, rhythm
lay bāṇṭ diminution of a composition (esp. *dhrupad*)
laykārī rhythmic manipulation or variation
madhya (1) medium (tempo), (2) middle section of a composition
mahā-āṛ based on division into 12s
mahā-kuāṛ based on division into 10s
mahā-viāṛ based on division into 14s
mañjhā, māñjhā middle section of a composition
mārga tāla the ancient *tāl* system
masītkhānī a type of *gat*
mātrā beat, time unit
matta a *tāl* of 10 beats
mīṇḍ, mīṛ glissando, portamento
miśra (jāti) septimal, i.e. based on divisions into 7
mizrāb plectrum
mohrā (1) cadential phrase or anacrusis (cf. *mukhṛā*), (2) part of *tihāī*
mṛdaṅga, mridaṅga (1) barrel drum (= *pakhāvaj*), (2) a variety of *yati*
mṛdaṅgam (K) barrel drum
mukhṛā anacrusis, particularly within a composition

muqām style of improvisation in which variations conclude at the beginning of the *mukhṛā* (rather than on *sam*)
nād sound
naḍai (svara) see *gati bheda*
naugun '9 times', i.e. with a maximum density 9 times the tempo
nauhār, nau Dhā *a tihāī* each of whose phrases itself includes a *tihāī*
nibaddh metred
nimeṣa moment, blinking of the eye
nom-tom ālāp *ālāp* sung to non-lexical syllables e.g. tā, nā, re
pad (1) song text, (2) text (usu. devotional) in free verse
padma āṛ based on division into 11s (Banaras *tablā bāj*)
pakhāvaj, pakhavāj barrel drum
pallā phrase from which *tihāī* is formed
pañcam savārī tāl a *tāl* of 15 *mātrās*
pāñcgun '5 times', i.e. with a maximum density 5 times the tempo
pañjābī tīntāl variant of *tīntāl* (16 *mātrās*)
paran composition type for the *pakhāvaj* drum
paunedugun '$1\frac{3}{4}$ times', i.e. with a maximum density $1\frac{3}{4}$ times the (3 : 4) tempo (7 : 4)
paunegun '$\frac{3}{4}$ times', i.e. with a maximum density $\frac{3}{4}$ the tempo
paunetigun '$2\frac{3}{4}$ times', i.e. with a maximum density $2\frac{3}{4}$ times the tempo (11 : 4)
pipīlikā a variety of *yati*
prastār permutation
pratyavāya 'ill effect'
qavvālī a genre of Sufi devotional songs
rāg mode, melody type
ras sentiment, aesthetic flavour
razākhānī a type of *gat*
rūpak a *tāl* of 7 *mātrās*
sādrā a vocal genre
sam beat 1 of a *tāl* cycle
sama a variety of *yati*
saṃnipāta, sannipāta a gesture (hands clap together) in the *mārga tāla* system
sañcārī 3rd section of a *dhrupad* composition
saṅkīrṇa based on division into 9s
sāraṅgī a bowed lute
sāṛhetigun '$3\frac{1}{2}$ times', i.e. with a maximum density $3\frac{1}{2}$ times the tempo (7 : 2)
sargam solfège
sarod a plucked short-necked lute
sātgun '7 times', i.e. with a maximum density 7 times the tempo
sāth saṅgat synchronized accompaniment
savāī, savāgun quintal, i.e. based on divisions into 5
savārī see *cārtāl kī savārī*
sīdhā 'straight', i.e. commetric
silsilā progression
sitār a plucked long-necked lute
sitārkhānī a variant of *tīntāl* (16 *mātrās*)
śṛṅkhalā see *silsilā*

srotovaha, śrotovahā a variety of *yati*
sthāyī 1st section of a composition
sūltāl, sūrphaktā a *tāl* of 10 beats
tablā a drum pair
tāl metre, metric cycle
tāla dasa prāṇa (K) 'ten vital breaths of *tāl*'
tālī beat marked by a clap
tān rapid vocalization, or its imitation on melodic instruments
tānpūrā a drone-producing long-necked lute
ṭappā a vocal genre
taraf sympathetic strings
tarānā a vocal genre
thāh see *ekgun*
thapiyā, thāpiyā *pakhāvaj* equivalent of the *ṭhekā*
ṭhekā diagnostic drum pattern associated with a particular *tāl*
ṭhoṅk 'hammer', a special stroke on the *sitār*
ṭhumrī a vocal genre
tigun '3 times', i.e. with a maximum density 3 times the tempo
tihāī, tīyā cadential figure comprising a phrase repeated three times
tilvāḍā a variety of *tīntāl*
tīntāl a *tāl* of 16 *mātrās*
tiśra, trayśra (jāti) ternary, based on division into 3
tīvrā (1) sharp (of pitch), (2) a *tāl* of 7 beats
tīyā see *tihāī*
toḍā instrumental technique featuring combinations of single and double strokes
trikāla(m) (K) 'three speeds', i.e. playing a phrase or composition at three different *lay* ratios
upaj improvisation, development (esp. in *dhrupad*)
vāk speech, utterance
vakra see *bakra*
varṇa one of the four classes of ancient Indo-Aryan society
vazan weight, emphasis
vi- intensified
viāṛ (-āṛī lay) based on division into 7s
vibhāg section of a *tāl* cycle
vilambit slow (tempo)
viṣam (1) off-*sam*, (2) a variety of *yati*
viśrānti sthān resting place (i.e. tone)
vistār development or improvisation, especially that immediately following statement of the *bandiś*
vyavasthā organization, arrangement
yati 'shape', see Ch. 10
zarb stroke, beat
zikr verbal invocation

Discography

AMIR KHAN (= Ameer Khan) (vocal, *khyāl*); ? (*tablā*) Rāg Mārvā *jhūmrā tāl* EMI EALP1253 [disc, n.d.].

AMJAD ALI KHAN (sarod); Samta Prasad (*tablā*) Rāg Nandkauns *tīntāl (drut)* EMI EASD1348 [disc, 1970].

——Sukhvinder Singh Namdhari (*tablā*) Rāg Bilāskhānī Toḍī *(ālāp)*; Rāg Brindābanī Sāraṅg *tīntāl (vilambit)* Navras NRCD 0027 [CD, 1994].

BHIMSEN JOSHI (vocal, *khyāl*); Vasant Achrekar (*tablā*) Rāg Durgā *tīntāl (drut)* EMI EASD1513 [disc, 1973].

BIDUR MALLIK (vocal, *dhamār*); Prem Kumar Malik and Ram Kumar Malik (vocal), Ramji Upadhyaya (*pakhāvaj*) Vinod Mishra (*sāraṅgī*), Sundarlar (harmonium) Rāg Jaijaivantī *dhamār tāl* Museum Collection Berlin CD17 [CD, 1993].

BUDHADITYA MUKHERJEE (*sitār*); Anindo Chatterjee (*tablā*) Rāg Pūriyā Kalyāṇ *tīntāl (drut)* Audiorec ACCD 1014 [CD, 1991].

DAGAR BROTHERS [Aminuddin and Moinuddin Dagar] (vocal, *dhamār*); S. V. Patwardhan (*pakhāvaj*) Rāg Darbārī Kanaḍā *dhamār tāl* EMI EALP1291 [disc, 1965].

DAGAR BROTHERS [Nasir Zahiruddin and Nasir Faiyazuddin Dagar] (vocal, *dhrupad*); Bithaldas Gujrati (*pakhāvaj*) Rāg Jaijaivantī *cautāl* EMI EALP1334 [disc, 1968].

DEEPAK CHOUDHURY; Arup Chattopadhyay (*tablā*) Rāg Pūriyā *jhaptāl* Private tape (London concert 7 Sept. 1991).

——Arup Chattopadhyay (*tablā*) Rāg Tilak Kāmod *rūpak tāl* Private tape (Birmingham concert 17 Sept. 1991).

——Kumar Bose (*tablā*) Rāg Bāgeśrī *jhaptāl*; Rāg Bhairavī *tīntāl (vilambit)* Concord 05–011 [cassette, 1989].

——Swapan Choudhury (*tablā*) Rāg Bhaṭiyār *tīntāl (vilambit)* Concord 05–021 [cassette, 1991].

K. G. GINDE (vocal, *sādrā*); Arjun Shejwal (*pakhāvaj*) Rāg Khaṭ *jhaptāl* EMI PSLP1365 [disc, 1985].

MALIKARJUN MANSUR (vocal, *khyāl*); Rajshekhar Mansur (vocal), Balkrishna Iyer (*tablā*), Baban Manjrekar (harm.) Rāg Yemenī Bilāval *tīntāl (vilambit)* EMI PSLP 1312 [disc, 1986].

——Nizamuddin Khan (*tablā*) Rāg Mārvā *tīntāl (drut)* Navras NRCD 0040 [CD, 1995].

MANILAL NAG (*sitār*); Sabir Khan (*tablā*) Rāg Jogkauns *tīntāl (drut)* HMV STCS 02B 6189 [cassette, 1987].

MUNAWAR ALI KHAN (vocal, *ṭhumrī*); Raza Ali Khan (vocal), Tanmoy Bose (*tablā*) Rāg Bhairavī *sitārkhānī tāl* Audiorec ACCD 1003–5 [CD, 1989].

NIKHIL BANERJEE (*sitār*); Swapan Choudhury (*tablā*) Rāg Megh *jhaptāl* EMI EASD1377 [disc, 1972].

PANDIT JASRAJ (vocal, *khyāl*); ? (*tablā*), ? (harm.) Rāg Miyān-kī-Toḍī *ektāl (vilambit)* CBS/ Swarashree PJ0001 [disc, 1988].

L. K. PANDIT (vocal, *ṭappā*); Deepak Nerurkar (*tablā*), Anant Rane (harm.), Dhruba Ghosh (*sāraṅgī*) Rāg Bhairavī *sitārkhānī tāl* CBS/ Swarashree LKP001 [cassette, 1988].

RASHID KHAN (vocal, *khyāl*); Samar Saha (*tablā*) Rāg Yaman *tīntāl (drut)* India Archive Music IAM CD 1003 [CD, 1991].

RAVI SHANKAR (*sitār*); Alla Rakha (*tablā*) Rāg Khamāj *tīntāl (vilambit)* EMI ASD2341 [disc, 1967].

——Kumar Bose (*tablā*) Rāg Gauḍ Sāraṅg *tīntāl (vilambit)* Chhanda Dhara SNCD 73688 [CD, 1988].

SABRI KHAN (*sāraṅgī*), Kamal Sabri (*sār.*), Sarwar Sabri (*tablā*) Dhun in Rāg Māṇḍ *dādrā tāl* Audiorec ACCD 1018 [CD, 1991].

SHRUTI SADOLIKAR (vocal, *khyāl*), Anant Krishna Kunte (*sāraṅgī*), Anindo Chatterjee (*tablā*) Rāg Miyān kī Toḍī *tīntāl (drut)* Nimbus NI 5346 [CD, 1992].

SHIV KUMAR SHARMA (*santūr*); Shafaat Ahmed Khan (*tablā*) Rāg Bhūpāl Toḍī *tīntāl (drut)* Music Today A91010 [cassette, 1991].

——Anindo Chatterjee (*tablā*) Rāg Miyān kī Malhār *jhaptāl (madhya lay)* Navras NRCD 0032 [CD, *c.*1994].

ULHAS KASHALKAR (vocal, *khyāl*); Suresh Talwalkar (*tablā*), Govind Patwardhan (harm.) Rāg Basant Bahār *tīntāl (vilambit)* HMV STCS04B 7449 [cassette, 1990].

VEENA SAHASRABUDDHE (vocal, *khyāl*); Vinayak S. Pathak (*tablā*), Pramod Marathe (harm.) Rāg Śrī *rūpak tāl* Rhythm House 240 355 [cassette, 1987].

——Sanjay Deshpande (*tablā*); Sudhanshu Kulkarni (harmonium) Rāg Bhūpāl Toḍī *tīntāl (madhya lay)* Navras NRCD 0031 [CD, *c.*1995].

C. R. VYAS (vocal, *khyāl*); Trimbak Jadhav (*tablā*), Purushottam Walavalkar (harmonium) Rāg Maluha Kedār *tilvāḍā tāl* CBS/ Swarashree CV001 [cassette, n.d.].

References

ABRAHAM, OTTO, and HORNBOSTEL, ERICH M. VON (1994), 'Suggested Methods for the Transcription of Exotic Music', *Ethnomusicology*, 38/3, 425–56 (trans. G. and E. List from 'Vorschläge für die Transkription exotischer Melodien', *Sammelbände der Internationalen Musikgesellschaft*, 1909–10, 1–25).

AGAWU, V. KOFI (1995*a*), *African Rhythm: A Northern Ewe Perspective*, Cambridge.

—— (1995*b*), 'The Invention of African Rhythm', *Journal of the American Musicological Society*, 48/3, Fall 1995, 380–95.

ALKUTKAR, MADHAVARAV SANKARARAV (c. 1960), *Mṛdaṅg vādan* (pt. 1), Durga, Madhya Pradesh.

AROM, SIMHA (1989), 'Time Structure in the Music of Central-Africa: Periodicity, Meter, Rhythm and Polyrhythmics', *Leonardo*, 22/1, 91–9.

—— (1991), *African Polyphony and Polyrhythm* (trans. M. Thom, B. Tuckett, R. Boyd), Cambridge.

BADDELEY, ALAN D. (1990), *Human Memory: Theory and Practice*, Hove.

BAGCHEE, SANDEEP (1998), *Nād: Understanding Rāga Music*, Mumbai.

BALSLEV, ANINDITA NIYOGI (1983), *A Study of Time in Indian Philosophy*, Wiesbaden.

BAMBERGER, JEANNE (1991), *The Mind behind the Musical Ear: How Children Develop Musical Intelligence*, Cambridge, Mass.

BERENDT, JOACHIM-ERNST (1987), *Nada Brahma: The World is Sound* (trans. H. Bredigkeit), Rochester, Vt.

BERRY, WALLACE (1976), *Structural Functions in Music*, Englewood Cliffs, NJ.

—— (1985), 'Metric and Rhythmic Articulation in Music', *Music Theory Spectrum*, 7, 7–33.

BHAGVHANDAS, MRDANGACARYA [and RAMSANKAR PAGALDAS, vol. ii only] (1960), *Mṛdaṅg tablā prabhākar*, 2 vols., Hathras.

BHATKHANDE, VISHNU NARAYAN (1953/58), *Hindustānī saṅgīt paddhati; kramik pustak mālikā*, 6 vols., Hathras.

BHOWMICK, K. N. (1975), 'Meaning of Sangat and the Role of a Tabla Player', *Bharata Manisha*, 1/2, July 1975, 37–42.

—— (1981), 'On Traditions of Tabla-riaz in Banaras School', *Journal of the Indian Musicological Society*, 12/1–2, 53–69.

BOLTON, THADDEUS L. (1894), 'Rhythm', *American Journal of Psychology*, 6.

BOR, JOEP (1988), 'The Rise of Ethnomusicology: Sources in Indian Music, *c.*1780–*c.*1890', *Yearbook for Traditional Music*, 20, 51–73.

BRAILOIU, CONSTANTIN (1984), *Problems of Ethnomusicology* (trans. A. L. Lloyd), Cambridge.

BROWER, CANDACE (1993), 'Memory and the Perception of Rhythm', *Music Theory Spectrum*, 15/1, 19–35.

BROWN, ROBERT E. (1965), *The Mṛdaṅga: A Study of Drumming in South India*, Ph.D. diss., UCLA.

CHANDOLA, ANOOP (1988), *Music as Speech: An Ethnomusicolinguistic Study of India*, New Delhi.

Chaturvedi, Mahendra, and Tiwari, Bholanath (1986), *A Practical Hindi–English Dictionary*, (13th edn.), New Delhi.

Chaudhary, Subhadra (1984), *Bhāratīy saṅgīt mẽ tāl aur rūp-vidhān: lakṣya-lakṣaṇmūlak adhyayan*, Ajmer.

—— (1997), *Time Measure and Compositional Types in Indian Music: A Historical and Analytical Study of Tala, Chanda, and Nibaddha Musical Forms*, New Delhi.

Childs, Barney (1977), 'Time and Music: A Composer's View', *Perspectives of New Music*, 15/2, 19–35.

Clarke, David (1989), 'Structural, Cognitive and Semiotic Aspects of the Musical Present', *Contemporary Music Review*, 3, 111–31.

Clarke, Eric (1987), 'Levels of Structure in the Organization of Musical Time', *Contemporary Music Review*, 2, 211–38.

Clayton, Martin R. L. (1993*a*), 'The Rhythmic Organisation of North Indian Classical Music: *Tāl, Lay* and *Laykārī*', Ph.D. diss., SOAS (London).

—— (1993*b*), 'Two Gat Forms for the Sitār: A Case Study in the Rhythmic Analysis of North Indian Music', *British Journal of Ethnomusicology*, 2, 75–98.

—— (1996), 'Free Rhythm: Ethnomusicology and the Study of Music without Metre', *Bulletin of the School of Oriental and African Studies*, 59/2, 323–32.

—— (1997), 'Le Metre et le tal dans la musique de l'Inde du Nord', *Cahiers de Musiques Traditionelles*, 10, 169–89 (English version available on the internet, url <http://www.open.ac.uk/arts/music/mclayton.htm>).

—— (1999), 'A. H. Fox Strangways and the Music of Hindostan: Revisiting Historical Field Recordings', *Journal of the Royal Musical Association*, 124/1, 86–118.

Clothey, Fred W. (1983), *Rhythm and Intent (Ritual Studies from South India)*, Madras.

Clynes, Manfred, and Walker, Janice (1982), 'Neurobiologic Functions of Rhythm, Time and Pulse in Music', in M. Clynes, ed., *Music, Mind and Brain*, New York.

Condon, William S. (1985), 'Sound-Film Microanalysis: A Means for Correlating Brain and Behavior', in F. H. Duffy, and N. Geschwind, eds., *Dyslexia*, Boston/Toronto.

Cone, Edward T. (1968), *Musical Form and Musical Performance*, New York.

Cooper, Grosvenor, and Meyer, Leonard B. (1960), *The Rhythmic Structure of Music*, Chicago.

Danielou, Alain (1957), 'Rhythm and Tempo in the Puranas', in *Aspects of Indian Music*, New Delhi.

—— (1968), *The Raga-s of Northern Indian Music*, London.

Delvoye, Françoise (1983), 'Research in Dhrupada: Towards a Critical Edition of Tānsen's Dhrupadas', in M. Thiel-Horstmann, ed., *Bhakti in Current Research, 1979–1982*, Berlin.

Deshpande, Vamanrao H. (1987), *Indian Musical Traditions* (trans. S. H. Deshpande, V. C. Devadhar), Bombay (2nd edn.; 1st edn. 1973).

Deva, B. Chaitanya (1974), *Indian Music*, New Delhi.

—— (1981), *The Music of India: A Scientific Study*, New Delhi.

Dick, Alastair (1984), 'Sitar', in *Grove 6*.

Dowling, W. Jay, and Harwood, Dane L. (1986), *Music Cognition*, London.

Dürr, Walther and Gerstenberg, Walter (1980), 'Rhythm' in *Grove 6*.

EKWUEME, LAZ E. N. (1975–6), 'Structural Levels of Rhythm and Form in African Music', *African Music*, 5/4, 27–35 (see also 'Guest editorial', 4–5).

ELLIS, CATHERINE J. (1984), 'Time Consciousness of Aboriginal Performers', in J. C. Kassler, and J. Stubington, eds., *Problems and Solutions: Occasional Essays in Musicology Presented to Alice M. Moyle*, 149–85, Sydney (Australia).

EPSTEIN, DAVID (1987), *Beyond Orpheus: Studies in Musical Structure*, Oxford.

—— (1995), *Shaping Time: Music, the Brain, and Performance*, New York.

FOX STRANGWAYS, ARTHUR HENRY (1914), *The Music of Hindostan*, Oxford (repr. 1965).

FRAISSE, PAUL (1978), 'Time and Rhythm Perception', in E. C. Carterette and M. Friedman, eds., *Handbook of Perception*, vol. viii, New York.

—— (1982), 'Rhythm and Tempo', in D. Deutsch, ed., *The Psychology of Music*, New York.

FRIGYESI, JUDIT (1993), 'Preliminary Thoughts toward the Study of Music without Clear Beat: The Example of the "Flowing Rhythm" in Jewish nusah', *Asian Music*, 24/2, 59–88.

FRISHMAN, MARCIE LEA (1985), *Patterning and Cadential Formulation in the South Indian Drum Solo*, MA diss., Wesleyan University.

GABRIELSSON, ALF (1993), 'The Complexities of Rhythm', in T. J. Tighe and W. J. Dowling, eds., *Psychology and Music: The Understanding of Melody and Rhythm*, Hillsdale, NJ.

GAUTAM, M. R. (1977), 'Evolution of Rāga and Tāla in Indian Music up to the 13th Century AD', Ph.D. diss., Banaras Hindu University.

—— (1989), *Evolution of Rāga and Tāla in Indian Music*, New Delhi.

GELL, ALFRED (1992), *The Anthropology of Time: Cultural Constructions of Temporal Maps and Images*, Oxford.

GERSON-KIWI, EDITH (1980), 'Cheironomy', in *Grove 6*.

GHOSH, NIKHIL (1968), *Fundamentals of Raga and Tala with a New System of Notation*, Bombay.

—— (1975*a*), 'Science and the Art of Keeping Time in Indian Music', *Journal of the Indian Musicological Society*, 5/2, 27–32.

—— (1975*b*), 'Rhythm in Indian Music: The Role of the Tabla', *Bulletin of the Ramakrishna Mission Institute of Culture (Calcutta)*, 26/9, 201–5.

GOTTLIEB, ROBERT S. (1977), *The Major Traditions of North Indian Tabla Drumming*, NGOMA Band 1, München-Salzburg.

—— (1985), 'Symbolisms Underlying Improvisatory Practices in Indian Music', *Journal of the Indian Musicological Society*, 16/2, 23–36.

—— (1993), *Solo Tabla Drumming of North India: Its Repertoire, Styles and Performance Practices* (2 vols.), Delhi.

GOULD, STEPHEN JAY (1987), *Time's Arrow, Time's Cycle: Myth and Metaphor in the Discovery of Geological Time*, Cambridge, Mass.

GROESBECK, ROLF (1999), '"Classical Music", "Folk Music", and the Brahmanical Temple in Kerela, India', *Asian Music*, 30/2, 87–112.

Grove 6 (1980), Sadie, Stanley, ed., *The New Grove Dictionary of Music and Musicians*, London.

HAMILTON, JAMES SADLER (1989), *Sitar Music in Calcutta: An Ethnomusicological Study*, Calgary.

HANDEL, STEPHEN (1989), *Listening: An Introduction to the Perception of Auditory Events*, Cambridge, Mass.

—— and LAWSON, GREGORY R. (1983), 'The Contextual Nature of Rhythmic Interpretation', *Perception and Psychophysics*, 34/2, 103–20.

HASTY, CHRISTOPHER FRANCIS (1997), *Meter as Rhythm*, New York.

HOFFMAN, STANLEY BRIAN (1978), 'Epistemology and Music: A Javanese Example', *Ethnomusicology*, 22/1, 69–88.

HOOD, MANTLE (1971), *The Ethnomusicologist*, New York.

HOPKINS, PANDORA (1982), 'Aural Thinking', in R. Falck and T. Rice, eds., *Cross Cultural Perspectives on Music*, Toronto.

HOULE, GEORGE (1987), *Meter in Music, 1600–1800: Performance, Perception and Notation*, Bloomington, Ind.

IMBERTY, MICHEL (1993), 'The Stylistic Perception of a Musical Work: An Experimental and Anthropological Approach', in 'Time in Contemporary Musical Thought', *Contemporary Music Review*, 7/2, 33–48, London.

INAYAT KHAN, HAZRAT (1991), *The Mysticism of Sound and Music*, vol. ii of *A Sufi Message of Spiritual Liberty*, Shaftesbury (Dorset) and Rockport, Mass.

JAIRAZBHOY, NAZIR ALI (1983), 'Nominal Units of Time; A Counterpart to Ellis' System of Cents', *Selected Reports in Ethnomusicology*, IV, 113–24.

JONES, MARI RIESS, and WILLIAM YEE (1993), 'Attending to Auditory Events: The Role of Temporal Organization', in S. McAdam and E. Bigand, eds., *Thinking in Sound: The Cognitive Psychology of Human Audition*, Oxford.

KAUFMANN, WALTER (1967), *Musical Notations of the Orient*, Bloomington, Ind.

KIPPEN, JAMES R (1985), 'The Traditional Tablā Drumming of Lucknow in its Social and Cultural Context', Ph.D, diss., Queens Univ., Belfast.

—— (1988), *The Tabla of Lucknow: A Cultural Analysis of a Musical Tradition*, Cambridge.

KOLINSKI, MIECZYSLAW (1959), 'The Evaluation of Tempo', *Ethnomusicology*, 3/2, 45–57.

—— (1973), 'A Cross-Cultural Approach to Metro-Rhythmic Patterns', *Ethnomusicology*, 17/3, 494–506.

KRAMER, JONATHAN (1988), *The Time of Music*, New York.

LASHLEY, K. S. (1951), 'The Problem of Serial Order in Behavior', in L. A. Jeffress, ed., *Cerebral Mechanisms in Behavior: The Hixon Symposium*, New York.

LATH, MUKUND (1978), *A Study of Dattilam: A Treatise on the Sacred Music of Ancient India*, New Delhi.

LEE, H. K. (1981), 'Quintuple Meter in Korean Instrumental Music', *Asian Music*, 13/1, 119–29.

LERDAHL, FRED, and JACKENDOFF, RAY (1983), *A Generative Theory of Tonal Music*, Cambridge, Mass.

LESTER, JOEL (1986), *The Rhythms of Tonal Music*, Carbondale, Ill.

LOMAX, ALAN (1982), 'The Cross-Cultural Variation of Rhythmic Style', in M. Davis, ed., *Interaction Rhythms*, New York.

LONDON, JUSTIN (1995), 'Some Examples of Complex Meters and their Implications for Models of Metric Perception', *Music Perception*, 13/1, 59–77.

MCGREGOR, RONALD S. (1993), *The Oxford Hindi–English Dictionary*, Oxford.

MAGILL, JONATHAN M., and PRESSING, JEFFREY L. (1997), 'Asymmetric Cognitive Clock Structures in West African Rhythms', *Music Perception*, 15/2, 189–222.

MANUEL, PETER L. (1983*a*), 'The Concept of Tala in Semi-Classical Music', *National Centre for the Performing Arts Quarterly Journal*, 12/4, 7–14.

—— (1983*b*), 'Thumri in Historical and Stylistic Perspective', Ph.D. diss., UCLA.

—— (1989), *Thumri in Historical and Stylistic Perspectives*, Delhi.

MARTIN, JAMES G. (1972), 'Rhythmic (Hierarchical) versus Serial Structure in Speech and Other Behavior', *Psychological Review*, 79/6, 487–509.

MERRIAM, ALAN P. (1964), *The Anthropology of Music*, Evanston, Ill.

MEYER, LEONARD B. (1956), *Emotion and Meaning in Music*, Chicago.

—— (1973), *Style and Music: Theory, History and Ideology*, Philadelphia.

MICHON, JOHN A. (1978), 'The Making of the Present: A Tutorial Review', in J. Requin, ed., *Attention and Performance*, vol. vii, 89–111. Hillsdale, NJ.

MINER, ALLYN (1990), 'The Sitar: An Overview of Change', *World of Music*, 32/2, 27–57.

—— (1993), *Sitar and Sarod in the 18th and 19th Centuries*, Intercultural Music Studies, 5, Wilhelmshaven.

MISRA, LALMANI (1973), *Bharatiya sangeet vadya*, New Delhi.

MURSELL, JAMES L. (1937), *The Psychology of Music*, New York.

NAKAMURA, HAJIME (1981), 'Time in Indian and Japanese Thought', in J. T. Fraser, ed., *The Voices of Time*, 77–91.

New Harvard (1986), *The New Harvard Dictionary of Music*, ed. Don M. Randel, Cambridge, Mass.

NIJENHUIS, EMMIE TE (1970), *Dattilam: A Compendium of Ancient Indian Music*, Leiden.

—— (1974), *Indian Music: History and Structure*, Leiden.

'PAGALDAS', RAMSANKAR (1964–7) *Tablā kaumudi* (2 vols.).

PANTALEONI, HEWITT (1987), 'One of Densmore's Dakota Rhythms Reconsidered', *Ethnomusicology*, 31/1, 35–55.

PARNCUTT, RICHARD (1987), 'The Perception of Pulse in Musical Rhythm', in Alf Gabrielsson, ed., *Action and Perception in Rhythm and Music*, Stockholm: Publications issued by the Royal Swedish Academy of Music, no. 55, 127–38.

PÖPPEL, ERNST (1989), 'The Measurement of Music and the Cerebral Clock: A New Theory', *Leonardo*, 22/1, 83–9.

POWERS, HAROLD S. (1980), 'India II, 5: Tala', in *Grove 6*.

PRESSING, JEFFREY L. (1993), 'Relations between Musical and Scientific Properties of Time', in 'Time in Contemporary Musical Thought', *Contemporary Music Review*, 7/2, 105–22.

QURESHI, REGULA (1994), 'Exploring Time Cross-Culturally: Ideology and Performance of Time in the Sufi Qawwali (Islamic Music)', *Journal of Musicology*, 12/4, 491–528.

RANADE, ASHOK DAMODAR (1984), *On Music and Musicians of Hindoostan*, New Delhi.

RANADE, GANESH HARI (1951), *Hindusthāni Music: An Outline of its Physics and Aesthetics*, Poona.

—— (1961), 'Some Thoughts about the Laya Aspect of Modern Music', in *Commemoration Volume in Honour of Dr S N Ratanjankar*, 121–3, Bombay.

RANADE, U., and CHAVAN, K. (1976), *Tāla Paintings*, Pune.

RATANJANKAR, S. N. (1967), 'Comparative Study of the Tala Systems of Hindustani and Karnatak Music', *Journal of the Music Academy, Madras*, 38/1–4, 113–29.

RENSHAW, ROSETTE (1966), 'Rhythmic Structures in Indian and Western Music', in R. Ashton, ed., *Music East and West*, New Delhi.

ROWELL, LEWIS (1981), 'The Creation of Audible Time', in J. T. Fraser, *et al.*, eds., *The Study of Time IV*, New York.

—— (1988*a*), 'Form in the Ritual Theatre Music of Ancient India', *Musica Asiatica*, 5.

—— (1988*b*), 'The Idea of Music in India and the Ancient West', in V. Rantala, L. Rowell, and E. Tarasti, eds., *Essays on the Philosophy of Music* (Acta Philosophica Fennica, vol. xliii), Helsinki.

—— (1989), 'Paradigms for a Comparative Mythology of Music', in R. C. Mehta, ed., *Music and Mythology*, Baroda.

—— (1992), *Music and Musical Thought in Early India*, Chicago.

ROYCHOUDHURY, B. (1975), *Bhāratīy saṅgīt koś*, New Delhi.

SACHS, CURT (1943), *The Rise of Music in the Ancient World*, New York.

—— (1953), *Rhythm and Tempo*, New York.

—— (1962), *The Wellsprings of Music*, The Hague.

SAHASRABUDDHE, VEENA (1999), 'Khyal and its Presentation', in M. Clayton, *Khyal: Classical Singing of North India* (OU Worldwide Video Cassette ETHNO VC01; accompanying texts by Martin Clayton and Veena Sahasrabuddhe), pp.12–18, Milton Keynes.

SAMBAMOORTHY, P. (1964), *South Indian Music*, vol. iii (of 6), Madras.

SARGEANT, WINTHROP, and LAHIRI, SARAT (1931), 'A Study of East Indian Rhythm', *Musical Quarterly*, 17, 427–38.

SCHOLES, PERCY A. (1938, 10th edn. 1991), *The Oxford Companion to Music*, Oxford.

SEN, ARUN KUMAR (1994), *Indian Concept of Rhythm* (trans. S. N. Gayatonde), Delhi.

SHANKAR, L. (1974), 'The Art of Violin Accompaniment in South Indian Classical Music', Ph.D. diss., Wesleyan University.

SHANKAR, RAVI (1969), *My Music, my Life*, New Delhi.

SLAWEK, STEPHEN (1987), *Sitār Technique in Nibaddh Forms*, Delhi.

SNELL, RUPERT (1983), 'Metrical Forms in Braj Bhāṣā Verse: The Caurāsī Pada in Performance', in M. Thiel-Horstmann, ed., *Bhakti in Current Research, 1979–1982*, Berlin.

—— (1991*a*), *The Eighty-Four Hymns of Hita Harivaṃśa: An Edition of the Caurāsī Pada*, Delhi.

—— (1991*b*), *The Hindi Classical Tradition: A Braj Bhāṣā Reader*, London.

SRIVASTAV, INDURAMA (1980), *Dhrupada*, Delhi.

STEWART, REBECCA M. (1974), 'The Tablā in Perspective', Ph.D. diss., UCLA (Ann Arbor, 1990).

STONE, RUTH (1985), 'In Search of Time in African Music', *Music Theory Spectrum*, 7, 139–48.

SUBRAMANIAM, L., and VIJI (1995), *Euphony: Indian Classical Music*, New Delhi.

SUCH, DAVID G., and JAIRAZBHOY, NAZIR ALI (1982), 'Manifestations of Cyclic Structures in Indian Classical Music', *Journal of Asian Culture*, 6, 104–17.

THOMPSON, GORDON (1995), 'What's in a Ḍhāḷ? Evidence of Rāga-Like Approaches in a Gujarati Musical Tradition', *Ethnomusicology*, 39/3, 417–32.

TOYNBEE, ARNOLD (1972), *A Study of History*, Oxford.

VAN DER MEER, WIM (1980), *Hindustani Music in the 20th Century*, The Hague.

WADE, BONNIE C. (1984*a*), *Khyal: Creativity within North India's Classical Music Tradition*, Cambridge.

—— (1984*b*), 'Performance Practice in Indian Classical Music', in G. Béhague, ed., *Performance Practice: Ethnomusicological Perspectives*, Westport, Conn.

WEGNER, GERT-MATTHÄUS (1982), *Die Tablā im Gharānā des Ustad Munir Khān (Laliyānā)*. Beiträge zur Ethnomusikologie, Band II.

WIDDESS, D. RICHARD (1977), 'Trikāla: A Demonstration of Augmentation and Diminution from South India', *Musica Asiatica*, I, 61–74.

—— (1981*a*), 'Aspects of Form in North Indian Alap and Dhrupad', in D. R. Widdess, and R. Wolpert, eds., *Music and Tradition; Essays on Asian and other Musics Presented to Laurence Picken*, Cambridge.

—— (1981*b*), 'Rhythm and Time-Measurement in South Asian Art-Music: Some Observations on Tāla', *Proceedings of the Royal Musical Association*, 107, 132–8.

—— (1981*c*), 'Tāla and Melody in Early Indian Music', *Bulletin of the School of Oriental and African Studies*, 44/3, 481–508.

—— (1994), 'Involving the Performers in Transcription and Analysis: A Collaborative Approach to Dhrupad' (with Ritwik Sanyal and Ashok Tagore), *Ethnomusicology*, 38/1, 59–80.

—— (1995), ' "Free rhythm" in Indian Music', *EM: Annuario degli Archivi di Etnomusicologia dell'Accademia Nazionale di Santa Cecilia*, III, 77–96.

YAKO, MASATO (1997), 'The Hierarchical Structure of Time and Meter', *Computer Music Journal*, 21/1, 47–57.

YESTON, MAURY (1976), *The Stratification of Musical Rhythm*, London.

ZUCKERKANDL, VICTOR (1956), *Sound and Symbol: Music and the External World* (trans. W. R. Trask), London.

List of audio examples

No.	Ex.	Details	Catalogue no.
1		Sabri Khan (*sāraṅgī*), *dhun* in *rāg māṇḍ, dādrā tāl* (extract)	Audiorec ACCD 1018
2	6.4	Amir Khan, *khyāl* in *rāg mārvā, jhūmrā tāl* (extract)	EMI EALP 1253
3	7.2	Amjad Ali Khan (*sarod*), *ālāp* in *rāg bilāskhānī toḍī* (extract)	Navras NRCD 0027
4	7.3	Amjad Ali Khan, *joṛ* in *rāg bilāskhānī toḍī* (extract)	Navras NRCD 0027
5	8.1	Dagar Brothers, *dhrupad* in *rāg jaijaivantī, cautāl* (first line)	EMI EALP 1334
6	8.2	Bidur Mallik, *dhamār* in *rāg jaijaivantī, dhamār tāl* (first line)	Museum Collection Berlin CD17
7	8.3	Bhimsen Joshi, *choṭā khyāl* in *rāg durgā, tīntāl* (first line)	EMI EASD 1513
8	8.4 a	Shruti Sadolikar, *choṭā khyāl bandiś* in *rāg miyān kī toḍī, tīntāl* (*sthāyī* only)	Nimbus NI 5346
9	8.4 b	Malikarjun Mansur, *choṭā khyāl bandiś* in *rāg mārvā, tīntāl* (*sthāyī* only)	Navras NRCD 0040
10	8.4 c	Rashid Khan, *choṭā khyāl bandiś* in *rāg yaman, tīntāl* (*sthāyī* only)	India Archive Music IAM CD 1003
11	8.5	Malikarjun Mansur, *baṛā khyāl* in *rāg yemenī bilāval, tīntāl* (first line)	EMI PSLP 1312
12	8.11	Ravi Shankar (*sitār*), *vilambit gat* in *rāg gauḍ sāraṅg* (first line)	Chhanda Dhara SNCD 73688
13	8.16	Deepak Choudhury (*sitār*), *madhya lay gat* in *rāg tilak kāmod, rūpak tāl* (first line)	private
14	8.17	Deepak Choudhury (*sitār*), *mukhṛā*-based *gat* in *rāg pūriyā, jhaptāl* (first line)	private
15	8.19	Amjad Ali Khan (*sarod*), *razākhānī gat* in *rāg nandkauns, tīntāl* (first line)	EMI EASD 1348
16	8.20	Manilal Nag (*sitār*), *razākhānī gat* in *rāg jogkauns, tīntāl* (first line)	HMV 02B 6189
17	8.22 a	Malikarjun Mansur, *baṛā khyāl* in *rāg yemenī bilāval, tīntāl* (*mukhṛā*)	EMI PSLP 1312
18	8.22 b	Pandit Jasraj, *baṛā khyāl* in *rāg miyān kī toḍī, ektāl* (*mukhṛā*)	Swarashree PJ0001
19	8.23	Shruti Sadolikar, *choṭā khyāl bandiś* in *rāg miyān kī toḍī, tīntāl* (*sthāyī* with variations)	Nimbus NI 5346
20	8.24	Deepak Choudhury (*sitār*), *madhya lay gat* in *rāg bāgeśrī, jhaptāl*	Concord 05–011

No.	Ex.	Details	Catalogue no.
21	9.1	Malikarjun Mansur, *baṛā khyāl* in *rāg yemenī bilāval, tīntāl* (extract of *bol ālāp*)	EMI PSLP 1312
22	9.2	Pandit Jasraj, *baṛā khyāl* in *rāg miyān kī toḍī, ektāl* (extract of *bol ālāp*)	Swarashree PJ0001
23	9.3	Deepak Choudhury (*sitār*), *vilambit gat* in *rāg bhaṭiyār, tīntāl* (extract of *gat sthāyī* and *vistār*)	Concord 05–021
24	9.5	K. G. Ginde, *sādrā* in *rāg khaṭ, jhaptāl* (extract of *bol bāṇṭ*)	EMI PSLP 1365
25	9.6	Munawar Ali Khan, *ṭhumrī* in *rāg bhairavī, sitārkhānī tāl* (extract of *bol banāo*)	Audiorec ACCD 1003–5
26	9.7	Veena Sahasrabuddhe, *khyāl* in *rāg śrī, rūpak tāl* (extract)	Rhythm House 240 355
27	9.8	Deepak Choudhury (*sitār*), *madhya lay gat* in *rāg bāgeśrī, jhaptāl* (extract)	Concord 05–011
28		Amjad Ali Khan (*sarod*), *vilambit gat* in *rāg brindābanī sāraṅg, tīntāl* (extract of *tāns*)	Navras NRCD 0027
29		Budhaditya Mukherjee (*sitār*), *drut gat* in *rāg pūriyā kalyāṇ, tīntāl* (extract of *tāns*)	Audiorec ACCD 1014
30	10.8	Veena Sahasrabuddhe, *khyāl* in *rāg śrī, rūpak tāl* (extract, *bol bāṇṭ* in *tigun*)	Rhythm House 240 355
31	10.9	Dagar Brothers, *dhrupad* in *rāg jaijaivantī, cautāl* (*bol bāṇṭ*)	EMI EALP 1334
32	10.10	Shiv Kumar Sharma (*santūr*), *madhya lay gat* in *rāg miyān kī malhār, jhaptāl* (*laykārī*)	Navras NRCD 0032
33	10.12	Deepak Choudhury (*sitār*), *madhya lay gat* in *rāg tilak kāmod, rūpak tāl* (extract featuring '*gopucchā yati*')	private
34	10.13	K. G. Ginde, *sādrā* in *rāg khaṭ, jhaptāl* (*tihāī*)	EMI PSLP 1365
35	10.14	Nikhil Banerjee (*sitār*), *madhya lay gat* in *rāg megh, jhaptāl* (*tihāī*)	EMI EASD 1377
36	10.15	Deepak Choudhury (*sitār*), *vilambit gat* in *rāg bhairavī, tīntāl* (extract)	Concord 05–011
37	10.16	Bidur Mallik, *dhamār* in *rāg jaijaivantī, dhamār tāl* (*nauhār tihāī*)	Museum Collection Berlin CD17
38	10.17	Shiv Kumar Sharma (*santūr*), *drut gat* in *rāg bhūpāl toḍī, tīntāl* (final *tihāī*)	Music Today A91010
39	10.18	Deepak Choudhury (*sitār*), *madhya lay gat* in *rāg tilak kāmod, rūpak tāl* (extract)	private

Index